Thealogy & Embodiment

Thealogy and Embodiment

The Post-Patriarchal Reconstruction of Female Sacrality

MELISSA RAPHAEL

Sheffield
Academic Press

To Verity

Published by
Sheffield Academic Press Ltd
Mansion House
19 Kingfield Road
Sheffield, S11 9AS
England

Typeset by Sheffield Academic Press
and
Printed on acid-free paper in Great Britain
by the Cromwell Press
Melksham, Wiltshire

British Library Cataloguing in Publication Data

A catalogue record for this book is available
from the British Library

ISBN 1-85075-757-7

CONTENTS

PREFACE

Like many writers, I have written the book I needed. Feminist spirituality is well supplied with historical, archaeological, psychotherapeutic and celebratory texts on the 'reflowering of the Goddess'. But in the course of my teaching, I have found that there is a lack of books that contextualize the thealogical construction of the female body as the embodied immanence of the Goddess within the history of feminism's criticism of religion. There has also been little to bridge the participant spiritual feminist texts—which are without critical distance—and the secular feminist studies of the social construction of embodiment. These latter studies, written over the last ten years, use largely Foucauldian theories of the body as a site on which the 'micro-physics' of power are played out, disciplining the body into the institutions of heterosexuality and male dominance. These secular texts are important and useful, but, like reformist religious studies of embodiment, they do not discuss the specificities of thealogy's post-Christian spiritual and political philosophy of embodiment. Both students of spiritual feminism and spiritual feminists themselves can learn a great deal from reformist religious feminism and from feminist social science. But ultimately spiritual feminists want to talk about the world using metaphors and types of truth claim which are either incomprehensible or incredible to secular thought or are overly separatist for reformist religious feminism.

Assuming the reality of divine presence and intention, this book will offer a non-reductionist but also non-confessional analysis of the feminist neo-pagan construction of embodiment as a matrix sustaining spiritual/ political agency. For it seems important that a sympathetic study of the ways in which a growing number of religious feminists experience embodiment be available to students of contemporary religion in a number of overlapping fields.[1] This is especially so since feminist

1. Cynthia Eller's book, *Living in the Lap of the Goddess: The Feminist Spirituality Movement in America* (New York: Crossroad, 1993) is an extremely valuable study, but its method is sociological and therefore does not attempt to analyse spiritual feminism from within the logic of the sacred itself.

academia (let alone patriarchal academia) commonly dismisses spiritual feminism on superficial readings of its texts. So as well as being written for the interested general reader and for spiritual feminists outside academia, this book also addresses students and their teachers (and their capacity to be both of these at once).

The standard critique of spiritual feminism is that it is essentialist, apolitical, and makes unwarranted historical claims. Although spiritual feminism is heterogeneous and one cannot make total judgments, it is not usually, in my view, simplistically essentialist. But equally it does not make the spiritually and politically self-alienating mistake of reducing the experiential continuities of female embodiment to a series of social constructions. My critical defence of spiritual feminism as a unique form of feminist activism and feminist historiography is not to be confused with apologetics. Rather, I intend to show that routine misunderstandings make the movement seem less spiritually, intellectually, and politically interesting than it actually is; not that it is, in any fundamentalist sense, finally true.

In company with the writers I cite, this book will renegotiate the meaning of female sacrality—those qualities of femaleness that mediate the sacred—as a structure by which we can imagine how the divine is immanent in the world through female embodiment and in 'female' modes of being and doing. This renegotiation is offered both as a contribution to the feminist study and practice of religion and as a way to trace the religio-political manoeuvres that have made and continue to make radical feminist religion unacceptable to mainstream believers, and politically suspect to non-radical feminists as an opportunity to extol motherhood and archetypal femininity. (My discussion of the sacral meaning of some forms of traditional female crafts in Chapter 3 is definitely not directed to that irritating end.) Spiritual feminism is, I am convinced, a profoundly political movement, though its invocation of power for political change is not typical of modern politics—feminist or otherwise.

If the term that summarizes that power, 'female sacrality', becomes more familiar to students of religion then the whole range of spiritual feminist discourses should come into clearer focus. It is a useful piece of shorthand to name female-referring transformatory powers. Because these powers have been unnamed, many, perhaps most, women are not conscious that they have ever been attributed to them. Arguably, we can only perceive a reality for which we have a conception; that is, perception follows conception. And a concept does not always name a fully actualized reality; it can bring it into existence. Conception names a cerebral process but also the beginning of a reproductive process located inside the female body. In this sense, I write not to clarify a spirituality or to describe an empirical quality of female bodies, but rather to quicken a spirituality.

Relatively speaking, a great deal of feminist research into the Western tradition of female holiness has focused on the self-sanctifying practices of medieval Christian women. As far as I am aware this is one of the first full-length studies of post-patriarchal female sacrality. In terms of the history of religion, post-patriarchal spirituality is far more significant than its growing numbers. Many involved in spiritual feminism are trying to do something unprecedented in the history of religion: to develop a gynocentric, feminist religion. In spiritual feminism women have ceased to wrestle with the difficulties of a tradition in which both the creator and saviour of the world are male. Here female sacrality is relatively self-defined, primary, and central rather than other, secondary or marginal. Conceptualizing the divine as 'female' allows a direct relation between divine generativity and its manifestations in women—a relation which has systemic political effects. For this reason I have not discussed the construction of female embodiment in the mainstream neo-pagan movement. (Spiritual feminists commonly feel that despite its welcome immanentism and green activism, mainstream neo-paganism can be almost as patriarchal as any other religion which venerates female divinities. It often honours only a stereotypical femininity that merely complements masculinity and is still not defined by women themselves.[2])

Nonetheless, thealogical models of embodiment are relevant to all religious feminist thinking and this book is intended for a much wider readership than those studying or practising feminist neo-paganism.

2.   Mainstream neo-paganism is not usually consciously feminist and male abuses of charisma and hierarchy do exist. The Goddess is often represented in sexist ways as a young, slim 'femme fatale'. See Cheryl Straffron's useful feminist critique: 'Pagan Philosophy and Women', *From the Flames* 13 (1994), pp. 26-27. However, the Goddess is generally given cosmological priority in mainstream neo-paganism and is revered in a multiplicity of forms that are not always stereotypically gentle and passive. The apparently misogynistic and racist tendencies of the Odinic Rites (two separate groups with the same name) and the Rune Gild are not typical of the rest of neo-paganism. (I am indebted here to Graham Harvey's lecture, 'Heathenism: a North European Pagan Tradition' given at the conference 'Paganism in Contemporary Britain' at the University of Newcastle upon Tyne, September 1994.)

'Female sacrality' is not a concept owned by any one religion. And it is a mistake to draw any final boundary between reformist feminism and post-Christian feminism. Christian and Jewish feminists have also resurrected the goddesses of the biblical period, they are also ecofeminist, and their spirituality also emphasizes divine immanence and embodiment. Like neo-pagan feminists, their prophetic critique is directed against those patriarchal social structures that generate social inequities of power, ecological devastation, and the marginalization of women in religion. There may be legitimate reasons for mutual criticism between radical and reformist religious feminists, but there is, I think, far more that unites them than divides them. And while we are suffering the present backlash against feminism, a lack of dialogue between religious feminisms will only dissipate feminist energy. I would hope, then, that Christian and Jewish feminists would also find much that is suggestive or usable within this discussion of female sacrality. Strictly speaking, this is not a book about the Goddess movement, but about that *idea* of female nature or being implicit in all religious feminism which celebrates the immanent divinity of the female body.

Masculine Sacrality

I could never claim that the divine only self-manifests in femaleness. While the female body might provide particularly apt metaphors for divine generativity, and more than that, become an actual medium of divine generativity, it is not the only thing to do so. It is not, then, that biological maleness is non-hierophanic, but that patriarchy has obscured and distorted maleness by the imposed structures of its will to power. Post-patriarchal men also have a history of damaged, sapped and distorted energies to reverse.[3]

Superficially, it might appear that I have discussed female sacrality without discussing male sacrality and have therefore been as myopic about maleness as patriarchal historians of religion have been about femaleness. Of course in actuality male sacrality and female sacrality cannot be separated: they usually coexist in systems, though rarely happily. 'Feminine' sacrality is usually a complementary element within patriarchal religions. And, as is often the case in spiritual feminism, the masculine sacrality that is manifest in war, sacrifice and celestiality has a

3. See M. Adler, *Drawing Down the Moon* (Boston: Beacon Press, 1986), p. 348.

tendency to become a set of negative symbols—a mere foil—against which positive female sacrality can be contrasted. I do, in fact, devote specific attention to masculine sacrality in Chapter 6. As my sources would, I have used the term 'masculine', as opposed to 'male', sacrality as more or less synonymous with patriarchal or masculinist religion. Whether or not the contrasts feminists draw between female sacrality and masculine sacrality are always justified, these contrasts are implicit throughout my discussion of female sacral processes.

Masculine and 'feminine' sacrality are at least politically related and should not be discussed in artificial isolation. Reformist feminist studies of religion are now beginning to move away from an exclusively woman-centred approach and are focusing more inclusively on the role of gender as a whole in religion. In the present study, however, for reasons of space and principle, male sacrality is not discussed in its own right, since the history of religion, theology and philosophy has been about little else. The time is long overdue for a study of female sacrality. Also, my woman-centred approach has been largely determined by the nature of my subject: radical feminist spirituality is itself woman-centred. This does not mean that men need read no further. 'Masculine' sacrality indicates a set of practices traditionally associated with biological males in patriarchal cultures. But patriarchal values are not a consequence of having a penis, any more than feminist values are limited to those in possession of a womb. The 'female' mode of religious being that I discuss here includes all those who are oriented towards biophilic relations with all living things.

Sources

In this book I give a *reading* of spiritual feminism, not a survey. And sometimes that reading might add something to spiritual feminism which was not explicit before. Nonetheless, I am aware that the spiritual feminist writers I quote write from a variety of positions. Some are far more critical of the patriarchal status quo than others who tend to celebrate the feminine before the feminist. My account of female sacrality is extrapolated from a selection of spiritual feminist writers (of whom Mary Daly, Jane Caputi and Barbara Mor writing with Monica Sjöö are the most significant). But none of their texts has a normative status. Spiritual feminists value their heterodoxy and, while of a common temper, their work comes from diverse positions. For example, Starhawk, Naomi Goldenberg, Zsuzsanna Budapest and Diane Stein are all feminist witches (though Goldenberg is more Jungian in her approach than the others, and 'Z' is a Dianic witch). Monica Sjöö is more of a thealogical realist than Naomi Goldenberg, and Asia Shepsut is less 'woman-identified' than the rest and wants to restore a traditional pagan balance between male and female energies. Or again, Naomi Goldenberg, Alix Pirani, Barbara Koltuv and Clarissa Pinkola Estés have all practised or been influenced by Jungian psychotherapy, though none of their texts requires the readers to be versed in Jungian analysis. Ultimately, though, these Jungian writers draw upon a shared view of the sacred, and it may only be their psychotherapeutic methodologies that distinguish them from other spiritual feminists.[4]

Mary Daly is out on her own. I have read her work as the best source and illustration of female sacrality and I refer to her work more often than any other (though my view is not identical to hers). She is a spiritual feminist metaphysician and perhaps too transcendental in temper for some. She is far more philosophically and theologically literate than any of the other writers I have used, and yet many of them

---

4.   I decided from the outset that I would not devote separate space to the Jungian element in Goddess spirituality. Like Jungian feminists themselves, I distrust Jung's views on the stereotypically gendered, archetypally unchanging, complementary anima and animus aspects of the unconscious or soul. His respect for 'the feminine' does not make him a feminist. His prescriptive view of women inhibits successful excursions into the 'masculine' realm of rational Logos, even though the 'feminine' qualities—Eros, connection, relationship and intuitive thought—are fundamental values for all religious feminists. But much of the material in Jungian spiritual feminist texts is more loosely Jungian in the sense that imagination, dreams and visions, rather than creeds or texts, are revelatory and produce an open, therapeutic self-directed religious experience. Jung's criticism of doctrinaire religion and its alienation of the subject's own mythopoeic and ritual capacities; his sympathy with heretics, and his attempt to create religious experience that would answer the needs of those who could not remain in the religions they were born to, have all served religious feminism well. Psychotherapy has strongly influenced the feminist spirituality movement and visionary material is properly included in its academic texts—both radical and reformist. Jung's concept of 'the Shadow' has suggested to many spiritual feminists that the feared, rejected or 'profane' part of the female self can be brought to consciousness and thereby transformed into energy and knowledge. See N. Goldenberg, 'Dreams and Fantasies as Sources of Revelation: Feminist Appropriation of Jung', in C. Christ and J. Plaskow (eds.), *Womanspirit Rising: A Feminist Reader in Religion* (New York: Harper Collins, 1992), pp. 219, 221. See also *idem, Changing of the Gods: Feminism and the End of Traditional Religions* (Boston: Beacon Press, 1979), pp. 47-71.

have been inspired by her and use motifs that have either been derived from her work or have emerged from the collective imagination and pooled scholarly research.

I am also aware that feminist spirituality is, in the sociologist Cynthia Eller's phrase, 'the civil religion of the lesbian feminist community', even though, as she notes, 'the majority of spiritual feminists consider themselves heterosexual'.[5] Lesbianism is central and at least implicit in many spiritual feminists' thealogies of embodiment. But I have not focused on lesbian theory in this study. Spiritual feminism is not synonymous with lesbianism and the female sacral processes I discuss here do not, in any case, assume any sexual or cultural complementary relation to masculine sacrality. Indeed, spiritual feminist sexuality and politics can be so gynocentric that heterosexual spiritual feminists cannot be sharply distinguished from their bisexual and lesbian sisters. Although I discuss the relation of lesbian sexual politics and the sacred where it is particularly relevant, I feel that this subject needs another book and a lesbian author to do it full justice. There is, in fact, such a distinctive mood and concern common to all spiritual feminist writers—the liberated operations of 'gynergy' or female energy—that I feel justified in putting a variety of spiritual feminist writers, lesbian and non-lesbian, alongside one another in order to emphasize or illustrate a given point.

Modernity's patriarchal scholars have rarely dropped the pretence of erasing from their finished manuscripts all traces of biography (and sheer opinion) in the interests of objectivity. By contrast, and in common with all postmodern scholarship, spiritual feminism respects not only written sources, but oral, local, plural, particular, changing, imaginal ways of knowing that have more often been characterized as 'female'. The whole personal experience of women is now as much a resource of feminist scholarship as other people's texts. My own experience of those religious (bad) manners that make women feel that they have jeopardized men's holiness has certainly shaped my feminist conception of holiness. My naively proffered teenage hand has been ignored by orthodox rabbis; I have slept out in the courtyard of a male *yeshiva* (seminary) in Israel while the men slept inside; I have sat next to a Buddhist monk at a conference who got up and moved several empty seats away from me. And nearly all women would be familiar with the expectation—often unconscious—that one's experience of a given religious event will probably be that of unnamed spectator.

5.   *Living in the Lap of the Goddess*, pp. 20-21.

If biography is a source that permeates all readings and all texts then it seems only fair to declare my spiritual interest from the outset. Like theology, thealogy is beset by philosophical and moral problems; nonetheless, although I do not practise Goddess religion, it has become an important determinant of my experience of the world and the way that I think about the world. There is perhaps a danger in being overly concise but, at present, the feminist Goddess is, for me, not a personal divinity but a symbol of the ultimate value of 'female' biophilic modes of relation and creation that derive from the nature of the divine. I find the Goddess a useful symbol of rebellion against patriarchal religion's construction of biddable femininity and its exploitative structures of relating and creating. For me, the 'return' of the Goddess marks a vision of the decline of 'masculine' modernity and its desacralization of 'female' materiality. In this, the Goddess is perhaps more a symbol of hope than of celebration: the postmodern spirit and intellect does not yet inhabit a post-patriarchal, post-capitalist or post-industrial world—the first being a precondition of the second two. Except where strictly relevant, I have tried to avoid imposing my own (shifting) reading(s) of the term 'Goddess' on those of my sources.

As a Jewish free spirit, politically sympathetic with the intentions of the Goddess movement if not always, in the end, persuaded by its practice, I have felt well placed to be a sympathetic commentator on spiritual feminism. The outsider status of a Jew has made me prone to the posture of commentator—all the more so as a feminist outsider among outsiders; an exile from the exiled. Alicia Ostriker also speaks for me when she says,

> To deny my Judaism would be, for me, like denying the gift of life...
> But I'm not a Jew, I can't be a Jew, because Judaism repels me as a woman. To the rest of the world the Jew is marginal. But to Judaism I am marginal. Am woman, unclean. Am Eve. Or worse, am Lilith.[6]

I might, then, be particularly sensitive to the anxieties and freedoms of female otherness as it is experienced and celebrated in spiritual feminism. I do not, however, write as a 'post-Jewish' feminist because, unlike some post-Christian feminists who may once have been baptized into Christianity and then left the church or ceased to take communion, my Jewishness is as spiritually and methodologically inalienable from my scholarship as it is from my identity.

6.   'Entering the Tents', *Feminist Studies* 15 (1989), p. 542.

Terminology

Given that this book is intended to be educative as well as, I hope, spiritually engaging, it has been necessary to use a certain amount of technical vocabulary. This is not intended to exclude or deter and I have tried to explain these terms either parenthetically or in the notes. (Some non-academic readers might prefer to skip over the methodological discussion in the first half of the Introduction.)

I am aware that I have used the term 'spiritual feminist' as a consensual term. As I have emphasized already, this is not intended to totalize all spiritual feminists as believing exactly the same thing: they do not. For many, the Goddess is the central focus; for others spiritual feminism includes, but is also something much wider than, Goddess worship. Thealogy does not just articulate beliefs about a goddess or goddesses. It is also more broadly concerned with imaging the divine with qualities traditionally or biologically associated with being female. There is considerable fluidity in thealogical thought and I have tried not to systematize it. However, it would have been impossible to say anything readable about the movement if I had constantly differentiated positions. So I have used the term collectively only where I have judged that all spiritual feminists would more or less assent to the given statement. I have used the term 'spiritual feminist' to refer to those women who are 'radical' in that they have left the patriarchal religions and are no longer trying to reform them from within. Their spirituality is consistently ecological and gynocentric.

I have also assumed that spiritual feminists are speaking from a more or less postbiblical position, but also (confusingly) see themselves as part of the 'feminist spirituality movement' which can include reformist feminists from all other religions. The line between reformist and radical is often blurred, so Eller's classification of spiritual feminists is to be welcomed. She counts as a spiritual feminist any woman who identifies herself as such, or without identifying herself as such, still adheres to at least three of the five main characteristics of feminist spirituality that she lists. These are: 'valuing women's empowerment, practising ritual and/or magic, revering nature, using the feminine or gender as a primary mode of religious analysis, and espousing the revisionist version of Western history favored by the movement'.[7]

---

7.   *Living in the Lap of the Goddess*, p. 6.

I have not consistently capitalized the word 'goddess'. Whether it is given a small or large 'g' will depend on how it has been used in my sources. But where I have written it myself without the capital letter, I am referring to a historical goddess or female divinities in general. With the capital, I am referring to *the* Goddess—namely the female divine principle of *contemporary* thealogy: a construction that may or may not include or refer to ancient goddesses. 'The Goddess' may refer to the Great Mother, the Great Goddess, a female psychological archetype, or a mixture of them all. Historians of religion may want to make careful distinctions between these but spiritual feminists do not. In thealogy, where divinity is characterized by traditionally and biologically female qualities and practices, the Goddess has many names and forms and is not exhausted by any one of them.

Although I am not convinced that the word 'God' is morally and spiritually redundant, spiritual feminism is deeply critical of the world religions, especially Christianity. Sometimes it fails to acknowledge that Christianity and other world religions are plural and their theologies come from a number of political and experiential contexts. I have tried to be more precise than most of my sources when it has been relevant to compare a given theology and thealogy. Nonetheless generalizations about theology have occasionally been appropriate, if only because listing the exceptions to a rule can be a tedious process for the author and trying for the reader. But to avoid confusion I have let the name 'God' stand—as spiritual feminists usually do—for the divinization of patriarchal power. For the sake of clarity I shall only use the word 'God' as a proper name for the masculine, monarchical father-deity of the biblical traditions: the god called God. I use the unspecific 'divine' to refer to the unimaginable, unconstructable, sexless inner being of what mysticism calls 'the Godhead'.

My use of the word 'female' also requires a brief explanation. Sometimes this word will simply refer to biological femaleness. At other times—and the difference will be apparent in context—the word 'female' is used to denote the value of practices, processes and modes of being that have been biologically or historically associated with women. However, biological femaleness is not always a precondition of female sacrality. Female sacral processes are metapatriarchally valuable and at least their meanings and intentions are available to anyone who consciously dissociates herself or himself from the patriarchal worldview.

ACKNOWLEDGMENTS

I am grateful to Lisa Isherwood and Dorothea McEwan of the Britain and Ireland School of Feminist Theology for commissioning this book with Sheffield Academic Press, and more generally, for setting up new and distinctive channels through which feminist theologians and thealogians can publish their work. I am also grateful to Rev. Stanley Rudman of the Centre for the Study of Religion at Cheltenham and Gloucester College of Higher Education for arranging the study leave that gave me a term to finish writing the book, to Sue Morgan who kindly agreed to take over my teaching during that term, and to the staff of the College's Information Services who helped me in numerous ways. Thanks are also due to Carol Smith and others at Sheffield Academic Press who have worked on this project, and to Veronica MacIntyre, editor of *From the Flames*, who kindly gave me permission to quote from her work.

This book has benefited from the friendship of women from the Oasis feminist spirituality group—especially Gisela Broers, Judith Cefalas, Rosie Mere and Sue Morgan, and from the friendship and encouragement of Dee Carter. As I wrote most of the book when my daughter Verity was a baby, it has also benefited from her happy disposition, her early willingness to sleep through the night, and, of course, the very fact of her being. Lastly, I would like to thank my husband, Michael, who has introduced me to ideas from postmodern science and deep ecology which have influenced this book and who has given me the loving support that greatly eased the process of its writing.

The publications committee of the Britain and Ireland School of Feminist Theology wish to thank Melissa Raphael for producing the third volume in our Occasional Series of books in Feminist Theology. This is an exciting work which will advance feminist theological scholarship. We wish the readers every joy in reading it and hope it will open new doors for them.

The Publications Committee
BISFT

INTRODUCTION

> The history of religion is, from the scientific aspect, largely the history of
> the devaluations and the revaluations which make up the process of the
> expression of the sacred.
>
> Mircea Eliade[1]

When Andrea Dworkin had finished writing *Pornography* she was in
despair. During its writing she had experienced 'the most intense
desolation' she had known as a writer. The material she had to read
gave her bad dreams. The research made her physically sick and silent; it
violated her. Pornographic images insidiously changed the signification
of things in her own everyday environment: the telephone wire became
an accessory of bondage;

> scissors were no longer associated with cutting paper but were poised at
> the vagina's opening...A doorway is a doorway. One walks through it.
> A doorway takes on different significance when one sees woman after
> woman hanging from doorways. A lighting fixture is for light until one
> sees woman after woman hanging from lighting fixtures. The common-
> place world does not just become sinister; it becomes disgusting,
> repellent.[2]

Dworkin's inner and outer world was profaned. But while, for Dworkin,
the everyday world began to deceive and repel her, I experienced the
reverse in writing this book: the everyday world began to tell me new
and different stories. It began to be resacralized: the property of mediating the sacred was restored to it. The sacral significance of ordinary
traditional domestic objects—brooms, cooking pots, needles and so
forth—became points of entry into another (largely heretical) women's
religious history, carrying other meanings and other possibilities. This
was not a nostalgic excursion into women's domestic heritage but a way

---

1. *Patterns in Comparative Religion* (London: Sheed & Ward, 1958), p. 25.
2. ('Afterword'), 'On the Writing of *Pornography: Men Possessing Women*', in
Pornography: Men Possessing Women (London: The Women's Press, 1981),
pp. 301-304.

into a ritual and political space in which women's generative energies can mediate and replicate divine cosmogonic energy through transposing the practices and metaphors of cooking, brewing, sewing, menstruation, gestation and birth onto those of political activism. While I was writing this book there were moments in which I felt as if I were coming out on the other side of the demonization and violation of women in conservative patriarchal religion and those social forms which are sanctioned by their worldview. Arguably, this is something Dworkin could not have done because she was not using the mutinous energetics of feminist spirituality: that momentum that hurled Mary Daly through her four Spiral Galaxies—out of the state of patriarchal possession and into the free feminist transcendence of 'continual expansion of thinking, imagining, acting, be-ing'.[3]

Dworkin says that pornography stole her dreams of freedom. In an oblique way, the history of religions has given them back to me. This may seem improbable—the history of religion hardly invites feminist confidence. Throughout recorded history the practice and study of religion has been at best androcentric and at worst misogynistic. Patriarchal religion (and indirectly the study of religion) has held women down on a Procrustean bed of self-sacrificial motherhood or lethal sexual magic. Women have not been, and by and large are still not, the subjects of their own religious experience. Patriarchal Western[4] religion has owned women's bodies but disowned the sacrality of those bodies.

To use Nancy Auer Falk's definition, female sacrality means the manifestation and use of transformatory divine energy in essentially or traditionally female activities such as generating new life or transforming raw materials into cultural artifacts through gardening, weaving and cooking.[5] But even her article, which is the most useful concise account of the subject, makes no reference to the contemporary feminist reconstruction of the sacral capacities of the female body.[6] Yet as Carol Christ has

---

3.   'New Intergalactic Introduction' to *Gyn/Ecology: The Metaethics of Radical Feminism* (London: The Women's Press, 1991), p. xxiv.

4.   All religions known to me appear to subordinate women to a lesser or greater degree, but as a white, middle-class Westerner I cannot and would not make literally global statements about all other women's religious lives. There are, of course, generalizations in this book, but if all exceptions were noted at all times writing could not proceed.

5.   M. Eliade (ed.), *The Encylopedia of Religion* (New York: Macmillan, 1987), V, s.v. 'Feminine Sacrality', p. 303.

6.   See U. King, 'A Question of Identity: Women Scholars and the Study of

written, when a spiritual feminist asks questions of her own being she 'opens herself to the radically new—possibly to the revelation of powers or forces of being larger than herself that can ground her in a new understanding of herself and her position in the world'. Using Doris Lessing's phrase, Christ describes the powers grounding the spiritual feminist quest as

> 'forces or currents of energy'... which operate in all natural and social processes. These forces are the energies of life, death, and regeneration and being, non-being, and transformation, which are most obvious in nature, but which also operate in the social world.[7]

If the mainstream history of religions names female sacrality at all, its recreative power is usually implicitly denigrated as a merely sexual/natural 'fertility'. Female sacrality is an accepted though peripheral technical description of what women and female deities do in *other* religions. This generative mode of being by which women work changes upon the world is left as unnamed non-data in secular culture; peripheral sub-data in the phenomenology of religions; and in Western religious culture it is something essentially pagan and suffused with the uncleanness of female sexuality. Although the term 'female sacrality' connotes female power it is hardly a title. Like the word 'witch' which negatively acknowledges female spiritual power, it is without honour. The only place where both terms have honour is within contemporary Goddess religion.

As Rosemary Ruether has observed, female sacrality is an immensely powerful idea in the human psyche, 'despite, and even because of its long repression'. But reaffirming it will not be easy:

> Patriarchal religion is built on many millennia of repressed fear of the power of female bodily processes. Any effort to admit the female in her explicit femaleness as one who menstruates, gestates and lactates, will create psychic time-bombs that may explode with incalculable force. One can expect cries of 'witchcraft', 'blasphemy', 'sacrilege' and 'idolatry' to be directed at those who seek to resacralize the female body.[8]

Religion', in *idem* (ed.), *Religion and Gender* (Oxford: Blackwell, 1995), p. 236.

7. C. Christ and C. Spretnak, 'Images of Spiritual Power in Women's Fiction' (part one by Carol Christ), in C. Spretnak (ed.), *The Politics of Women's Spirituality: Essays on the Rise of Spiritual Power within the Feminist Movement* (New York: Doubleday, 1982), p. 329.

8. 'Women's Body and Blood: The Sacred and the Impure', in A. Joseph (ed.), *Through the Devil's Gateway: Women, Religion and Taboo* (London: SPCK, 1990), pp. 18-19.

Although 'female sacrality' is not a familiar term to those outside the history of religions it seems to me that even where its capacities have not been named as such, it is this idea of the female body as a locus and medium of the sacred that informs the thealogy and practice of spiritual feminism (and, it is often believed, that of ancient matrifocal societies as well). As Christine Downing has put it: 'What provoked goddess veneration was recognition of female energy as transformative energy'. The manifestation of this transformatory energy was both spiritual and corporeal and as such, 'the most potent exemplification of divine power'.[9] In short, the resacralization of female embodiment answers both a historical and an ontological need of many religious women: 'We are starved for images which recognise the sacredness of the feminine and the complexity, richness, and nurturing power of female energy.'[10]

A Different History of Religions

Religious feminism is unanimous in arguing that androcentric studies of religion are skewed by the scholars' life-long acclimatization to an academic culture in which only masculine methods and the values which inform them are considered objective and normative.[11] Consequently, when historians of religion discuss female sacral experience through an androcentric lens—as they usually do—they are adding another layer of patriarchal mediation to the religious experience of the female members of a given religion which is already generally controlled by men.[12] Feminist criticism of religious studies does not allow that the study of men simply includes the study of women.[13] In the words of Rita Gross, '*homo religiosus* as constructed by the history of religions does not include women as religious subjects, as constructors of religious symbol

9. C. Downing, *The Goddess: Mythological Images of the Feminine* (New York: Crossroad, 1990), pp. 11, 13. On p. 11 Downing gives a useful summary of the meaning of female sacrality.

10. Downing, *The Goddess*, p. 4.

11. V. Saiving, 'Androcentrism in Religious Studies', *Journal of Religion* 56 (1976), p. 179.

12. See M. Raphael, 'Feminism, Constructivism and Numinous Experience', *Religious Studies* 30 (1994), pp. 514-15.

13. R. Gross, 'Androcentrism and Androgyny in the Methodology of History of Religions', in *idem* (ed.), *Beyond Androcentrism: New Essays on Women and Religion* (Missoula, MT: Scholars Press, 1977), pp. 7-19.

systems and as participants in a religious universe of discourse'.[14]

The feminist revision of the politics and substance of religious experience cannot allow masculine sacral experience to encompass that of women. Instead, 'it is just possible that the unheard testimony of that half of the human species which has for so long been rendered inarticulate may have something to tell us about the holy which we have not known—something which can finally make us whole'.[15] In other words, a revived concept of female sacrality would do much to correct and balance scholarly conceptions of the sacred, which until now have worked on the assumption that female sacral experience is either unworthy of note or the same as men's.

Because it is strongly immanentist, thealogy has little in common with traditional methods in religious studies. In thealogy a woman's embodied finitude is holy in that it belongs to the intramundane processes of divine creativity: 'There is no division of the spiritual and the profane; all is related in the universe, and none stands apart from nature. All is nature.'[16] When nature is impregnated with the numinous the feminist sacred cannot simply be translated into that of men. Moreover, female sacrality is not just different but profane to the holy in male-dominated religious rituals. Feminist spirituality experiences female embodiment and its connectedness with other natural forms, not historical revelation, as its source of sacral empowerment.

Religious feminists celebrate the mediation of the divine presence by ordinary natural things as opposed to special sanctified objects which have been set apart from daily life. Because the divine is not an alien presence the medium becomes integral to the meaning of the experience. As Meinrad Craighead puts it, in and through finite things 'we may apprehend the incarnate presence of the holy in all of creation. Through them God our Mother communicates with us through her body, within her own mysterious creation.'[17]

Immanentism breaks down the traditional binary oppositions of spirit and flesh, heaven and earth, sacred and profane, where the value of one element in the duality—the transcendent—is secured at the expense of

14. Androcentrism and Androgyny', p. 10.

15. Saiving, 'Androcentrism in Religious Studies', p. 197.

16. Z. Budapest, *The Holy Book of Women's Mysteries* (Oakland, CA: Wingbow, 1989), p. xxv.

17. 'Immanent Mother', in M. Giles (ed.), *The Feminist Mystic and Other Essays on Women and Spirituality* (New York: Crossroad, 1982), p. 81.

the other—the immanent. The establishment of the transcendent value
of the spirit at the expense of the flesh is a classic example of this. Even
without its erotic overtones, the word 'flesh' was and is read in the West
as a signifier of sexuality and therefore finitude: mutations from which
the holy is ritually protected. To be of 'flesh' in traditional Christianity is
to have been born of woman, profaned by her blood, distracted by her
embodiment and generally in a state of rebellion against God.[18]

Both the androcentric *and* the feminist historian of religion would
agree (though for different reasons) that the passage of female sacral
power is not through priestly mechanisms of sacrifice, purification and
atonement.[19] If female sin is not the same as male sin (in a patriarchal
society the social structures do not offer opportunities for female
hubris—raising oneself to the status of the gods[20]) then women will not
need the same kind of purification rituals as men who associate sin with
pride, ambition and varieties of dirt. In any case, in Judaism, Islam and
the priestly Christian denominations, a woman's menstruality alone
would remind her of her naturalness or profanity: a quality inseparable
and irremovable from her embodiment.

Although the Western history of religions includes a variety of theories,
methods and interests, it has not appeared to be aware of the inadequacy
of these to describe women's religious lives. The feminist study of religion
has criticized the Western history of religion as a metanarrative united
by androcentrism and largely rooted in the history of Christendom. A
metanarrative is an agreed, foundational story that explains all other
stories. Any metanarrative is an imaginative construction by the
members of a given discourse community, providing them with a stable
rhetoric that supports their own values. Underpinning the metanarrative
of the history of religions have been the patriarchal narratives of conquest, ideologically permitting patriarchy, in God's name, to use (female)
nature (and therefore women) as servants of its own projects.

But spiritual feminism also has its own (alternative) metanarrative—
that of the origins of patriarchy and the demise of female sacrality. The

18. See P. Brown, *The Body and Society: Men, Women and Sexual
Renunciation in Early Christianity* (London: Faber & Faber, 1990), p. 48.

19. See R. Otto, *The Idea of the Holy* (New York: Oxford University Press,
1958), p. 57.

20. See V. Saiving, 'The Human Situation: A Feminine View', in C. Christ and
J. Plaskow (eds.), *Womanspirit Rising: A Feminist Reader in Religion* (New York:
HarperSanFrancisco, 1992), pp. 25-42.

high level of agreement and participation in this metanarrative is evident in the fairly predictable contents of most books on the Goddess. Whether or not this metanarrative is verifiable is largely beside the point. (Anyway, metanarrative claims are too comprehensive in scope to be subjected to normal empirical testing.) The purpose of any metanarrative is, I think, ultimately hermeneutical. That is, it is a means of deciphering future possibilities in the record of the past. The spiritual feminist meta-narrative is not a straightforward sequential chronicle of women's religious lives from prehistory to the present. There can be no neutral chronicling if all experience, including that codified in primary sources, has been ideologically mediated. Meanings cannot be simply 'read off' from the past.

Notwithstanding the patriarchal dynamics of the androcentric history of religion, the concept of female sacrality relies heavily upon it, both as a repository of imaginally suggestive materials, and as a way of maintaining global and historical connections with all women. The relationship between androcentric and post-patriarchal history of religions is a dialectical (not always hostile) one. For spiritual feminism also carries within itself a different history of religion: a spiralling underground passage of rewritten, reversed, recycled knowledges, much of which derives from the patriarchal history of religions. This passage runs from a golden matrifocal *Urzeit* (both researched and imagined) in which female sacral energies were part of the meaning of the created world; onto the beginnings of patriarchy about 5000 years ago; up to the present day and onto a post-patriarchal utopian beyond.

Spiritual feminism's historical claims are not ordinary historical claims. The gynocentric history of religion is narrative as incantation. Refusing not only modernity's positivist disenchantment of nature, but its disenchantment of *women*, it has been 'singing' women into the fullness of existence since the early 1970s: across the United States and Canada, parts of Europe—particularly Germany, Holland and Britain—and in Australia and New Zealand. The ontological continuity of women, the Goddess, and those quasi-timeless processes through which she is manifest entail that history and present psycho-religious experience are inseparable in contemporary spiritual feminist experience. Asia Shepsut dated a channelled poem '2279 BC, Ur/AD 1990, Watford',[21] and, equally dramatically, Jean Mountaingrove wrote of her menstrual

---

21. *Journey of the Priestess: The Priestess Traditions of the Ancient World* (London: Aquarian, 1993), p. 80.

connection with female history: 'I have heard a call across a million years, I will answer it'.[22] As such, the radical feminist history of religion bears unique witness to all historiography's unceasing negotiation and dialogue with the past. (Even to the point of undermining the historiographical project altogether.)

In its willingness to negotiate with the past, spiritual feminism is deeply postmodern and must be understood as such. Most of the texts used in this book have been written since the mid-1970s—in precisely the period that the postmodern interpretive shift has taken root. The most important future purpose of the spiritual feminist metanarrative is to generate new social and political realities. So even if the metaphors and analogies by which female sacrality is evoked motivate or 'fiction' female becoming more than metaphysically fixing what women *are*, either way the concept of female sacrality abolishes the notion of women as passive victims of their own religious history. This metanarrative also assumes that sacral transformations have actually been played out in a number of politically oppressive contexts even when misnamed or unnamed.

In their different ways, Michel Foucault and Mary Daly are right that the operations of (patriarchal) power are omnipresent; but neither Foucault nor Daly would accept their omnipotence, hence, again, the invigoration I experienced in writing this work of feminist counter-imagination. Foucault's relational concept of power as a constant process of negotiation, manoeuvre and resistance has abolished the simple historiographical dualism of oppressor and victim. (Though patriarchy is actually remarkably difficult to shift and the experience of victimization by a powerful and violent oppressor is absolutely real and must not be forgotten.) Foucault has offered postmodern theorists a sense that the operations of power are more complex, dynamic, unpredictable and resistible than those of sheer force. His expression of the shifting boundary between fiction and political reality would also characterize that of spiritual feminist historical discourse:

> I am well aware that I have never written anything but fictions. I do not mean to say, however, that truth is therefore absent. It seems to me that the possibility exists for fiction to function in truth, for a fictional discourse to induce effects of truth, and for bringing it about that a true

22. In (Cornwoman) Celu Amberston's compilation of accounts of menstrual experience, *Blessings of the Blood: A Book of Menstrual Lore and Rituals for Women* (Victoria, BC: Beach Holme, 1991), p. 86.

discourse engenders or 'manufactures' something that does not yet exist, that is, 'fictions' it. One 'fictions' history on the basis of a political reality that makes it true, one fictions a politics not yet in existence on the basis of a historical truth.[23]

To enter sympathetically into spiritual feminist historical discourse one must also appreciate the nature of the magical thinking that inspires it. The word 'magic' comes from the Chaldean *magdhim* meaning philosophy. The words 'image' and 'imagination' also derive from this term.[24] Hence to visualize a different social patterning, whether past or future, but freed from patriarchal domination and realigned with the divine cosmic energies, is magically to conceive, gestate and give birth or consciousness to new conditions of possibility. This is the postmodern magic of (literally) making wishes come true. And it is a practice encouraged by the 'reenchantment' of nature in postmodern science. Where positivist modernity confined the 'real' to the observable properties of matter, postmodernity has reunited energy, imagination and matter. The world is (re)opened to magical suggestion. The energies of heavenly and human bodies, flesh and the cosmos, are (re)made continuous with one another. Changes in the body effect changes in the world and vice versa.[25] In this context, 'magic' is not to be confused with the solitary masculinist mastery or manipulation of the natural world by high magicians. Feminist magic releases and directs the energy of living things that 'flows in certain patterns throughout the human body, and can be raised, stored, shaped and sent. The movements of energy affect the physical world, and vice versa.'[26] When I refer to female sacrality as a 'magical' energy it will be in this feminist, erotic sense alone.

I would use the phrase 'spiritual feminist *religion*' guardedly because most spiritual femininists would prefer to see their practices as spirituality rather than the more institutionalized 'religion'. Spiritual feminism is non-centralized, without a formal canon of sacred texts, and

23. In *Power/Knowledge: Selected Interviews and Other Writings 1972–1977* (ed. C. Gordon; London: The Harvester Press, 1980), p. 193.

24. S. Roney-Dougal, *Where Science and Magic Meet* (Shaftesbury: Element, 1993), p. 212.

25. D. Mariechild, *Mother Wit: A Guide to Healing and Psychic Development* (Freedom, CA: Crossing Press, 1988), p. 32.

26. Starhawk, *Truth or Dare: Encounters with Power, Authority, and Mystery* (New York: HarperSanFrancisco, 1987), p. 24.

determinedly non-dogmatic. However, Goddess feminism has most of
the other ingredients of a religion even if they are informal and non-
authoritarian: thealogy, ontology, sacred history, cosmology, ritual,
favoured texts, ethics, priestesses and so forth. The spiritual feminist
historiography of its own religion is as eclectic as the other elements of
its religion. It is a mixing—a kind of spell—by which women re-call their
embodiment of the collective female past: in the vocabulary of female
sacral crafts, each contemporary woman is an 'aggregation of scraps', a
'patchwork' of myths, a 'basket containing millennia'.[27] Although its
sacred history is not a myth in the strict sense of a fixed narrative explanation of the origins of the present, its historiography uses mythopoeisis
to bring together personal and cosmic history as structurally identical.
This kind of remembering is a process of taking the metanarrative of
women's religious history into the body; of re-membering or fleshing
out one's own story, and in so far as biology collectivizes, other
women's stories too. However, although it is sometimes accused of
doing so, its elision of prehistory, modernity and postmodernity actually
prohibits spiritual feminism from prescribing a return to primal social
and intellectual conditions that are politically and geographically alien to
our own.

One of the purposes of this book is to make a contribution to this
different history of religions by extrapolating a theory of 'female' being
from a combination of androcentric and feminist religious texts. To
make these different sorts of texts cohere, I will have to straddle at least
two forms of discourse. The first of these are the participant poetic texts
in which metaphors are unravelled and re-spun, not merely for literary
effect, but in recognition that all abstract thought is and can only be
metaphorical. We conceive the world in its unexperienceable totality in
terms of our own experiences of the world around us—and more often
than not in terms of our embodiment. The second form of discourse is
that of the more conventional conversation with other writers that has
traditionally characterized academic texts. Although my task of extrapo-
lation and exposition will be a 'rational' process, spiritual feminists do not
usually rely on linear thinking for initial inspiration. To subject the ludic
poetics of spiritual feminism to positivist or reductionist logic would be
to make a textual category mistake. Esther Harding, Christine Downing
and Irene de Castillejo are, for example, representative of the majority of
spiritual feminists whose thealogy is psychologically derived from

27. Ostriker, *Entering the Tents*, p. 546.

divination of dreams, biological experience and numinous experience.[28]

Yet spiritual feminism also draws inspiration from a number of academic disciplines, and I have therefore done so as well. Like any transdisciplinary writing this can be problematic in that each discipline has its own methodological conventions. I have chosen, therefore, to let the spiritual feminists' own method of giving 'free' reconstructive readings govern all other sources, provided that there are sufficient conditions for this transposition of meaning and the original meaning of the text has not been distorted out of all recognition.

Historians of religion have been using a similar method to this one for some time: the phenomenological method of studying religion. The phenomenology of religion is a branch of the history of religions and its primary concern is to organize religious data so as to grasp their religious value and meaning. Although some historians of religion suspect that the phenomenological method pays insufficient attention to the historical context of its data, phenomenologists are not so much indifferent to historical context as determined not to reduce religious phenomena and hierophanies (manifestations of the sacred) to their sociohistorical meanings alone. Phenomenologists also try to avoid letting personal prejudices obscure the object of enquiry. A feminist phenomenology would not, of course, suspend moral or political judgment. Even if absolute detachment *were* possible it would be immoral in the face of oppressive religious practices. However, in my own phenomenological presentation of spiritual feminist experience I have usually let remarks stand without interposing my own opinion of their validity.

But what is most significant for my present purpose is that phenomenologists of religion are more likely to construct theological or thealogical and philosophical meanings for religious phenomena than those historians of religion who are more strictly historical and philological in their methods. In its greater emphasis on intuition, empathy, and a willingness to understand religious experience from within, the phenomenology of religion is more of an art than a science.[29] This study is

28. See, for example, Downing, *The Goddess*, pp. 2, 5.
29. K. Rudolph, *Historical Fundamentals and the Study of Religions* (New York: Macmillan, 1985), p. 37. Rudolph does not approve of this more experiential method and on p. 44 he complains that 'historians of religion display an increasing propensity to wander in directions that are not scientific'. The history of religions is sharply divided on issues of method. The 'scientific' wing, of which Rudolph is a part, attempts to be independent of theological and philosophical presuppositions. He

typically phenomenological in that I have not given a sequential history of the construction of female sacrality or given historico-causal explanations of its suppression. I have wanted to present and illustrate a contemporary religious *idea* of femaleness. It has not been my task to give an exhaustive historical account of *how* patriarchy has tried to keep female sacrality under its control as pious femininity or as an alliance with demonic power that must be broken. As such the phenomenological method seems to be appropriate to the spiritual feminist mood.

It was common for early twentieth-century historians of religion to search for one interpretive category by which all religious phenomena could by understood. Most famous of these was Rudolf Otto's category of the Holy. He has been justifiably criticized for using this category to select material that corroborated his theory in an ahistorical and non-contextual manner. Because most spiritual feminists have a spiralling rather than a linear conception of the passage of time, they also tend to use data from anthropologists and historians of religion in an a-contextual manner. Despite its shortcomings, I too have used a 'hermeneutical' method to study feminist religion. I have used the concept of female sacrality as a category by which to unify spiritual feminist texts and reported experience of the recovery and exercise of 'gynergy' or female energy.

It may, in fact, be possible that diverse data from the androcentric history of religions *can* be read as evidence of a historically continuous sub-tradition in patriarchal religious history. But it has not been my task to *prove* that is the case. Nor have I wanted to make any *a priori* claim that female sacral agency is the defining characteristic of any radical feminist religious phenomenon, such that whatever does not fit its criteria is *therefore* not radical feminist religion. More modestly, I want to say that the concept seems to summarize the ontic, discursive, ritual and political dynamics of radical feminist religion. Wanting to tether my argument to a specific historical context, I have only attempted to show how the female body has been resacralized in the postmodern context of (mainly) anglophone spiritual feminism from the late 1970s up to the mid 1990s.

---

and others criticize such historians of religion as Rudolf Otto, Gerardus van der Leeuw and Mircea Eliade for failing to work independently of these presuppositions.

Using Androcentric Texts

I am inclined to share Daly's distrust of academic methodologies as being 'social and cultural institutions whose survival depends on the classification of disruptive and disturbing information as non-data'.[30] This is particularly true of female sacrality which is a paradigm case of patriarchal non-data. But all sustained research requires some method of selection and presentation by which to make sense of information. So it seemed appropriate for a book on female sacral processes, of which various sorts of 'cooking' are a central part, to use one of the libertarian methodologies of feminist spirituality. Here the body of the text becomes, like the female sacral body, a cauldron into which political, poetic and thealogical elements are stirred and brewed rather than explained away. The cauldron is a metaphor for an inclusive, eclectic, provisional text-as-process rather than product. The text is a crucible of words in which each reader's imagination combines and reacts with the material to create new conditions of possibility.

Because renewal and change can come through 'mixing' it was important that androcentric texts should go into the pot as well. Throughout this book I will use androcentric discussions of the relation of the sacred and the profane to advance a gynocentric discussion. Like many other feminists working in religious studies, I feel ambivalent about using theories that have been articulated by men who (on occasion) state things *about* women rather than 'hearing them to speech'. Many of these theorists have also classified religious phenomena according to their own, sometimes implicit, ranking of religions, in which Christianity is judged to be the world's most evolved religion.[31]

30. *Beyond God the Father: Towards a Philosophy of Women's Liberation* (London: The Women's Press, 1985), p. 11.

31. Otto, Gerardus van der Leeuw and Nathan Söderblom's studies of the holy are helpful to the present purposes, but it is worth remembering that their phenomenology was not neutral. All of their work was ultimately conditioned by Christian theology and had been influenced to varying degrees by the nineteenth- and early twentieth-century history of religions' imposition of evolutionary schemes and hierarchical rankings on the world's religions. This, and a widespread search for the essence of religion, has all but disappeared today. Rather, as Kurt Rudolph points out, the 'ideological-critical' function of the history of religions is being revived where it is recognized that ideologies of dominance have manipulated religion to suit their purposes (*Historical Fundamentals*, p. 75).

Two of the best-known twentieth-century theorists of the sacred, Rudolf Otto and Mircea Eliade, are not merely androcentric in their methods of selecting material, they also devalue traditional female modes of existence and at least implicitly exclude them from the authentic or normative sphere of the sacred which is masculine in character. Eliade, who is reputed to have been associated with Romanian fascism in his youth,[32] describes women's sacrality as biologically and domestically grounded in 'the sanctity of life and the mystery of childbearing and universal fecundity'.[33] This is depicted as peculiar to women and is contrasted with the dynamics of male sacrality, which is depicted as a bid for freedom from the natural state of 'man'—'to break the bonds that keep him tied to earth'.[34] And female sacrality is implicitly denigrated as less than fully human since the achievement of transcendence is also, for Eliade, the achievement of authentic humanity.[35] Carol Christ has, therefore, rightly objected to the 'dualism, idealism, and false universalization of male experience' that distorts Eliade's historiography of religions.[36] (For Durkheim as well, sacredness is virtually defined by its exclusion of women who would profane the sacred merely by looking at it.[37] And although Arnold Van Gennep concedes that a

32. See A. Berger, 'Mircea Eliade: Romanian Fascism and the History of Religions in the United States', in N. Harrowitz (ed.), *Tainted Greatness: Anti-Semitism and Cultural Heroes* (Philadelphia: Temple University Press, 1994), pp. 51-74. My inserting this information into the mere clause of a sentence does not indicate indifference to the seriousness of the charge. Indeed Eliade must be read in the light of it. But my use of Eliade's work is not deferential to Eliade *himself*. Rather, his knowledge—however strongly mediated by sexism and nationalism—can be strongly suggestive when either transposed into a new context or used to confirm feminist suspicions about patriarchal scholarship.

33. *Rites and Symbols of Initiation: The Mysteries of Birth and Rebirth* (New York: Harper & Row, 1965), p. 80.

34. Eliade, *Rites and Symbols*, p. 132.

35. See Saiving, 'Androcentrism in Religious Studies', pp. 190-93; Eliade, *Rites and Symbols*, p. 135.

36. 'Mircea Eliade and the Feminist Paradigm Shift', *Journal of Feminist Studies in Religion* 7 (1991), p. 94.

37. See *The Elementary Forms of the Religious Life* (repr.; London: George Allen & Unwin, 1971 [1915]), pp. 120, 126, 138-39, 303-305, 319. Durkheim concedes in a footnote that women are not absolutely profane, but are profane in relation to men (p. 138).

woman can become sacred in specific relations to others, she is still 'congenitally impure'.[38])

A spirit/flesh dualism structures Eliade and Otto's work. The profane is not simply the mundane, but what is illusory (Eliade) or 'flesh' and 'creaturehood' (Otto). As I have argued elsewhere,[39] in *The Kingdom of God and the Son of Man* Otto is even more emphatic than in his more famous book *The Idea of the Holy* that the life of the flesh is utterly opposed to the life of spirit: 'holiness or righteousness are not possible in the present, earthly, fleshly, worldly existence, or in an existence and situation of an earthly kind', but rather, in the 'wholly other' existence 'in heaven'.[40] He does not appear to be aware that a male divinity would be less 'wholly other' to men, whose culture allows them to dissociate themselves from their embodiment, than to the majority of women who are mothers. Or again, the male experience of holiness has tended to demand the self-abnegation of the subject. In Otto's account of numinous experience the spiritual inadequacy of the 'creature' is experienced in an inverse ratio to the fullness of divine holiness. Women who have traditionally been disqualified from religious office and who are 'creatures' of the Father God and of male culture would feel this inadequacy more sharply than men.

In *Redeeming the Dream* Mary Grey rejects Otto's account of numinous experience as 'totally opposed to what women have experienced'.[41] The experience of the divine as *mysterium tremendum et fascinans* is, she argues, modelled on separation from the object of experience: 'the deeper the experience the greater the awe and terribleness of God as wholly other. Spirituality will then consist in recognizing that one is dust and ashes before the deity.'[42] It is difficult to know whether women *do* have typically Ottonian numinous experiences or not.[43] If Western

38. A. Van Gennep, *The Rites of Passage* (repr.; London: Routledge & Kegan Paul, 1965 [1908]), p. 12.

39. This paragraph and the next paraphrase parts of my article, 'Feminism, Constructivism and Numinous Experience', pp. 519, 524-25 respectively.

40. *The Kingdom of God and the Son of Man* (London: Lutterworth, 1938), p. 49.

41. *Redeeming the Dream: Feminism, Redemption and the Christian Tradition* (London: SPCK, 1989), p. 44.

42. *Redeeming the Dream*, p. 44.

43. See, for example, T. Beardsworth, *A Sense of Presence* (Oxford: Manchester College: Religious Experience Research Unit, 1977), pp. 116-28. All female respondents reported a comforting, markedly non-numinous divine presence.

women *have* been accustomed to experiencing the holy in this manner, these experiences may have been continuous with a sense of personal insignificance in the presence of the masculine, and therefore sub-religious. Nonetheless, if women do have theistic numinous experiences, it seems unlikely that theirs would be essentially the same as men's if for no other reason than that numinous experience, as Otto evokes it, is linguistically and conceptually funded by male values and experience.

However, it may be possible to transpose Otto's evocation of the numinous into thealogy without taking his theology and politics of religious experience as well. In *The Idea of the Holy*, Otto describes how the numinous—the pre-rationalized, pre-moralized sacred—evokes a particular emotional reaction of awe, terror and attraction or love, all of which he summarizes as the *mysterium tremendum et fascinans*. Thealogically expressed, Goddess is holy: as *mysterium* she eludes human categories of value; as *tremendum* she is the destroyer, the Crone; as *fascinans* she is Mother and Virgin: she 'pours out her love on the earth' and she enchants the soul. And the lack of moralistic judgment implicit in 'primitive', Ottonian and feminist concepts and experience of the sacred liberates female sacrality from idealized moral expectations, especially in relation to sexual behaviour. It is not important to correlate radical feminist religious experience with the history of scholarship simply to make it respectable. The correlation is to show that spiritual feminism is a coherent spiritual worldview having continuities with the collective history of the world's religions as well as strong political differences.

Reversing the History of Religion

The feminist manipulation (a word used almost literally—not pejoratively) of androcentric scholarship is well exemplified by Mary Daly. Daly has good grounds for her hostility towards those historians and anthropologists of religion who record but do not condemn 'religious' barbarisms like *suttee* or female genital mutilation as the atrocities against women that they are. Although her use of quotation is the reverse of obsequious, she does, however, do patriarchal scholars the honour of quoting their words with some frequency. But her method of quotation is idiosyncratic. Androcentric words are caught and held in her textual web-spinning. And at the centre of her heretical operations she rereads, rewrites and reverses the androcentric concept of the sacred. She expends energy on patriarchal texts—catching (them out), deciphering and digesting them—precisely because the patriarchal defamation or demonization of female sacrality is the clue to its feminist power:

> In order to reverse the reversals completely we must deal with the fact that patriarchal myths contain stolen mythic powers. They are something like distorting lenses through which we *can* see into the Background. But it is necessary to break their codes in order to use them as viewers; that is, we must see their lie in order to see their truth.[44]

Daly's work sets out to reverse the patriarchal sacred, just as witches were accused of dancing counterclockwise or destructively reversing natural laws. Here her methodological adaptation of witchcraft into scholarship has the biophilic intention of reversing a nature disenchanted and perverted by patriarchy to its own magical naturalness. In her auto-biographical work *Outercourse* Mary Daly records: 'I unravelled reversals, finding the Archaic Origins of myths and symbols that had been stolen and twisted to serve the masters' purposes'.[45]

Post-patriarchal reconstructions of female sacrality can often be summarized as 'reversing the reversals'. And such reversals can even be made *within* the history of feminism itself. The equal rights or Enlighten-ment feminist tradition argues that the patriarchal construction of female otherness has provided naturalistic justifications for attributing stereo-typical qualities to women (such as irrationality) which have kept them on the margins of society. Where equal rights feminism has blurred equality and sameness in order to remove the stigma of otherness it has greatly improved the integration of women (albeit mainly white middle-class women) into social institutions.

However, that patriarchal construction of female otherness need not be reversed into sameness but into a positive celebration of otherness as a mark of holiness. In this, radical spiritual feminism partially unravels the work of reformist feminism. While spiritual feminism accepts that female otherness has been used against women, that term also has a spiritual/prophetic meaning that needs to be retrieved and reversed on feminists' own terms. Then female otherness is no longer a mark of denied subjecthood, but a mark of the numinous power of female being.

44. *Gyn/Ecology*, p. 47.
45. *Outercourse: The Be-Dazzling Voyage* (London: The Women's Press, 1993), p. 221.

Reversing Otto's use of the phrase 'wholly other' to evoke what is essentially a male experience of the numinous, Mary Daly uses the phrase to evoke the holiness of women who separate *themselves* from society because they know themselves to be

> 'wholly other' to those who are at home in the kingdom of the fathers. Dreadful women are 'quite beyond the sphere of the usual, the intelligible, and the familiar'. Indeed women becoming 'wholly other' *are* strange. Myth-living/loving Hags are members of the 'Outsiders Society'.[46]

The process of reversal does, however, need to be used with care. As I shall discuss at the beginning of Chapter 3, there is a tendency for Goddess feminists to define their own sacrality by assuming that because female sacrality is biophilic, male sacrality is simply the reverse— necrophilic. At its most basic, it is held that where women use their power to foster growth and health in the face of death and disease, male power accelerates death and disease by repeated acts of destruction and the invention of ever more efficient methods of destroying. But despite the overwhelming reality of war and other predominantly male atrocities, I cannot allow that even quite politically conservative men have no sense at all of the sanctity and beauty of life. Patriarchal cultures have, in spite of themselves, produced sublime art and music and count- less instances of heroic love. To deny that (even implicitly) is to resurrect the kind of dualism that feminism has sought to deconstruct. 'Reversing the reversals' should not mean simply blaming all men for what all women have been blamed for: the entry of sin into an otherwise perfect world. It might be preferable to say that erotic, biophilic experiences associated with (but not automatic to) being a woman should shape our concept of the sacred rather than, say, revealed and then highly elaborated patriarchal codes of law or blood sacrifice.

The spiritual feminist method is one which not so much reverses *everything* that is valued under patriarchy as looks for clues within anthropology and the history of religions which imply some original, sub-textual recognition of female *mana* or supernatural power. That positive *mana* has been gradually alienated from women and turned negative or sour in a series of patriarchal sexual-political rationalizations: mythical, moralistic and finally scientific.[47] But any discussion of female *mana* can be lifted out of a given text and 're-meant' by setting the

46. *Gyn/Ecology*, p. 50.
47. K. Millet, *Sexual Politics* (London: Sphere, 1972), p. 51.

material to work within the different religio-political trajectory of feminism in the urban, late-industrial West. So that when women *as speaking subjects* use important source documents like, say, Eliade's *Patterns in Comparative Religion* (1958), or Erich Neumann's Jungian study *The Great Mother* (1955), there are inevitable changes in the signification of these works.

Again, this process of transposition is open ended. The spiritual feminist reconstruction of female sacrality—or at least my synthesis of it—is far from foreclosing conversations about women. It is more gymnastic than magisterial: a linguistic, imaginal, textual play with androcentric anthropology, archaeology, mythography and the history of religions in the unpredicted and unpredictable situation of Western women celebrating and sometimes worshipping goddesses for the first time in about 1500 years. It is true that this reverted knowledge is still 'ideological' knowledge in that the theory and method consciously serve the interest of the knower. Yet it is quite unlike ideology in being *altruistically* constructed in the interests of justice for nature and the oppressed, not individual women alone. It is at once a local narrative of women's liberation and an eschatological metanarrative of the redemption of nature from patriarchy.

This seems to me to be a more promising approach than that of attempting spontaneous generation of new religious 'woman-words' which could easily degenerate into a private language. Even Mary Daly's neologisms derive their power from irony and reversal. Ricoeur was right in saying that self-understanding is mediated through the appropriation and re-contextualizing of texts that express humanity's struggle for the fullness of being, rather than immediately intuited.[48] And knowledge is not only textual: language generated from the experiences of female biological difference can accommodate multiple, expansive 'maternal' knowing that is epistemologically distinct from that of patriarchal scholarship.[49]

So I have not, in my turn to speak from the academic centre (or thereabouts), excluded from my discussion those texts or religions in which women are simply profane in relation to men. On the contrary,

48. See E. White, 'Religion and the Hermeneutics of Gender: An Examination of the Work of Paul Ricoeur', in King (ed.), *Religion and Gender*, p. 78.

49. For a useful discussion of maternal epistemology see B. Miller-McLemore, 'Epistemology or Bust: A Maternal Feminist Knowledge of Knowing', *Journal of Religion* 72 (1985), pp. 229-47.

they contain allusive subterranean meanings. What Alicia Ostriker has said of the biblical narratives is also true of the androcentric narrative of the history of religions:

> Inside the oldest stories are older stories, not destroyed but hidden. Swallowed. Mouth songs. Nobody knows how many. The texts retain traces, leakages, lacunae, curious figures of speech, jagged irruptions. What if I say these traces too are mine?[50]

Like Daly and Ostriker, Ruether has also wanted to read patriarchal texts 'from the underside and note their hidden message'—namely the reversal of female speaking subjects into silent or absent objects.[51] And like Ruether, I am not using this method to prove the existence of a lost feminist religion. It is likely that those ancient texts which bear witness to worship of female divine principles or goddesses also serve patriarchal interests to some degree. If this is the case, 'the past provides us only with a dark mirror on which to show our own images but yields no developed texts by which to verify our imagination. Better then to claim that imagination as our own.'[52] The method I have used in this book closely corresponds with this religious feminist method of using a variety of texts which, at least in their capacity to trigger new metaphors, are equally educative whether they are feminist or not. Their words and images are all available to the imaginative reconstructions that transform one's sense of the possible.

Liberating the Sacred

To say that female embodiment has sacred qualities is, whether one likes it or not, to participate in the long history of religious ideas that has classified the world by degrees or divisions of sacredness and profanity. Of course these divisions have also sanctioned the marginalization of women with other profane things in opposition to the sacred. And feminists are rightly suspicious of any hierarchical division of reality, especially this most fundamental religious division of the sacred and the profane. Whatever is profane in patriarchal religions is available for everyday non-cultic use. Not surprisingly, that everyday use is often *female* use. The vicious circle runs like this: women are excluded from

50. 'Entering the Tents', p. 547.
51. R.R. Ruether, *Womanguides: Readings Toward a Feminist Theology* (Boston: Beacon Press, 1985), p. xi.
52. Ruether, *Womanguides*, p. x.

the powerful male cults and so whatever they use or issue from their bodies is more or less profane. And the profane is defined as that which is beneath divine notice and so cannot be consecrated to the cult—the very cult women have been excluded from. And so it goes on.

Feminism must question all religious dualisms or binary oppositions—especially that most fundamental of binary oppositions: the sacred and the profane. This is because binary oppositions are typically gendered, with the feminine side providing the derivative or pejorative meanings, the antonym. Penelope Margaret Magee is right that philosophy, theology and the church have defined the relation of the sacred and the profane to their own advantage by setting them at war with one another. And, as she says, 'feminism should not sell arms to the combatants'. If forms of violence have been constitutive of the distinction between the sacred and the profane then she is right in warning that

> [t]he politics of subversion will be a dangerous undertaking—the pleasure of keeping our shoes on and striding towards the burning bush. If 'Being in their place is what makes [things] sacred'... 'but so, equally, does their being *out* of place'... who knows what disorder might result?[53]

As the liberation of the sacred is the central theme of this book, it might seem more congruent with feminist immanentism to only use the work of those writers who affirm the sacredness of all things, times and places, rather than include those whose work describes and proposes a distinction between the sacred and the profane where the profane is always something less valuable than the sacred. Of the former, Irene Javors has eloquently evoked the Goddess who transcends our rational divisions of the world into the dualities of creation and destruction, beauty and hideousness, sacredness and profanity: 'In so loving the world, the Goddess in the metropolis dances amid the concrete and the garbage embracing us all.'[54]

Nonetheless, the post-patriarchal sacred, by virtue of being 'post', will still bear a close, even if profoundly critical, relation to the patriarchal sacred. Post-patriarchal feminists name the sacred and the profane on their own terms, but those terms can derive their power by

53. 'Disputing the Sacred: Some Theoretical Approaches to Gender and Religion', in King (ed.), *Religion and Gender*, p. 117.
54. 'Goddess in the Metropolis: Reflections on the Sacred in an Urban Setting', in I. Diamond and G.F. Orenstein (eds.), *Reweaving the World: The Emergence of Ecofeminism* (San Francisco: Sierra Club Books, 1990), p. 214.

reconfiguring the old topography of the sacred. Daly, for example, calls women to reclaim their own profanity and find their sacrality therein:

> The term profane is derived from the Latin *pro* (before) and *fanum* (temple). Feminist profanity is the wild realm of the sacred as it was/is before being caged into the temple of Father Time. It is free time/space... Since it is not confined within the walls of any spatial or temporal temple, it transcends the 'accepted' dichotomies between the sacred and the profane.[55]

Actually Daly offers only a very limited etymological analysis of the Latin word for the profane. Even so, it is clear that some of the multiple meanings of the sacred/profane distinction need to be understood before they can be transformed. Texts cannot be deciphered and altered without knowledge of the codes that they are written in. A feminist concept of the sacred will not appear *ex nihilo*, but in spite or in defiance of previous uses of the concept. For myself, I am not convinced that the sacred/profane duality *originates* in the distinctions of gender even though it is often *used* by a given ideological system to promote the interests of a sex. While that cannot be proved, I would agree with Nathan Söderblom's classic statement that 'holiness is the great word in religion, it is even more essential than the notion of God. Real religion may exist without a definite conception of divinity, but there is no real religion without a distinction between the holy and the profane.'[56] In this sense, 'the sacred' is an important (perhaps the *only*) way of attributing specifically and irreducibly religious value and meaning to an object or phenomenon. And it is spiritual feminism's (usually implicit) distinction between sacred things and things that have been profaned by patriarchy that makes it a spirituality or religion for women before it is a political pressure group.

So it is not that feminist spirituality should do away with the sacred/profane distinction; rather it should redefine it. Daly is surely right in saying that

> we have to be free to dis-cover our own distinctions, refusing to be locked into these mental temples. To try to fit metapatriarchal process into these categories is attempting something analogous to fitting natural feet into footbindings which at first deform and later function as needed supports for contrived deformity.[57]

55. *Gyn/Ecology*, p. 48.
56. In J. Hastings (ed.), *The Encyclopaedia of Religion and Ethics*, VI (Edinburgh: T. & T. Clark, 1913), s.v. 'Holiness: General and Primitive', p. 731.
57. *Gyn/Ecology*, p. 48.

I am not sure that the old categories are, in themselves, as tight-fitting as she seems to think. A new setting for the sacred/profane distinction alters its shape and reference quite dramatically. This setting is a new/old religion for women; a religion that has set out to 'glory in femaleness, to proclaim the spiritual potential inherent in womanhood, to take the "weak vessel" of Christianity and make her the holy chalice of the great goddess'.[58] The embodied immanence of the divine in women-as-goddess means that they are no longer excluded from the mediation of the sacred. A woman's body can mark the passage of the sacred through the world in the numinosity of her experience of its continuous change: conception, birth (not only of babies), ageing or decay, death, rotting, and rebirth into non-human life forms.[59]

Given that the profane has usually been associated with 'female' impurity of various kinds, it is not surprising that spiritual feminists talk a great deal more about the sacred than about precautions for avoiding the profane. For on the one hand, the resacralization of the whole body and its organic byproducts deprives the category of the profane of much of its traditional content. But on the other hand, in the feminist religious worldview whatever has been distorted by patriarchy (and very little has not) has been to a lesser or greater degree profaned. The sphere of this 'true' profane is what Daly calls the 'foreground'—the everyday, flattened, boring zone of alienation. The foreground is opposed to the sacred Other dimension of the 'Background': 'the Realm of Wild Reality; the Homeland of women's Selves and of all Others; the Time/Space where auras of plants, planets, stars, animals, and all Other animate beings connect'.[60]

In effect, spiritual feminism synthesizes a number of theoretical approaches to the sacred. Daly's division of 'foreground' and 'Background' is a powerful sacred/profane opposition. Although a radical feminist opposition of the sacred and the profane has moral elements, they are not straightforwardly so. The relation of the spiritual feminist sacred and the morally good is an important one—especially as feminism is an inherently moral critique of patriarchal powers. Yet something that spiritual feminists would hold in common with anthropologists and historians of religion is the recognition that a tabooed object is not

58. Eller, *Living in the Lap of the Goddess*, p. 33.
59. See E.D. Gray, 'Women's Experience and Naming the Sacred', *Woman of Power* 12 (1989), p. 11.
60. *Outercourse*, p. 1.

necessarily dirty or morally unclean; it simply has a powerful charge and must therefore be treated in particular ways. In other words, a taboo acknowledges and respects the power of any object which is literally out of the ordinary. As such it inspires dread (which can in some circumstances tip into hostile fear) and must be treated with special precautions. Roughly speaking, the Western moralization of the sacred and the profane began with the eighth-century BCE Judaean prophets who detached the meaning of the sacred from its narrower cultic context and moralized it as social righteousness. Eventually, in Judaism and Christianity, a holy person or saint with the privileged status of separation from ordinary social duties would be expected to conform to ideal moral standards as well as (in some denominations) incarnate semimiraculous powers of wisdom and healing. But in the primal religious forms (to which spiritual feminists often look for inspiration) the sacred has not been moralized and only implies that the tabooed object has had close contact with the divine and must not be approached without special precautions.

In a feminist context, where that 'object' is the female body, that and all cognate natural forms are forbidden to the 'touch' of patriarchal desecration. Yet the perception of a person, time or space as temporarily, or by its nature, sacred does not entail that it is of itself morally superexcellent. Spiritual feminists, like all feminist ethicists, are suspicious of moralism. Feminist ethicists have rightly refused to adopt the posture of moral omnipotence and omniscience that privileged male philosophers and theologians have been able to do from the high places of academe. Letting (a very few) feminists into the academy has exposed the particularly 'masculine' nature of moral imperatives applied universally and regardless of context. However, I would not have undertaken to write this book if I had entirely accepted the most radical deconstructionist position that one cannot be morally *right* about something. One has moral obligations to the holy, even if they are not named as such. Despite its enjoying the liberation of postmodern interpretive practices, feminism cannot afford its most radically relativist conceits. There *are*, in all feminisms, two final and related moral adjudicators: the full humanity of women and the absolute value of all living things; neither of which has, until very recently, informed mainstream liberal ethics and theology.

So a feminist sacred/profane distinction does have an ethical dynamic in sacralizing the humanity of women and the value of nature, but not a moralistic one. Thealogy liberates the sacred from puritanical virtuousness but reinforces the religio-ethical dynamic of the distinction. As in any immanentist spirituality, where Goddess feminism perceives, say, a forest as sacred, that will entail a particular religio-moral orientation towards it—such as refusing to clear-cut it for timber or otherwise subordinate it to human profit. Or again, if the female body is sacred then to abuse its sexuality, or misappropriate what it produces, is a violation as well as an injustice.

The anthropologist Mary Douglas demarcated the profane as that which is—like a pair of boots on a dining table—in the wrong place.[61] But feminists would want to say that patriarchal desecration has done more than put contaminants in the wrong place—they have no place. Patriarchy contaminates both consciousness and the environment and in doing so creates the spiritual, aesthetic and environmental wastelands that banish the sense of the divine presence. So one could not say that diesel oil is profane when it clogs a seagull's eyes and feathers but neutral when it is in an engine. Given that the uncontrolled production of engines is substantially contributing to the degradation of the plane-tary environment, this kind of distinction is not adequate. Patriarchal subjects feel empowered to dominate creation—the world of objects— through conquest and colonization: the means and results of continual acts of desecration. Patriarchy then holds onto its misappropriated source of power by subsuming natural and female sacrality into its coercive apparatuses and mechanisms of power.

But this powerful subject/powerless object dualism loses meaning in the 'maternal' dissolution of the boundaries between me/not me. Women in the generative sacral mode cannot be walled cities. They are individual persons but they express themselves in and through their connectedness with what lives. The feminist sacred refers to a standard of value and practice that is 'wholly other' to the patriarchal values which have recruited as much of the social order as they can (including our idea of the divine) to the pursuit of power and all its gratifications. So the restoration of divine presence to the world demands more than a new ethic alone; it demands the healing of resacralization. Female sacral acts regenerate or re-energize what has lost life or energy by desecration and profanization. For if profanization of the sacred is destructive of its object, then its opposite, sacralization, returns the natural potency or inner *telos* to the object in an act closely akin to re-creation.

61. M. Douglas, *Purtiy and Danger* (Harmondsworth: Penguin, 1970), p. 48.

The feminist liberation of the sacred is not achieved by simply eradicating the category of the profane as if it were in itself an immoral, patriarchal category. I am not convinced that all distinction and division is *a priori* unfeminist. The spiritual distinction between sacredness and profanity is, I think, necessary to the liberation of the sacred on at least two counts. First, it is precisely the *loss* of the sacred/profane distinction in post-Reformation and Enlightenment secularization which—coupled with a transcendentalist theological tradition—has been largely responsible for environmental destruction. The *hubris* of male mastery over a disenchanted nature has left creation unable to command reverence as sacred and therefore available to those with sufficient power to degrade it as property at their sole disposal.[62] The resacralization of nature has, then, a spiritual/political function in protecting it from the apparently limitless capitalist predation that has polluted (profaned) it.

Secondly, the sacred/profane distinction does not have a fixed or predetermined reference. Although tabooed things will always 'belong in some way to a different order of being, and therefore any contact with them will produce an upheaval at the ontological level',[63] what is sacred in one context can be profane in another. As Van Gennep puts it, 'Characteristically, the presence of the sacred (and the performance of appropriate rites) is variable. Sacredness as an attribute is not absolute; it is brought into play by the nature of particular situations.'[64] The methodological reversals I have described above are a manifestation of that variability. It is the reversible, pivotal nature of the category which makes it such an important and adaptive tool in spiritual feminist criticism, reclamation and reconstruction of religion. The sacred is socially determined by human perception; from where a person stands. Plutarch, for example, remarked that the Greeks could not tell whether the Jews worshipped or abhorred the pig: whether they abstained from its flesh because it was sacred or because it was profane. Of course the pig is actually profane in Judaism, but it could equally have been the reverse: the Cretans did not eat pigs because they were sacred.[65]

Likewise patriarchy might call menstrual or postpartum bleeding

---

62. See M. Raphael, 'Doing Green Justice to God: Immanentism in the Contemporary Feminist Spirituality Movement', *Theology in Green* 5 (1993), pp. 34-42.
63. Eliade, *Patterns in Comparative Religion*, p. 17.
64. *The Rites of Passage*, p. 12.
65. Söderblom, 'Holiness', p. 736.

unclean, and spiritual feminism might call it sacred. But both responses stem from the same belief that in these states a woman has a powerful 'charge' because she has come very close to the divine source of life and death. So radical religious feminism *does* actually share something of the structure of the patriarchal sacred/profane distinction but reverses the patriarchal denigration and segregation of female power. In believing that the female body is particularly close to the source of life, radical religious feminism shares with far more conservative commentators on the sacred the belief that menstruating women have *mana*; they are powerfully charged by their contact with the life force. But it is not the ascription of *mana* to women which is, in itself, patriarchal, but the methods by which that *mana* is misnamed and therefore misused as the profane. When a person is called profane, she or he is, like all profane things, available for common use. Profane persons (like the 'Untouchables' in Hinduism) are the *Lumpen* of religious systems. Without charismatic power or moral reliability they are disqualified from social power and responsibility. Indeed, patriarchy's association of profane things with the contagion of organic corruption (a process that remains outside its control) requires that they are controlled by religious ordinance or harnessed to the service of the (male) sacred.

But the sacred and the profane are dynamically related. So, for example, in a gynocentric scheme, the 'dangerous' power of the profane as manifest in menstrual blood can come to be *perceived* as a beneficent power revealing something important about the workings of the divine and therefore sacred. Conversely, if what has been called sacred in the patriarchal scheme (perhaps 'holy war' the spilling of Jesus' blood under torture, or ascetic sexual abstention and fasting) is perceived by feminists as spiritually and politically harmful they will (non-violently) separate from it or exorcise themselves of its power over their consciousness. The sacred is, then, a shifting boundary open to reconstruction and new religious intention. Most cultures have regarded menstrual blood as profane and have accordingly subjected women to varying degrees of segregation from the sacred. But religious feminists (both Jewish and neo-pagan) now choose to experience their menstruation as a time to recharge themselves through the beneficent power of their blood. Jewish feminists celebrate the new moon (Rosh Chodesh) as a monthly rebirth and even contemporary orthodox Jewish women have come to regard their monthly visit to the *mikvah* (ritual bath) as a positive means of honouring and refreshing their bodies.[66] Perhaps indirectly influenced by Jewish feminism, these female apologists for *Taharat HaMishpachah* (codes of family purity) perceive their being *niddah* (separate) during menstruation as a way of giving them space to recover their bodily integrity as individuals who are not always sexually available to their husbands.

Neo-pagan feminists also refuse to see menstruation as a curse, profaned by its removal from the protected sphere of divine things. They welcome their menstruation as a time of magical 'dragon' energy and perceive this lunar blood as a sign of the cosmic dimension of their embodiment. Accordingly menstrual blood is treated with respect—vaginal sponges are sometimes used instead of bleached, non-biodegradable towels and tampons and when the sponges or cloths are washed the water can be used as a fertilizer for plants or for rituals, rather than being flushed away in private like other excreta.

It should be remembered that spiritual feminism did not begin this dialectic of desacralization and resacralization. Historically, female sacrality has been matrifocally constructed (perhaps), patriarchally deconstructed, and in the late twentieth century reconstructed again in spiritual feminism. It is a central tenet of spiritual feminist history that patriarchy broke the first taboo against desecrating the female earth—the Great Mother. To take the case of mining: in prehistory the earth was regarded as being too sacred to rip apart. (In the late nineteenth century a chief of the Wanapum tribe refused to till the ground for the same reasons.)[67] According to Rupert Sheldrake, when mining began, men *did* practise purification rites before entering the mine, seeing it as the Goddess's sacred womb and feeling obliged to honour the fairy protectors of the underground realm. The metal-workers understood theirs to be a 'female' gestatory task of transforming raw materials into cultural goods by the heat or energy of the womb-like furnace. As Sheldrake puts it: 'In ancient societies metal-workers and smiths were at once feared and held in high esteem; their powers were regarded as both

66. See, for example, Linda Sireling's article, 'The Jewish Woman: Different and Equal', in Joseph (ed.), *Through the Devil's Gateway*, pp. 87-96; T. Abramov, *The Secret of Jewish Femininity: Insights into the Practice of Taharat HaMishpachah* (Southfield, MI: Targum, 1988), pp. 97-109.

67. R. Sheldrake, *The Rebirth of Nature: The Greening of Science and God* (London: Rider, 1993), p. 6.

sacred and demonic.'[68] With the advent of patriarchal warriors the taboos that imposed respect for the earth and its ores slowly dissapeared.

Spiritual feminists now choose to (re)gain power for the sacred when, in their turn, they break patriarchal taboos, for example by attaching used menstrual pads to the perimeter fences of nuclear installations, painting designs on their bodies with menstrual blood, or using phials of it in rituals. These taboo-breaking acts are using the health-giving power of the holy (the Anglo-Saxon root of this word, *hal*, means healthy or whole) to protect life from the sickness and death that follows patriarchal desecration. By definition, sacred things require reverent care, and ecofeminists, among others, manifest their care of the sacred in direct actions such as the establishment of peace camps around the gates of the Cruise missile site at Greenham Common, an encirclement that protected everything outside the installation; or, in California, the blockade of the Diabolo Canyon Nuclear Power Plant.[69]

Although, within human perception, the sacred is a relative category, spiritual feminists, like all religious people, want to say that their perception of the sacred is the closest human perception can come to the reality of the sacred in itself. In other words, spiritual feminists *are* making a truth claim about the sacred and for the authenticity of their own spirituality. Medieval theologians developed intricate procedures by which they could tell whether supernatural power came from God or the devil. The truth of the spiritual feminist claim is, however, self-authenticating in that if the effects of female sacral processes are that planetary and human degradation is visibly healed and life flourishes, the sacred will show itself as an authentic displacement of the false sacred.

Another way in which the sacred was traditionally demarcated was in its separation from ordinary or common things and its appointment to divine use. Religious feminism, by contrast, never distinguishes the sacred from the profane by removing it from ordinary daily life and ordinary use. This practice drastically devalues everyday (usually female) experience and denudes it of religious meaning. But religious feminism does or could distinguish sacred and profane things by attention to their effects within a given scheme. Patriarchal power is profane because of the sickness and death it inflicts on living things. For example, scientific research—especially vivisection, arms manufacture and testing, and the

---

68. *The Rebirth of Nature*, p. 8.

69. See Starhawk, *Dreaming the Dark: Magic, Sex and Politics* (London: Unwin Hyman, 1990), pp. 151-53.

'development' of 'green field' sites for roads and commercial building—inflict a particular sort of death. It is not the cyclic death that is found in nature where one life-form is transformed into another life-form. Patriarchal desecrations inflict an abrupt end on the cycle. These are ends without biophilic transformatory intentions and only serve the interests and profit of an elite. The tangible effects of the patriarchal profane can be seen in the way that, like all violations, it brings the fall-out of sickness and extinction in its wake. It has been estimated that by the middle of the next century over half of all existing species will be endangered or extinct. Overhunting, the introduction of new species into habitats where they did not previously occur (causing disease and exterminating other species), and habitat destruction are all profanations of the earth. As ever, the profane is contagious and here produces a 'domino' effect in which the extinction of one species brings, in turn, the extinction of many of its predators.[70]

To any immanentist, the smoking, amputated remains of a rainforest, a six-lane motorway cut through an English woodland, bloated dead fish washed up on the side of a lake, a tiger languishing in a cage, are all the sacred made visibly profane. Used by feminists, the relation between the sacred and profane can provide an indispensable distinction between the biophilic and the necrophilic: what manifests the divine and what violates it. That feminist taboo-breaking is healing in intention and effect, and patriarchy's is destructive and self-serving, is evidence of the authenticity of the feminist sacred. For female sacrality derives its magical or sacred power from the natural forces of the universe, not the human will to power. As Cynthia Eller puts it, the spiritual feminist exerts her will for good by positively manipulating the energies of the created universe:

> Psychically moving the energetic forces of the universe, she enters a trance state and opens herself up to communion with unseen forces that drive her life...the life of the world. And sometimes, in small ways—in gradually larger ways—she makes a difference.[71]

The sacred is a beneficent creative power that can be ritually 'tapped into' for healing and empowerment against evil. In this sense, the feminist Wiccan concept of magic as 'divine power accessed and directed by

70. J. Diamond, *The Rise and Fall of the Third Chimpanzee* (London: Vintage, 1991), p. 323.

71. *Living in the Lap of the Goddess*, pp. 12-13.

the will and the actions of its practitioners'[72] is closely akin to other traditional practices of the sacred.

Perhaps Durkheim was not entirely wrong in his reductionist, dualistic, androcentric contention that the sacred originates in a community's projection of itself as a transcendent unity. For this is clearly true of patriarchy's will to deify its own political values by projecting them, and patriarchal maleness itself, onto God. However, I would argue that the sacred *itself* is mediated only through the spiritual capacity to feel and nurture the presence of the divine. That is, the authentic feminist sense of the sacred is a response to the transsubjective reality of the divine—a reality that stands over and against the necrophilic political values of patriarchy. Where 'God' is the proper name of the god constructed to serve patriarchal dominance, Kate Millet may have been right that 'patriarchy has God on its side'.[73] But religious feminism conceptualizes the divine not simply as an ally in the struggle for liberation but as the meaning of that liberation itself.

Where the sacred is not only a social construction of meaning and value but also a true revelation of the divine, it suffuses human values and practice with healing 'biophilia'. In other words, the sacred mediates the healing/holiness of divine presence. That presence entails ethical obligations—namely that the sacred should not be treated as if it were the profane. Indeed, divine immanence in nature means that nothing should be used as if it existed to serve the patriarchal will to power.

But when the sacred is subsumed into patriarchal dogma it is almost inevitably distorted or negated and serves to absolutize the false values of that ideology. And by correlation, whatever opposes those patriarchal values becomes marginalized as the profane other. This is certainly the case in fundamentalist circles today, where, with echoes of the witch-hunts, religious feminism's biophilic practices are cast as demonic. Yet the ferocious energy with which the patriarchal sacred has set upon the female sacred by naming it as profane and therefore marginalizing it, screening it off, secluding it, or (during the Witchcraze) torturing it into invisibility, is also an admission of its power. Perhaps spiritual feminism wants to say that women's exclusion from the cult has been less because they are too profane, but because patriarchy has sensed that they are *too sacred* and so would disorder the false sanctity of their own cult.

In sum, religious feminism has described a process in which women

72. *Living in the Lap of the Goddess*, p. 116.
73. *Sexual Politics*, p. 51.

have been profanized or set apart from the patriarchal sphere of the sacred—a public and cultic realm sanctified by its own religious projections. The result is that in patriarchal religions human sacrality is sharply dichotomized and unequally valued along lines of gender and female sacral energies have been dissipated or contained as 'feminine' sanctity by restrictive ideological divisions of religious labour. It is important to remember that women are not absolutely profane in patriarchal religions. They are usually profane in relation to the cult—especially during menstruation. But feminine virtues such as virginity, chastity, obedience, silence, stillness, serenity and self-sacrificial dutifulness can all sanctify women, their homes and their families. How spiritual feminism is liberating, regenerating and transforming 'feminine' sanctity into female or feminist sacrality will be the subject of this book.

Chapter 1

FEMALE SACRALITY IN A FEMINIST CONTEXT

> Then in my usual way, I called upon the Great Original Witch in every woman, who Howls:
> *Flieg mit meinen Winden*—Fly with my Winds
> *Ströme mit meinen Wasser*—Rush with my Waters
> *Umarme meine Erde*—Hug my Earth
> *Entzünde mein Feuer*—Light my Fire!
> Since Germany was the country in which the witchcraze in Western Europe had been most cruel and most violent, I felt a special Be-Witching power in the uttering/Howling of those words there, on that ground. The women also Heard that power.
>
> Mary Daly[1]

In 1976 Valerie Saiving observed that there was almost no material available on women's experience of the sacred, and that the little there was had usually been interpreted by men. Consequently, she felt that feminist scholars of religion would encounter serious difficulties in giving an account of women's experience and understanding of sacrality.[2] I doubt that Saiving could say the same today. Since 1976 a great deal has been written by women which is, broadly speaking, about the retrieval of their capacity as women to manifest sacred powers. Indeed, although the term 'female sacrality' is rarely used, its recovery in contemporary religious feminism as 'womanpower' is an event in the history of Western religion whose importance should be recognized by all students of religion. At present, however, it is mainly discussed by those in the womanspirit movement whose writings seem to me to have the recovery of female spiritual power (or female sacrality) as their unifying theme.

In my introduction to the present study I adopted Nancy Falk's summary of the use of the term 'female sacrality' in the history of religions

---

1. *Outercourse*, pp. 308-309.
2. 'Androcentrism in Religious Studies', p. 191.

as the manifestation of transformatory divine energy in essentially or traditionally female activities. These activities might be biological: gestation, lactation and so forth; or they might be cultural derivations of biological processes such as transforming raw materials into cultural products through gardening, spinning, weaving, potting, brewing, boiling and baking. This is how the term is used in the history of religions, but clearly, in the process of its retrieval and practice within a green, feminist, post-Christian and postmodern paradigm its meaning will be altered. (And as such the term is significant to any study of the politics of late twentieth-century religion.)

Feminist neo-paganism[3] reveres female power and its flourishing is seen to be a precondition and a sign of the health of the whole biosphere in whose energies the divine is immanent and which is either imaged as female or named as 'the Goddess'. And where the divinized earth is held to gestate and feed all life-forms in an essentially female manner, the human female body images or 'is' the Goddess in its own biological and cultural processes. The religious and social status of women is therefore dramatically upgraded by these eco-spiritual assumptions. Female being becomes a conduit of sacred power: a boundary point at which magical or supernatural powers are mediated into and through the world.

But under Western patriarchy the absence of a self-defining female divine principle from the practice and study of religion has either rendered this ontology of women absent, or has subjugated it into feminine piety and sexual purity. A combination of feminist emancipatory critique, postmodern theories of power and experiential witness has led to the consciousness that the authority of priests, rabbis, taboos and purification rites has been imposed upon women because there is something 'other' in women that patriarchy wants to keep in check. This 'otherness' is debilitating to men and male systems unless it is redirected to serve their own ends. It may best be described as female sacrality: a kind of embodied energy or 'womanpower' (a participant term for female sacrality.)

Theoretically at least, once women begin to restore this energy to themselves it will not only eventually entail their equal social and religious status, but will also restore health to the natural world from

---

3.   I am using the word 'pagan' fairly loosely to suggest diverse groups of spiritual feminists who are no longer monotheist; do not credit the Bible with any more authority than any other ancient text—and often less; and who affirm a female divine principle which women embody whether they bear children or not.

which it is drawn and whose energies, like those of women, are plundered by men. In short, the academic programme which seeks to restore women's religious experience to our knowledge of religion can be fruitfully coupled by spiritual feminist scholars with the feminist spirituality movement whose purpose is to generate spiritual empowerment by re-presenting the female divine principle in women's lives.

It needs to be stressed that in the creation of new systems of value, all religious feminists, not just radical religious feminists, are to some extent engaged in 'a re-sourcing of energy'. But the implication that *female* power is in and of itself salvific (in the sense of a healing ointment or 'salve'—not as a redemption from death) is more prevalent in radical spiritual feminism. As the radical feminist Sally Gearheart puts it,

> there is a source or kind of power qualitatively different from the one we have been taught to accept and to operate with; further, the understanding, the protection, the development of that source and the allowing of it to reach its full dimensions could mean the redemption of the entire globe from the devastation of the last ten thousand years.[4]

Female Sacral Activity

In Goddess religion and feminist witchcraft women's transformative powers are used in a number of connected ways: domestic, ritual and political. None of these is, in itself, more important than the others because they are essentially the same: the patriarchally separated spheres of religion, home and political activism have all been sacralized as one sphere of spiritual/political praxis.

The domestic forms of sacrality—cooking, weaving, gardening and other such activities—are familiar from the history of religions and have been reclaimed (albeit in a conservative form) by Kathryn Allen Rabuzzi. She suggests that a woman who has been alienated from the traditional religious institutions may find that 'something [else] in her life serves as a conduit to a level of experience she recognises as sacred'.[5] In consciously creating a clean sanctuary whose threshold divides the home from the profane public world, the traditional homemaker takes on the role of priestess and through the rituals of housework enters into a mode

4. 'Womanpower: Energy Re-Sourcement', in Spretnak (ed.), *The Politics of Women's Spirituality*, p. 196.

5. *The Sacred and the Feminine: Toward a Theology of Housework* (New York: Seabury Press, 1982), p. 32.

of being which Rabuzzi names as the goddess Hestia—the goddess of the hearth. Housework, she claims, can be hierophanic (revelatory of the sacred) when it is properly valued as an act with specifically religious intentionality. Rabuzzi interprets a woman's creation of shining order out of the chaos made by a young family as her participating once more in what Mircea Eliade has described as the mythic time of creation. Transcending the profane time of everyday history, a woman sacralizes her home by 'ritually returning as a priestess to the time of origins, the primordial time in which the gods and goddesses originally created order out of chaos'.[6] Or again, by her cooking (especially on high days and holidays) a woman provides an abundance of food and pleasure and so enters 'the sacred realm of the great goddesses'.[7]

That female sacrality unifies the domestic, biological and cosmic realms is made clear by the poet, artist and ex-Benedictine nun Meinrad Craighead. She summarizes the common dynamic of female sacrality—whether Goddess-referring or otherwise—with the following:

> Our feminine existence is connected to the metamorphoses of nature: the pure potential of water, the transformative power of blood, the seasonal rhythms of the earth, the cycles of lunar dark and light. Within nature too we transform matter, giving form to elemental energy, handling water and fire, cooking and baking, bearing and healing, tending and gathering, making from the earth's materials.[8]

Although Rabuzzi's and Craighead's work may be insufficiently political for some, their account of female sacrality is not patriarchal. Theirs is not just a domesticated form of, say, priestly sacrificial sacrality. Female sacrality is cultic in that, like the ancient cults, it is considered essential to the maintenance of the health of the whole community and the land. But it is not propitiatory. Instead of sacrificing women's needs to those of husband and family (or sacrificing any living thing), spiritual feminist practice is to work transformations in and through the natural cycles of birth, death and decay. The 'ordinary' is at once ordinary and non-ordinary reality. Divine energies are channelled through the female body and imagination in domestic crafts and biological and political relationships—each of which is modelled on the other. So it is only when female sacrality is subjected to the patriarchal separation of home and cult/culture that it (dis)*appears* as sub-religious. The spiritual feminist model

6.   *The Sacred and the Feminine*, p. 97.
7.   *The Sacred and the Feminine*, p. 126.
8.   'Immanent Mother', p. 79.

of immanent holiness is quite different. Feminist spirituality does not regard the earth as the dust of the grave, or homes and landscapes as mere backdrops for historical rebellions and reconciliations with God. Instead, the earth is experienced as a womb-like divine mother of all possibility. With that paradigm shift comes a revaluation of biophilic generativity as the greatest good.

Goddesses, Mothers and Magic

In spiritual feminism, especially Goddess feminism, female reproductivity divinizes women without transcendentalizing them. In this it is more than a kind of mystical humanism. Female sacrality must, I think, mean more than the sum of a woman's best physical and mental capacities. Sacrality is a religious phenomenon and here originates in a divine source immanent as the ground of the created order (not bestowed on privileged individuals as an act of grace from above). This is why the religious term 'Goddess' is so often used to indicate that the source of female sacral energy is both identical with and transcendent to the self as immanent in all that is alive. As Carol Christ made clear in her ground-breaking article 'Why Women Need the Goddess: Phenomenological, Psychological and Political Reflections', it is not necessary to make final pronouncements on the precise nature of the Goddess, but more to understand her as the unifying symbol 'of the legitimacy of female power as a beneficent and independent power' in harmony with the energies of nature and the wills of all beings.[9]

Mary Daly takes the word 'Goddess' even further as that which can name 'active participation in the Powers of Be-ing'. The word 'Goddess' can be a 'metaphor', namely, a word that literally (from the Greek *meta* and *pherein*) carries women out of and beyond 'phallocracy' to where they can realize their Elemental powers.[10] The very word 'Goddess' has magical transformatory power. Like a witch's broom the word is a vehicle in which to quest for the recovery of female energies. Daly does not postulate a 'real' divine Mother with a will and purpose of her own whose body is the world. Others are more inclined towards thealogical realism. In fact it is often difficult to be precise about a witch or Goddess religionist's 'position' because their texts are not precise philosophical treatises and there is an understandable suspicion of dogmatism

9. In Christ and Plaskow (eds.), *Womanspirit Rising*, p. 277.
10. *Beyond God the Father*, p. xix.

encroaching into areas of intuitive and mythopoeic experience. So although there is no orthodoxy in the Goddess movement (indeed heresy is often promoted to the status of methodology) there *is* a unifying theme: that of the recovery of the divinity of female power. Whether that power is channelled from one or many female deities or whether it arises simply from the intrinsic sacredness of the cycles of female and cosmic existence is of secondary importance. Starhawk's account of the *effect* of the Goddess as an idea and an experience would, I think, be accepted by all postbiblical writers:

> The image of the Goddess inspires women to see ourselves as divine, our bodies as sacred, the changing phases of our life as holy, our aggression as healthy, our anger as purifying, and our power to nurture and create, but also to limit and destroy when necessary, as the very force that sustains all life.[11]

The concept of the Goddess is inseparable from the spiritual feminist concept of motherhood (in all its forms) as a cosmic generativity. Human culture and history are female issues, as are the vegetation and other animals that are brought forth from the body of the earth. Broadly speaking, the difference between divine maternal creativity and the creativity of a father god is that female powers transform elements in nature, whereas in the biblical creation stories God does not create the world by transforming parts of his body or pre-existent matter, but more or less *ex nihilo* by his will or reason. This latter form of creation ensures that God is credited with the creation of a perfect world whose imperfections are then attributable to human disordering.

But mothers do not produce perfect people. (In traditional Catholic theology Jesus' moral perfection has owed a great deal to Mary's abnormal reproductivity.) Thealogy has no concept of perfection, or the material stasis an object's perfection implies. Its conception of female sacral power originates in the pagan celebration of flux, where women—especially in their mother and 'crone' aspects—guard the inseparable mysteries of life and death. When a woman experiences the transformation of her body into the vehicle of new life, transforming plant and animal matter into blood that will create a new being, she incarnates and summarizes the transformation mysteries that sustain life.

The human mammal is born helplessly dependent on the loving and

---

11. 'Witchcraft as Goddess Religion', in Spretnak (ed.), *The Politics of Women's Spirituality*, p. 51.

protective attentions of its mother. The mother has the power to kill her offspring by neglect or rejection; if women are perceived to give life they can also take it away. Thealogy is unsentimental about mothers. Just as the thealogical trinity of Virgin, Mother and Crone is a formal or conceptual distinction rather than a description of three separate states, a mother can also be (or feel like) the raging crone or still as unattached and free as the virgin. She may not instantaneously love her baby; she may resent its absolute intrusion into every aspect of her life. In short, thealogy recognizes in its trinity that motherhood is rarely, if ever, purely a gift of life (and the mother's own life) to a child.

Patriarchy does not accept this account of motherhood and has often projected its sense of the ambiguity of motherhood onto old women who have ceased to be responsible for their children's welfare. The demonization of old mothers as witches or—in the twentieth-century West—rendering them culturally invisible betrays the patriarchal religions' recognition that femaleness signifies death as well as life. Old women have been profanized and set apart as a way of distancing masculinity from the fact of its mutability and mortality. Simone de Beauvoir argued that men in 'high' civilizations like to see themselves as abstractions or as immortal gods fallen from the brightness of an infinite heaven into the mud of the female earth. The womb then signifies a prison, cave or abyss from which a man's birth marks the beginning of his death.[12]

The philosophical/political context of female sacrality is crucial to its meaning for a given period. In a culture or period that celebrates the mysteries of fertility a woman can be a divine guardian or priestess of those mysteries even if that culture is basically male-dominated. But in a culture that seeks to conquer, control and exploit nature by reason, female sacrality either has no function at all (as in secularism) or it is downgraded to mere sorcery and those who honour it are called super-stitious rather than religious. Indeed, in the biblical traditions the sacrality of motherhood can only be accommodated in marriage sanctified by a male religious authority. In the traditional Jewish or Christian marriage a woman 'loses none of her primitive attributes, but these are reversed in sign; from being an evil omen, they become of good omen, black magic turns to white. As servant, woman is entitled to the most splendid deification.'[13]

12. *The Second Sex* (Harmondsworth: Penguin, 1982), pp. 177-79.
13. *The Second Sex*, p. 204.

That female being seems to reflect the workings of divine creativity has been an ambiguous benefit in the history of women since 'the ancient, continuing envy, awe and dread of the male for the female capacity to create life has repeatedly taken the form of hatred for every other female aspect of creativity'.[14] By their biological association with the lunar cycles women become, as de Beauvoir put it, 'part of that fearsome machinery which turns the planets and the sun in their courses'.[15] Although this female reproductive energy is not like that of the theistic God's creativity, it is so much a function of divinity that the patriarchal will to power has sought to take it for itself. Patriarchy abstracts natural energy to fuel its own systems, and projects its own will to power onto God as Father: it not only colonizes female power, it also colonizes or takes back the powers it has projected onto its own god. The patriarchal appropriation of nature's energy and God's will has allowed biblical cultures to ignore or discredit female sacral powers. It seems telling that Catholicism in particular evidently considers it less ignominious that the son of God should have died with thieves on a city rubbish dump than that he should have been defiled by the blood of a normal birth. The very defiling squalor of Jesus' death is inseparable from its sacrificial power. The defilement of menstrual blood is not assimilable into this scheme of salvific reversals—indeed it would deprive the scheme of its power.

An example of the male appropriation of female powers is seen in the prohibition of abortion. Under patriarchal monotheism babies become a gift of God the Father and much of the religious basis of anti-abortion laws assumes that life is only in the gift of the male God. This means that if women have no stake in the divine creative processes then the baby is resident in, but is not a part of, their own body and they can have no say in its fate. Women are, so to speak, merely the wrapping paper for this gift. Only when the baby emerges from the mother can a christening—or, for Jewish boys, the rite of circumcision—offer God's gift back to him, cleansed and prepared to enter patriarchal sacred history. On the whole, that grand narrative has not served biophilic relationality: as feminists have observed for over a hundred years, when baby sons grow up, mothers are traditionally expected to socialize them into practices of competition and domination. Relationality has to

14. A. Rich, *Of Woman Born: Motherhood as Experience and Institution* (London: Virago, 1992), p. 40.
15. *The Second Sex*, p. 181.

become a private 'feminine' mode in contrast to which mature masculinity is defined.

Feminist criticism of modern patriarchal religion has argued that in Protestantism and Judaism particularly, the only authority or power allowed to women has been sentimentalized, contained and defused as maternal and domestic. The purity of a wife's maternal love is (usually implicitly) set against the impurity of her bodily discharges. But if a woman does not donate her reproductive power to the maintenance of patriarchal socio-religious systems, its energies can be subject to a number of false namings. Without being channelled into motherhood, a woman's sexual power can be feared as that of a temptress or marriage-breaker. Or if she (or her husband) is infertile, she forfeits much of that power and becomes an object of pity.

But the spiritual feminist conception of female sacrality is by no means exclusively maternal—just as female religious office in the ancient patri-archies was not solely maternal. The Mesopotamian goddess Innana exercised a power which fused love and sex: she was the king's lover and his power was born of the blessing of her love and the united energies of their sexual desire.[16] Sumerian goddesses as well as ordinary women living in ancient Israel were mourners and lamented whole destroyed cities, not just private, familial deaths. (Ritual lamentation was, and is, more significant than a cathartic expression of grief. It can be intercessory, whereby the woman mediates between the dead and the divine powers who hold the fate of the living and the dead.[17]) Or again, prophetesses, mediums and women attuned to the subterranean voices are attested throughout the ancient world. The palm reader or clairvoyant sitting in a shabby caravan hung with tawdry bits of old cloth, pretending to look into her crystal ball, is a caricature much beloved of children and comedians. But this degraded archetype is a distant memory of ancient female divination. Despite Yahweh's prohibitions, women mediums like the Witch of En Dor were consulted by kings anxious to know the outcome of future wars.

The Dianic priestess Zsuzsanna Budapest summarizes female sacral powers not in the word 'mother' but in 'witch', as it is 'the only word in English that denotes "woman with spiritual power".'[18] The manifesto

16. T. Frymer-Kensky, *In the Wake of the Goddesses: Women, Culture, and the Biblical Transformation of Biblical Myth* (New York: The Free Press, 1992), p. 62.
17. *In the Wake of the Goddesses*, pp. 36, 38.
18. *The Holy Book of Women's Mysteries*, p. xvii.

of her coven, the Susan B. Anthony coven no. 1, opens with the words: 'We believe that feminist witches are women who search within themselves for the female principle of the universe and who relate as daughters to the Creatrix.' It goes on, 'We are committed to defending our interests and those of our sisters through the knowledge of witchcraft: to blessing, to cursing, to healing, and to binding with power rooted in woman-identified wisdom.' The Manifesto ends with the witch's pledge to remember her past and renew her powers.[19]

Given that the English language does not possess respectable words for female spiritual authority and power, their retrieval is bound to appear subversive and eccentric. In the modern world words like 'medium', 'priestess', 'witch', and even 'prophetess' all connote a degree of fraudulence or crankiness. But the very fact that spiritual feminism is so easily dismissable as 'cranky' is an integral part of the patriarchal derogation of female power. Postmodern criticism has, however, served spiritual feminism well in arguing that the dominant discourse community maintains its interests by mocking or suppressing those discourses which pose a threat to its authority and universality. In the present case, those subjugated discourses are gynocentric and are recovered or reconstructed by feminists committed to the emancipation of female sacrality. For where female religious titles are taken seriously, their occultism reinforces the Jewish and Christian distrust and even hatred of the independent exercise of female knowledges. In fundamentalist ideology, the word 'occult' is not simply applied to arcane 'hidden' practices, but to any practice that is perceived (in this case, wrongly) to manipulate God and serve the interests of the self over and against God's. In this context, Mary Daly's restoration and reinvention of such spat-upon terms as Spinster, Weird-Sister and Hag in her lexical *Wickedary*[20] is a religio-political act. Daly makes language a tool with which women can once more name and own their elemental, magical powers.

The Erasure of Female Sacral Power

To say that female sacral power has 'declined' may be too mild a way of expressing what, to spiritual feminists, has been less a decline than a

19. *The Holy Book of Women's Mysteries*, pp. 2-3.
20. *Webster's First New Intergalactic Wickedary of the English Language* (Boston: Beacon Press, 1987).

long process of erasure of female sacral power by patriarchal mono-theism whose history represents the outworking of intentional 'Goddess murder'. The spiritual effects of that murder can be summarized in Mary Daly's words as that 'deep and universal attempt to destroy the divine spark in women'.[21] Her work documents the manifestations of Goddess murder where the destruction of female life-powers is con-tinually re-enacted in the raping and killing of women and nature.[22] As with all spiritual feminist theories of female power, the deep past and the present, the collective and the individual, are inextricably woven together. Linda Barafuldi, for example, remembers how she had been taught as a young Catholic girl to recite 'The Angelus' three times a day. As an adult feminist she writes: 'I was horrified to realize that I had been taught to recite the rape of the Goddess and to cooperate in the mutilation and killing of my own self-image—of my Self.'[23] As Daly does, Barbara Starrett names the gynocidal power that drains female and natural energies as 'the Vampire'. It is urgent, she says, 'that we understand that the power held and used by the masculinist society is ours: *We* are the Vampire's energy source.'[24]

Perhaps Mary Daly's use of the term 'gynergy' (a term coined by Emily Culpepper in the 1970s) summons some of the deepest meanings of female sacrality and how it has been sapped. 'Gynergy' is 'the female energy which both comprehends and creates who we are; that impulse in ourselves that has never been possessed by the patriarchy nor by any male; woman-identified be-ing'.[25] In Daly's scheme (which does not paraphrase well) patriarchal socialization works to sap, stunt and tame this energy, leaving successfully adapted women as little more than 'fembots' or 'feminized artifacts' who have become the products and commodities of patriarchal 'necrophilic' sexual fantasy. At the opposite pole from the fembot is the radical feminist who realizes her own 'volcanic' sacrality on the boundaries of patriarchal institutions and, more, learns to live by cross-dimensional voyaging into other, liberative, dimensions of reality.

Patriarchy's erasure of female sacrality has never been complete and

21. *Gyn/Ecology*, p. 315.
22. *Gyn/Ecology*, pp. 107-11.
23. *Gyn/Ecology*, p. 108.
24. 'The Metaphors of Power', in Spretnak (ed.), *The Politics of Women's Spirituality*, p. 188.
25. *Outercourse*, p. 43.

spiritual feminism derives some of its greatest satisfactions in restoring images of the female sacred through a cross between archaeology and (spiritual) gardening, in which the buried roots and seeds of the female sacred are located, germinated and replanted to reflower in the present. This process will involve textual study and, where possible, journeys to Goddess sites. (As female embodiment is itself a sacred site, that journey need only be introspective.) Daly recovers sacrality by 'Metamemory'. This process is described as

> Deep, Ecstatic Memory of participation in Be-ing that eludes the categories and grids of patriarchal consciousness, Spiralling into the Past, carrying Vision forward; Memory that recalls Archaic Time, Re-Calling it into our be-ing; Memory beyond civilization.[26]

In this, Daly does not rely on historical evidence of cultures in which women may or may not have enjoyed the full exercise of their own sacrality. She is not interested in resurrecting the role of pagan priestess or resacralizing motherhood. Although she engages in a certain amount of feminist archaeology, her recovery of the female sacred is in the leaping, incendiary imagination; in the 'Otherworld journey' into 'self-transcending immanence'. This is not a roundabout journey into the old transcendent supernatural which relegates the natural to the realm of the salvifically irrelevant. In the *Wickedary* the word 'supernatural' is written as 'Super Natural', namely: that supremely natural 'Elemental order which directs history from inside'. A woman enters that order through memory, or, more expressively, 'Re-Calling'. This is a process of 'giving voice to Original powers, intuitions, memories' without which women cannot 'Spin'.[27] In spinning a Craft in which to voyage into other realms, women 'Dis-Cover' the lost threads of their cosmic con-nectedness. In the 'Third Passage' of Daly's *Gyn/Ecology* the energy of female becoming is generated by volcanic rage and the courage to be a blaspheming heretic; a lunatic; a witch or 'Revolting Hag', borne on 'the Great Wind which Calls and Carries Wild, Deviant Women on our True Course'.[28] Women's existential realization will be achieved in a separate 'Women's Space' where women are free to actualize their 'Archimagical Powers'. The 'other side of the moon', the 'uncharted Zone', the 'Fairy Space', the 'Subliminal Sea' are all images which name the magical

---

26. *Outercourse*, p. 52.
27. *Outercourse*, pp. 130, 195.
28. *Outercourse*, p. 52.

place where women (or Daly and her familiars at least) can live out the female sacred.

This re-calling of women's spiritual energies is, I think, most powerfully expressed by Daly. But she is not alone: it is a central theme in feminist spirituality. For example, in Clarissa Pinkola Estés's *Women Who Run with the Wolves: Contacting the Power of the Wild Woman* (1992), Estés proclaims: 'Bone by bone, hair by hair, Wild Woman comes back. Through night dreams, through events half understood and half remembered, Wild Woman comes back.'[29] But despite its grounding in observed Western sexual-political realities, Daly's is a far more abstract, mythical scheme than that of any other writer in this field. (Daly rightly recognizes that myth and philosophical abstraction are not oppositional modes of thought—her philosophy is properly poetical.) Her theory is also far less rooted in female embodiment than any other kind of religious feminism. Daly's prophetic call is for women to realize their own 'elemental powers'; powers which include but also transcend embodiment. In *Gyn/Ecology* she documents atrocities in which women's bodies have been the target of patriarchal butchery (such as female genital mutilation or Chinese footbinding). But it is above all the mind, imagination or spirit which is the source of female magic and sacrality, and it is the mind which has been 'mummified' by the layers of 'mindbindings' imposed by centuries of patriarchal patterns of thought.[30]

It might be helpful to illustrate how female sacral activity is held to have been taken over by men and its peculiarly female meanings removed or demonized. The feminist history of pottery is a case in point. There is evidence to suggest that pottery or the making of sacred vessels was a sacred female activity which was invented by women and taboo (or forbidden) to men in prehistory. Pottery is one of the clearest illustrations of how the gendering of a sacred activity is not an arbitrary division of labour, but actually reflects and participates in female transformatory activity. The act of moulding a pot seems to symbolize the mother moulding the child in the pot-like womb: a 'vessel' containing female blood that magically coagulates into new and separate flesh. The finished pot (a revolutionary invention in itself) was a magical object in which vital transformations could occur—such as the storage, cooking and fermentation of food and drink. The bones of the dead could also be kept in pots.

29. London: Rider, 1992, p. 26.
30. *Gyn/Ecology*, pp. 6, 42, 331.

At Eleusis the *kernos* was a sacred pot symbolizing the womb from which the dying god Adonis would be resurrected. The sacramental fluid it contained may have been a mixture of female blood and milk.[31] The pot was associated with the Great Mother in most parts of the world. The Potter was one of the titles of the Sumero-Babylonian goddess known, among many names, as Ninhursag or Mammitu (Mother). She made the first human beings out of clay or earth. The sky god Yahweh who vanquished her also made men out of the earth and called the first man Adam—*adamah*, meaning 'bloody clay'. Earth—the material from which pots can be made—has been almost globally feminized as a 'Mother' (though in the West the phrase 'Mother Earth' is used either vacuously or disparagingly since it is associated with pagan or 'primitive' religion.)

Biblical monotheism cannot allow life and order to come from any other source than God. And although new life does not fall out of the sky (the traditional masculine divine space) but comes from the earth or from female animals on or close to the earth's surface, theism cannot tolerate a divine female counter-creator. God may in some non-literal sense 'live' in the sky, but he rules the earth by giving men dominion over it on his behalf. The earth, as clay, is a malleable substance that can symbolize matter's subjection to human design and fashioning. It is no coincidence, then, that monotheisms commonly liken God to a potter, and in the Hebrew Bible particularly, the experience of God's wrath is likened to a pot being smashed to pieces.[32] To secure its ownership of the valuable functions of this transformatory craft, patriarchy then demonizes the female association of women and magical pots. The priestesses' and witches' cauldron which once brewed healing and ritual herbal infusions becomes a vessel of death and destruction, completely reversing the life-giving meaning of female vessels. This cauldron is filled with a boiling brew of things named as unclean in the Hebrew Bible—blood, reptiles, insects and bits of human cadavers. So too, in a parallel

---

31. For further details on the sacral significance of pottery see B. Walker, *The Woman's Dictionary of Symbols and Sacred Objects* (New York: HarperCollins, 1988), pp. 150-51; Rich, *Of Woman Born*, pp. 96-98; R. Briffault, *The Mothers: A Study of the Origins of Sentiments and Institutions*, I (repr.; New York: Johnson, 1969), pp. 473-74, 466. For the significance of the cauldron in feminist witchcraft see D. Alba, *The Cauldron of Change: Myths, Mysteries and Magick of the Goddess* (Oak Park, IL; Delphi, 1993), pp. 87-90.

32. See Ps. 2.9; Isa. 30.14; Jer. 18.2-7; Rev. 2.27.

symbolism, the female vessel of the womb becomes an unclean place whose menstrual and human issue is subject to taboos and purificatory rites. And where the womb-pot once signified an active, fermenting, churning generativity, under patriarchy it signifies passivity. In patriarchal sex, the reproductive act is one in which the penis symbolizes the active probe and the vagina and womb simply receive the probe, the sperm, and the offspring who will take the father's name.

The Christian feminist Rosemary Ruether offers a compelling historical explanation of the desacralization of women:

> The more one studies different religious traditions and their early roots, the more one is tempted to suggest that religion itself is essentially a male creation. Could it be that the male, marginalized from direct participation in the great mysteries of gestation and birth, asserted his superior physical strength to monopolize leisure and culture and that he did so by creating ritual expressions that duplicated female gestating and birthing roles so as to transfer the power of these primary mysteries to the male?[33]

Ruether believes that this might explain why, despite the predominance of Mother Goddess figures in early religion, they seem to establish the power of king figures, but do little to establish truly gynocentric cultures or promote the autonomous humanity of women. Moreover, she claims that even in the pagan religions the priesthoods have always been predominantly male. Ruether traces three main stages in the development of ancient Near Eastern, Graeco-Roman and Judaeo-Christian religion. First, the male sublimates or channels the female life-giving powers into a Great Mother Goddess figure and pictures himself as her son or lover. The power of the Mother typically rescues him from death and enthrones him as king. This can be seen in the ancient Near Eastern myths of Innana, Ishtar, Anath and Isis and of course in Christian Mariology, where Mary is an object of cultic devotion but also sacralizes female submission to the Son and Father. This takes us onto the second stage, where the Great Mother is no longer the Great Goddess but is forced into a subordinate role as say, Mother Earth or 'the church'. The church is typically characterized as female and often as a bride under the control of the transcendent Christ who, ascended to God's right hand, is no longer limited by earthly embodiment. As pure rational spirit he rules and dominates the earth-bound female. In the third stage—that of

33. 'Renewal or New Creation? Feminist Spirituality and Historical Religion', in S. Gunew (ed.), *A Reader in Feminist Knowledge* (London: Routledge, 1991), p. 278.

modernity—the male elite assumes direct power over the cosmos through science, while making religious piety a private concern in the lives of women.[34] The privatization of piety is actually far less marked in Orthodox Judaism where *Torah* pervades all of family life. Nonetheless, in this and most other religious traditions, female piety is variously domesticated and controlled by men with authority to bless, teach and lead.

Even if we do not accept every detail of what is, after all, set out as a very broad hypothesis, the general theoretical pattern of men imitating and taking over feared but desirable female powers for their own cultural ends has been traced by ethnographers and historians of religion since the end of the nineteenth century. J.J. Bachofen's *Das Mütterecht* (1870) was followed by Robert Briffault's *The Mothers* (1927). Erich Neumann propounded the 'female principle' as an alternative to destructive male power in *The Great Mother* (1955), as did Robert Graves' *The White Goddess* (1966). In *Symbolic Wounds* (1968) the psychologist Bruno Bettelheim regarded male initiation rituals as profoundly expressive of male envy of female power and of men's attempt to share in it through imitation.

The twentieth-century countercultural interest in Jung and Eastern philosophies has also encouraged men to cultivate their intuitive, relational, 'feminine' side as a balance to their rationalism and aggression. This alternative material is not feminist in itself, though it is far less patriarchal than that of established and fundamentalist religion. And the recovery of the 'feminine side' has, nonetheless, strongly influenced the spiritual feminist movement—especially in its more essentialist moments. One of its first applications to feminist discourse was in Elizabeth Gould Davis's *The First Sex* (1971), which itself drew on Helen Diner's *Mothers and Amazons* (1929). Drawing on Bachofen and Briffault both of these writers argued for the existence of pre-patriarchal matriarchies in which female embodiment was revered as a source of divine power. This book will not attempt the virtually impossible task of proving or disproving the accuracy of these large claims. What seems more significant is the way in which such claims have inspired spiritual feminist utopian visions of cultures empowered by an alternative spirituality which is distinctively ecological and female in character.

34. Ruether, 'Renewal or New Creation?', p. 279.

The Eternal Feminine Revisited?

Reformist religious feminism has directed a good deal of energy to the reclamation of sacred texts, to the ordination of women to the priesthood and the rabbinate, and above all, to the struggle for planetary justice and relationality. But it has, on the whole, shown little explicit interest in the sacrality of women as such. Despite its insistence that feminist knowledge, spirituality and ethics are rooted in embodied experience, reformist feminism tends to be apprehensive of celebration or sacralization of female reproductivity, fearing to slip into essentialist neo-conservative thinking. Female sacrality that is grounded in biology or in biological metaphors seems too closely associated with traditional constructions of female embodiment as mindlessly cyclic rather than historically engaged. To image the body as a reproductive container— even a magical one—seems to confirm those passive, holding, patient 'feminine' qualities to which patriarchy has claimed women are 'naturally' fitted.

Alex Owen's (mis)reading of spiritual feminism as a movement that can 'readily be interpreted as antagonistic to a strategy for change'[35] is typical of many reformist feminists'. Owen rightly denies that women's political power and the representation of the female principle in women's bodies 'flow unproblematically one from the other'. Power does not, she writes, 'proceed automatically from the female body, and spiritual power is not to be equated with sexual equality'.[36] But thealogy does not (or should not) propose the automatic empowerment of simply happening to be female. In thealogy, power arises from the ecological *labour* of restoring human connectedness with the whole cosmos in the Goddess. The spiritual feminist has not arbitrarily deified her 'essential femininity' or her biology. She uses her biology as a metaphor for a number of material and spiritual transformations. These are also inherently political transformations because the feminist sacred is absolutely, and by its own logic, egalitarian. As Starhawk insists in all her writing, 'every being is sacred—meaning that each has inherent value that cannot be ranked in a hierarchy or compared to the value of another

---

35. *The Darkened Room: Women, Power and Spiritualism in Late Nineteenth-Century England* (London: Virago, 1989), p. 241.
36. *The Darkened Room*, pp. 240, 242.

being'.[37] The embodied immanence of the sacred entails a political end: that of a just social organization which refuses to permanently privilege the interests of any one species or class of being.

The postbiblical preoccupation with female embodiment and biological function does not unwittingly collaborate with those patriarchal thinkers who have insisted upon the essentially pre-civilized naturalness of women. Spiritual feminist concepts of female sacrality do not collaborate with hierarchical conservatism: they subvert and attack the systemic suppression of female sacrality by renaming the processes of female becoming through the metaphors and experience of sexual reproductivity and change. Their construction of these processes is transgressive, allowing women to define and represent themselves as the subjects of their own experience. That spiritual feminism is grounded in female physiology stems not from a neo-conservative derogation of female intellect, but from the foundational claim of radical feminism that, in Adrienne Rich's words, 'The woman's body is the terrain on which patriarchy is erected'.[38]

Certainly, the claim that female collective energy is uniquely life-giving is a very big claim and it is essentialist to the extent that a specific quality of power is attributed to female being. But these claims are not simplistically essentialist. For in recognizing that contemporary Western woman is to a large extent a product of historical forces, spiritual feminists also recognize that women can reinvent or reproduce themselves. Sally Gearheart justifies her claim that female power is biophilic on the basis that women's exclusion from the competitive 'man's world' has allowed women to develop greater resources of relational energy. And if women reject the self-hatred engendered by patriarchy and gladly accept that 'we *are* what the patriarchy has labelled us'—receiving, nurturant, incubatory beings (though not *only* that)—these qualities will achieve political power when they are not distorted by the counter-power of patriarchal aggression.[39]

Nonetheless, any book that proposes an idea of female *being* rather than contingent modes of female existence is, even before it has been read, open to the charge of making falsely universal, total, ahistorical statements about all women. It should be conceded that some of the more popular writers in the feminist spirituality movement speak generically,

37. *Truth or Dare*, p. 21; *The Fifth Sacred Thing* (New York: Bantam, 1994), p. i.
38. *Of Woman Born*, p. 55.
39. 'Womanpower: Energy Re-Sourcement', pp. 197-98.

apolitically, and transhistorically of an essential 'woman'. But to derive meanings from female biological processes is not essentialist if one assumes, as I have done, that female being does not have one fixed essence but is suggestive of and open to a number of biophilic ways of being. It is only the fixing or ossification of being that is an invitation to conservatism.

Brief consideration of an actual *patriarchal* ideology of femininity should make it clear that although thealogies of embodiment might sometimes bear *superficial* resemblances to conservative constructions of female embodiment they draw wholly different conclusions about the meaning, value and relations of almost everything: divinity, nature, history and politics. Werner Neuer's widely read study, *Man and Woman in Christian Perspective*, was written in 1981 and was published in Britain in 1990 having been through four German editions. In this book Neuer, a German systematic theologian, draws heavily on studies of sexual-genital difference (significantly) published in Germany by Theodorich Kampmann during the 1940s. Following Kampmann, who summarizes male and female difference as (respectively) spontaneity and receptivity, Neuer summarizes femininity as receptive and reproductive as opposed to masculinity which is spontaneous and creative: 'While a man is more strongly equipped for creative or destructive remodelling of his environment, the woman is more strongly equipped for arranging what the man has acquired for her or she has received from him.'[40] Men's and women's 'innate gender-specific endowment' constitutes their 'nature and their destiny'. If they rebel against this 'one can and must speak of degeneration'.[41] He warns women of the dangers of rebelling 'against their position in creation, which is to be the man's support and to be mothers'.[42]

With Kampmann and others, Neuer insists, for example, that women's brain structure equips them for linguistic aptitude, but not for mathematics: 'there is not a single known case where "mathematical talent has been inherited from the mother"'.[43] This unverifiable genetic claim would be risible were it not that 'science' is coupled with superstitions that strongly recall the notorious witch-hunting manual *Malleus Maleficarum* of 1486. Neuer repeatedly asserts that a woman's recep-

40. London: Hodder & Stoughton, 1990, p. 38. See also pp. 44, 47, 49.
41. *Man and Woman*, p. 53.
42. *Man and Woman*, p. 167.
43. *Man and Woman*, p. 54.

tivity and openness to influence (first evident at the Fall) 'shows women as a creature in special need of protection and *particularly open to Satanic seduction*'.[44] In Eden the serpent singles out the woman not the man, and the serpent's conversation with the woman 'creates the *inner disposition in the woman to transgress God's command in the given situation*'.[45] (I would urge the reader to spend a moment or two contemplating this dangerous contemporary defamation of one half of humanity in order to let its full implications sink in.) Neuer concludes that women's subordination to men is not to be understood so much as a punishment than as 'a blessing'. Female subordination apparently protects all of humanity by, in effect, subordinating Satan and helping women to use their receptivity for good rather than occult purposes. The subordination of women to men is, he says, 'a helpful ordinance for both sexes. The story of the fall shows that to upset this order ends in catastrophe for both sexes.'[46]

The absolute political difference between this truly conservative ideology of femininity and spiritual feminism's reconstruction of female sacral power is too obvious to be spelled out. Linguistically perhaps, there is some commonality between the patriarchal and the spiritual feminist discourse. The power of female witchcraft to disorder systems is, for example, a preoccupation of them both. But feminist witchcraft is directed towards the biophilic transformation of systems. Magical energy is directed towards justice and healing the damage that systems such as Neuer's have inflicted on women, nature and subject classes and peoples. Any overlap between the two systems is only in their mutual but opposed interest in the relation of sexual politics to the social order. This book will show how, in a number of ways, spiritual feminism is absolutely committed to change; to upsetting the patriarchal order that Neuer calls a 'blessing'. The resacralization of the female body as microcosmic of the generative purposes of the divine is not a new twist on the old theme of the complementary eternal feminine. Spiritual feminism is indeed interested in female biology but does not limit female regenerativity to

44. *Man and Woman*, p. 77. (Italics mine.)

45. *Man and Woman*, p. 76. (Italics mine.) This kind of statement legitimated the witch burnings and if applied to minorities could equally legitimate genocidal persecution today. A radical feminist could, however, read this statement in the spirit of Lilith as an ontological confirmation of women's capacity to defy the patriarchal policing of the spirit.

46. *Man and Woman*, p. 78.

sexual reproduction. Its construction of the body is not (or should not be) that of a 'natural' body, where 'natural' would mean that the meaning of the body was unmediated, inevitable and without a history. The naturalness of spiritual feminist embodiment is its organic connectedness to the non-human world, but it is also a refusal of what patriarchy means by nature, namely, what is sub-intelligent and infinitely available.

Reformist feminism should not, therefore dismiss *a priori* all discussion of sexual difference as back-door conservatism. And it should be remembered that the recurrent use of the word 'female' in this and other texts is not a synonym for femininity. 'Female' refers to positive biophilic qualities or activities that are analogous to female biological processes, or that are traditional, but not necessary, to female modes of being. Therefore, although the word 'female' may have vestigial continuities with patriarchal 'femininity', the difference between the two words liberates powerful qualities and practices for new ends. If, as Adrienne Rich has argued in *Of Woman Born*, civilization is a struggle in which men seek to contain female spiritual power, then this attempt to recover and liberate it is a revolutionary process.

I have argued that the spiritual feminist resacralization of female embodiment is not essentialist in the way that it might, superficially, appear. Nonetheless, in spiritual feminism 'gynergy' is being celebrated and described as an ontological capacity: what it means to *be* a spiritually/ politically active woman in a given time and place. Given that 'being' and 'essence' are closely related terms, we need to consider what the word 'ontological' means in the spiritual feminist context.

Ontology has traditionally been understood as a metaphysical discipline: the science of essential being preceding and abstracted from the existential contingencies of embodiment. Postmodern epistemology has shown that no discourse, including ontology, can any longer be abstracted from its spiritual/political context. 'Being itself' is not a gender-neutral idea. It has been a male pretension of primacy, necessity, individuality, and transcendent independence, allowing men to repudiate their origins inside women's bodies. Femaleness is cast as a complex, secondary, derivative, immanent existence that lacks the purity of a stable essence. Under patriarchy, female ontology is determined and flawed by its biological capacity to become compound: two in one. Because it is mixed it is impure; it is confused and therefore destabilized by multiplicity. And because, biologically, women create by chemistry or *mixing* rather than by verbal/rational fiat, the sacral acts of the female body are cast as primitive, deviant, sub-religious productions, or more precisely, mere re-productions (fakes). The demonization of female sacrality may, finally, be traceable to patriarchal ontology, and it is here in the ontic dimension that spiritual feminism reclaims its power.

In the patriarchal scheme female being does not have the privileges of the self-defining subject. A woman's being is a historical self-for-others. She is constituted by a variety of other people's desires; at worst she is a pornographic non-subject, a screen of flesh for male sexual projects. The political conditioning of ontological discourse is visible in the very historical reluctance of men to ascribe a stable ontology or 'being itself' to women. Its exclusions have relied upon myths like those of Pandora or Eve which reduce female being to a fall—an accident waiting to happen. And now, in its historical turn, spiritual feminism is refusing the secular capitalist ontology of woman as consumer and consumed, and is using archaeological and anthropological texts to advance a peculiarly female, religious mode of being, production and exchange. Perhaps most people do not want to feel that their 'inner' being as well as their body is sexed. This would seem to delimit choice and transcendence. It is customary to see sex as contingent: an addition to our extension in time and space. In dualistic religious ontologies this redeems at least part of the self as being something like God. However, in Goddess religion divinity is immanent in nature/embodiment and is therefore sexed in so far as nature is sexed. It is not literally so, but the metaphors and processes by which Goddess spirituality describes how things come into existence are sexed and sexual in ways that theism is not.

So it may be that this spiritual feminist ontology is also an anti-ontology in its deliberate political (con)fusion of physiology and trans-cendence. Certainly it is an idiosyncratic ontology. It proposes female sacrality as the most comprehensive agency of radical change: one that transforms not merely the procedures and apparatuses by which we live, but what we can be. Feminist hierophanies are a sign of the sacred power to ferment political change or transmutation—rather than revolution. (Despite their noble intentions, twentieth-century communist revolutions have usually degenerated into violence, state capitalism, and have rarely brought justice for women.) Spiritual feminist mutation changes political relationships in and through a series of ontological redefinitions. The remythologization or reenchantment of women is a process of purification from the patriarchal false consciousness that is ultimately an ontological pollution. In so far as spiritual feminism has an essentialist element this informs its political stance in two senses. First, in ontologizing female subjecthood, it refuses patriarchy's metaphysical denial of any ontological essence to women. And secondly, its use of the term 'femaleness' invokes the political effect of re-evaluating and re-viewing the states of being associated with biological femaleness.[47]

However, as Susan Bordo has argued, it is dogmatic to attack in the name of difference 'all gender-generalizations as *in principle* essentialist or totalizing'.[48] Constructing an ontological concept of sacrality assumes the sort of unitive female possibility that at least spiritually or emotionally transcends or precedes the historical differences of women's race, class and locality. Bordo rightly asks, 'Do we want to delegitimate *a priori* the exploration of experiential continuity and structural common ground among women?'[49] Without some notion of the global solidarity and collectivity of women the feminist movement would disintegrate. Too heavy an emphasis on female difference forgets that patriarchy is virtually omnipresent across races and classes—even if its effects can differ widely. While the way we think about and practice religion has been oxygenated by postmodernism, taken to its relativist extremes deconstructive postmodernism would suffocate the religious and political impetus of feminism altogether.

And because they are religious as well as political agents, spiritual feminists must attribute holy power to female *being*, rather than contingently to some exceptional women, in order to make sacrality an inalienable (though not automatic) possibility of femaleness. Any feminist project must to some extent take on the traditional, Western religious metanarrative of an eventual liberation from the forces of alienation and injustice—whether these are called states of sin or not. All religious feminisms prescribe some absolute relational values which teach one to be what one *should* be. Both reformist and radical feminism have to resist a possible postmodern erasure of womankind as a meaningful or coherent category to which the project 'feminism' refers.

But none of that makes female sacrality a conservatively essentialist attribution. On the contrary, spiritual feminism's construction of female sacrality constitutes a highly particular ontological construction mediated

47. Cf. D. Fuss, *Essentially Speaking: Feminism, Nature and Difference* (London: Routledge, 1989), pp. xi, 5, 50, 71.

48. 'Feminism, Postmodernism and Gender-Scepticism', in L. Nicholson (ed.), *Feminism/Postmodernism* (London: Routledge, 1990), p. 139.

49. 'Feminism, Postmodernism and Gender-Scepticism', p. 142.

by left-wing politics after the so-called 'collapse' of socialism, by green criticism of the human relation to the environment, and by late twentieth-century feminist criticism of the Judaeo-Christian politics of religion.

The preceding discussion may go some way to answering the question of whether the phrase 'female sacrality' refers to a transsubjective quality of femaleness. I can only give my own view here. While I would deny that it is a straightforwardly physiological female capacity like ovulation, it is 'real' in two senses. First, female sacrality is real or actual as an interpretive tool that helps us to understand the true—that is, the most biophilic—religious meaning of female physiology and the traditional gestatory modes of production (such as pottery or spinning) which imitate female reproductive biology. Secondly, the phrase 'female sacrality' assumes the actuality of divine immanence which can be manifest through the processes of female embodiment and those cultural creative processes which are modelled on female biology. But my *concept* of female sacrality is a dateable, socially conditioned construct—a reading, not a description, of female embodiment.

It is in reconstructing female sacral power that spiritual feminism makes its bid for socio-religious change. Modernity has overthrown the sacred as the source and guide of biophilically balanced social power. Modern patriarchy rules by technological reason buttressed only where necessary by a divine king. But the ancient vision of organic community, blessed by the Shalom of the sacred, is a counter-tradition within the biblical text itself.[50] And it is a vision that persists not only in religious feminism, but in the emergent liberal religious view as a whole, and especially that of the contemporary creation spirituality movement. In spiritual feminism, where divinity is female in character, female sacrality is the central medium of this blessing. Because this spirituality has been born from the planetary struggle for life—an unprecedented situation—one cannot say that contemporary spiritual feminism regards women (as Marx did religion) as 'the heart of a heartless world'. Where nineteenth-century evangelicalism made womankind the heart of a particularly heartless capitalism, spiritual feminism changes the religio-political paradigm itself.

---

50. See, for example, J. Armstrong, *The Idea of the Holy and the Humane Response* (London: George Allen & Unwin, 1981), pp. 5, 16.

Chapter 2

THE SACRAL BODY

Christ loved the church and gave himself up for her, that he might sanctify
her, having cleansed her by the washing of water with the word, that he
might present the church to himself in splendour, without spot or wrinkle
or any such thing, that she might be holy and without blemish.

Eph. 5.25-27

I have endeavored for many years to 'make the feminine holy', and one
way I have expressed that is by making images of a female god.

Judy Chicago[1]

A New Somatic Spirituality

One of the most positive consequences of Goddess spirituality has been
the awakening of women's pleasure in their own bodies as they pass
from youth to sexual maturity to old age. Imaging the Goddess as
virgin, mother and crone reintegrates the female bodily transmutations
of shape-changing and waxing and waning energies within the divine
economy. Jewish-Christian feminism also refuses to participate in a
religious history that damages and distrusts the female body, and instead
celebrates embodiment as a locus of religious meaning: 'in reclaiming
our bodies we are stating not only that the material, the physical, is a
vehicle for the divine, but that change is holy, that passion is sacred and
self-direction the path of divinity'.[2] This is a contemporary worldview—
in some ways unprecedented—in which the *normal* functions of the
female body are both metaphors and manifestations of a divine
generativity imaged as female. The sacred is power and therefore the

1. *The Birth Project* (New York: Doubleday, 1985), p. 177. Quoted in
G.F. Orenstein, *The Reflowering of the Goddess* (New York: Pergamon, 1990),
p. 94.
2. L. Isherwood and D. McEwan, *Introducing Feminist Theology* (Sheffield:
Sheffield Academic Press, 1993), p. 113.

sacralization of female embodiment is a means to individual and collective religious feminist empowerment. Of course to a secularized worldview, whether feminist or non-feminist, the religious perception of the world/body as holding within itself the radiance of the sacred has become incomprehensible. This is not a reading of embodiment which could persuade a non-religious feminist.

Although spiritual feminist somaticism has continuities with other somatic spiritualities, it is also specific to its period and politics. It should not be interpreted as if it were simply a more holistic version of, say, fourteenth- or nineteenth-century Christian sacralizations of female embodiment. Some of the medieval female saints seem to have used their bodies as means by which to endure self-inflicted pain and so demonstrate their sanctity and gain access to God.[3] Or again, in the nineteenth century, mothers and female philanthropists exhausted their bodily energies in sacrificial service to the poor, diseased and fallen.[4] These spiritual experiences and their intentions are complex and are not to be lightly dismissed, but the spirituality described here is a far happier one: as the Goddess says, 'all pleasures are my rituals'. Thealogy refuses to attribute salvific value to bodily suffering, or less dramatically, to the self-sacrificial drudgery required by traditional Catholic and Protestant constructions of female embodiment.

And nor does the physiological nature of spiritual feminist sacrality once more render women the mere nexus of natural energies; the mere object of irresistible natural forces. The spiritual feminist account of female sacrality, especially in its biological manifestations, does indeed make women a conduit of divine creativity: that is an irreducibly religious claim, but not one which empties women of will and person-hood. Where a woman's embodiment is a manifestation of the Goddess, that has a very different meaning than if that divinity were imaged as

3.   See C.W. Bynum, 'The Female Body and Religious Practice in the Later Middle Ages', in *Fragmentation and Redemption: Essays on Gender and the Human Body in Medieval Religion* (New York: Zone, 1991).

4.   See, for example, R. Barrett, *Ellice Hopkins: A Memoir* (London: Wells, Gardner, Dalton & Co., 1907). In her biography of the nineteenth-century high church evangelical philanthropist and reformer, Ellice Hopkins, Barrett dwells on the bodily infirmity and pain Hopkins suffered on account of her great labours in a manner reminiscent of medieval hagiography (pp. 195, 197-99) Ultimately, 'she gave her life to the service of GOD, to the purifying and uplifting of the human race' (p. 199; cf. p. 6.).

male. Certainly, a spiritual feminist's religious experience of her body is not immediate: it is mediated by language and concepts like any other religious experience. But its mediation does not have to overcome the imaginal and epistemological estrangements of religious experience in a masculinist context. For example, in a guided meditation, Lara Owen says, 'Feel the Goddess within you. She loves your full round belly; she loves the femaleness of you, the fecund weightiness of that full soft belly. Let it go even more.' She explains the spiritual and psychological harm caused by women constantly sucking in and tensing their bellies to flatten them.[5] Here the Goddess releases the flesh into religious meaning, whereas under the influence of Hellenistic philosophy traditions in Judaism and Christianity have depicted the spirit as a prisoner of the flesh.

But spiritual feminist somaticism does not alienate femaleness and intellection. For here matter is not the inert particles and lumps of Newtonian physics. It is experienced as magical—that is, form changing, intelligent or conscious, and pervaded by divine immanence. As such, it is neither a mere (traditionally pagan) container or an incitement to mono-theistic sexual sin. Perhaps for the first time in history, and certainly since the rise of Christendom in the West, female bodies are sacramental of a self-identifying, self-generating female power. So contemporary religious feminism is hardly returning to the definition of female being as, and no more than, body. The Goddess, the earth, the female body are unified and charged with sacral powers for the transmutation of matter, for shape-shifting, and for the production of cosmogonic effluvia: blood, milk and water.

This spiritual physiology of women is original but it is also subversive of and oppositional to its Western inheritance. The friction between patriarchal and feminist models of embodiment has generated new inter-pretive possibilities and the religious and cultural ramifications of spiritual feminism's 'high' theory of female embodiment are extensive and in process. That friction is not simply between old and new models of embodiment. There are still oral, native cultures that sacralize female embodiment—even if they are not feminist cultures. Among these sacralizations are the North Canadian Eskimo goddess, Sedna; the Lakota Buffalo Maiden; the mother goddess Eschetewuarha of the

5. *Her Blood is Gold: Reclaiming the Power of Menstruation* (London: Aquarian, 1993), p. 153.

South American Chamamoco; the Australian Rainbow Snake and the Nigerian river goddess Oshun.[6]

On the whole, the Judaeo-Christian West does not sacralize female embodiment. It does, however, sacralize male embodiment in so far as Jesus was an incarnation of God and redeemed the world through his bodily pain; circumcision marks Jewish men's bodies as closely related to the purposes of God; and the exercise of moral will and reason sacralizes men's minds as made in the image of God's. Yet although it is difficult to interpret, there *is* a legacy of female sanctity in the Western mystical patriarchal traditions—especially those of Christianity and Islam. Some would also argue that Hochmah and Shekhinah are constructable as Jewish goddesses, and that Mary, though a historical woman, has or could become a Christian goddess. Whether or not the biblical traditions represent sufficient and redeemable images of female holiness is not a question I need to address here. For post-Christian feminists, the biblical context does not do justice to these 'goddesses', especially where it offers images of the female sacred whose reproductive processes, like Mary's, are crucially incomplete.

It is worth remembering, then, that there are vestiges of female sacrality in the patriarchal traditions and that this complicates the feminist resacralization of the body. Thealogy is a reaction against a residual religious worldview—still robust in conservative religious circles—which treats the natural (that is, uncontrolled) female body as profane. But at the same time thealogy reacts against a more secular worldview which prefers to see the female body as a resource for the sexual and aesthetic satisfaction of men at leisure. In this latter case the body has been finally emptied of its religious meaning. Although 'flesh' is no longer a synonym for weakness and sin, neither is it a paradigm of divine and human connectedness.

However, it is my conviction that the West is not distant enough from the Jewish and Christian worldview to argue that the religious signification of the female body (or anything else) has simply and straightforwardly disappeared. It is not simply that fundamentalism exists and is increasing. An absolute dichotomy between religious and secular conceptions of the world does not exist in Western modernity. Among many others, Mircea Eliade has pointed out that we still have superstitions and taboos, 'all of them magico-religious in structure', and a 'large

6.   D.L. Carmody, *Mythological Women: Contemporary Reflections on Ancient Religious Stories* (New York: Crossroad, 1992), pp. 130, 150.

stock of camouflaged myths and degenerated rituals'.[7] For the present purpose I will assume (for this is not the place to prove it) that the two worldviews of a sacral and a desacralized universe are continuous and interconnected. Moreover, my discussion of *post*biblical religious thinking cannot omit all reference to the biblical religions against which postbiblical religion is defined. New religious traditions are created in dialogical and polemical relation with other traditions. So to understand spiritual feminism's conception of embodiment as a religio-aesthetic sign of its own sacrality (which is the purpose of this chapter) we need to sketch in some of its antecedents in the history of Western religious aesthetics of the body—of which the thealogical is one of the most recent developments.

Western culture has inherited both a pagan and a biblical tradition. From classical paganism, women inherit two sorts of images of the body. There are, for example, the exquisite, if rather formalized, representations of the female numinous in, for example, images of Aphrodite and Demeter. But classicism has also left a more enduring Western preoccupation with the disciplined, symmetrical, athletic young man—an aesthetic subject to periodic revivals, most recently in twentieth-century fascism. In fascist art the Aristotelian conception of women as mere passive mothers/matter and men as energetic, intellectual historical movers resurfaces again. Women are depicted as stationary, rural mothers who stay at home to breed while their husbands and sons depart for conqest. In contemporary pagan artistic representations of the body, the classical Southern pagan heritage is not especially evident. In neo-pagan art the Goddess has regained her ancient dynamism but women often protest the recurrent depiction of her by male artists as a fiercely beautiful, slim, usually semi-naked young woman complementing a usually clothed male god.[8]

Judaism, Islam and Protestantism (Puritanism especially) have resisted the pagan 'idolatry' of natural forms. Their worship is aniconic and all representations of bodies—male and female—more or less disappear. Catholicism is more interested in female embodiment and allows statues and paintings of Mary and the female saints. If the latter are naked, their flesh is usually redeemed by its meritorious patience as it undergoes the

7. *The Sacred and the Profane* (New York: Harcourt, Brace & World, 1959), p. 204.
8. C.M. McGlynn, 'Nudity', *The Deosil Dance: The Journal of Pagan Beliefs Today* 36 (1993), p. 4.

agonies of martyrdom. Although the Enlightenment period was less spiritually distrustful of bodily beauty, its aesthetics could still exclude women by predicating beauty on the rationality of the male mind and body. Male rationality was projected onto the natural world, harmonizing reason and the beauties of nature, but colonizing nature by the operations of reason in the process. As in antiquity, the beauty of reason or *logos* belonged to free male citizens, and women consisted essentially of body and emotions, making their beauty more ambiguous.

Material and emotional volatility is an inevitable attribute of women if their bodies are represented as little more than the flux of organic matter. Without the full operations of reason, women become ahistorical, cyclic, sometime animals, and are therefore marginal to the dynamics of culture.[9] Within this patriarchal history, and that of modernism's attempt to establish its own rational 'eternity in the midst of flux',[10] neo-pagan feminism's celebration of all female bodily transformations (notionally unmediated by patriarchal culture) is an aesthetic as well as a religious heresy.

The feminist spirituality movement has rejected the dualism which dis-spirits women's bodies and redeems their sexuality by subordinating it to ecclesiastical and state control. Feminist spirituality questions the basic patriarchal configuration which masculinizes mind, words and cultural creation. It is in making these alone revelatory of God that female embodiment has been desacralized. The history of the doll can be read as a reproduction of that process in minature. Under contemporary patriarchy the biological plasticity of the female body has rigidified into a plastic doll: a girl's toy which she will quickly outgrow. But the doll is probably a degraded form of the figurines that once symbolized the Goddess and which priestesses carried about with them.[11] Moreover, dolls as toys are intended to evoke feminine qualities in little girls. The maternal qualities evoked by baby dolls are laudable in themselves, but they are not the qualities that are evoked by dolls (crude replicas of offending bodies) in many pagan traditions. Among the small minority of feminist witches who are prepared to hex rapists and other such

9.   See E. Kuryluk, *Veronica and her Cloth: History, Symbolism, and Structure of a 'True' Image* (Cambridge, MA: Blackwell, 1991), pp. 14-17.

10.   See D. Harvey, *The Condition of Postmodernity: An Enquiry into the Origins of Cultural Change* (Oxford: Blackwell, 1989), p. 206; see also Part 1, pp. 3-118.

11.   See A. Walker, *Possessing the Secret of Joy* (London: Jonathan Cape, 1992), p. 188; Budapest, *The Holy Book of Women's Mysteries*, p. 43.

criminals by sticking pins into a male doll,[12] the doll uses embodiment as a form of (covert) moral agency that can establish 'natural', pre-civilized justice by its own powers. The feminist witch's doll is intended to model the retributive power of the human female body who made it and the divine female body that established the cosmic codes of right-living that the rapist has offended against.

But patriarchy has made sure that the doll has, so to speak, come back to haunt women. Like the doll stuck with pins, the female body has been constituted by its numinous ambiguity. And where the female body is deficient in reason and absent from public discourses, it becomes a surface in which to 'stick' a history of dangerous meanings of which it is not the author. Religious feminism argues that female embodiment as 'natural' rather than civilized has been marked or inscribed by Judaeo-Christian anxieties about nature as a source of disease and sexual/social chaos. As such it has had to be regulated by law. Western logocentrism makes female embodied generativity at best a secondary power by its own emphasis on the power of reason and language to bring things into existence. In the first chapter of John's Gospel a holy Word begins time; and although Trinitarian doctrine is various and complex, God seems to have generated his son through the rational power of the Word or *logos* circulating within the divine pleroma. Christ is incarnate as flesh but a flesh characterized as Word. Mary, as *theotokos*, carries but does not generate or speak that Word.

This kind of cosmology renders female flesh dumb. In the biblical traditions, a woman's body lacks verbal fluency: unlike the male Jew, the female Jewish body is uncircumcised (*arel*), one meaning of which is 'obstructed'—a word connoting deafness to reason and impeded speech. And uncircumcised she is, like the uncircumcised foreigners of the Hebrew Bible, the other: by implication, a foreigner to Israel and therefore to culture.[13] In Judaism, circumcision and Bar Mitzvah honour the passage of masculinity through time. But Western culture does not celebrate menarche. Indeed, the female passage through (cyclic) time is a mark of its mutability and therefore profanity. Lacking the sacral, ritual legitimations of the passage of the female body through time, many Western women try to sacralize their embodiment by fixing themselves in time. The apparent stasis of permanent youth is, however, a kind of parody of the sacred which, like a relic on velvet and preserved under

12. See Budapest, *The Holy Book of Women's Mysteries*, p. 43.
13. Kuryluk, *Veronica and her Cloth*, pp. 20-21.

glass, does not rot. Women who profoundly fear the effects of time on their bodies fear being feared as women who have lost the will and energy to withstand their own profanity or naturalness. Patriarchal concepts of female embodiment are notorious for their casting women as negative magical space bounded by flesh. Certainly patriarchy can idealize the young, married, pregnant female body that holds an even younger body within itself. But when the patriarchal female 'hold-all' loosens and softens she loses her aesthetic value and becomes an 'old bag' of mere skin.

However, a Foucauldian account of women's bodies as essentially victimized flesh, 'inscribed', branded and stamped (on) by the history of patriarchal sexual projections, can undermine feminist historiography, thealogy (or theology) and spirituality, all of which offer instances and explanations of female creativity within the constraints of patriarchy.[14] The central thesis of spiritual feminism has, after all, been that female spiritual agency and creativity has never been finally destroyed and is now resurgent in the late twentieth century. This assumes a sacred history of a suppressed, sometimes heretical, informal, private, but continuous and relatively autonomous 'subculture' of female religious experience. And now spiritual feminism's reassertion of female sacrality counters the reductionism of some postmodern representations of flesh as infinitely malleable/manipulable. Because the Goddess is eternally immanent and 'female', spiritual feminism makes the body a powerful site of resistance to its own desacralization and the energetic source of its own resacralization. This thealogy of empowerment is confident that even if women have internalized the dis-ease of false representations of the ideal female body, they have never been entirely infected by them. Women store sufficient powers of resistance, healing and self-regenerativity to become the subjects of their own representation in the Goddess. In the image of the Goddess a woman's bodily sacrality becomes both figurable in its material immanence, and un-figurable in that, as the popular Goddess chant goes, 'She changes everything she touches, and everything she touches changes'.[15] In other words, in spiritual feminism, materiality is honoured but cannot be objectified.

---

14. See L. McNay, *Foucault and Feminism: Power, Gender and the Self* (Cambridge: Polity Press; Oxford: Blackwell, 1994), p. 12.

15. This lyric is quoted in Eller, *Living in the Lap of the Goddess*, p. 98.

Carving up the Female Body

Although, to some extent, women may have privately reconstructed patriarchal religions to suit their own theological and experiential purposes, the public Western patriarchal history of female sacrality is a history of misnamings, defamations, exploitations and suppressions. One of the most recent attacks on female sacral embodiment has been the diet: a phenomenon mediated indirectly through institutionalized religion and directly through the diet industry. This particular attack on women has been sustained through the literally reductive patriarchal aesthetics of the female body.

It has not always and everywhere been fashionable to be thin. Body shape is differently interpreted in different cultures. In some cultures, fatness can be a sign of prosperity, or in children, of being well loved. The present discussion relates to Western women particularly and to a wave of dieting that began among nineteenth-century elite women who wished to look as slight and delicate as their (sexual) appetites.[16] Until recently, it was white women between the ages of about 10 and 50 and from the upper working class to the upper class who have been the most affected by the desire to be thin. But as Sandra Bordo argues, 'obsessive relations with food' are now increasingly common across the divides of class, race and sexual orientation.[17] Religious feminism would want to say that all women under patriarchal domination have been spiritually as well as physically shaped by patriarchal practices against the female body. Spiritual feminism has not put a critique of the diet industry at the centre of its struggle, but it seems to me that its resacralization of embodiment is best understood in relief against the contemporary desacralizing culture it inhabits but opposes.

There have been several strands in the secular feminist critique of the diet culture—political, ethical, psychological. But perhaps the most helpful place to begin is not with the diet, but with a cultural critique of the social construction of embodiment itself. Any contemporary feminist account of the patriarchal construction of female embodiment will be indebted to Foucault's analysis in *Discipline and Punish* of the way in

16. For the nineteenth-century background to the contemporary diet see S. Bordo, *Unbearable Weight: Feminism, Western Culture and the Body* (Berkeley: University of California Press, 1993), pp. 112-17.
17. *Unbearable Weight*, p. 103.

which disciplinary methods produce 'subjected and practised bodies, "docile" bodies'. Most significantly for our purposes, Foucault claims that discipline 'dissociates power from the body...*it reverses the course of the energy, the power that might result from it, and turns it into a relation of strict subjection*'.[18] In its most generalized form, the 'disciplines' of the body can be a useful preliminary model for discussing the diet as a 'relation of subjection' of women to their own bodies and to their culture. An artificially thin female body is one which has been disciplined and punished by the institution of dieting. Although the tabloid press regularly puts fat women in the (figurative) stocks, most women do not actually need the threat of public humiliation to diet or 'watch' what they eat, because they have internalized their punishment through the discipline of the self-policing diet culture.

According to Sandra Lee Bartky, the 'disciplinary regime' of femininity is unbounded by any one institution. The techniques practised on the female body are a function of 'a far larger discipline, an oppressive and inegalitarian system of sexual subordination. This system aims at turning women into the docile and compliant companions of men just as surely as the army aims to turn its raw recruits into soldiers.'[19] Foucault has been criticized by Bartky and other feminists for his blindness or indifference to the role of gender in the cultural construction of the body. But his concept of the body as a site and means of modern coercive power has profoundly influenced feminist discourse. And it is not difficult to see how naming a woman 'beautiful' within a patriarchal social structure is not a disinterested aesthetic judgment, but is also— perhaps primarily—an aesthetic ordering of hierarchical social relations. The patriarchal aesthetics of the female body are also ideological judgments in that they associate beauty with specific ages, colouring, ethnicity, sexuality, (relatively low) levels of educational achievement and political awareness, affluent styles of dress and, perhaps above all, body shape.

Dieting is one of the most widespread disciplines practised on and against the Western and Westernized female body. The slightness of the female form may be intended to mirror the slightness of her impact on

18. M. Foucault, *Discipline and Punish: The Birth of the Prison* (Harmondsworth: Penguin, 1977), p. 138. (Italics mine.)

19. 'Foucault, Femininity and the Modernisation of Patriarchal Power', in I. Diamond and L. Quinby (eds.), *Feminism and Foucault: Reflections on Resistance* (Boston: Northeastern University Press, 1988), p. 75.

the world, just as the 'proper' heftiness of men is an image and instrument of masculine force. Certainly the trained and exercised male body is also subject to exacting disciplinary techniques. But far fewer men train their bodies than women diet—especially if dieting is defined as a behaviour ranging from being 'careful' not to eat fattening foods, to the semi-starvation of crash dieting, and finally to fatal anorexia. Masculine disciplines usually have more the character of a hobby and confirm men's confidence in themselves and their bodily strength, whereas female dieting breeds distrust of and hostility to the body whose appetite for food constantly eludes control. Unlike 'female' dieting, 'masculine' training usually generates more physical energy, not less. The recent fashions for female weight-training and boxing may foster a superficial confidence in the body, but unlike women's self-defence classes, they co-opt women into the values of patriarchal aggression and are, in fact, nonfunctional. A female body-builder's power is more or less ornamental. It does not present a serious moral and physical challenge to male violence; it is a flattering imitation of the violent male body.

Since the late 1970s there have been a number of secular attempts to explain the phenomenon of obsessive female dieting. In 1978 Susie Orbach popularized the claim that fatness is not a failure of self-control, but is 'a response to the inequality of the sexes', such that overeating can be a deliberate attempt to avoid aggressive sexual objectification. Her book was popular in both appealing to women's sense that dieting is politically and psychologically problematic, but setting out to help them to lose weight nonetheless.[20] Others have understood obsessive dieting as women's succumbing to the pressures of the contemporary Western aesthetic of the body, and even as a form of depression resulting from a biochemical imbalance. The psychological analysis of anorexia as rooted in a woman or girl's dysfunctional relationship with her mother has been highly influential, though it has been rightly criticized by feminists for blaming women—mothers and daughters—for the distorted behaviours that patriarchy has imposed on them.[21]

20. *Fat is a Feminist Issue: The Antidiet Guide to Permanent Weightloss* (New York: Paddington Press, 1978), pp. 18, 21.

21. See, for example, A. Spignesi, *Starving Women: A Psychology of Anorexia* (Dallas: Spring, 1983). This study summarizes the literature of the mother–daughter relationship through the diet. Spignesi herself traces ritual and sacrificial elements in female eating disorders as service to an archetypally raging, hungry mother who is working out her frustrated ambitions through her daughter. Kim Chernin's *The*

Chernin's *Womansize* may place too heavy an emphasis on the mother–daughter relation, but more significantly, the book also celebrates female mass as a 'memory' of primordial power and recognizes that the revival of forgotten pagan images of mother goddesses could restore women's pride in their fleshiness. In common with spiritual feminism, Chernin argues that the diet is a result of male jealousy of the cosmic meaning of female embodiment and that to starve the body is to reduce and subdue its power.[22]

Chernin also asks the political question of why women are now, in the late twentieth century, suffering the equivalent of pre-revolutionary Chinese footbinding: the intention to 'keep women from developing their bodies, their appetites and their powers'.[23] Chernin notes the crucial historical juxtaposition of two female activities that arose in the mid-1960s (the period in which anorexia and bulimia became widespread social diseases). The first was that of feminist consciousness-raising, where women gathered to support one another and *develop* their public presence and power. The second was the growth of weight-watching groups, where women gathered to support one another and *reduce* their presence and restrain their power.[24] As Chernin points out, both activities are manifestations of the political struggle for and against women's liberation that is waged on the terrain of female embodiment.

Since then, Naomi Wolf and Susan Faludi have also convincingly represented the diet culture of the last 25 years as a 'backlash' phenomenon against the women's liberation movement.[25] It is no coincidence that this assault on women's bodies has taken root at precisely the same time that women (even if usually white and middle-class) have achieved

Hungry Self: Women, Eating and Identity (London: Virago, 1985) also describes what she calls a daughter's hidden 'bitter warfare against the mother' and was influenced by Spignesi and by Hilda Bruch's *The Golden Cage: The Enigma of Anorexia Nervosa* (London: Open Book, 1980). Chernin also discusses obsessive dieting as a daughter's way of turning anger against her mother onto her own body in *Womansize: The Tyranny of Slenderness* (London: The Women's Press, 1993. First published in 1981 in America as *The Obsession: Reflections of the Tyranny of Slenderness*).

22. *Womansize*, pp. 148-49.
23. *Womansize*, p. 96.
24. *Womansize*, pp. 99-100.
25. See, for example, Susan Faludi's discussion of the beauty industry as a backlash phenomenon in *Backlash: The Undeclared War against Women* (London: Vintage, 1992), pp. 237-57.

some success in the job market. As the 'ideal' weight is placed at least a stone below most women's natural weight, their bodies become, almost by definition, fat. The vast majority's failure to achieve the ideal shape— extreme slimness with relatively exaggerated breasts—becomes 'failure as defined as implicit in womanhood itself'. [26] There are very few women between adolescence and menopause who can remain cheerfully oblivious of the diet culture.[27] Indeed, '[i]f anorexia is defined as a compulsive fear of and fixation upon food, perhaps most Western women can be called, twenty years into the backlash, mental anorexics'.[28]

Although working-class women and mothers at home do diet, it is educated middle-class girls who are still the most likely to become obsessive about their weight. If the 'backlash' theory is correct, these young women will be the diet culture's central ideological targets as they are the most likely to become feminists and to pursue a career. These young women can also afford the time and money to maintain a low body weight through exercising several times a week and eating a diet high in expensive fresh fruits and vegetables. (Apart from apples, Leslie Kenton's fruit-fast, for example, uses grapes, pineapple, pawpaw, mango and watermelon[29]—all of which are expensive luxury imports for Northern European women.)

Patriarchy intends that middle- and upper-class women, instead of competing with men for prestigious jobs, should compete with one another for physical perfection so that they can marry money rather than earn it through their skills and intelligence. Where masculine power is expressed as financial or physical force, a woman can achieve cultural power of a limited and paradoxical sort when she is most weak. Unless she is an athlete, a dieting woman can attract men by the appearance of a cultivated physical powerlessness that seems to promise sexual compliance. Of course the rewards for successful dieting are considerable. 'Trophy' wives and girlfriends of very rich men, successful fashion models and pornography models at the 'top end' of the market can all

26. *The Beauty Myth: How Images of Beauty are Used against Women* (London: Vintage, 1991), p. 186.

27. See, for example, statistics relating to American female college students' dissatisfaction with their bodies in O. Wooley, S. Wooley and S. Dyrenforth, 'Obesity and Women—II. A Neglected Feminist Topic', in R. Klein and D. Steinberg (eds.), *Radical Voices: A Decade of Feminist Resistance from Women's Studies International Forum* (Oxford: Pergamon, 1989), pp. 26-27.

28. Wolf, *The Beauty Myth*, p. 183.

29. L. Kenton and S. Kenton, *Raw Energy* (London: Century, 1985), p. 137.

profit from their ability to control their own shape. The smallness or angularity of most parts of their bodies is a mark of first world affluence. Indeed, in the West, obesity is most common among the poor and especially among poor women.[30] 'White' thinness signifies a glut of food, whereas 'black' emaciation is the result of malnutrition or starvation.

For Wolf, the 33 billion dollar diet industry in the US is a political solution to feminism that is driven by fear of women.[31] Wolf argues that psychological theories of dieting miss 'the tactical heart of this struggle' against food.[32] Women who are starving to death are incapacitated and have no will to participate in the organized feminist movement or 'to infuse energy into second-wave burnout and exhaustion'.[33] As Wolf points out, women who are besieged in their bodies become disorientated and depressed. During the Holocaust, the Jews in the Lodz ghetto were given rations of between 500 and 1200 calories a day. In the Treblinka extermination camp inmates were given 900 calories a day; in weightloss clinics women are put on diets of only 100 calories more than that.[34]

Wolf's comparison of the calorific intake of a people suffering genocide with that of a chronic dieter is suggestive as an analogy (though not as a direct historical comparison). For if, as Mary Douglas has argued, the body is a bounded system symbolizing the community or the social body,[35] then attacks on the individual body can be the strategic preliminary skirmishes of a total attack on the social body to which that body belongs. The Third Reich attempted to purify the body of Europe of its 'verminous' and 'diseased' Jewish, Gypsy and disabled bodies. Jews dematerialized into thin bodies invisible behind ghetto walls and then dispersed as ash from crematoria chimneys. Or their bodily energy was used up more slowly and usefully as slave labour. Nazis referred to the Jews they were exterminating as *Figuren*—human shapes without the dignity of personhood. Without making offensively direct comparisons between the 'Final Solution' and dieting, I would want to say that some of the logic, intentions and effects of these are held in common.

30. Wooley, Wooley and Dyrenforth, 'Obesity and Women', p. 22.
31. *The Beauty Myth*, esp. p. 196.
32. *The Beauty Myth*, p. 198.
33. *The Beauty Myth*, p. 208.
34. *The Beauty Myth*, p. 196.
35. *Purity and Danger* (Harmondsworth: Penguin, 1970), pp. 118-23.

The eradication of space-taking 'other' flesh by long-term dieting is a slower and less obvious process than that of deportation and murder. But its effects can be similar to that of racial persecution. Psychiatrists have found that 'overweight' women show the same chronic symptoms of 'helplessness, anxiety, and impending doom experienced by victims of racial discrimination and anti-Semitism'.[36] Both racial persecution and the pressure to diet evacuate the patriarchal social body of a body of 'other' people who are perceived to be taking up spaces and opportunities that have already been sacralized, consecrated and occupied by patriarchal men. By making racial bodies and bodies of a certain shape(lessness) profane, the dominant group justifies the marginalization of the minority as a way of protecting the *Lebensraum* of the sacred.

Long-term deprivation of food leads to mental disorientation, physical weakness, loss of libido and infertility. Even pre-pubescent girls can become diet-conscious through peer pressure and the example of women's eating patterns around them. Dieting as a way of life, or rather as a way of living out death, is thus the most comprehensive single means of nipping not only feminism and its unwelcome successes in the bourgeois labour market in the bud, but also of extinguishing the possibility of girls' developing into mature spiritual/political agents. The following journal entry of a contemporary anorexic girl exemplifies the gynocidal effect of the diet culture. Describing herself as 'a mountain of fat', the young woman writes:

> Buried within is a bit of joy slowly drowning in the emollient folds. Hope too is suffering the death agony, going down for a third time in the enormous body of fat. There is only one cure for the indignities... Marking time, counting calories... avoiding people, hiding misery, extravagantly wasting my life (29 December).[37]

Girls and women who are disgusted by their bodies lose respect for themselves and relationships with others are often filtered through envy and obstructed by their flesh. They become other to themselves, let alone to those around them. When a woman is reduced to a shape, she and the women around her turn into outlines bigger or smaller than herself. Thus Jo Ind: 'Everything that I saw in the world, I saw through fat and thin.'[38] She describes the divide-and-rule dissociation of self and

---

36. Wooley, Wooley and Dyrenforth, 'Obesity and Women', p. 28.
37. Cited in Wooley, Wooley and Dyrenforth, 'Obesity and Women', p. 28.
38. *Fat is a Spiritual Issue: My Journey* (London: Mowbrays, 1993), p. 9.

body that effectively defuses spiritual/political resistance. Her self-hatred became ritualized as constant self-examination: 'looking with disgust at my protruding breasts and extended belly. I grimaced at the white, fleshy thighs enhanced for extra ugliness with stretchmarks. I was loathsome to myself. The bare truth was revealed and I could bear it no more.'[39] Ind's evangelical Christianity added further refinements to her pain, compelling her to meditate on 'how perfect and beautiful Jesus was and how ugly and obscene [she] was by comparison'.[40]

In 1975 the radical therapist Aldebaran (no forename given) argued that the 'mass starvation of women is the modern American culture's equivalent of foot-binding, lip-stretching, and other forms of woman mutilation'. In an open letter to all therapists treating fat women, Aldebaran wrote: 'You see fat as suicide, I see weight loss as murder—genocide, to be precise—the systematic murder of a biological minority by organized medicine, acting on behalf of the law- and custom-makers of this society.'[41] It seems strange, then, that when Mary Daly documents the gynocidal crimes of the 'sadostate' she largely ignores one of its most obviously necrophilic devices: culturally prescribed starvation, known euphemistically as 'slimming'.

Here patriarchy's gynocidal intentions are at their most contemporary, pervasive and lethal. When anorexic women become sufficiently 'mad' to take the message of dieting to its rational conclusion, they reduce themselves to a skeletal, corpse-like form, or to the final disappearance of death where the flesh is cremated or eaten away. Dieting as a means of burning and consuming the flesh is inherently funereal. Burning off weight or flesh is a way of sacrificing one's own person as a burnt offering: literally, a holocaust. And when, as in spiritual feminism, that weight/flesh also generates sacral energy, its burning becomes redolent of the witchburnings where female flesh was burnt off to liberate and redeem the soul.

By contrast, a fat woman is unavoidably *there*. For by 'fat' I do not necessarily mean obese, but any female body which will not negotiate its size or shape with patriarchy. A politically and/or actually fat woman is one who is unvigilant; indifferent to the patriarchal fear that femaleness is not only reproductive of things it can use, but can also self-reproduce

39. *Fat is a Spiritual Issue*, p. 5.
40. *Fat is a Spiritual Issue*, p. 4.
41. Quoted by Wooley, Wooley and Dyrenforth, 'Obesity and Women', pp. 30, 32.

and expand its own field. The backlash, then, marks and damages female embodiment in more than political ways. It is also a *religio*-political backlash; a counter-attack on the contemporary reclamation of women-spirit which removes women's bodies from the confinement of small patriarchal sexual and cultural spaces for women and situates them as obstructive prophetic presences at sites of patriarchal power.

Dieting as a Pseudo-Religious Behaviour

If asked, most contemporary dieting women would say that they were dieting in order to look and feel more attractive to themselves and others. They would be very unlikely to give religious reasons for what is an apparently cosmetic practice. Some are dieting in order to feel lighter and more energetic. And it is not for feminists to tell women that there is a moral or political sense in which it is better to be 'overweight', whatever that term might mean. Nor should Goddess feminists unwittingly imply that women who are congenitally thin image the Goddess less clearly than rounded, capacious bodies. Without prescribing any ideal bodily form, an embodied spirituality will nonetheless be concerned to tend the body and not to fill it with, say, junk foods or meat that has been lovelessly farmed and killed without respect. Thus Mary Farkas: 'Remember that the Female Principle symbolizes LIFE. Cook your own food; nourish your body. Don't eat the dead food that patriarchy serves up consistently.'[42]

It is not so much that any feminist would want to determine other women's shapes, as to point out that dieting is a response to an oppressive gender ideology: a way of reproducing gendered inequalities. All dieting is an act of conscience; not the moral conscience, but the sense that an intangible authority is insisting that one *ought* to control the appetite. Correspondingly, many foods represent a temptation of the will. However secularized and cosmetic the intentions of dieting may be, there are obvious and well-documented connections between dieting and religious asceticism.[43] Among others, Shelley Bovery in *Being Fat is Not a Sin* has detected religious under- and overtones in the rituals,

42. Budapest, *The Holy Book of Women's Mysteries*, p. 210. This quotation is from Farkas's contribution to the book, 'The Politics of Food', pp. 201-10.

43. See, for example, R. Bell, *Holy Anorexia* (Chicago: University of Chicago Press, 1985). This is a psychological study of the self-starvation of eleventh- to seventeenth-century women as a purification behaviour.

confessions and penances of dieting.[44] To varying degrees food becomes a source of toxicity from which the body must be emptied and purged by dieting or meticulously regulated eating patterns.

Leslie and Susannah Kenton's *Raw Energy* was an influential book of the mid-1980s. It is not primarily a diet book, though it contains diets. It prescribes a dietary regime by which a transformation of the unhealthy body to a state of beauty, health and renewed energy (quasi-holiness) can be attained through the consumption of particular sorts of whole, raw foods. It is markedly ascetic and is even hopeful that a diet consisting almost entirely of raw fruit and vegetables may eventually 'liberate' women by stopping menstruation.[45] The Kentons recommend that 'toxic waste' from food be eliminated by their '10 day diet' (an 'intestinal broom') and by brushing it from the *dry* surface of the skin with 'a long-handled natural bristle brush or a rough hemp glove... When your body is used to it you can increase the firmness of your brush strokes.'[46] They make no secret of the rigours of this programme and the side-effects of such a dramatic purge.[47]

In the story of Eve's creation from Adam's body, women's bodies are at one further remove from divine perfection than those of men, and it is not difficult to see how women would internalize the messages of a diet culture whose doctrines are, superficially at least, continuous with those of conservative Christian culture. Jo Ind, reflecting on her alternating compulsive eating and self-starvation, writes in a transcendental, ascetic idiom: 'I was not contemplating suicide, just wishing I was dead. I imagined a land where there was no food, a place without diets, binges or fat. If I did not have a body I would enjoy living there. That would be heaven itself.'[48] At a time when the authority of religion in women's lives has been eroded by secularism, Wolf sees the diet industry as patriarchy using the *forms* of religion to keep women in order. By reinforcing women's obedience to the prevailing ideology of femininity, patriarchy once more induces a sense of the sinful, polluting quality of women's bodies.[49]

And the contemporary diet culture borrows as much, or more, from

44. London: Pandora, 1989, pp. 21-27.
45. *Raw Energy*, p. 119.
46. *Raw Energy*, p. 113.
47. *Raw Energy*, p. 135.
48. *Fat is a Spiritual Issue*, p. 6.
49. *The Beauty Myth*, pp. 90-91.

the evangelical idiom as it does from asceticism. The momentum of the diet is largely derived from presenting food as a quasi-sexual indulgence to be sinfully and guiltily consumed and then confessed to others. Thinness signifies membership of a reborn, saved, elect group of women who have triumphed over the temptations of the flesh.[50] Yet Naomi Wolf regards the relation between dieting and religion as more than the borrowing of metaphors. She argues that the diet culture actually supplants and reconstitutes the forms of religion to control women's minds and bodies with a new creed: 'that there is such a thing as beauty, that it is holy, and that women should seek to attain it'.[51]

Our contemporary panoptical culture of media and security surveillance seems to be continuous with religious traditions in which God is imagined as a male judge of the naked sinner. The combination of religious and secular elements is an exacting one—especially when that sinner is a woman. The diet culture expects women to spy on themselves and constantly to assess their progress. So too, right-wing American evangelical Christians urge women to look beautiful for their husbands, and so, indirectly, for God. The surveillance common to both secular and religious culture ensures that, as Starhawk puts it, 'our value becomes dependent on how closely we conform to the rule; our unique beauty is rendered invisible, worthless. A woman's own body becomes her enemy, her betrayer, by its insistence on shaping itself according to its own organic imperatives.'[52] Throughout the world, and especially in ancient religions, the mirror has been feared and revered as an instrument for soul-trapping; a doorway into a confusingly reversed reality.[53] Here its function is similar. The mirror is co-opted by the diet culture as an instrument of surveillance and a judgment on female vanity. In a quasi-magical sense, the mirror lies to anorexics by reversing reality: the starved body is clothed in fat.

The diet may also be an indirect result of the way in which traditional Judaeo-Christianity's spiritual dissociation from the dominated earth has been coupled with modernity's industrialized relations to the earth. It is characteristic of modern patriarchal attitudes to both the earth and women's bodies that any respect for their life is subordinated to their

50. See Bovery, *Being Fat is Not a Sin*, p. 27.
51. *The Beauty Myth*, p. 88.
52. *Truth or Dare*, p. 73.
53. Walker, *The Woman's Dictionary of Symbols and Sacred Objects*, pp. 145-46.

perceived utility to industrial forms of production. The monocultural worldview which resists the inconveniences and delayed profits of bio-diversity also demands and farms only one kind of female body.

But when the earth is the body, intelligence and soul of the Goddess, as it is in pagan religions, spiritual feminism understands any attack on the female body as an attack on the earth itself. Clarissa Pinkola Estés (who gracefully describes herself as being 'built close to the ground and of extravagant body') correctly identifies the diet culture as a parallel process to that of ecological destruction. The demand that a woman should 'carve' her body 'is remarkably similar to the carving, burning, peeling off layers, stripping down to the bones the flesh of the earth itself. Where there is a wound on the psyches and bodies of women, there is a corresponding wound...on Nature herself.'[54] In a matrifocal religion whose purpose is to enable things to thrive and grow, a woman's biological connections with her mother and grandmothers are important and should not be broken by hatred of the body they have fed and passed on through half of their genes. For if body size is inherited, rejection of one's own body is to attack what Estés calls the 'sacred history' of the female line: 'In essence, the attack on women's bodies is a far-reaching attack on the ones who have gone before her as well as the ones who will come after her.'[55]

The diet industry uses women as role models and spokeswomen to give other women reversed truths. Women are encouraged to consume the 'goods' created by wasteful, toxic modes of production: and the degree to which they consume becomes an index to their status as women. At the same time they are warned against consuming the organic food substances that the diet industry claims will toxify and swell their bodies. In other words, the satisfaction of eating is poisoned, and the environment is poisoned to satisfy all material desires other than food. But the woman who has retrieved her 'wild nature', as Estés describes it, 'would never advocate the torture of the body, culture, or land. The wild nature would never agree to flog the form in order to prove worth, prove "control", prove character, be more visually pleasing, more financially valuable.'[56] But where the earth is reduced to inert matter, the female body will also be treated as mere flesh to be shaped and pornographically consumed.

54. *Women Who Run with the Wolves*, p. 204.
55. *Women Who Run with the Wolves*, p. 203.
56. *Women Who Run with the Wolves*, p. 204.

A belief that this may not always have been so can be seen in contemporary feminist matrifocal readings of the Stone Age figurines whose fleshiness was probably revered for its promise of fertility, but perhaps also for its beauty—the Venus of Willendorf, ironically named by male archaeologists, is fat but does not appear to be pregnant. (Veronica MacIntyre, writing in an experimental style, questions the interpretation of the Venus of Willendorf as a fertility symbol: 'fertility fecundity as though they can imagine nothing else for fat women no other reason that 30,000 years ago some loving sculptor shaped her... what if she's not a "fertility goddess" but a self-portrait? what if she was a fat dyke sculpted by her lover?')[57] Spiritual feminism consecrates flesh as something more than passive 'fertility'. The word 'fertility' cannot evoke the patriarchally uncontrollable generativity and proliferation of flesh. Spiritual feminism celebrates the bounty of flesh in the same moment that it celebrates the earth and the foods the earth produces in generous abundance.

The ancient Greek association of the underworld, the invisible world of Earth, with the female body remains inspirational for spiritual feminism's sense of the capaciousness of femaleness:

> As a vessel, a container, a body filled with an interiority itself full of potential for holding, for entreasuring or warming, the woman's body was seen [by the Greeks] as analogous to the earth, with its caves, crevasses, openings into an invisible world from which the living emerged, into which the dead departed.[58]

While other feminisms might be uneasy at the characterization of women's bodies as ever-welcoming and ever-receptive, spiritual feminism honours the enveloping, protective motherliness of the Goddess—an aspect which is imaged as amplitude. Food, flesh and earth symbolize and are media of immanent divine generativity. This is an ancient pagan worldview and one which would regard modern patriarchy's quasi-aesthetic refusal of female bodily maturity, sexuality and fertility as ingratitude to the Goddess. And more than that, the materiality of the spiritual feminist sacred means that the flattening and diminution of matter—especially the belly (the *omphalos* or navel of the cosmos)—is also a diminution of all power and energy: 'the belly is the spiritual as well as physical centre that unites us to the universe. Through our

---

57. 'writing at risk', *From the Flames* 11 (1993), p. 21.
58. P. DuBois, *Torture and Truth* (London: Routledge, 1991), p. 78.

bellies, we can hear the voice of our higher universal power speak to us.'[59] The diet industry's physical and axiological diminution of matter eradicates female sacral energy and is therefore doing the work of patri- archal religion, even in spheres where the influence of such religions is negligible. A spiritual feminist might, then, read a body that refuses to make itself thin as a transgression and transvaluation of patriarchal ideologies of the body. Here 'fatness' is a sign of feminist spiritual/ political power and mass and at least a liberation from the aesthetics of patriarchal religio-sexual politics.

The Profanity of the Fat Body

As I pointed out earlier, the political, physical and psychological harm done to women by the diet and cosmetics industry has been fairly well documented—though not as much or as often as it should have been. Rather than rehearse this material again I would like to give a religious reading of the industry as having been particularly conditioned by the sacred/profane dichotomy, and to draw out the implications of that for a thealogy of embodiment.

The disciplines practised on the female body are essentially spatial. The 'secular' diet pushes a woman into a visual corner, it deprives her body of (breathing) space. So too, in fundamentalist or traditional religions women disappear under veils or scarves and behind screens. All patri- archal religions approve of the seclusion of women in the home to some degree. These religious practices save advantageous spaces for men and have a similar effect on women to that of the more secular diet. Spatial separations of women and men usually have religious roots in the fear of or reverence for female *mana* that is primarily manifest at the transformatory boundaries of life: the menarche, reproduction and menopause. As these processes are biological and not under the direct control of men, patriarchal religion controls women's bodies by colonizing these magical, reproductive energies through a variety of taboos. And, in biblical cultures, the meaning of the body has been re- presented to women as functional rather than positively sacral or revelatory in its own right in order to appropriate those magical powers.

There is a feminist consensus that patriarchy holds power by owning and controlling the form and products of the female body (hence its resistance to contraception and abortion on demand). Religious feminists

59. Amberston, *Blessings of the Blood*, p. 69.

have long argued that this legislative control over women's bodies is at the same time a means to control nature or chaos. If this is so, I would suggest that fear of female fatness or abundant fleshiness is a fear of natural materiality which is not ultimately subject to patriarchal morality and aesthetics. (Aethetic and moral value come together in the ideology of 'feminine' beauty: the princess of fairy tales is captivatingly pretty because she is sexually virtuous.) Being outside male/divine control the 'shapeless' fat body signifies chaotic formlessness and therefore profanity. In turn, that profanity justifies the 'fat' female body's outcast/ cast-out social status from a community that legitimates its political structures and protects them from change by sacralizing its identity as a fixed order.

In Europe and America the woman of 'perfect' body attracts some of the qualities of the well-ordered Christian church—another female container. In the 'Pauline' letter to the Ephesians, the church is imaged as the obedient bride of Christ. As a holy female body, the collective Christian body or church has had her unreasoning flesh purified by his reason: a reason which has the magical/aesthetic effect of removing the imperfections of female embodiment. In a sexual sense, Christ takes the Church into his rational embodiment by 'present[ing] the church to himself in splendour, without spot or wrinkle or any such thing, that she might be holy and without blemish' (Ephesians 5.27). By implication physically marred female bodies are profane or unassimilable into a sacrificial cult, church or semi-secular society. Christ's body cannot enter a blemished or profane female body because his body is sacred. It is unblemished by sin and has been set aside by God for his own use. It is lacerated and pierced only by the sins of others; a sacrificial marking that purifies his incarnation with his/God's own blood.

This aestheticization of the sacred is common in the world's religions. One common criterion for both sanctity and profanity is unusualness or rarity. A body which is 'freakishly' without flaw is set aside for divine use and therefore set apart from common use. Mary, for example, was immaculately conceived. That is, she was conceived without the taint or 'spot' of original sin. In Latin, a *macula* is a spot. So again, Mary's sinlessness was inseparable from her physical perfection. In the cultic biblical scheme only what is fresh and without blemish can be set before the divine king, so Mary can only have the status of a sacred woman set aside for divine use if she is physically flawless.

Modern female bodily perfection will not carry the full sacrificial-salvific meanings of a perfect male body like that of Jesus, but it is still elevated out of the sphere of ordinary imperfect women. The perfect body still carries residual but sub-religious meanings and privileges. Western culture is only partially secularized and the sacred/profane dichotomy continues, if subliminally, to serve a useful function in the construction of ordered social hierarchies with their respective rewards and punishments. Since the rise of popular feminism these hierarchical orderings of women have become ever more significant: the women's liberation movement is a modern confirmation of patriarchy's anxiety about women as being 'naturally' disobedient (after Eve) or otherwise difficult to assimilate into a given social order.

The perfectly disciplined, obedient, female body that has resisted its unruly naturalness and propensity to change has achieved some of the characteristics of masculine holiness: the full exercise of (quasi-) moral will and transcendence of the body. This female body has been purified of its irrational hungers and has kept perfectly within its appointed spatial boundaries. This trained body can then earn the rewards of leisure or set-apartness by being paraded as a model before the less perfect or by marrying a rich man. One measure of her success is that she not need to do any menial work at all. Her non-ordinary position is maintained in part by punctilious attention to diet, make-up and exercise, all of which are designed to create an illusion of the immortality that the masculine sacred is premised upon.

Conversely, the ordinary, non-elite woman whose body bears no sign of training through exercise or special diet, but is clearly subject to organic change, is profane. She eats cheap starchy foods; foods that are profane to the elite dieter. (Bordo recounts how, after eating sugar, a woman felt 'polluted, disgusting...as if something bad had gotten inside'.[60]) The non-elite fat woman's body is placed outside the sphere of the sacred and is therefore available for common use. She performs the menial, dirty tasks like lavatory cleaning and washing floors for herself, her family and sometimes for elite quasi-sacred women.

Elite slim women occupy a privileged separate space that is prohibited to all non-elite bodies except cleaners. These prohibitions (marked out by fences, gates, security systems and so forth) protect the elite body and the space she sacralizes. But the fat woman is also subject to (different) prohibitions. The treatment of female fatness can be similar to that of the profane or taboo object. When a religious system removes or separates

60. *Unbearable Weight*, p. 148.

an object from ordinary use it becomes either sacred or taboo depending on whether its powers are perceived to be controlled and beneficent or uncontrolled and threatening. In the case of a woman whose body has clearly eluded patriarchal discipline, she is set apart for social invisibility, whereas the immaculately maintained body of, say, a model, is set apart for public admiration. The 'perfect' body can be exposed to view in tight and revealing clothes whereas the fat woman must shroud her profanity from sight.

But despite science's best efforts, even a 'perfect' female body is subject to organic change. Most models and actresses (other than character actresses) retire, or are made to retire, from public view when they begin to age. For a model this can be as young as 23. For the sacred should not corrupt or decay; indeed, decay—especially female decay—is a sign of profanity. The 'degeneration' of 'ordinary' female bodies (and finally, non-ordinary bodies) in their passage from pre-pubescent slimness to pregnancy and old age places them *by definition* into the realm of the profane.

At the end of the twentieth century the secular Western media are probably more powerful mediators of patriarchal values than the church, which once performed some of the same ideological functions. And unless the fat/profane woman has an unusually pretty face or is a successful comedian, the media keeps her from view. With the odd exception, fat women's sexuality is not depicted; it is unthinkable. Ordinary, that is, profane women, with heavy thighs, stretch marks and round bellies do not *appear*. Like old women whose bodies are also marked by organic change, those women who will not render them-selves invisible (slimmed down or shrunk) are simply removed from sight. Their naturalness is too fearful to look upon. The Hebrew concept of *herem*—the banned object isolated for its destruction—is exemplified in secular form by the practical anathematization of fat women. Research has repeatedly shown that from an early age people judge fatness as a socially 'bad' quality and slimness as 'good'. Psychologists have found that children maintain a far greater 'personal space distance' from fat people than any other body shape. Fat children are subject to 'extreme ostracism':[61] precisely the means of separating the profane from the sacred by excommunication or *herem*.

Fear of fatness is usually rationalized as concern for its putative risks

61. This research is summarized in Wooley, Wooley and Dyrenforth, 'Obesity and Women', pp. 23-25.

to health. It is doubtless true that extreme weight-gain puts undue strain on the heart and bodily systems. But if fatness is also a socio-religious signifier, then fear of ill health through fatness is an ideological as well as a medical concern: a fear of the corruption or degeneration of bodily/ social form by sensual indulgence or sloth. The equation of fatness and the unhealthiness of the (social) body has a certain logic: the word 'unhealthy' comes from the same root as the Gothic *heils* (holy) and the Old English *hal*, whole. An unhealthy body is one whose wholeness/ holiness is under threat. But where the German *heil* valorizes physical wholeness as having spiritual meaning, modern patriarchy valorizes wholeness more literally as the orderliness of physical perfection. When this is achieved through dieting, patriarchal dualistic concepts of embodi- ment have the effect of sanctifying spiritual dis-integration; of making the will an enemy of the body. It is this dis-integration that disconnects not only the mind, body and emotions, but also the human body from the earth, thereby causing personal and planetary ill health. Under nominally Protestant modern patriarchy, good health/holiness is too often reduced to a synonym for fitness. To be 'fit' is to have worked hard to expend large reserves of energy in losing weight as much as it is to be sacred/fit to come into the divine presence.

The patriarchal God is a god who imposes order on chaotic nature. The sacred/profane dichotomy may pivot or be subject to the reversal of its elements, but it does not fuse them. The patriarchal sacred stands for what is ordered and can therefore sometimes stand for positive human values like peace and beauty. But as an imposition of order, organization can also have more authoritarian meanings than that of peaceful coexistence as such. And as Nancy Jay has noted in her critique of the patriarchal sacred, human ordering is not represented in the natural empirical world where life is neither wholly ordered nor wholly chaotic; neither wholly sick nor wholly healthy. As she says, 'in the empirical world, almost everything is in a process of transition: growing, decaying, ice turning to water and vice versa'.[62] Since femaleness is constructed as non-rational and natural, women occupy time and space in ways that men-as-god do not. Female bodily changes demarcate the profanity of an organic as opposed to a civilized space. Organic spaces are constantly in the profanity of process, as when women are swelling and multiplying in pregnancy or are 'putting on weight'. The patriarchal sacred is, as

62. 'Gender and Dichotomy', in Gunew (ed.), *A Reader in Feminist Knowledge*, p. 93.

Durkheim described it, an exclusive reality which must be isolated and protected from profane disorder. And it is in doing this that patriarchy structures and demarcates its own ordered space and justifies its deprivation of space to female flesh as nature.

Religious feminism has argued that women suffer the political effects of exclusion from the sacred. Arguably, women who diet are compensating for that exclusion in their attempt to emulate the changeless perfection of the holy. Opposition to dieting is therefore at once a spiritual and a political stance of resistance to patriarchy's desacralization of organic change. It is a religious protest on behalf of the sacrality of the body. For as Clarissa Pinkola Estés puts it, 'the body is no dumb thing from which we struggle to free ourselves. In proper perspective, it is a rocket ship, a series of atomic cloverleafs, a tangle of neurological umbilici to other worlds and experiences.'[63] The untamed female power *in* the body gives it locomotive energy; an 'ability to transport us elsewhere'; to be 'a series of doors and dreams and poems through which we can learn and know all manner of things'.[64]

Those magical or transformative embodied powers are weakened or destroyed with the dieter's (usually) notional or imitative death. Living matter is volatile and if it is preserved by being 'frozen' in time it will die. The obsessive dieter attempts to 'freeze' her body by stopping its transformatory passage through time and effectively ceasing to occupy the space in which time is operational. (An anorexic friend of mine not only deprives her body of food, she also believes that she will lose weight if she 'freezes' her body in another way: by keeping it cold. By switching off the heating in her house she compels her body/furnace to work harder and so burn off more calories.) Time turns a girl into a woman, then usually into a mother, and then into an old woman. All of these processes involve changes of shape. To arrest embodied change the dieter has to enclose her body within tightly controlled diet regimes—each of which has its own calender that must be observed for a fixed duration of days or weeks.

The diet forcibly contains the shape of the body and wastes its energies. And as such it bears a more than analogous relation to the Iron Maiden. The Iron Maiden was manufactured during the witchcraze for the torture and murder of witches. It was a cast iron coffin-like replica of the female body that killed the woman imprisoned inside it by means of

63. *Women Who Run with the Wolves*, p. 205.
64. *Women Who Run with the Wolves*, p. 208.

its interior spikes. This was a cruelly ironic death, in which patriarchy turned the tables on a woman's capacity to hold another human being inside her and give it life. That patriarchy (especially where it has been influenced by Hellenistic philosophy) understands pregnancy as the beginning of death is apparent here. In the Iron Maiden patriarchy took its revenge on women for the crime of incarcerating the eternal soul in the consumptive sarcophagus of flesh. (In Greek the word means literally a stone eater of flesh. Flesh itself—as *sarx*—can mean a prison.) Women's flesh reduces essence to existence—the finite, mutable realm of the profane. When an anorexic feels her 'conscience' pricking every time she eats, or when a non-anorexic woman feels uneasy about eating rich foods, the Iron Maiden's spikes are still piercing and punishing female flesh and consciousness for this fall.

The Iron Maiden was also a cannibal. She sunk her metal teeth into her own kind. Again, in the global mythologies of female cannibalism, the mother who gives her bodily fluids and her cooking to feed others in turn becomes the great eater. Joseph Campbell draws with apparent relish on this model of womankind as eaten turned eater in his discussion of the world folklore of female cannibals and of course the archetypal devouring goddess—Kali:

> The Hindu mother-goddess Kali is represented with her long tongue lolling to lick up the lives and blood of her children. She is the very pattern of the sow that eats her farrow, the cannibal ogress: life itself, the universe, which sends forth beings only to consume them.[65]

This ambivalence about mothers may in part explain why our culture fears fat women and makes nervous jokes about the archetypally suffocating Jewish mama who fattens her family with her self-sacrificial love and her delicious, copious food. For in fattening the bodies of her sons with her love she also softens their bodies; she feminizes them, and so produces the studious, unsporting, cake-eating, mother-loving, stereotypical sons of popular Jewish and anti-Semitic humour. Whether a woman 'starves' her children by becoming fat herself or whether she fattens them into a state of (social) vulnerability, her feeding is liable to put her in the wrong; it is in danger of profaning her and her offspring.

Nonetheless, it is a common oversimplification of religious feminist discourse to assert that in patriarchal religion women's bodies are,

65. *The Masks of God*. I. *Primitive Mythology* (New York: Arkana, 1991), p. 70.

almost by definition, profane or devouring of the sacred order. In fact, patriarchy can in some senses be explained as a response to its own perception of the *sacredness* of female bodies. After all, the reproductive cycle brings a woman unnervingly close to the processes of divine generativity. And female religious behaviours can themselves be complex, paradoxical and difficult to interpret. Some medieval female saints seem to have assumed the possibility of female bodily sanctity in their apparently contradictory readiness to defile their own bodies. Dorothy of Montgau made herself literally profane to the church by bricking herself into the cathedral walls. There she froze her body into sacred stillness by refusing blankets against the winter night. Clare Gambacorta ate only refuse, Mary Alacoque relished drinking the excrement of a man with dysentery, and Catherine of Siena drank bowls of pus from the cancerous sores of a woman who had abused her.[66] These gross defilements were evidence of these women's being miraculously set apart as saints— a mark of whose sanctity was to possess the supernatural power of eradicating normal bodily reactions and desires.[67] By taking the profane into their own bodies, these female saints could redeem or at least diffuse the negative charge of their bodily profanity by their sacrificial gestures. Playing on the ambiguity of the sacred/profane distinction, they sacralized their bodies by defiling them.

Or again, in the nineteenth century women manifested their Christian sanctity by ministering precisely to the profane: those excluded from the operations of the established Christian cult. Deaconesses, female nurses, district visitors and 'rescue workers' (who reformed prostitutes) all laboured with those whom they knew would contaminate them whether through immorality, disease or simply being socially and cultically outcast. Their ministry was an act of confidence in the power of industrious female presence to *transform* the profane; to bring it into the sphere of the sacred by compassion and healing, cleansing touch. These are not the only possible readings of these acts, and nor would I claim

66. For further examples and discussions of this type of *acta* see R. Keickhefer, *Unquiet Souls: Fourteenth Century Saints and their Religious Milieu* (Chicago: University of Chicago Press, 1984); D. Weinstein and R. Bell, *Saints and Society: The Two Worlds of Western Christendom 1000–1700* (Chicago: University of Chicago Press, 1982).

67. In *The Idea of the Holy*, p. 158, Otto notes that holy persons create a spontaneous impression of the numinous; of 'a being of wonder and mystery, who somehow or other is felt to belong to the higher order of things, to the side of the numen itself'.

that there is any inherent merit in a *via dolorosa* of self-defilement. These examples are intended to show that in patriarchal religions the female body does not have one fixed meaning. Rather, female flesh has plural, shifting meanings and these are dependent on who is articulating that meaning and whose interests it serves. My interpretation of the diet culture and pornography (below) may seem unremittingly negative, but even here male and female assumptions—albeit distorted and misconstrued—of the reality of female sacredness can be found. The diet industry is founded upon religious significations for female embodiment: it assumes that women's bodies are accustomed to fasting for others; that it is part of the sacrality of femininity to make sacrifices. Or again, pornography's desecration of female embodiment assumes that the female body is owed some sort of religious honour, without which the pleasurable *frisson* of its dishonouring would be considerably diminished.

Pornography and the Desecration of Female Bodies

The diet culture is less socially transgressive and apparently less violent an assault on female embodiment than pornography. Diet books are not shrouded in the 'brown paper' that protects society from the profanity of the 'dirty' material beneath. The diet's assault is simply a part of 'normal' everyday life and few are immune to its rhetoric. Women are not physically coerced into dieting—indeed it can be a mark of (pseudo-) virtue manifest as self-control. If for this reason alone, it is possible that the diet culture is as insidiously damaging to women as pornography. The two cultures are, in any case, continuous with one another in several respects. Both food (especially cakes) and female bodies are photographed in magazines where they are presented as illicit pleasures designed to awaken salacious desire. However, men and women are differently situated as voyeurs to these objects of desire. Men are not expected to deprive themselves of food or of the female bodies that are laid out for their pleasure. Women are expected to prepare delicacies (good food and good bodies) to satisfy other people's appetites but not their own. In other words, sexual pornography assumes male dominance, and food pornography, female subordination.[68] Women have to reduce their size if they are to be 'successful' objects of the male gaze,

68. See R. Coward, 'Naughty but Nice: Food Pornography', in E. Frazer, J. Hornsby and S. Lovibond (eds.), *Ethics: A Feminist Reader* (Oxford: Blackwell, 1992), pp. 132-38.

but in becoming lovably small they are, symbolically at least, left more vulnerable to its pornographic intrusions.

Pornography's gross imbalances of gendered power have led radical feminism particularly to make pornography a central issue in feminist politics. There are, of course, feminists—usually liberal feminists—who do not object to pornography as such, and indeed encourage women to produce self-defining pornography under equal conditions of labour. But radical feminism has traditionally sought to ban or restrict pornography not only because it institutionalizes sexual inequality, but also because it ontologically defines women's existence *as* sexual availability. As Catherine MacKinnon has said, in pornography 'women exist to the *end* of male pleasure', it 'purports to define what a woman *is*'.[69] Feminist objections to pornography are not puritanical. One of the central objections is that pornography cannot represent the woman as a subject of her own experience because it seeks genital sensation at the expense of mutual feeling, whereas feminist eroticism may include, but is not defined by, penetrative sex. For religious feminism the erotic is an essentially biophilic capacity to spark and generate love through a wider connectedness than the genital union of bodies alone: that of erotic power-in-relation.[70]

The opposite of the biophilic touch which soothes and excites is the pornographic desecratory touch which excites male bodies irrespective of female desire. Desecration of any sort is a violent attack on the sacred. It is an attempt to deny or destroy the essential power of a sacred thing. And where the sacrality of an object is embodied, that is, inseparable from its life, then desecration attempts to destroy a woman's bodily substance as well as her essence or meaning. The classical radical feminist critique of patriarchy is still exemplified in Andrea Dworkin's claim that women are subdued by the threat and actuality of male violence. Physical power put to the service of patriarchy is 'the capacity to terrorize, to use self and strength to inculcate fear, fear *in* a whole class of persons *of* a whole class of persons'.[71] A woman's mere femaleness can be a sufficient screen on which to project male fantasy. A woman does not have to be beautiful or have an unusually slim figure

69. 'Pornography: Not a Moral Issue', in Klein and Steinberg (eds.), *Radical Voices*, p. 160.

70. See C. Heyward, *Touching Our Strength: The Erotic as Power and the Love of God* (New York: Collins, 1989), p.3.

71. *Pornography*, p. 15.

to appear in pornographic material (at the lower and harder end of the market at least).

To this critique I would want to add that pornography debases female sacral power by recasting it as the power of sexual attraction. Patriarchy may pay homage to this but is also threatened by the power of the female body to provoke sexual excitement; to have power over men's bodies. Pornography violently defuses that power by acts of desecration. A woman's sacral power to change the form and function of matter then dwindles to the particular and limited power to provoke an erection. A patriarchal man conquers what is left of those 'shape-shifting' powers by reducing the woman to a subordinated sexual object: 'he forces her to become that thing that causes erection, then holds himself helpless and powerless when he is aroused by her. His fury when she is not that thing, when she is either more or less than that thing, is intense and punishing.'[72]

Both the fetishization of breasts as sexual toys and the tabooing of mature or elderly breasts are instances of the unnaming and rejecting of female sacral power. The changing, maturing (already owned) body of the wife-mother is not usually an object of pornographic attention. Her breasts have swollen to feed and comfort new life and the skin may have lost some of its elasticity in the process.[73] The breast which is not youthful or airbrushed or inflated with silicone becomes taboo, unphotographable.

But the bodies of certain types of women, namely prostitutes, Jewish women and black (read 'slave') women, have a kind of 'distilled' profanity. The more profane or out-caste a woman is, the more dangerous is her sexuality. Colonized women and prostitutes are multiply profane as 'available' for common use and dangerous in their genetic impurity and their moral and venereal contagiousness. In the Western pornographic imagination, this profanity and its prohibitions make 'other' women more, not less, sexually arousing than the white Protestant wife. The bodily profanity of women who are other to Christian culture has not been contained by church and state. These women, argues Dworkin, are arousing because they are 'seen as pure and dangerous sexuality, used, reeking with violation'. This is one of the ways in which patriarchy reads 'natural' women: as being on heat; what Baudelaire called

72. Dworkin, *Pornography*, p. 22.
73. See Susan Brownmiller's discussion of breasts as objects of pornographic desire in *Femininity* (London: Hamish Hamilton, 1984), pp. 44-45.

'abominable'.[74] The abuses of the master/servant relationship in the British colonies were paradigmatic of all patriarchal sexual relations in that patriarchy is an inherently colonial or parasitic system. But in the colonies the profanity of female embodiment could be enjoyed and abused with relative social impunity. The 'primordial', rampant, exotic, pagan sexual energies of black and Asian women could be used up in ways that white middle- and upper-class women's could not. White virtuous wives were those who would perpetuate the legitimate white male line, making their bodies prohibited to all but their white husbands.

In the late twentieth century, the masculine potency and autonomy of the penis is still protected from the demystification of repeated exposure. There is strong legal resistance to subjecting the penis to the routine objectification suffered by women's genitals. It is perhaps to protect its sacral potency that it is illegal in Britain to show an erect penis. If it is to be seen at all it must be flaccid and usually sheathed in its foreskin, that is, like many other sacred things, shielded from direct view. But in biblical cultures female nakedness has already been given over to the realm of the profane. Eve, for example, is always depicted as naked whereas Mary is clothed. And the *ritus paganus* of nocturnal, heathen magic has always been imagined to be—and weather permitting, still is—practised unselfconsciously 'skyclad'. In paganism, nakedness represents paradisal freedom and the purity of the natural. (Skyclad ceremonies do not, in fact, occasion sexual arousal though it would not be morally problematic to pagans if they did.[75])

Pornographers are often at their most brutal when fantasizing about having a feminist 'bitch' (an 'Amazon' or 'castrator') at their mercy. All of these words are abusive epithets for a woman who demands the ownership of her own sexuality and reproductivity. These fantasies of humiliation imply patriarchy's fear that it has not, finally, conquered women's bodies and show that it (mistakenly) 'postulates that [feminist] women will do to men what men have done to women'.[76] Male dominance is thereby justified once again. But perhaps Dworkin comes still closer to the religious heart of the matter in her gloss on a quotation from Georges Bataille:

74. Dworkin, *Pornography*, p. 119.
75. On ritual nakedness in contemporary witchcraft see T. Luhrmann, *Persuasions of the Witch's Craft: Ritual Magic in Contemporary England* (London: Picador, 1994), pp. 50-51.
76. Dworkin, *Pornography*, p. 35.

'Beauty is desired in order that it may be befouled; not for its own sake, but for the joy brought by the certainty of profaning it.' Beauty, then, consistently has meaning in the sphere of female death or violation. An object is always destroyed in the end by its use when it is used to the fullest and enough; and in the realm of female beauty, the final value of the object is precisely to be found in its cruel or deadly destruction.[77]

Although she does not pursue her point, Dworkin hints at what may be the primary intention of pornography: the deliberate desecration of the female body. For a woman's embodiment, her 'naturalness', is an affront to culture: her mutability is a sign of her freedom. The pornographic photograph in particular freezes female flesh in one frame; one space and time in which she is disconnected from her environment and permanently available to patriarchy *in that form*. The pornographer might also intuit that female sacrality is meaningless outside its relationships of emotion and change with the human and natural environment. Pornography, by contrast, is non-contextual. In pornographic texts and films the narratives and characters are thin or non-existent; the images of the bodies far more anatomical than those of erotic art. Like the Baconian scientist's examination of nature, 'penetrating' its 'caverns and corners when interrogating the truth',[78] the pornographer takes a woman's body out of its relational context and positions it in a series of *tableaux* (non) *vivants*. It is this non-contextuality that makes pornography—ultimately—monotonous as well as distressing.

Yet the meaning of desecration alters across different religio-moral contexts. In the feminist neo-pagan context the application of the word 'desecration' to the female body is not the same as its application to, for example, a Christian female body/house such as the church. J.T. Gulczynski has enumerated the grounds on which Canon Law judges a church to have been desecrated and violated. Among murder, the unjust shedding of blood, and other 'sordid uses' (such as the burial of excommunicants within its boundaries), Gulczynski also lists using the church for irreverent theatrical productions, circuses, markets or 'any other type of boisterous revelry' as acts of desecration.[79] It seems

77. *Pornography*, pp. 117-18.
78. The quoted phrases are from Bacon's 1623 *De Dignitate et Augmentis Scientiarium*, quoted in C. Halkes, *New Creation: Christian Feminism and the Renewal of the Earth* (London: SPCK, 1991), p. 28.
79. *The Desecration and Violation of Churches: An Historical Synopsis and Commentary* (Washington, DC: Catholic University of America Press, 1942), p. 78.

significant that all sexual ('sordid') acts are forbidden except those between married couples in times of war when the woman has been made homeless.[80] In this instance it would seem that the profanity of sex is overlooked because patriarchy is in danger of consuming more young men than it is replacing.

A spiritual feminist would not understand pornographic desecration of her body as patriarchally as this, though the sense of the trauma of violation is just as strong. Yet feminist spirituality is not puritanical and rarely stands on its dignity. In feminist Wicca ritual boisterousness and humour is normal and the sexual nature of divinity is celebrated. Pornography profanes feminst sacrality in a different sense to that of Christian desecration. The mystic Simone Weil's asceticism bears little relation to pagan women's erotic spirituality. However, her suggestion that 'vice, depravity and crime are nearly always...attempts to eat beauty'[81] provides a clue to the offense of pornography to the spiritual feminist worldview. Where pornographic desacralization is a metaphorical eating and digestion it reduces women's bodies *qua* sacred 'food' to prey—food captured and consumed. In a common pornographic extended metaphor women are hunted, skinned (or stripped of clothing), and consumed.[82] This digestive process destroys its object's personhood and she is metaphorically turned to excrement—patriarchal men hold ageing sex workers and other used women in contempt. Pornography typifies all wasteful, consumerist patriarchal interventions in nature. In pornography the female body's sacral capacity to become food for babies in the womb and at the breast and, traditionally, to turn ingredients into meals, is subjected to male force, used and then, in a pseudo-ethical judgment on female sexual availability, wasted; spat out. (Similarly the word 'de-flower' suggests the deliberate bruising and crushing of petals and fruit—among the great beauties of nature's reproductivity.)

Daly's development of Jo Freeman's analysis of women as members

---

80. *The Desecration of Churches*, pp. 35-36.

81. 'Forms of the Implicit Love of God', quoted in J. Herik, 'Simone Weil's Religious Imagery: How Looking Becomes Eating', in C. Atkinson *et al.* (eds.), *Immaculate and Powerful: The Female in Sacred Image and Social Reality* (Boston: Beacon Press / Crucible, 1985), p. 260. Weil blames Eve for beginning the sin of eating rather than looking so I have taken her words almost, but not entirely, out of context.

82. See Dworkin, *Pornography*, pp. 25-30.

of a sexual caste system[83] is an important contribution to understanding pornography as a function of the desacralization of women and the earth. The root of the Latin word *castus* is 'pure' or 'chaste'. Under patriarchy women are ideally chaste, that is, pure and untouched or untouchable in respect to their being the property of one man. Yet they are also paradigmatically touchable. Daly argues that the female caste is, like that of nature, that of the touchable—what is always available. This becomes clearer when one considers the Latin and Greek terms related to caste: *carere*, 'to be without', and *keazein*, 'to split'. Daly claims that the language of caste permits the patriarchal male to sever women, as a caste, from the processes of their becoming by inflicting a variety of more or less pornographic practices upon their bodies.[84]

Any caste system is also a function of the patriarchal division of the sacred and the profane which separates out different classes of object for different sorts of treatment. There are many sub-castes within the female caste: all women may be touchable, but some are more touchable than others—dependent on their race, class and (dis)abilities. It is in this sense that pornography needs to be understood; not simply as disguised violence against women—though it is that—but as a deliberate desecration of womanhood in order to establish the male as the ultimately privileged god-like subject within a spiritual hierarchy. This is a parodic version of classical theism which for all its faults does not praise *hubris*. But the most distorted patriarchal models of God have shared with pornography the fantasy of unlimited penetration: where the all-seeing, all-knowing, all-judging male subject has the whole sinful female body/earth spread out before him and awaiting judgment. Neo-pagan feminism, however, can utilize a very old method of magically tricking, escaping and disempowering objectification, whether through pornography or the diet industry: that of shape-shifting.

Feminist Shape-Shifting

Even in an age of 'equal opportunity', only very occasionally and under special circumstances has Western patriarchy permitted women significant political authority over men. The exclusion of women from the process of direct social transformation, means that they, and non-

---

83. *Beyond God the Father*, p. 2; *Pure Lust: Elemental Feminist Philosophy* (London: The Women's Press, 1984), pp. 232-35.

84. *Pure Lust*, p. 233.

elite men, enjoy little or no sense of their creative historicity. In fundamentalist households particularly, women do not even have the final say
over the more significant domestic decisions. So, in the patriarchal
context, a woman's apparent authority to shape (though not to own) her
own body through dieting can be some small compensation. Of course
this is a false compensation, as drastic reduction of the body size actually
drains magical energies from the living form. But it may be that the diet
culture contains another distorted religious element: that of promising
shape-shifting powers to women; in this case, the capacity to transfigure
the body to reveal the 'true' slim identity of the woman.

Shape-shifting is a transreligious phenomenon, assuming a different
meaning in each tradition and context, but at its most general it refers to
'the alteration in form or substance of any animate or object'.[85] Shape-
shifting can be used to escape a seducer or to seduce; it can liberate
from bondage, or reveal divinity through transfiguration. In patriarchal
mythologies, the Cinderella figure turns into a princess, liberating her
from the menial profanity of her place in the ashes of the kitchen hearth
and revealing her sacred goodness and beauty. A more contemporary
form of this story is that of the Hollywood waitress who is liberated
from her drudgery by being 'seen' by a customer who turns out to be a
producer and transforms her overnight into a glittering film star.[86] Diet
manuals also utilize the shape-shifting motif in the cliché that inside
every fat woman a thin woman is hammering to get out. (Perhaps
unwittingly, Daly turns this metaphor, familiar from the diet industry, on
its head by insisting that 'the fembot-shell' must be cracked open before
'the Original Witch springs free'.[87])

The diet culture reverses the divine shape-shifting or changing powers
inherent in the meaning of female sacrality. Shape-shifting is traditionally
the prerogative of pagan gods, goddesses, shamans, witches and the
menstruating women who in folklore could change into hares.[88] The
Goddess is, above all, a shape-shifter. Not only does she age in and with
women,

85. J. Carse, 'Shape Shifting', in Eliade (ed.), *The Encyclopaedia of Religion*,
XIII, p. 225.

86. These two examples are from Carse, 'Shape Shifting', p. 227.

87. *Pure Lust*, p. 391.

88. See Michele Jamal's account of a group of contemporary female shamans in
Shapeshifters: Shaman Women in Contemporary Society (New York: Arkana,
1987).

> She has a thousand names, a thousand aspects. She is the milk cow, the
> weaving spider, the honeybee with its piercing sting, She is. . . the snake
> that sheds its skin and is renewed; the cat that sees in the dark; the dog that
> sings to the moon—all are Her.[89]

Masculine divine shape-shifters like Dionysus, Tammuz and Christ also
transform their bodies in a 'female' way, that is, in accordance with the
annual death and resurrection of nature. The transformation of Christ's
body into bread and wine in the Eucharist also sacramentally feeds and
gives new life to his church. The cyclic suffering of these gods may be
modelled at least in part on the 'sacrifice' of women's blood shed in
menstruation and its transubstantiations for gestation and lactation.
Feminist shape-shifting can be a sacramental act, but it can also be an
experience of ontological shift. Feminist witches experience a shifting of
the boundaries of their personal and physical identity when they are
initiated into Wicca. As Margot Adler has described it, 'the clear line that
separates you from bird and tree and small lizards seems to melt.
Whatever else, your relationship to the world of living nature changes.
The Witch is the changer of definitions and relationships.'[90]

The meaning of shape-shifting shifts with each new context. We find it
at work in Daly's feminist-ontological scheme as a moment of psychic
transformation when a woman who is becoming a radical feminist
recognizes and celebrates her otherness to all things patriarchal: 'The
shape-shifting acts of Be-witching women create vortices of gynergy
which can help pull women away from the traps of labeldom into
Realization of their/our magnificent Otherness.'[91] In the spiritual feminist
worldview, women are *ontologically* equipped with the power, or
'Active Potency', as Daly would put it, to overcome patriarchy through
metaphor itself—the linguistic-locomotive power of shape-shifting in
which 'crones crack the man-made shells. Maenads chew them into
better shape. Brewsters cook them, Dragons melt them, Spinsters spin
their substance into verbs.'[92]

Women's liberation as a form of shape-shifting refers to the power of

89. Starhawk, *The Spiral Dance: A Rebirth of the Ancient Religion of the Great
Goddess* (New York: Harper & Row, 1979), p. 80.
    90. *Drawing Down the Moon*, p. 44. Shahrukh Husain has collected a selection
of stories about witches' shape-shifting powers in Part 4, 'Transformations', of her
edited collection, *The Virago Book of Witches* (London: Virago, 1994), pp. 93-120.
    91. *Pure Lust*, p. 398.
    92. *Pure Lust*, p. 399.

the female body to change in its own seasons, uninterrupted by patriarchal ideology. It is an ontological and artistic act of self-creation, and as
female being *is* also embodiment, then shape-shifting is at the same time
manifest in women's reclaiming their own body shape and sexuality.
That shape-shifting is not about turning into a princess but into a woman
of power has mythical precedence in European and Indian folklore. The
femme fatale witch, for example, enchants men with her bewitching
beauty, but she can also move in and out of youth, beauty and humanity
at will and often for retributive purposes.[93] The very words for women
that have been revived as metaphors of female numinosity—hag, crone,
spinster, Gorgon and so on—deliberately evoke unredeemed, gnarled
female 'ugliness'. Radical feminist metamorphoses do not invite a prince
to transform a crone with a kiss into a patriarchal beauty: a marriage-
able, biddable princess with pale golden hair. That would be an
intolerable loss of numinous 'crone' authority.

Jane Caputi also finds the meaning of female shape-shifting in magical
acts of resistance and mutation. 'Mutation' is a word associated with
nuclear catastrophe. This word, rather than the more positive
'transformation', rids the concept of female sacrality of any domesti-
cating tendency to moralize it as a feminine virtue. That mutation is
exemplified in the transfiguration of the face into that of the Gorgon—
an ancient divinity of the underworld: the symbol which will 'repel,
petrify, and immolate those who would capture, disrespect, and exploit
female Powers'.[94] The threat of an untamed, unowned woman is so
terrifying to patriarchy that the confrontation of her sheer presence is
defused most effectively by naming her hideous. Such naming does
indeed isolate, silence and literally efface a woman.

But where female flesh appears 'repulsive' to the patriarchal eye it
cannot be a temptation to male desire; a belief differently shared by
patristic theologians, the popular press, and radical feminist spirituality.
But for the latter, 'ugliness' (as a political metaphor; a strategy rather
than a literal description) liberates women from the hierarchical aesthetics
of patriarchal art which has never represented women as the subjects of
their own experience. 'Ugliness', that is self-defining, mutational female
presence, deflects the pornographic gaze and, more, petrifies or

93. See Husain (ed.), *The Virago Book of Witches*, pp. xiii-xiv.
94. *Gossips, Gorgons and Crones: The Fates of the Earth* (Santa Fe: Bear &
Co., 1993), p. 167. See also Kuryluk, *Veronica and her Cloth*, pp. 153-61 on the
power of the Gorgon image.

incapacitates male aggressors by its Gorgon stare. In 1980 the radical feminist philosopher Emily Culpepper found herself confronted by a male attacker. In her journal she recounts how she repelled or petrified the rapist by instinctive shape-shifting. Her face turned into a Gorgon: 'My face is bursting, contorting with terrible teeth, flaming breath, erupting into ridges and contortions of rage, hair hissing. It is over in a flash.'[95]

No one is suggesting that any woman deliberately and literally abuse or neglect her embodiment. Nor does the 'appearance' of the numinous extinguish female sexuality, as did that of some female ascetics in the early church who made themselves 'repulsive' to men. They did this by becoming *ersatz* men: by fasting they stopped menstruation and androgynized their bodies. They cropped their hair, masculinized their names and sometimes wore male clothing.[96] By contrast, the Gorgon is a symbol of a woman's existential freedom to claim, name and own her embodied powers as a woman in terms that are longer defined by patriarchy. As Gorgon, or having Gorgonish capacities, her body is no longer pitted against women who have come into (false) being in the (false) protection of the patriarchal gaze—where a woman *is* when she is seen and when she is pleasing to the male eye. As we shall see in the next chapter, spiritual feminists do not abuse the body to make it 'ugly'. On the contrary, by crafting their own beauty they liberate it from the abusive practices that are supposed to make it beautiful. In reclaiming the aesthetic power of the sacral body, spiritual feminists can redefine the meaning of bodily transformations as signs of divine activity through change.

Although spiritual feminist shape-shifting is at one with the post-modern will to reconstruct, recode and reinvent the body, this spiritual feminist body is still a body of determinate sex; a biological identity that has nothing to do with the technologized, reassembled identity of Donna Harraway's feminist Cyborg: half human, half machine.[97] The spiritual feminist may physically and imaginally transform her body to transgress patriarchal boundaries and to elude the patriarchal touch, but she is not adrift in the flux of technological change. The shape-shifting spiritual

95. Quoted in Caputi, *Gossips, Gorgons and Crones*, p. 170.
96. See Bovery, *Being Fat is Not a Sin*, p. 24.
97. See D. Haraway, 'A Manifesto for Cyborgs: Science, Technology, and Socialist Feminism in the 1980s', in Nicholson (ed.), *Feminism/Postmodernism*, pp. 190-233.

feminist is an epistemologically unified subject in pursuit of a just, organicist future. And those who refuse to suppress their female Powers, as Caputi calls them, enter a sacred space: they 'journey to her island of rock and stone and there face a laughing, welcoming, and gorgeous Gorgon. As we do, we turn not to stone, but to sentient flesh, sensual mind, and boiling blood.'[98] In other words, the Gorgon freezes or stops patriarchal oppression in its tracks, but thaws and stirs feminists into new life. If, as Eliade defined it, a hierophany is a manifestation of the sacred within the profane or ordinary sphere, turning into a Gorgon can be a symbolic feminist hierophany. The gendered selves of those who face the Gorgon 'die' in that 'they transmute—change into beings beyond patriarchal classification and containment'.[99] To face the Gorgon is to face unmasked femaleness:

> [those] traits that the godfathers fearfully and mendaciously have deemed shameful, ugly, or monstrous in ourselves: our sexualities, our unruly bodies, our agedness, our energies, and our Powers, not only of life but also of *death*. Gazing into the Gorgon's eye, we acknowledge the workings of sacred female Powers in the self, in the cosmos.[100]

In sum, spiritual feminists refuse to falsely sanctify their embodiment by making it available to God (that is, in effect, to patriarchy). In that refusal they are evolving a pagan sacral aesthetic: a self-generating, self-defining, fluid, transmutational beauty-as-power that patriarchy will not find attractive.

The Hierophanic Body

In all religions the state of the body—male and female—is, to some degree, an index of personal holiness. Even within misogynistic patriarchal schemata (exceptional) female bodies have, against all odds, been hierophanic. Medieval saintly fasting is an example of this phenomenon and one which is particularly relevant to the present discussion. Fasting may be more complex than sheer capitulation to misogynistic doctrine. In fact, Catherine of Siena's self-starvation was theologically ambivalent even at the time. She herself referred to her inedia as an infirmity. And sometimes, on the basis of her ability to survive without food, she was accused of witchcraft and of attempting the mortal sin of suicide. Inedia

98. *Gossips, Gorgons and Crones*, p. 156.
99. *Gossips, Gorgons and Crones*, p. 213.
100. *Gossips, Gorgons and Crones*, p. 198.

was not always a religious virtue even in the medieval period.[101] On the whole, though, the medieval period understood self-torture as an *imitatio Christi*, or so argues Caroline Walker Bynum.[102] Although the typical symbolization of flesh as female and therefore in subjection to male reason/spirit was a factor in female inedia, Bynum believes that it was not so much dualistic misogyny that drove women to fast as the possibility of achieving power and meaning.[103] Although fasting practices often began at puberty, medieval female saints were not attempting to become metaphorical males but to model their bodies on Christ's crucified body. Medieval Christian ontology associated a woman's body with food—especially milk as the 'fluid of life that coursed through her veins'. In this, the Eucharistic food of Christ's blood and wounds assumes a feminine character.[104] By his death Christ fed the world. In Christian art of the period Christ displays the salvific, nurturing wounds in his side, just as Mary displays her breast to feed the baby Jesus. There are, then, certain Christian theological schemata that can sacralize the female body to a very high degree. As Bynum remarks, it is 'no wonder women manipulated their bodies; in doing so, they became God—a God who feeds and saves'.[105]

Although it is highly specialized, Bynum's work is important because it shows that women *can* construct meanings which override misogynistic meanings. Of course, Bynum is too careful a historian to claim that a woman who refuses to eat anything but a Eucharistic wafer is any sort of model for contemporary women's spirituality. But these hierophanic bodies show that women in patriarchal societies can and do have *self*-understanding—they are not simply the objects onto which meaning is projected without opposition and subversion. Here medieval Christianity as an incarnational theology, in which Christ's suffering flesh redeems the world, appears to sacralize female embodiment as a representation of the humanity and therefore immanence of God.

Nonetheless, the patriarchal signification of female fasting seems to me to ultimately override the loopholes or susceptibilities to (proto)feminism

101. C.W. Bynum, *Holy Feast and Holy Fast: The Religious Significance of Food to Medieval Women* (Berkeley: University of California Press, 1987), pp. 196-97.
102. *Holy Feast and Holy Fast*, pp. 221-23.
103. *Holy Feast and Holy Fast*, pp. 212-14.
104. *Holy Feast and Holy Fast*, pp. 270-71.
105. *Holy Feast and Holy Fast*, p. 275.

that exist within its own theology. That Simone Weil apparently starved herself to death in 1943 seems to indicate that Catholicism can still idealize female asceticism as reversing the Fall: where Eve's hunger brought sin into the world, another woman's refusal of the sensual/sexual pleasure of food could save it.[106] Crossculturally, women have always and still do fast. Among others, Hindu women fast for their family's prosperity and well-being. And globally, wherever families live in great poverty, women are expected to sacrifice their own need for food so that the children and husband will not go hungry. (Male fasting is typically less self-renouncing—it is more likely to be a hunger strike in political protest.[107]) If women's bodies are, in the religious imagination, food, then they do not need food—they can live on themselves.

Radical feminism could hardly accept this violent, if heroic, sacrifice of female energies (indeed it is one of Daly's central contentions that patriarchy is precisely vampiric of female energies). Feminism may refuse any patriarchal expectation that women be prepared to die or weaken themselves to feed others in the womb or to nourish young life.[108] But spiritual feminists do derive a spirituality from their choice to feed life through the normal biological/sacral functions of their own embodiment. That is not a weakening or draining experience. If the body is properly tended it replenishes its own energy.

Apart from the womb, perhaps the two most sacrally charged parts of the female body have been the female head of hair, which has had particular sexual powers invested in it, and the skin, which is by its very nature a sacramental boundary between self and world. Some brief remarks on each must suffice to illustrate how spiritual feminists can playfully (mis)use and reverse the traditional meanings of body symbols to affirm the sort of new/old construction of embodiment this chapter has described.

Long hair has been an almost universal symbol of supernatural strength. Medusa, or the Gorgon, was sometimes bearded and had live snakes for hair. It was in her writhing red snake-hair that her menstrual/monstrous powers resided. Barbara Walker documents how Mother

106. See Herik, 'Simone Weil's Religious Imagery', p. 271.
107. See Bynum, *Holy Feast and Holy Fast*, p. 192.
108. Cf. Luther's well-known remark in *The Estate of Marriage*, 'let [women] bear themselves out. This is the purpose for which they exist.' Quoted in E. Clark and H. Richardson (eds.), *Women and Religion: A Feminist Sourcebook of Christian Thought* (San Francisco: Harper & Row, 1977).

goddesses and witches were believed to bring on thunderstorms, summon demons and generally control the spiritual world with their unbound hair. Tantric writers believed that the binding and loosing of women's hair wrought cosmic creation and destruction. It may be that these kinds of belief in the sacral power of female hair survived in the Christian, Jewish and Islamic injunctions for women to shave or cover their hair to protect God's ordered creation from female chaos.[109] (Though in a quirk of religious history, the orthodox Jewish woman's wig often surpasses her cropped natural hair beneath in style and luxuriance.) In the West, long female hair became profane in its association with pagan sexuality: 'out of control—unpinned, dishevelled or free from a concealing cap—it was invested with dangerous powers. In myth the beautiful Lorelei, who sang while she combed her long blonde hair, lured sailors to wreck their boats on treacherous rocks.'[110]

Under traditional Christian and contemporary Muslim patriarchy long hair concealed under a cap or veil satisfies the will to both suppress and exploit female sexuality. In Paul's first letter to the Corinthians (1 Corinthians 11.6-16) he says that long hair is a woman's pride or glory and it is a sign of her femaleness. But it is acceptable only in so far as it is covered with a veil or it is cut off. Women must be subject to husbands as husbands are subject to Christ. The covering of female hair is a sign of the subjection of the female will to men and God. That it must be covered may also testify to the ancient investment of female hair with sacral power. That female sacral power is profane within masculine monotheism is particularly apparent in Paul's insistence that women must not pray, or come into the divine presence, with uncovered hair. Covered and bound hair is a mark of owned and therefore safe female sacrality. Until the end of the First World War for a woman to cut her hair short was an act of self-profanation. She had rid herself of an important sign of her biblically ordained difference. (Deuteronomy 22.5 forbids cross-dressing as an abomination to the Lord, and in conservative religious cultures where males have short hair, for a woman to cut hers is tantamount to cross-dressing. It is a threat to the meticulously classified stable order.) But in cutting off her inconvenient long hair, an early twentieth-century Protestant woman had also rid herself of a symbol of subjection to men which denied her any sanctity except that

109. *The Woman's Encyclopedia of Myths and Secrets* (New York: Harper-SanFrancisco, 1983), pp. 367-71.

110. Brownmiller, *Femininity*, pp. 60-61.

defined by married maternity. Nowadays, apart from women in orthodox Jewish communities and in some Christian sects, few women in
contemporary Europe and America cover or bind their hair. But they
do, however, conceal its changing colour with hair dyes to maintain an
appearance of permanent youth.[111] This is surely another form of
covering natural female hair—here an index to crone power and a sign
of numinous vitality and the passage of time, both of which Western
patriarchy fears in women.

Historically, female hair seems to be charged in itself whereas the skin,
by its nature, seems to mediate that charge. It acts as a boundary
through and on which the sacralized body manifests and transmits its
energies. Female skin stretches with pregnancy and dries and sags with
age. It heals through contact and gentle touch. It is marked by physical
and spiritual trauma. Ewa Kuryluk has suggested that Christianity has
appropriated some of these qualities for its own saviour. The incarnate
Jesus has a skin which suffers in the manner of battered women:
stripped, bleeding, and often chronically forgiving, it still has a magical,
healing touch. Its holiness is much anointed, washed and cared for by
women. For as Kuryluk observes, 'skin destruction is predominantly a
male business', but skin preservation is usually a female labour.[112]
(Indeed, many of the Christian miracle stories may derive their meaning
from that of female sacrality. And not only the healing miracles: the
feeding of five thousand people with the multiplied loaves and fishes
may also be a case in point.)

This chapter has discussed the two industries that most desecrate
female flesh—pornography and the diet industry. Both of these damage
the skin. Pornography is sometimes known as 'the skin trade'—a
metaphor evoking the removal and selling of the skin of hunted animals.
And the crash diet shrinks the skin, leaving it prematurely loose. The
diet industry grows fat on women trying to get thin. It has to make
women and men at least anxious and at best disgusted by expanding
expanses of female skin. Thus Jo Ind: 'I watched myself squeeze my

---

111. See A. Gerike, 'On Gray Hair and Oppressed Brains', in E. Rosenthal (ed.),
Women, Ageing and Ageism (New York: Harrington Park Press, 1990), p. 40.
Gerike summarizes recent American research on hair colouring. In 1990, 45 per cent
of American women in their 40s and 50s coloured their hair, whereas only 8 per cent
of men coloured theirs. As concern with appearance is still considered effeminate in
older British men I would guess that less than 8 per cent of men would dye theirs.

112. *Veronica and her Cloth*, pp. 218-19.

newly rounded cheeks and felt my fingernails press into the flesh that covered them. Looking at myself was not enough. The fact that I was disgusting had to be confirmed by touch as well.'[113]

Profane things cannot touch sacred things without having taken the proper precautions against their power. If touched correctly sacred things can heal, but if they are touched irreverently they can destroy. In 2 Sam. 6.6-7 God smote the well-meaning Uzzah who dared to touch the ark to steady it when the oxen stumbled. Conversely, when the Hemorrhissa touches Jesus, power goes out of him but he is not angered by her violation of his sacred power because she approaches him in trust and faith (Mt. 9.20-22; Mk 5.25-34; Lk. 8.43-48). Or again, the most profane (outcast) caste of India, who are treated as sub-religious beings, are also called 'untouchables' because it is believed that contact with their skin would contaminate the sacred. Sacred things are usually protected in some way: often by shrouds and the erection of material and social boundaries. We have seen how Culpepper exercised her sacrality when she petrified an attacker by displaying her rage at his attempt to violate her flesh by touch. Yet she would also affirm that women are, like the Goddess, healers as well as destroyers. Touch that recognizes sanctity (like that of the Hemorrhissa) is rewarded with new life.

Feminist spirituality is often also a lesbian spirituality. For Daly, a lesbian, the skin has repressed capacities of spiritual ignition. The soul is not something that is buried or abstracted within the flesh: 'The Surface Soul is in Touch with the Air, Earth, Fire, and Waters. She is in Contact, Communion. Her tactics are tactile; her triumphs and trials tangible... She cannot be tracked down, trod upon, trained.'[114] So that, 'deprived of our powers of Touching, women have in fact been skinned alive'.[115] For Daly, the lesbian reclaims both her skin and soul by breaking the social taboo against women touching the bodies of other women. In doing so she makes contact—'Contagion spreads; the Touchers move'— passing on her own sacral-political power to other women by her positive spark or charge. It is in offering a psychic and political empowerment to women that in no sense complements masculine power that lesbianism is an abomination to conservative religion. Whereas, in different ways, patriarchy fears to touch both the profane and the sacred, lesbian touching becomes, for Daly, the sacral mechanism by

113. *Fat is a Spiritual Issue*, p. 1.
114. *Pure Lust*, p. 245.
115. *Pure Lust*, p. 246.

which the contagious *mana* of the 'Archimagical influence' of 'Wild and Free women' is liberated.[116]

Buried Treasure

Page DuBois has described how in antiquity the Greeks tortured their slaves to extract evidence for trials—a phenomenon reflected in the European philosophical tradition, in which the pursuit of truth 'leads almost inevitably to conceiving of the body of the other as the site from which truth can be produced, and to using violence if necessary to extract that truth'.[117] The subjugated flesh holds 'a hidden truth, one that eludes the subject, must be discovered, uncovered, unveiled, and can always be located in the dark, in the irrational, in the unknown, in the other'.[118]

I find this a suggestive conclusion to the present chapter. To use the word 'torture' as a *metaphor* of the pornographic and dietary abuses of the female body is not to suggest that these are the same as the immediate agony of undergoing torture. (Though in the case of pornography it can be.) In its demonization of the unregulated female body, patriarchy has and continues to desecrate the magical secret(ion)s of women through forms of torture. Thus DuBois: 'The psychotic pursues women's truth through torture'.[119] The witchcraze was paradigmatic of this. It is as if patriarchy senses that the reproductive processes of the female form are a kind of *gnosis*—the secret of creativity. But this cosmic explanation is obscured by flesh and its truth must be extracted by torture—whether through diets, pornographic violence, excised clitorises, shroud-like veils or any number of gynocidal practices.[120] Patriarchy fails to recognize that the truth and the body are in fact inseparable; that the goose can only lay her golden egg while she is alive.

116. *Pure Lust*, pp. 247-48. Daly's account of lesbianism may be more of an ideal of 'creative political ontophany' than, as yet, a widespread reality in the lesbian community as a whole. Using Baba Copper's research findings, Ann Gerike notes in 'On Gray Hair and Oppressed Brains', p. 40, that although young lesbian women are less likely to be obsessed with their appearance than heterosexual women, ageing lesbians still suffer prejudice within their own communities.

117. *Torture and Truth*, p. 6.

118. *Torture and Truth*, p. 147.

119. *Torture and Truth*, p. 149.

120. See Daly, *Gyn/Ecology*, pp. 93-96.

It is in contemporary desecrations of the earth and women's bodies that the ancient and the modern intentions of torture come together. Where traditionally the body was tortured to yield truth, an answer to a question, modern torture generally uses pain as an instrument of fear. The victim of torture is dumped back into the world physically and mentally damaged or broken. Victims of torture are a warning to others not to challenge the dominant ideology.[121] The totalitarian quality of the diet culture is a form of domination by (indirect) violence. Its victims have yielded up the truth of their bodily energies. But like victims of torture they are left thin, exhausted and disoriented—no longer knowing the truth of their thinness from the lie of their fatness. The extraction of abundance and juice from the female body is a sign that its power and its truth have been taken from it; the will has consumed and dispersed the body, and its power blows away like weightless powder. The body has answered the patriarchal question.

Women's bodies are caught both ways. The dieter's pain (slicing and mutilation by plastic surgeons, stomach stapling, jaw wiring, periodic starvation and gorging and vomiting) should be understood by feminism as both a patriarchal warning and an example to the whole community of women. But so too, those who do not submit to the ideology of thinness and to the suffering that it requires, who keep the secret of their sacrality within their flesh, are warned of the punishment of being cast out—becoming untouchable. When a woman is disowned by patriarchy altogether, she is, like all outlaws and outcasts, profane and therefore left without protection. This latter is a fearsome prospect but it might also be the beginning of a feminist existential liberation.

Finally, I would like to give a feminist reading of one more image from the history of religions: that of the traditional Indonesian practice of ritual male flute playing. Their flute (a symbol or word for the vagina in several languages) has a female name and is perceived by the Indonesian men themselves as being full of the power of life. The flute has the power to bring forth spirits, and even to get a note out of it is regarded as miraculous. The men play it in secret, circling around the sacred post in the middle of the home. Women are forbidden to see this sacred flute and any angry man can threaten to punish any woman's misdeed with death by his choosing to pronounce the sacred name of the flute. Van der Leeuw's casually bracketed gloss on this custom, 'it is typically

---

121. See DuBois, *Torture and Truth*, p. 148.

masculine to keep a woman's own secret from her',[122] summarizes the meaning of this parable of the desacralization of the female body.

But spiritual feminists are now themselves pronouncing the forbidden name of the flute and are not dying. On the contrary, they are blowing life into—inspiring—their own bodies. This is no Derridean, post-structuralist semiosis or metaphorization of the female body, or of difference as a whole, but is directly related to the historical experience of actual women. Here the body is 'concrete', but not fixed in essentiality: its sexuality both constitutes the truth of the body and the possibilities of its reconstruction. The cosmogonic meanings of the female body are being newly and transgressively written and danced as the abundance of the immanent sacred:

> matter is energy alive and kicking knows itself intelligence incarnate we are made of rocks mountains streams soil breath and sweat sacred and heady earth spins and spirals vibrant mass thru teeming space...this is what I call sacred now.[123]

---

122. *Sacred and Profane Beauty: The Holy in Art* (London: Weidenfeld & Nicolson, 1963), p. 214.

123. MacIntyre, 'writing at risk', p. 21.

Chapter 3

WOMEN IN LABOUR

Now my mother, she doesn't go for cleanliness, orderliness, static have-come-from-nowhere objects for use. She shows you the production, her production. She is always in the middle of it and you will never see the end... You'll have to follow her through her path in the chaotic production, you'll have to know her comings and goings, her fluidity through the production.

Maria Lugones[1]

A Fearful Symmetry?

One of the most frequent criticisms of spiritual feminism is that it dualizes the cosmos into an unequal sexual struggle in which women make and men unmake women's making in acts of war. This duality is either reflected in or has constructed (it is difficult to tell) Goddess religion's sacred history as narrated, for example, by Barbara Walker:

if women's religion had continued, today's world might be less troubled by violence and alienation. Gods, including Yahweh, tended to order their followers to make war; whereas the great mother Goddesses advocated peaceful evolution of civilised skills.[2]

At its most essentialist, the contention that women make and men unmake moralizes and cosmologizes the gendered divisions of labour and production. This has been criticized (with some justice) as a kind of feminist gnosticism in which women embody peace and goodness and men embody war and evil. Janet McCrickard, once a born-again Christian, turned Goddess worshipper, turned secular humanist, accuses the Goddess movement of being fundamentalist in its 're-writing of history as a dualistic battle between good (us) and evil (them)'. She goes

1. 'Purity, Impurity and Separation', *Signs* 19 (1994), pp. 460-61.
2. *The Woman's Encyclopedia of Myths and Secrets*, p. x.

on to claim that women allocate for themselves all the 'feminine' qualities of the lunar principle in opposition to those of the fierce masculine
solar principle. This would sustain a new dualism in which women and
men are divided up as signifiers of either life or death; co-operation or
aggression; left-wing or right-wing politics; creative magic or destructive
science.[3]

Certainly bloodshed can appear to be neatly split along lines of
gender.[4] There is a widely held belief among spiritual feminists that war
is a means for men to spill blood and so achieve the sense of empowerment that women already experience in menstruating, or that men kill
sacrificial animals and enemies for their blood because they have no
magical blood of their own. And feminist anthropology can seem to
support this duality. Peggy Reeves Sanday observes that in pre-literate
societies 'women give birth and grow children; men kill and make
weapons. Men display their kills (be it an animal, a human head, or a
scalp) with the same pride that women hold up the newly born.'[5] In
cultures where myths prescribe male dominance, social equilibrium is
preserved by bloody strife and the perceived need to harness the chaotic
power of female reproduction. Men will, according to Sanday, 'go to
extraordinary lengths to acquire some of the [female] power for themselves so that they will not be impotent when it is time to fight. Men
attempt to neutralize the power they think is inherent in women by
stealing it, nullifying it, or banishing it to invisibility.'[6]

The gendered opposition of blood-power subsequently informs spiritual
feminism's view of modernity as a paradigmatically masculine period.
Modernity is interpreted as having precipitated a gendered dualism
within technology: that of life-giving (female) crafts and death-dealing
(male) science whose effluents of toxins and war pollute and disorder
female biological craft. When Rosalie Bertell wrote the poem *A
Micronesian Woman* she named the atom bomb as the 'father' of a
baby who had been born with severe abnormalities. The bomb *is* a man

3. 'Born-Again Moon: Fundamentalism in Christianity and the Feminist
Spirituality Movement', *Feminist Review* 37 (1991), pp. 62-63.
4. See, for example, Amberston, *Blessings of the Blood*, p. 61; L. Francia,
Dragontime: The Magic and Mystery of Menstruation (Woodstock, NY: Ash Tree,
1991), p. 26.
5. *Female Power and Male Dominance: On the Origins of Sexual Inequality*
(Cambridge: Cambridge University Press, 1981), p. 5.
6. *Female Power and Male Dominance*, p. 35.

and he 'raped our land / He killed our trees / He saps my life'. Here the masculinity of war can destroy female making even before it is done.

My baby, the fruit of my womb—
   for nine months I longed for it

I sang to it
I laid out clothes
I dreamed sweet dreams

My baby, the fruit of my womb—
   it had no face for me to kiss.[7]

The businessman Alan Sugar once remarked, 'if there was a market in mass-produced portable nuclear weapons we'd market them too'.[8] If his words are juxaposed with Bertell's lament, a gendered ethical and spiritual dualism becomes understandable even if it is ultimately an inadequate explanation of evil. Modern technology has made patriarchy ever more dangerous in the scale and impact of its means. But modernity did not create patriarchy. There is no doubt that men have, historically, been the prime movers in domestic, inter-tribal and international violence. But if spiritual feminism really thought that masculine destructiveness was congenital that would fatally undermine the point of its own practices and its hopefulness for the future. For war can destroy more quickly and efficiently than birth can replenish, especially if women's reproductive systems are damaged in the process. In addition, the predictive stabilities of any such dualism would fix and sentimentalize femaleness as something very close to patriarchal 'femininity', permitting an ideology that wastes female labour and then expects women to replenish the population when the war is over. So where spiritual feminism is essentialist and dualistic (as it can be). sexual-political solutions may indeed be more straightforwardly won by egalitarian democratic reform than by a cosmic opposition of the sexes.

However, it seems to me that thealogy does not allow for self-righteousness or any other sort of fastidiousness. Goddess feminism may construct primal divisions of labour, but these cannot exempt femaleness from the power of (ecological) death because nature precisely consists of destruction and creation held in balance. Natural predation is usually proportionate to the predator's needs, but spiritual feminism is not

---

   7.   In L. Caldecott and S. Leland (eds.), *Reclaim the Earth: Women Speak Out for Life on Earth* (London: The Women's Press, 1983), p. 111.

   8.   Quoted in Harvey, *The Condition of Postmodernity*, p. 352.

sentimental about nature as a killing field of sorts. Moreover, traditionally female and traditionally male crafts are interconnected: women have processed dead animals for use in human culture by tanning and sewing skins and cooking meat, and masculine hunting, scavenging and butchering can also belong within the ecological process in transforming dead flesh into new life forms.

So the spiritual feminist understanding of ecology forbids reducing every individual man to a programmed element of the patriarchal super-organism. Death is a part of nature. Moreover, the kind of anti-ecological 'megadeath' or total destruction of life on earth that spiritual feminism associates with men is an industrial evil—a historical phenomenon that is not necessarily biologically inherent in men as a sex. Patriarchy is not, I think, primarily biological; it is a political institution controlled by men which skews male personhood and exploits the higher or lower levels of aggression that are, arguably, a product of physiological and hormonal gender differences. If this is so, it is not the case that, say, lunar and solar principles are a gendered opposition inherent in the created structure of the universe. In its contemporary forms that opposition is a historical product of modernity. As Monica Sjöö puts it, ' We are now threatened by nuclear death at the hands of a contemporary solar priesthood, the nuclear physicists, who want to finally defeat the Earth and turn Her into a nuclear furnace like the sun itself.'[9] It is patriarchy—a political system before it is a sex—that has done this. The accusation that the Goddess revival has simply ascribed the power of making things and giving life to women, and that of unmaking them and taking life to men, is a misrepresentation. Although like most exaggerations it contains elements of truth, the Goddess movement does not reject ecological 'female' destruction (which is not to be confused with evil). Indeed female destructions are instituted within the thealogical trinity as the Crone.

Spiritual feminism, no less than reformist and socialist feminism, is a *political* struggle against patriarchy—not a purely sexual one. This system is named quite categorically as evil. But not because it is male, but because it is inherently parasitical on nature beyond its needs—hence its power over plants, animals and subject humans is disproportionate to its numbers. Of course patriarchy is intellectually, economically and militarily run by men. But as a historical phenomenon it is in

9.   *New Age and Armageddon: The Goddess or the Gurus? Towards a Feminist Vision of the Future* (London: The Women's Press, 1992), p. 156.

process. And now in the name of fundamentalism some right-wing women have adopted typically patriarchal ideologies into their religious ways of life. And in the name of reformist feminism, some right-wing women have adopted typically patriarchal attitudes into their working practices. Perhaps, then, instead of saying that spiritual feminism constructs simplistic sexual-moral dualisms, it is fairer to say that spiritual feminists interpose their bodies between sacred nature and the political system—patriarchy—which is responsiblefor its profanation. Symbolically, this establishes the female body and its productions as mesocosmic—belonging to a mediating 'cosmos' of meaning in which the microcosmic individual is brought into relationship with the macrocosmic whole. That is, spiritual feminists make themselves into what Joseph Campbell called (in a different context) 'a kind of poem, hymn, or icon of mud and reeds, and of flesh and blood, and of dreams'. In this sense spiritual feminists, like Campbell, believe that 'life on earth is to mirror, as nearly perfectly as is possible in human bodies, the almost hidden—yet now discovered—order of the pageant of the spheres'.[10]

The Spiritual Politics of Craft

In this chapter I shall elaborate what I understand to be a spiritual feminist ecological politics of production. In modelling production on divine and biological maternity, spiritual feminism transforms all forms of production into a cyclic, and therefore sustainable, self-renewing reproduction. This erotic re-vision and re-mythologization of labour benefits women and nature in at least two ways. First, the immanent divine intelligence of materiality is restored. In its reenchantment of matter, religious feminism is at one with postmodern science. The material world is not just as Descartes would have had it, an aggregate of lumps and particles of various sizes and velocities; it is conscious energy. The postmodern scientific and spiritual fusion of consciousness, spirit and matter radically changes the meaning of any new associations of women and materiality. If that association ever was demeaning to the female intellect, it cannot be any longer. And secondly, whatever labours in and with the natural process refuses hierarchical ownership of the means and modes of production.[11] The sacred is inherently unownable and establishes a

10. *Primitive Mythology*, p. 150.
11. Cf. Ruether, *Womanguides*, p. 44.

system of value that has nothing to do with monetary value. As the old woman Maya says in Starhawk's novel, *The Fifth Sacred Thing*, 'When something is sacred, it can't be bought or sold and nothing that might harm it is worth doing. What is sacred becomes the measure by which everything is judged.'[12]

In ecofeminist and other green philosophies, nature has become an ethical model for human relationships and modes of production. The traditional evolutionary model of nature—and implicitly society—as a history of warfare over resources has been replaced by a more symbiotic, cooperative model of nature as a web. In the modern context, the web is a 'female' image in that women's relational faculties have not, on the whole, suffered the alienations necessitated by having to compete in the public sphere. But when spiritual feminists reclaim the spiritual signifi-cance of domestic crafts as 'female' (spinning and mending the web rather than tearing it) that does not mean that they intend, in any right-wing sense, to return active, politicized women to the marital home. It is more that when the earth/cosmos is reimaged and resacralized as 'our home' then the sphere of female sacrality is infinitely expanded. The 'culture of the hearth'—to use Lin Simonon's phrase—entails a 'new ecology of sexual energies' which promises '"re-production" rather than production, a science of the hearth; creating a well-balanced, well-functioning organism—be it the family, the tribe or the earth of which we are a part'.[13]

In some languages the term for 'mother' is 'producer-procreatrix'. This would suggest to spiritual feminism that women were once not only biological mothers, but 'the prime producers of the necessities of life: the *social mothers*'.[14] Feminism often likes to make an etymological con-nection between matter and mother (*mater* in Latin). Some etymologists have argued that this connection is erroneous and that the word 'matter' originated in a word approximate to 'heart of wood'. But as Eliade remarks, the etymological origins of the word 'matter' are not significant, since 'matter does the work of a mother, for it unceasingly gives birth'.[15] I am not sure that the work of any maternal person is to

12. *The Fifth Sacred Thing*, p. 18.

13. 'Personal, Political and Planetary Play', in Caldicott and Leland (eds.), *Reclaim the Earth*, p. 199.

14. E. Reed, *Woman's Evolution: From Matriarchal Clan to Patriarchal Family* (New York: Pathfinder, 1975), p. 129.

15. *Patterns in Comparative Religion*, p. 253.

'unceasingly' give birth, but certainly spiritual feminism is a productive activism in which female divine energies are expressed in biological and cultural generativity. A nine-month pregnancy requires about 800,000 calories and further calories to produce breast-milk; female sacral energies are not just a religious abstraction or metaphor—they actually burn food. Labour, the bringing to birth of any new thing, is magical and that brings consciousness and materiality together as one reproductive process.

Maternity is also magical/sacred in the pre-modern sense, in which the sacred is not so much a quasi-moral quality of physical purity as a quality 'related to magic simply because both [magic and the sacred] are experienced as energy arts: techniques of gathering and directing energy toward a numinous or transphysical goal'.[16] By contrast, theistic faith is predicated on a transcendent reality yet to be—or only partially revealed. 'Faith' is not, therefore, spiritually compelling in the neo-pagan or thealogical context. In Goddess feminism the transformatory dynamics of renewing/remaking life are an intensely *realized* form of religion. Labour is not simply work; in the fullest sense of the term it is the cosmogonic work of regenerating the world.

The casting of femaleness as an active *process* is at the heart of spiritual feminist politics. This politics rejects the dualistic patriarchal philosophy of labour which is premised on its division of body and soul. Patriarchal ontology dictates that an ensouled elite think; robotic slaves do; and matter has things done to it. Modern patriarchy separates imagination from labour. Inventors are privileged in not having to make more than one of the things they have invented. In protest against the modern industrialized relations of nature and production, spiritual feminists are reclaiming the practice and the metaphor of craft as at once a cosmogonic and an egalitarian culture-creating process: one which reflects a thealogy of the world itself as a conscious, relational, 'female' artifact.

Thealogy's magical ontology of matter has informed feminist witchcraft, which is dependent on a 'primitive' view of women as, by definition, witches by virtue of their powers of biological and social production. Thus Robert Briffault:

> The power of witchcraft is universally regarded as appertaining specifically to women. The witch is a woman, the wizard is but a male imitation of the original wielder of magical power...every woman,

16. M. Sjöö and B. Mor, *The Great Cosmic Mother: Rediscovering the Religion of the Earth* (New York: HarperSanFrancisco, 1991), p. 272.

wherever magic powers are believed in, is credited with the possession of those powers because she is a woman.[17]

Of course the *patriarchal* view of female sacral craft and witchcraft as synonymous and demonic has had terrifying results. But thealogy refuses the defamation of (witch)craft as demonic. The Goddess 'pours out her love' as the Creatrix and as the witch in women. And making witchcraft a biophilic, regenerative labour entails that women and the Goddess are ontologically continuous in ways that men and God are not. Patriarchy has both projected and amplified its political power in its image of God, but the dynamics of this model have also allowed God to centralize creative power in his own being. It is not only feminists who have observed the self-aggrandizing posture of the dominant biblical model of God. God is, according to John Armstrong, the proper name of one who has centralized all holy power into his own will, 'controlling the forms and forces of nature but present in none':[18]

> The heightened psychic strength which [holiness] denotes is the prerogative of heroic and pre-eminent supermen—the mighty warrior, the great chieftain, the prophet and the priest—and that typically in brief visitations of quite exceptional forcefulness, radically discontinuous with their normal performance, and associated with ritual isolation from everyday life.[19]

Armstrong's account of the transcendental monarchical concept of holiness is, in its effect on the status of female reproductivity, precisely what thealogy resists. Traditional theology's dual subordination of matter and centralization of power in God has alienated human productivity from divine purposes, whereas thealogy unites them. Women and the Goddess multiply, heal and mend things not through the kind of temporary miraculous suspension of the 'laws' of nature that are described in the Gospels, but through normal immanent processes. The late twentieth-century Goddess is not a centralized, exclusive locus of power but represents the wholeness or health of what lives and thrives. Just as the Goddess is in nature but is more than the sum of nature's parts, female craft is an organic expression of, but not exhaustive of, the meaning of women's being. Special historical revelations and interventions are not a

17. *The Mothers: A Study of the Origin of Sentiments and Institutions*, II (London: George Allen & Unwin, 1952), p. 556.
18. *The Idea of the Holy and the Humane Response*, p. 17.
19. *The Idea of the Holy and the Humane Response*, p. 6.

necessary or even meaningful element of thealogy, because the Goddess does not centralize power and will as God does in his messiahs. (Admittedly God's messiahs—especially Jesus as the Suffering Servant and divine son—have had to suffer sacrificially for their status. In this sense theology has, perhaps, a greater dramatic profundity and pathos than thealogy. However, in thealogy, power is generated biophilically, not in a paradoxical state of temporary defeat nor at the expense of putting another community—the Jews—in the eternal wrong.)

Thealogy incorporates and transforms elements of socialist feminism, extending its concern for human justice to concern for planetary justice and well-being. Thealogy traces one of the causes of patriarchy's systemic injustice to the Judaeo-Christian legitimation of the exploitative use of women's sacred power of multiplication. Here female sacrality provides the bodies that will believe in and work for the centralized hegemonic power of patriarchy's theological and economic systems. It is spiritual feminism's emancipatory critique of patriarchal production (both theological and material) that funds its discussion of the relation of thealogy and craft.

Religious radical feminists challenge the patriarchal ownership of objects made by subject labour—including the biological making of children. Motherhood is an alienated power of biological and social reproduction which has been controlled or bought cheap as marital labour. (The socialization of children into patriarchy is another sort of quasi-maternal reproduction.) In conservative religious marriages the personhood of mothers has been secondary to the biblical requirement that they redeem their female sexuality by obedience to the divine command that they multiply—not to make more women, but, ideally, sons—and then in due pain.

The belief that women's place in patriarchy has been one of, more or less, reproductive slavery has always been a cornerstone of radical feminism. The (non-)relation of slave and master is not of course confined to women's relations with patriarchal men. But radical feminism has argued that the bought and owned productivity of male workers/slaves is modelled on the reproductive slavery of women's bodies. In modernity the factory has been a (parodic) model of the reproductivity of women's bodies. In the factory mass production is systemically loveless: its products are rapidly dispersed and its accelerated reproduction produces effluents which, unlike menstrual and lochial blood, are truly polluting. Profitable monetary exchange for goods which the vendor has had no hand in making allows vast accumulations of capital and, for the vendor, an inflated sense of his own importance. It also creates a 'sacred' caste of people, the rich, who only visit and rarely *touch* the profane or soiling apparatuses that reproduce their goods and wealth.

Of course radical feminism has been theoretically diverse. Spiritual feminism departs quite drastically from socialist radical feminism in defining the female energies of reproduction as divine or cosmic in nature and origin. Spiritual feminism differs markedly from, say, Shulamith Firestone's revision of Marxist theories of the relations of production. For Firestone, the primary class distinction is a sexual class distinction between men and women, where women's reproductive roles (rather than essence) constitute the first division of labour and the cause of their subordination.[20] Spiritual feminism *does* follow Firestone in believing that if women take control of their reproductive power they will eliminate gender discrimination and break down the oppressive structures of the patriarchal family. But Firestone's vision of a biological revolution in which women move towards androgyny through new technologies of artificial reproduction is not that envisaged by spiritual feminism. In the interests of equality, Firestone radically devalues motherhood, the womb and all biological labour. Spiritual feminists do not want to be detached in any sense from the meaning of the womb, since it is metaphorically and actually the central locus of female sacral power. (Reproductivity may not be comfortable and giving birth may, in fact, feel, as Firestone graphically described it, like 'shitting a pumpkin',[21] but sensation and meaning are not to be confused.)

Today, as reproductive technologies become ever more powerful, complex and (still) male-dominated, radical feminists as a whole are more likely to adopt the sort of arguments proposed by Mary O'Brien,[22] Robyn Rowland[23] and Adrienne Rich,[24] namely that patriarchy compensates men for their alienation from and dependence on the female power of reproduction. Biological motherhood can be a joyous

20. *The Dialectic of Sex* (New York: Bantam, 1970), pp. 1-12.

21. *The Dialectic of Sex*, pp. 198-99.

22. *The Politics of Reproduction* (Boston: Routledge & Kegan Paul, 1981).

23. 'Reproductive Technologies: The Final Solution to the Woman Question', in R. Arditti *et al.* (eds.), *Test-Tube Women: What Future for Motherhood?* (London: Pandora, 1984).

24. *Of Woman Born*, pp. 11-12.

experience, giving profound spiritual satisfaction and an experience of
unity with all other mothers that ultimately transcends ethnicity and
class. And as patriarchy is still dependent on female reproduction, it may
be the only strong card that women hold as a sexual class. Reproductive
technology would further reduce femaleness to breeding. It would give
patriarchy final control over nature, culture and women of the sort that
can already be seen in contemporary India and China where ultra-sound
technology enables doctors to abort unwanted female foetuses.

Patriarchy's relation with nature is that of an owner of a cosmic
means of production. Nature can represent the growth of capital; patriarchy takes nature's goods or buys them cheap. Patriarchy finds
existential self-realization or subjectivity through possession (I am
because I own). Radical feminism has argued that patriarchy posseses
the world in and through female reproductivity. In *Being and
Nothingness* Jean-Paul Sartre describes an existential orientation which
precisely typifies patriarchal attitudes to women as objects of desire and
exchange to be classified with a slice of bread or a car.[25] Sartre's
analysis of ownership encapsulates what spiritual feminism refuses: 'The
possessor is the raison d'être of the possessed object. I possess this pen;
that means this pen exists *for me*; it has been made *for me*.'[26] The spiritual feminist critique of patriarchy as a system defined by possession is
more than a critique of the capitalist sanctification of property; it is an
existential critique of a system in which you *are* what you have or what
you do not have. In spiritual feminist discourse women's subjecthood is
not dependent on possession. Women's biology and cultural practice
signify the making of things which are ultimately unownable because
they are biodegradable. Female crafts are organic in all senses. They do
not produce the toxic pollution that patriarchy has attributed to biological reproduction but is now actually the result of its own modern
productions.

Patriarchy takes everything that God or the Goddess has made for its
own use. It is the paradigm case of its own type of profanization: it
makes everything available for its own use. But to be more interested in
having than generating breaks the rhythm of divine continuous creation.
The feminist spirituality of being-as-making attempts to swim with the
flow of continuous divine creation where, in the Goddess, persons and

25. *Being and Nothingness: An Essay on Phenomenological Ontology* (London:
Methuen, 1969), p. 576.
26. *Being and Nothingness*, p. 589.

things coming into being as one continuous process.

This is truly a sexual politics because it posits material reproductivity itself—rather than *logos*—as the source of cultural generativity. And it is a sexual politics because it protests the pornographic nature of capitalism and science which treat the earth's resources and women's bodies as objects to be contained, dismantled, examined and redistributed for use. (The disembodied, impersonal, mechanistic quality of scientific enquiry may explain why even today a majority of schoolgirls find science lessons boring and are more likely to go on to study subjects in the humanities.[27]) The pornographic quality of reification resides in patriarchal epistemology where to know is to own or to possess. 'Possession' is a term that encompasses sexual invasion, economic power and an omnipotent subject's literally exhaustive knowledge of its object. In *The Male Birth of Time*, Francis Bacon, a founding father of patriarchal science, fantasizes about a scientist offering the body of Nature to his son: 'In truth, I have come to bring you nature and all her children, that you may have her serve you and be your slave.'[28]

The alienations of masculine technologies of reproduction are perhaps a logical outcome of a theology in which the patriarchal sky god opens history with commanding words but not with his body. The chthonic mother goddesses, by contrast, create from the depths and hollows of their bodies which, like the earth, already contain growing things.[29] Gerardus van der Leeuw gives a classic (non-feminist) expression of this gendered division of creative labour:

> Religions that are intensely orientated towards Will turn away from the mother to the father... The father acts with power; the mother is merely potent. The father leads his people to their goal: the mother's child-bearing renews the cycle of life. The mother creates life: the father history.[30]

27. See M. Watts and D. Bentley, 'Humanizing and Feminizing School Science: Reviving Anthropomorphic and Animistic Thinking in Constructivist Science Education', *International Journal of Science Education* 16 (1994), esp. pp. 84-86. See also E. Fox-Keller, 'Feminism as an Analytical Tool for the Study of Science', *Academe* 69 (1983), pp. 15-21; *idem*, *Reflections on Gender and Science* (New Haven: Yale University Press, 1986).

28. Quoted in Halkes, *New Creation*, p. 29.

29. See E. Neumann, *The Great Mother: An Analysis of the Archetype* (Princeton: Princeton University Press, 1955), pp. 3-25.

30. *Religion in Essence and Manifestation* (London: George Allen & Unwin, 1938), p. 100.

The gendering of historical creative agency as male has not served women well. Nor is it entirely the case: the Egyptian Ma'at and other goddesses like her unified cosmic and social ordering under their rule. But spiritual feminism does not counter this gendered division of creative labour by disproving it. Instead it refuses to relegate fertility to a state of ontological and social stagnation where natural abundance swamps personality and obstructs history (much as the Sleeping Beauty slept behind an impenetrable thicket of briars and thistles).

Patriarchy has derogated fertility as sub-historical and has exalted economic and military manoeuvre as paradigmatically historical. But it is patriarchy's grandiose sense of its own historical destiny that has ravaged 'female' modes of production. These modes of production were profoundly changed or brought to an end by patriarchy's global colonization and industrialization of women's bodies, land, animals and all 'other' peoples. Spiritual ecofeminists have argued that the desacralization of women's crafts has alienated production from the organic cycles of the female body/earth. Patriarchal patterns of mechanized mass production and consumption are parasitic on nature in that they extract the power of materiality and turn it into wealth. Whatever material cannot be 'digested' or turned into money is excreted as pollution into the planetary 'female' containers: the sea or landfill sites. The spiritual principle of showing respect and gratitude for the natural sources of human prosperity is quite alien to capitalism, as is any will to replenish what it has taken or to redistribute equitably the profits it has yielded. Profit relies on the production of goods at a rate and in a quantity that rapidly depletes the earth's resources. It also institutionalizes social injustice for the women and men who process the goods. Although post-industrial technology is now making a great deal of human labour redundant, capitalism is not yet a post-industrial economy and still requires a vast subject labouring class; and the worst paid of that class are usually women.[31]

The colonization of the female body/earth has ended or at least disrupted indigenous patterns of 'female', that is, socially and ecologically cooperative, spiritually expressive modes of production.[32] For example,

---

31. This inequity has had to be demonstrated yet again by Kate Figes in *Because of Her Sex: The Myth of Equality for Women in Britain* (London: Macmillan, 1994).

32. See, for example, Alice Walker's discussion of the demise under slavery of traditional black female crafts such as quiltmaking, herbal medicine and midwifery in *In Search of Our Mothers' Gardens* (London: The Women's Press, 1984).

the Maori feminist Ngahuia Te Awekotuku is well aware that traditional Maori society is and was male-dominated and, like the colonialists, regards (female) land and women as prizes for successful warfare.[33] But what Awekotuku wants to preserve and revive is the way in which women take care of the earth's resources because their bodies are analogous, and more than analogous, to the earth. She describes the traditional Maori woman cutting and weaving flax by setting her description in the metaphor of midwifery:

> Trimming cautiously, she ensures that the *rito*—the youngest, finest shoot that emerges coyly between the two larger parent leaves—remains untouched and undamaged. The parent leaves are also respected, for they will keep the youngest warm, and ensure the life of the plant.[34]

From this flax women make baskets, clothes, floor coverings, plates and medicines. Nothing is wasted (the unusable offcuts are tied together and 'placed within the bosom of the plant—once again to ensure its life'): all is eventually given back to the earth.[35]

What makes this ecofeminism distinctively religious is the way in which its account of female craft fuses biography and mythology. The source of these skills is both cosmological as the craft of the Goddess, and personal as a mother's gestatory crafting of a child. The mother then (ideally) teaches female skills and crafts to her child as a continuing oral tradition. These are crafts which she herself learnt from her own mother who learnt them from the foremothers who learnt them from the prehistorical foremothers who learnt them from cocoon- and web-spinning insects and nest-building birds. And these animals learnt their crafts from the Goddess as she spun and wove the fabric of existence from her own body/loom. Even without a thealogical perspective that draws women, nature and the cosmos into a reproductive circle, crafts can still connect past and present generations of women. Female crafts are trivialized in patriarchal culture as hobbies, make-up and fashion, and then placed outside or on the very edge of high culture. But when women use the sewing skills and recipes that their mothers and grand-mothers have taught them, this can give a profound feeling of connection with those women—especially if they are no longer alive. Similarly,

33. 'He Wahine, He Whenua: Maori Women and the Environment', in Caldicott and Leland (eds.), *Reclaim the Earth*, p. 139.
34. 'He Wahine, He Whenua', p. 137.
35. 'He Wahine, He Whenua', p. 137.

Judy Grahn describes her mother's 'hope' chest: a wooden box filled with female oddments and paraphernalia. She writes,

> I assume there must have been a long line of such chests with wedding gowns, crocheted and knitted items, embroidery, recipes perhaps— women's things passed along a distaff line that, increasingly, forgot the origins and greater significance of their paraphernalia.[36]

Again the comparison of female productive knowledge with patriarchal productive knowledge is stark. Workers are 'trained', but children are taught. Businesses are traditionally passed on to sons whom the father fondly hopes will develop the business even further by 'taking out' the competition. The business will prosper by consuming ever more resources to make a product that must be consumed in ever larger quantities. Money (a word derived from the name of the Roman Great Mother Juno Moneta) is *made* at the expense of nature. Patriarchal economics are a necrophilic parody of the life-giving unbilical and lactatory connection between mothers and babies. And it is money, not blood, water and milk that supplies the consumers' demands and circulates around the economic body of capitalism.[37]

Of course spiritual feminism is well aware that most Western women have to 'buy into' capitalist mass production because they have neither the time to make, nor the money to buy, hand-made objects. The point here is that of a comparison between the intentions and the processes of 'female' and patriarchal modes of production. Feminists reclaim craft production as an act of spiritual-political dissent and as a form and metaphor of transformatory praxis. In the words of the feminist weaver Faith Gillespie, 'within the power to change raw materials by our hand into things both pleasing and useful lies an intimation of the possibility of transforming our lives'.[38]

Just as nineteenth-century Christian feminism believed that women would morally regenerate society, contemporary neo-pagan feminism endows female craft with the power to regenerate not only political relations, but culture's relation to nature as well. Certainly, the reclamation of craft has utopian elements. But it is not merely romantic bourgeois *nostalgie de la boue* that drives the ecofeminist 'back' into

36. *Blood, Bread and Roses: How Menstruation Created the World* (Boston: Beacon Press, 1993), p. 85.

37. See Sheldrake, *The Rebirth of Nature*, p. 22.

38. 'The Masterless Way: Weaving an Active Resistance', in G. Elinor *et al.* (eds.), *Women and Craft* (London: Virago, 1987), p. 178.

primal culture for a guide to praxis and a vision of a culture in which female knowledge is honoured. If the earth is to be a source of human goods, then ecofeminism wants to make their exchange a 'green' exchange. Domesticated craft production is at least a model of vegetal, biodegradable production which spares the earth from the burden of permanently polluting, deathless artifacts like plastics and nuclear waste which will long outlive the men and the cultures who made them.

Re-Sourcing Women's Sacral Labour

I am not convinced that contemporary Western spiritual feminist politics need to be validated by a prehistorical past or by pre-modern native practices that persist today. However, there is no doubt that for most spiritual feminists the precedent of female modes of production is significant, however temporally, culturally or geographically remote this might be. Yet the meaning of female sacrality in non-Western practices is even more difficult to retrieve and interpret than it is in more familiar traditions. Evelyn Reed notes that in most anthropological texts, the 'pages are filled with descriptions of the hunting and fighting activities of men, their blood rites, their games and ceremonies, while the activities of women are slighted'.[39] And as Nancy Falk has noted, 'materials on the transformative powers manifested through women's cultural activities are still sparse'.[40] Even so, what can be reconstructed and revalued from anthropology's account of pre-modern female sacral activities is crucial to spiritual feminism's sense of its spiritual inheritance and its ecological future. Because spiritual feminist religious politics depend in some measure on anthropology it is necessary to consider how anthropological insights are transposed into this contemporary spiritual scheme.

Howard Eilberg-Schwartz has argued that American feminist neo-paganism represents a culmination of twentieth-century cultural anthropology's attempts to understand its own culture by studying other cultures. Feminists may, he says, take its results more seriously than the anthropologists themselves. While anthropologists rarely 'go native', neo-pagans have enthusiastically adopted the cosmologies and native practices of witch-believing cultures.[41] This is basically true, but it also an

39. *Woman's Evolution*, p. 127.
40. 'Feminine Sacrality', p. 312.
41. 'Witches of the West: Neopaganism and Goddess Worship as Enlightenment Religions', *Journal of Feminist Studies in Religion* 5 (1989), pp. 87-88.

exaggeration to say that spiritual feminists treat these anthropological texts much as the traditional religions treat the Scriptures.[42] Spiritual feminism is a good deal more eclectic than that and its use of anthropological texts is heavily indebted to the postmodern collapse of the distinctions between 'primitive' and 'civilized', and scientific and mystical thinking.

Nonetheless, spiritual feminist politics of production *are* to some measure dependent on an anthropological assertion: that when female technologies can be combined with childcare, as in cultures dependent on hoe-cultivation, women's status can be high or equal to that of men because they are doubly productive. But once cultures are directed towards herding animals and ploughing land owned by men, and women are left to take care of children, their status is low and they are dominated by men.[43] Spiritual feminism has utilized the available (but contested) evidence that from around 7000 BCE Europe enjoyed about 3000 years of peaceful, ceramic-producing, agricultural matrifocal life where settlements were unfortified and did not need to manufacture weapons. Patriarchy is believed to have arrived in Southern Europe, India and the near East with horse-riding warriors who worshipped sky-gods and demoted women and the earth goddesses as subordinates of husbands and gods within the patriarchal family and pantheon.[44] The women who, it is claimed, made the technological advances that trans-formed hunting societies to gardening or agricultural societies, and who developed language, pottery, ovens, leather tanning, brewing, mathe-matics, calendars, the domestication of animals, and so on were no longer the mistresses of their own inventions.

For our present purpose, the political intention behind such claims is more important than their strictly historical status. Even if there is insufficient evidence to show that women were, historically, the mothers of all invention, a more subtle argument remains, namely, that the first human societies produced goods in a 'female' mode. Goods were produced in a rhythmic, tactile and therefore sustainable fashion. The *idea* of craft as a means by which women transformed humankind from

42. 'Witches of the West', p. 88.

43. See J. Lorber, 'Dismantling Noah's Ark', in J. Lorber and S. Farrell (eds.), *The Social Construction of Gender* (Newbury, CA: Sage Publications, 1991), pp. 357-58.

44. I am indebted here to Rupert Sheldrake's concise account of the matrifocal 'Golden Age' and its demise in *The Rebirth of Nature*, pp. 10-11.

its basically animal condition to a distinctively human one means that their labours must be understood quite differently from the normal patriarchal and equal rights feminist view of female labour as drudgery. Thus Evelyn Reed: 'Far from being "drudgery", woman's work was esteemed as supremely creative; it created nothing less than the human species.'[45]

The idea that the first made things were 'female' productions is at the political heart of radical feminist sacred history. As Faith Gillespie puts it, 'further back than we can know, before the Mother-god was called "Father", in the time when there were no masters, the power of making was ours'.[46] In this sense women are proposing an ambitious heresy: that female divine reproductivity in the Goddess made the human world, not God. The *actual* Fall of women came with the first patriarchal reversal. For as Sjöö and Mor put it,

> it was women who were biologically endowed to create human society, language, and culture. And then it was men, who were socially endowed by women, who turned around and declared women unfit for culture, using women's biological endowment as a justification for our oppression.[47]

The debate among anthropologists over the existence of ancient matriarchies has been going on for over a hundred years. It is not within my competence to take sides in this debate. What is more important to the present purpose is to examine the way in which arguments such as that of Evelyn Reed, who proposed that the maternal clan system was the original form of social organization, have percolated through to spiritual feminism and are being remade as a gynocentric, 'gyn/ecological' tradition. While not being slavishly dependent on scientific scholarship, spiritual feminism makes a scholarly investment (of sorts) in this material because female sacrality is far more evident in the records and current practices of most primal religions than it is in Western logocentric traditions in which God and elite men make with words, not hands. Of course the pagan attribution of transformatory powers to women or goddesses does not make those traditions feminist. Anthropology has shown that under patriarchy female *mana* cuts both ways. It may redeem femaleness from insignificance, but the perceived power of female sacrality can

---

45. *Woman's Evolution*, p. 128.
46. 'The Masterless Way', p. 186.
47. *The Great Cosmic Mother*, p. 239.

also mean that women's bodies are invested with attributes considered dangerous to the stability of the group, so justifying practices such as menstrual seclusion that would be intolerable to liberal secularism.

So although all but the most recent anthropological scholarship is without feminist intentions, it does at least recognize that there *are* cultures in which women have *mana* or positive supernatural power— even if it is a *mana* apparently defined by men. This scholarship is at least a textual reminder that not all societies are premised on a myth in which women end a golden age by their sin. Writers like Briffault, Neumann, Eliade, Campbell and Reed offer at least textual possibilities for contemporary reconstructions of a 'female' sacred.[48] For example, the anthropologist Peggy Reeves Sanday has shown that female power roles can be derived from (but would not be the same as) pre-modern conceptions of nature:

> In societies where the forces of nature are sacralized...there is a reciprocal flow between the power of nature and the power inherent in women. The control and manipulation of these forces is left to women and to sacred natural symbols; men are largely extraneous to this domain and must be careful lest they antagonise earthly representatives of nature's power (namely, women).[49]

In past and present paganisms the association of women and nature as the mysterious matrices in which life flourishes is the beginning of religion. And the contention that female craft was originally a religious mode of production is supported by Marija Gimbutas's archaeological findings. She argues that in the temples of matrifocal Old Europe female skill was used to make the religious artifacts for the worship of the Goddess—goods of great value not belonging to any chief but to the Goddess alone. Baking, pottery and weaving were sanctified because

---

48. The spiritual feminist articulations of the religious meanings of female transformations are substantially dependent on the anthropology and history of religions produced in the first 60 years or so of the twentieth century. These texts are androcentric, if not androcratic. According to Falk, who was writing in 1987, the most comprehensive studies of female sacrality are still the Jungian psychologist Erich Neumann's *The Great Mother* (1955) and Mircea Eliade's *Patterns in Comparative Religion* (1958). Joseph Campbell's *Primitive Mythology* in his series *The Masks of God* (1959) is also useful in its scheme of the rise of male dominance, breaking and controlling the elemental powers of women once regarded as 'no less a marvel than the universe itself' (p. 315).

49. *Female Power and Male Dominance*, p. 5; see also pp. xv-xvi.

'the routine acts of daily existence were religious rituals by virtue of replicating the sacred models'.[50]

Or again, baking the circular or Goddess-shaped sacramental cakes was important in the cults of the ancient Near Eastern goddesses.[51] But unlike the meaning of the communion wafer, the meaning of this sacrament is as much in the making of the cake as in the eating. Bakery is traditionally a metaphor for pregnancy; for thealogy this implies that sacramental communion is continuous with all biological processes as contact with the energy of life. This is subtly different from traditional Catholic Eucharistic theology in which the communion wafer mediates salvation through a priest's conjuring the presence of one man who is both dead and alive, or in Protestant theology the memory of that one man. Of course the Christian Eucharist is life-giving in intention, and is like thealogy in so far as it recognizes that life is resurrected through death. But the Eucharistic sacrament concentrates the power of life not in the material food (which in Catholicism transubstantiates into spirit) but in the sacrificial pain of one particular man. In thealogy, however, life continually resurrects through matter itself: the transubstantiation is one in which one sort of material energy becomes another, whether in nature or craft.

In its new/old feminization of nature, thealogy shows that the association of women and nature is not *necessarily* and of itself politically disabling, even if it has been in Western religion and culture, and in the reformist feminist commentary on them. Some studies of pre-modern societies make it at least possible that the devaluation and subordination of women as immanently 'natural' and the male rule of nature as transcendently 'cultural' are historical phenomena. And as historical, such an ordering is neither universal nor inevitable.[52] Indeed, female sacral crafts are a fusion of natural and political power. Craft is the product of a philosophy of labour in which consciousness no longer controls nature but, ideally and symbolically, is 'taught' by nature. The way in which dust or mud turns into a rock-like substance when baked is one example

---

50. 'Women and Culture in Goddess-Orientated Old Europe', in Spretnak (ed.), *The Politics of Women's Spirituality*, p. 24.

51. A. Long, *In a Chariot Drawn by Lions: The Search for the Female in Deity* (London: The Women's Press, 1992), pp. 124-25.

52. See S. Ortner, 'Is Female to Male as Nature is to Culture?', in M.Z. Rosaldo and L. Lamphere (eds.), *Women, Culture, and Society* (Stanford, CA: Stanford University Press, 1974), pp. 69, 83-84.

of a magical/natural transubstantiation that creates the conditions for cultural development.[53] If both nature and culture are the craft of the Goddess then the two cannot be wholly distinguishable categories.

The ecological and spiritual significance of craft as female sacrality-in-process transcends the modern distinction between the public and private spheres and the ideology which took cultural industry out of the home and into the factory. The study of women living in places and periods where the home is not a marginal space can be used by feminists to show that modern social organization is not inevitable or laid down with the created order. So too, technology, now a masculine preserve—and usually a destructive one—was once a practice which was not separate from domestic life in a time when domesticity and culture were one. Recalling pre-modernity, spiritual feminism fuses spiritual, green and socialist politics to (re)feminize technology for sustainable, just and spiritually rewarding modes of production.

The spiritual feminist revision of craft can be illustrated by looking briefly at how anthropological data can be reconstructed to give evidence of notionally pre-patriarchal, pre-industrialized women's lives and of an ontology of femaleness that is being recovered for postmodern conditions. Anthropologists are more or less in agreement that in nearly all societies men engage in the 'hard' technologies of butchering, mining, quarrying, and making stone and metal into tools for smashing, pounding, killing and dismembering. Spiritual feminism politicizes this evidence, arguing that mining and smelting defaced the earth's surface (and therefore the Goddess) with spades and swords, and in doing so inscribed the beginning of the end: the opening paragraphs of

> imperialistic, centralised and warlike city states. With iron weapons and iron tools such as ploughs to rip the Earth open for agriculture on a large scale and axes to cut down the vast forests, patriarchal men could finally take over and impose their own anti-life values based on left-brain, linear thinking.[54]

By contrast, female technologies tend to be 'soft': transforming or processing pliable plant materials by cooking, spinning or weaving vegetal products.[55] To combine craft with childcare women need to stay near the home or work in places where it is safe for children to play and help

---

53. See Reed, *Woman's Evolution*, p. 119.
54. Sjöö, *New Age and Armageddon*, p. 158.
55. See Sanday, *Female Power and Male Dominance*, pp. 77, 79.

with the work. Our image of prehistory is admittedly a means by which we gauge our own evolution or degeneration; it is riddled with stereotypical expectations of gender roles and nostalgia for slow, apparently uncomplicated lives. Accounts of prehistory must be read with a critical eye. Nonetheless, in the popular imagination it was pre-historical men who went on dangerous hunting, exploring and scavenging expeditions. This picture is not groundless: hunting requires concentration, silence and sudden bursts of movement and speed that the presence of children would prevent. Mothers would stay within the community encampment because they were breast-feeding or unwilling to leave children unprotected. So women's crafts would probably have had to use immediately available materials which could then be processed in the communal setting of talkative circles and clusters of other women and children. Whether or not this picture of prehistorical organization is 'true' is of secondary importance to its power as an evocative image of female production-in-community.

Situating femaleness in and around the house and its garden localizes but does not limit female sacrality. For contemporary religious feminists, the garden is not just the ornamental space for leisure that it is in the modern suburb.[56] The garden is revered as a place for growing healing herbs and flowers and fruit, as it was and remains in agricultural societies. Linked to the family's survival, the garden in primal religions can be a sacred space—a place reserved for the enactment of female craft and therefore endangered by masculine presence. When, for example, Trobriand women garden—'an activity which is reserved for them alone—[they] have the right to attack and knock down any man who comes too close to their gardens'.[57]

The garden as sacred space engenders sacred knowledges. For example, women's knowledge of horticulture and cookery developed magical/medicinal distillatory skills by which the poisonous properties of plants could be boiled off to leave a residue that could be compounded with other plants as medicine.[58] Recipes, spells or instructions could be

56. For a discussion of gardening as a symbol and a fruition of religious feminist praxis see M. Raphael, 'At the East End of Eden: A Feminist Spirituality of Gardening Our Way Past the Flaming Sword', *Feminist Theology* 4 (1993), pp. 101-10.

57. Eliade, *Rites and Symbols*, pp. 79-80.

58. See M. Chamberlain, *Old Wives' Tales: Their History, Remedies and Spells* (London: Virago, 1981). This is a comprehensive feminist survey of the history of female healing.

passed orally, and therefore without male scrutiny, from one woman to another. This heritage is traced back to the ancient Near Eastern priestesses who were also physicians. They were required to be knowledgeable about botany and chemistry; their prayers and incantations for the sick were also prescriptions.[59] Contemporary feminist witchcraft images women as healers or witches (if not by nature then by inheritance). Their horticultural skills are both inherited knowledge and also modelled on women's physiological capacity to grow or cultivate living things from inside their bodies. The female reproductive process is profane to the patriarchal cult and so too are these horticultural skills. Independent female herbalism has been topographically and cultically marginal; it has been practised in the immediate space around the home or village and outside the authority of the church.

The thealogy of healing has been a threat to the masculine power to work miracles. In Exod. 15.26 God shows that he has taken over the healing prerogative of the goddesses when he proclaims 'For I am the Lord, your healer'. In the biblical period sickness was viewed as the punishment of sins and was only cured by faith in God's forgiveness and by repentance and obedience. So later when women brewed herbal remedies to try to alleviate parturant women's pain, their implicit disregard for God's command that women be punished for Eve's sin by pain in childbirth was *prima facie* evidence of witchcraft. And more generally, to cure sickness with vegetal products rather than prayer was paganism (that is, witchcraft). This slur on female medicine has contributed substantially to the gradual desacralization of gardens as sacred spaces and female healing as sacred knowledge and a craft.

Sophie Laws, a social constructionist[60] radical feminist, rightly warns against any essentialist biologism which romanticizes the physical sources of female oppression, 'mythologising other women's experience without fully understanding their circumstances'.[61] But spiritual feminism does not do this. On the contrary its *own* account of domesticity exposes patriarchal domestic labour as unsalaried, repetitious work without economic or self-defining status as an appropriation and degradation of female power.

59. *Old Wives' Tales*, p. 11.

60. A social constructionist is one who regards inequality as the result of the interrelation of social power between men and women rather than a biological given.

61. *Issues of Blood: The Politics of Menstruation* (London: Macmillan, 1990), p. 28.

If the spiritual feminist critique of patriarchal culture places a greater reliance on archaeological and anthropological texts than these can strictly support, is because spiritual feminist discourse is far more prescriptive than either of these disciplines. Spiritual feminists are not social scientists *manquées*. They intend that women should create or return to a possibility of labour which is not spiritually and politically alienated and which requires the ingenuity and imagination that women in putatively matrifocal societies expended on craft or other domestic transformations. Of course any feminist hesitates to sacralize female cleaning and the removal of stains in case it should look as if she were fetishising purity and hygiene. No feminist would want to offer religious compensations for the countless women whose intellect and skills have been wasted on an unchosen life of scrubbing, bleaching and polishing. This would be comparable to those who hallow poverty as a religious virtue; a hollow praise for those whose poverty was not elected and whose lives have been stunted by poverty.

It was to show that domesticity need not be patriarchally conceived that in 1973 the performance artist Mierle Laderman Ukeles chose to sacralize the profane pavement by ritual cleansing. The movements she made with the water and the cloths were those she would have used in painting.[62] Her gesture implied that domestic purifications are an art; a transformation mystery with a religious significance that secular modernity has lost sight of in its removal of any spiritual meaning or status from female acts of purification. Ukeles' performance made clear that feminist craft makes no distinction between menial acts of reproduction and the making of goods which are useful, beautiful or both.

Feminist craft is, then, a very different thing from the domestic accomplishments that once gilded the cage of the bourgeois marriage and which are now hobbies for those who have spare time for them. Indeed, as we will see, the passage of craft to hobby can be traced as one of the ways in which women have been separated and diverted from the religious and economic power-broking of the public sphere. But spiritual feminism's historico-poetical readings of archaeological and anthropological texts begin not with modernity and women's experience of embourgeoisement or industrial labour, but with the argument that 'the impressive labor record of women is obscured by the usual description of it as "household" work'. In pre-industrialized societies women's

62. Orenstein, *The Reflowering of the Goddess*, p. 124.

household production could hardly be called 'handicraft'.[63] To attribute biological and cultural powers of transformation to women is not, then, a limitation of being. In her preface to the revised edition of *Ancient Mirrors of Womanhood*, Merlin Stone wrote that if ancient goddess cultures could become 'a familiar part of general education' that would 'expose and refute many simplistic stereotypes and views of womanhood that have come to be accepted by both women and men'.[64] That the magical nature of women causes things to *change and multiply* offers the liberation of unlimited existential possibilities.

Sewing the World Together

Spiritual feminist schemes do not have linear beginnings and ends—the life-giving circulation of both material and intellectual life is kept moving as a circular or spiralling process. The beginning and the end of spiritual feminist historical discourse cannot be separated. Perhaps the word 'history' is not properly applicable to this discourse at all. For here descriptions of the past and prescriptions for the future are mutually informing. Prehistory can be transposed to women in a nuclear age because in the radical feminist spiral concept of time, prehistory loses its place in the evolutionary scheme of lost beginnings and becomes a future utopian possibility of ends. (A woman can spin a primal umbilical rope within her womb through which she passes life-energy to the future.) How a feminist can move in and out of history at will is particularly well exemplified in Mary Daly's work, where the deepest meanings of spinning and cooking are metaphors of psychic/cosmic renewal and re-creative political ferment. Weaving, for example, is a way of repairing women's split, torn, fragmented consciousness—it re-weaves 'our Original Integrity'.[65] And gyn/ecological creativity is a form of spinning; a way of 'dis-covering the lost thread of connectedness within the cosmos, repairing this web as we create'.[66]

The discourse of craft (especially that involving the use of spun thread) typifies how spiritual feminism weaves together biology, cosmogony and politics into one mythical, metaphorical and practical discourse that also narrates a complete history of female sacrality. This narrative is mythical

63. See Reed, *Woman's Evolution*, pp. 124-25.
64. Boston: Beacon Press, 1991, p. x.
65. *Gyn/Ecology*, p. 423.
66. *Gyn/Ecology*, p. 390.

in character. Myth forms a matrix or web of stories that holds together the contemporary feminist reconstruction of craft and its history.

The mythology of spinning includes Hebrew women weaving hangings for Asherah (2 Kgs 23.7); the Greek goddess Athena—a weaver *par exellence*—and Ariadne who led Theseus through the labyrinth of life with her ball of thread; the Scandinavian Norns spinning the thread of life and fate; and the Navajo Grandmother Spider spinning out the fabric of the universe. In Navajo mythology the threads of time are knotted together by Navajo women, who still weave unique blankets, which are 'valued as organic expressions of the special powers of the makers. Each blanket with its inspired design has a spiritual significance, and is thought of as giving power and protection to the person who wears it.'[67] Or again, there may be threads connecting the European folklore in which women spun all sorts of magical cloths to the Christian women who maintain a tradition of sacred sewing in making tapestry hassocks and hangings for their local church.

There is perhaps a stronger thread connecting the magical cloths of European folklore and the women who used menstrual blood-cloths to tie together the gates at Greenham Common. Symbols never have just one meaning, but these cloths seem to have symbolized women's binding together the fabric of a world that the missiles within the installation were threatening to blow apart. So too, the blood on the cloths 'profaned' and thereby diffused male sacral powers of destruction. The tied and bloodied locks became 'untouchable' to patriarchy and so took the power of the site and its weapons of mass destruction captive. Moon, a travelling woman in her fifties, has always used her blood-cloths during political actions at military bases. At Greenham she tied a fresh one to the gates each month. The men inside the base were 'absolutely stunned and repulsed' by this, but none of them touched the cloths and they were eventually removed by cutting.[68]

The Latin word for religion, *religare*, means 'to bind up'—a meaning as close to the 'female' healing work of bandaging a disinfected wound as it is to 'female' mending and sewing. Indeed it is in the nature of all

67. Sjöö and Mor, *The Great Cosmic Mother*, p. 51.

68. From Amberston, *Blessings of the Blood*, pp. 60-61. When Moon used her blood-cloths as art at a spiritual feminist event in New Mexico, painting patterns on them with the blood, some of the women were deeply appreciative; 'other women thought it was absolutely disgusting, repulsive, and gross' (p. 61). Clearly not all spiritual feminists find the blood-cloth politically helpful.

religious discourse and practice that cosmic beginnings, present alienations and resolving ends are tied together. Again, Greenham demonstrated how weaving and spinning can be metaphors for the healing
power of spiritual reconnection. Here as well webs were woven onto the
perimeter fences and wool was wound around the sentry boxes.
Similarly, the American Donna Henes's environmental process sculp-
tures have used web- and cocoon-spinning to mediate on ecological connectedness. On one occasion she created a healing event called
'Wrapping Our Wounds in Warm Clothes', on an island where 1459
psychiatric patients were housed. There she knotted strips of cloth or
bandages onto the trees—one tree for every patient. Commenting on
Henes's web-spinning Gloria Orenstein writes, 'she is making visible the
force-fields, energy fields, and networks of nature that are like the blood
vessels of the human body'. As such, the webs reconnect human power
to planetary and then cosmic power.[69] So spinning rituals are religious in
the best sense of that word: their purpose is to remake, tie or sew a torn,
unravelled world back together.

Like spinning and weaving, knitting can be similarly understood as
having a magico-religious function as well as a practical one (feminist
magic is after all a practical activity). Knitting is one of many female uses
of spun thread, and in Western culture it is an activity strongly associated with sedentary post-menopausal women. Again it is both a practical
craft and a biological metaphor. In Job 10.11 Job attributes to God the
female capacity to knit flesh: 'Thou didst clothe me with skin and flesh,
and knit me together with bones and sinews.' And grandmothers often
clothe a new baby by knitting elaborate blankets and numerous pairs of
mittens and boots. Here the practical and the metaphorical nature of
knitting come together. For it is as if, no longer fertile themselves,
grandmothers begin to knit, often at the very beginning of a pregnancy,
with the quasi-magical intention of aiding the knitting of flesh in the
younger woman's womb.

The spiritual feminist use of the web motif itself belongs to a web of
connected uses. Webs of all sorts have become perhaps the most prevalent postmodern model for ecological relationship: for non-centralized
communication or networking (as on the Internet's World Wide Web)
between groups of like-minded people. The web is also an ethical symbol
and a model of natural holistic justice in that each connected element of
the web is as important as another. Carol Gilligan's *In a Different*

69. *The Reflowering of the Goddess*, p. 106.

Voice[70] has been one of the most influential expositions of the 'female' web as a feminist ethical alternative to unequal masculine hierarchy. But the spider is an emblem of female sacrality in its ambiguity as well as its ecological functions. As cosmogonic spiders, women spin and mend life, but at the centre of the web they can, in trapping and eating their mate or prey, also consume it—making spideriness a quality of the Goddess as the Crone who devours time and its creations.

For spiritual feminism, the mythical dimension of sewing is intertwined with its own socialist historiography. Rozsika Parker's remark that 'to know the history of embroidery is to know the history of women' is not simply rhetorical. Parker has documented how the medieval embroiderers, many of them women, produced theologically expressive and highly prized works of art. But during the Renaissance art was separated from household craft and transcendentalized as 'high art'—a prestigious male activity of the public sphere. By the nineteenth century needlework was a lady's pastime or a working-class woman's sweated labour. By then, middle- and upper-class needlework signified women's inactive seclusion in a private sphere in which ornamental women made ornamental objects. The cottage industry of spinning and weaving had been industrialized and sewing became what it remains: low-paid work or a work which signifies not working.

The domestication of sewing was one means of inculcating femininity. Needlework 'instructed a girl in docility and accustomed her to long hours sitting still with downcast gaze'.[71] And yet the feminist historian finds herself ambivalent in trying to assess how successful a means of suppression sewing actually was. The silent, hunched shoulders of the (leisured) embroiderer can be read as a posture of submission. Or they can be read as the autonomous self-containment of a woman (or sorority of women) concentrating on the meticulous creation of a beautiful item that would have been highly prized within a female culture at least.[72]

Under patriarchy, what can distinguish art from work, and male labour from female labour, is where artifacts are made and who makes

70. *In A Different Voice: Psychological Theory and Women's Development* (Cambridge, MA: Harvard University Press, 1982).

71. *The Subversive Stitch: Embroidery and the Making of the Feminine* (London: The Women's Press, 1984), p. 151. Parker is a feminist but not, as far as I know, a spiritual feminist.

72. *The Subversive Stitch*, pp. 10, 11.

them.[73] In the nineteenth century working-class women often sewed at home. Their sewing was not cosmogonic; on the contrary, it fuelled a capitalist economy. Charlotte E. Touna's novel *The Wrongs of Women* (1844) illustrates the anti-sacral process by which Kate Clark, a lace-maker's apprentice, is forced to sell her craft so cheaply and in such poor working conditions that her vitality is destroyed. In German *Kraft* is a feminine noun meaning vigour, strength and power. But patriarchy's exploitation of female craft broke Kate's mind and body. She became white and 'crooked' like the women who made the white lace with her in the dark and dirty cottage. Finally, when she was unfit for anything else, Kate sold the last of her sexual *Kraft*. With tragic logic she profaned herself absolutely as a prostitute.[74] Under patriarchy female craft does not renew women's power but exhausts (or profanes) it. Christianity reversed the relation of craft and female power by demonizing its apparatuses and products. Women's spinning, cleaning (broomsticks), gardening (poisonous herbs) and cooking (cauldrons) become the signs of witchcraft. But it is not the female crafts which are demonic, but the religio-economic system that is parasitic upon them.

Spiritual feminism restores the biophilic *Kraft* to craft, making the imaginative weaving of ideas, words and images pro-creative in every sense. Daly's prose is a (witch)craft in which she spins magical meanings: 'It became increasingly evident that my Craft as a Radical Feminist Philosopher is also Witchcraft.'[75] Her craft is a magical vessel in which she sails out into the 'Subliminal Sea' of metapatriarchal consciousness. So too, in *Feminist Revision and the Bible* Alicia Ostriker biologizes texts by observing that the Latin *textus* also means tissue— another word for flesh. The authorial weaving and critical unweaving of a text is a maternal labour. It fashions a textual material that itself has a magical capacity to self-revise hermeneutically; to generate multiple meanings.[76] To 'feminize' fabric is, then, to multiply or fabricate its meanings and functions beyond that of protective covering for our fur-less skin (though that is necessary to our survival).[77] A piece of fabric

73. *The Subversive Stitch*, p. 5.

74. Parker uses this novel as an illustration of the degradation of the embroiderer's craft: *The Subversive Stitch*, p. 77.

75. *Outercourse*, p. 198.

76. Oxford: Blackwell, 1993.

77. See Kuryluk, *Veronica and her Cloth*, pp. 179-98, for an analysis of the manifold mythic meanings of cloth.

can be a shape-shifting cloak or shroud, a veil, or a sail—all accessories of feminist *Wanderlust*. Daly unites some of these purposes when she writes, 'I was Sinspired to Sail further and further Out on my Quest as an Outlaw, as a Terrible Taboo-breaking Radical Feminist Philosopher/ Pirate. I found that the Courage to Sin is also the Courage to Spin.'[78]

Veiled Bodies

The meaning of cloth also has a capacity to self-revise in the different intentions with which it is used to cover women's heads, and sometimes bodies, as a veil. Men may cover their heads and faces for protection in war and against inclement weather, but they do not wear veils. Veils are 'female' pieces of cloth. This piece of cloth is perhaps the most ambivalent of all signifiers of female sacrality and so merits particular attention. In each of the three Abrahamic faiths women are differently veiled, though all patriarchal veiling is at least a requirement of modesty. In other words, the veil protects a man's sexual property by hiding its charms from other men. In this sense veils can be read, like diets, as another female disappearing act. (It is no coincidence that heavily veiled women are not under the Western compulsion to diet, since they have already disappeared.) The *patriarchal* veil shrouds the erotic vitality of women. It is, I believe, gynocidal in that the personhood of the woman is blanked—blacked or whited—out. She becomes a shadow, a shade or a ghost. She not only becomes literally invisible in the public sphere, she is also silenced—we 'draw a veil' over that which we prefer to ignore.

It is in Islam that the meanings of veiling are closest to the contemporary social surface. Here the degree of veiling varies according to geography and religio-political allegiance. And Moslem women wear the veil with a variety of motivations, styles and religio-political nuances.[79] Geographically too, the veil takes a variety of forms. Some of the heaviest veiling is in Mzab where women are totally veiled and even turn their heads away as they pass; in eastern Algeria where the veil is black and covers the entire face and body except for one eye; and in Dhofar where women are fully veiled and wear embroidered leather masks over their faces.[80]

78. *Outercourse*, p. 198.

79. L.A. Odeh, 'Post-Colonial Feminism and the Veil: Thinking the Difference', *Feminist Review* 43 (1993), pp. 34-35.

80. J. Minces, *The House of Obedience: Women in Arab Society* (London: Zed, 1982), pp. 50-51.

A great deal has been written on the subject of Islamic veiling, but one of the most relevant studies for the present purpose is Fatima Mernissi's *Beyond the Veil*,[81] in which she argues that Islam does not so much regard women as biologically inferior as actively and dangerously sexual. In Morocco women are associated with *fitna*—chaos. This is significant: in Islam, and in many other traditions, the female mouth is imaged as a castrating *vagina dentata*—a vagina with teeth. This image symbolizes women's fearsome mythical capacity to swallow men as they 'swallowed' the babies in their swollen abdomens. The mouth is an image of devouring chaos and a return to cosmic, pre-patriarchal beginnings (and therefore male disempowerment). The covering and shutting of the mouth with a veil therefore protects the social order. As symbols of disorder women are a threat to the stability of society unless they are 'covered' by Qu'ranic law. A woman who is without a husband or male kin to discipline and control her *fitna* is truly an outcast (the paradigm status of profane persons).

In effect, and perhaps in intention, veiling produces an image of female formlessness. So it seems ironic that heavily veiled women then seem to embody visually the formless chaos that the veil is intended to protect men from in the first place. However, it seems clear that the patriarchal veil is intimately connected with patriarchy's fear of death. Patriarchy claims that it veils women because men will be sexually distracted if they do not. This distraction from piety might result in the forfeiture of eternal life. But sexual arousal also brings life into the world whether it is wanted by men or not. And with life comes death, as the cycle of creation requires death to make life. In the biblical myth of the Fall, Eve tempted Adam to know his own mortality. She offered him knowledge—a *revelatio*; the drawing back of the veil that had protected his innocence of death. This female power to 'tempt' men into the existential abyss—to face the *tremendum* of their own mortality—is an agency that can de-generate society into the spiralling chaos of primal abundance. This is a tangled, proliferative state in which the regulatory straight line of patriarchal rationalism cannot survive. Modern patriarchy has to regulate nature by turning the planetary 'home' into a giant factory: an institution which contains and uses 'female' generativity, but also stops it unravelling the patriarchal order.

The veil is also used to shield the social order from women who are in

81. *Beyond the Veil: Male–Female Dynamics in a Modern Muslim Society* (Cambridge: Schenkman, 1975).

a liminal or boundary phase and therefore vulnerable to possession by evil spirits or their more abstract equivalents. Patriarchy metaphorizes women's bodies—and the earth—as bounded empty space that must be colonized and filled up with *something*. In ancient Hellenic cultures widows were veiled (symbolically closed) because they were without a husband's control over their bodies. And brides are still veiled on their wedding day—a reminder that their *mana* is not yet under the control of a husband but is in the process of passing out from the control of the father. On the day of a patriarchal marriage the woman's hymen (Greek for veil) is lifted/broken. The Latin word *nupta* connotes that after the wedding or nuptials the woman is to be overshadowed—her master will overcloud her sacrality, and where there are laws of coverture, her property.[82] Covering the bride's body with a veil and perforating the inner veil of her hymen, the husband takes possession of, and thereby diffuses, the bride's sacral threat to his power. He closes her body to everything but himself.

Out of a similar fear of its stimulus to chaotic sexuality, Judaism shaves or crops married women's natural hair and keeps it covered from public view by a wig or scarf—the equivalents of a veil. Christian nuns traditionally shaved off their hair and took the veil as a sign of the quasi-marital renunciation of their sexuality to God in Christ. In many cases, the religious and the political appropriation of female sexual power belong together. The cropping or shaving of the head is significant here. It may be that recruits into the armed forces and those entering prison camps have their hair cropped as a sign that their energies have been brought under patriarchal discipline. In this, hair cropping is more than a way of preventing the spread of lice; it is 'a cleansing rite placed upon a taboo person'. That the French female collaborators had their heads shaved when France was liberated at the end of the Second World War 'may likewise be traced to primitive magic'.[83]

Fundamentalist Moslem women put on the veil because for them it offers freedom and protection from the objectification by the male gaze that is suffered by Western women and Islamic women in Western clothes.[84] However, Western feminism would be more likely to argue that the veil interferes with male lust but does not reform it. The veil

82. See Rabuzzi, *The Sacred and the Feminine*, p. 178.

83. K. Seligmann, *Magic, Supernaturalism and Religion* (London: Allen Lane, 1971), p. 19.

84. Odeh, 'Post-Colonial Feminism and the Veil', p. 29.

seems less likely to banish patriarchal sexual fantasies than to provoke them. Covering a body which is without the political power of autonomous subjecthood, the veil offers at least one man the privilege of its unveiling. Tearing off a veil is a desecration that traditionally symbolizes rape (especially of a virgin). The image of the torn veil reveals the profound connection between pornography and profanation: both are what Sartre called a 'violation by sight'.[85] So too, the desecration which tears the covering of grass and trees from nature's surface and the clothes from women's bodies is at least metaphorically enacted in the scientific dis-mantling or unveiling of nature. Jane Caputi calls science 'pornoscience and pornotechnology', both of which are 'predicated upon disrespect and profanation. [Scientists] are obsessed with penetrating, displaying, possessing, and exposing sacred mysteries—with baring the nakedness of the Goddess / Universe.'[86] Only, like all desecrations, the pornographic unveiling of femaleness is anti-climactic; it misses the point. Under the veil there is 'just' a woman's body. A sacred thing is not an accumulated 'stock' of holiness, but a sign or a point in space and time through which the holy suffuses the world.

Yet the fact that the basic function of a veil is to protect the sacred points to the possibility that this piece of cloth may not *in itself* be necessarily suppressive of women. Women under patriarchy often claim to use the veil to protect themselves from violation by male lust and conservative religion has no quarrel with this use. So too, spiritual feminism can interpret the veil as protecting women's sexual *mana* from patriarchal violation. This interpretation of the veil is superficially similar to that of Moslem women who put on the veil to avoid sexual harrassment on the streets. Yet for spiritual feminists the veil is more than protection form the violatory gaze: it is also a temporary accessory for a rite of emergence; something akin to the piece of cloth conjurors place over a magical object that is about to turn into something else. In this, the veil is abundantly polysemic (yielding manifold meanings) and includes metapatriarchal meanings that subvert its other meanings. Veils give men power over women, but, as we will see, they can also take it away.

The veil has a multiplicity of contexts even in the patriarchal politics of religion. But in the context of spiritual feminism the veil gives women freedom to shape-shift; to change the boundaries of the female form, allowing women to be elusively there and not there at the same time.

85. See *Being and Nothingness*, pp. 578ff.
86. *Gossips, Gorgons and Crones*, p. 238.

The veil or cocoon of spun silk can be a symbol of ontological meta-morphosis and emergence. It can represent that intermediate stage when a woman uses the psychic energy she has stored as a metaphorical caterpillar to emerge from the chrysalis of her former persona and fly off like a butterfly into the light of liberated feminist consciousness.[87] (About two thirds of animal species are insects and the vast majority of these insects undergo metamorphosis: this would appear to be a highly successful evolutionary strategy.)

Clarissa Pinkola Estés is one writer who has reclaimed the sacrality of the veil for spiritual feminism. For her, a Jungian feminist, this symbol preserves the sanctity of the female psyche. The veil is about 'not giving one's mysterious nature away. It is about preserving the eros and *mysterium* of the wild nature.' Just as a veil or cloth placed over a bowl of dough allows the yeast to ferment and rise, so too the veil activates the transformative powers of the female psyche: 'To be behind the veil increases one's mystical insight. From behind the veil, all human beings look like mist beings, all events, all objects, are coloured as though in a dawn, or in a dream.'[88] Like the Ottonian numinous, a veiled woman is awesome, terrifying, infinitely attractive, but also powerfully repellent of any irreverent touch. Estés remembers being eight years old and seeing her cousin Éva preparing for her wedding:

> My uncle Sebestyén stopped in the doorway aghast, for Éva was no longer a mortal. She was a Goddess. Behind the veil her eyes seemed silvery, her hair starry somehow; her mouth looked like a red flower. She was of only herself, contained and powerful, and just out of reach in a right way.[89]

Or again, when the artist Barbara Otto was making a sculpture out of webs, she received a gift of some old silver veils from a friend. When she put one over her face and looked at herself in the mirror she had a vision of the web-like interconnectedness of all things in the universe in her own image.[90]

Above all, the veil *presupposes* the sacrality of the body beneath it. It is only the most sacred objects that require veiling to protect the naked eye, so to speak, from the charge or shock of their holiness. It is true of both the patriarchal God and the Goddess that none shall look upon

87. Cf. Daly, *Pure Lust*, pp. 333-35.
88. *Women Who Run with the Wolves*, pp. 441-42.
89. *Women Who Run with the Wolves*, p. 442.
90. Cited in Eller, *Living in the Lap of the Goddess*, p. 36.

them and live. The covering of ancient goddesses was not to preserve
their decency. Their veiling protected the worshippers from their power.
In Greek tradition, the Goddess names herself as 'no one has lifted my
veil', that is, she is not the sexual property of any man; her sexual
autonomy is a function of her sacral power. Hence when, in legend, a
young man removed the veil of the Goddess at the Egyptian temple of
Sais he was struck permanently dumb.[91] The Goddess's face was
particularly dreaded because to see her face was to see one's own death.
Or again, in Ovid's *Metamorphoses* a young hunter watched the goddess
Diana bathing in a pool. When she caught him looking at her she turned
him into a stag and his own hunting dogs tore him to pieces.[92] It is a
common feature of religions that death or sickness of one sort or
another is the punishment for violation of the sacred. Modernity's
desecratory unveiling of nature also seems to be causing sickness in
many species: a contemporary form of a very old phenomenon.

But in reverent hands the veil is at least a symbolic accessory of
female sacrality. Whether materially or metaphorically, feminist veils are
conceived and spun to protect women's autonomy and the processes of
metamorphosis and emergence. This is a crafted artifact that at once
signals and conceals female sacral process.

Crafting the Female Self

Yet female sacral self-expression can also be more outwardly
hierophanic—more defiant of the profaning gaze—than veiling alone
would suggest. The form of outward sacral self-expression that would
come most readily to mind is feminist ritual. But a great deal has already
been written on neo-pagan ritual in the feminist spirituality movement.
And although the meaning of the individual body cannot be separated
from its social meanings, this book focuses on the resacralization of
female bodies more than that of the social institutions they participate in.
So I would like to end this chapter with a discussion of the aesthetic
possibilities of inscribing sacral meanings on the surface of the female
body itself—inscriptions that can themselves constitute rituals of
emergence.

As I argued in my last chapter, patriarchal 'beauty' resists organic
change, particularly decay or swelling. The word 'hag' is derived from

91. See Campbell, *Primitive Mythology*, p. 63.
92. *Primitive Mythology*, p. 62.

the Greek word for a saint or holy person but has come to mean an old and ugly woman. Yet the dual meaning of 'hag' may suggest a meta-patriarchal association of holiness and change where cosmeticized, sanitized beauty will not be a prerequisite of feminist sacrality. Generally, only women from the age of about 14 to about 35 can count as 'beautiful'. Contemporary Western patriarchy most admires whatever reflects its own modernist geometries: flat stomachs, sharpened cheek-bones and hips, and high round breasts without any elongation of their form. Women who do not labour to obstruct the organic ageing process are women who, like decaying food, have 'gone off'; have 'let themselves go'. This latter phrase images ageing women as those who have lost or let go of their female identity as if it were a balloon on a string. Yet this image is also oddly precise in that patriarchy has made female self-identity inseparable from the power to attract. Women who have 'let themselves go' have been defeated by the engulfing chaos of female materiality/nature that wipes all historical identities off the face of the earth.

Patriarchal make-up restores a disappearing picture of youth—one that is being engulfed by nature as time. A 'fembot' (to use Daly's word) constantly re-creates herself by painful self-sacrifice: 'paralyzing potential E-motion into mummified, canned, glamorized de-formed forms'.[93] 'Glamour' once referred to a magic charm or spell. But here the female power of metamorphosis is a debased art. The glamorous *fascinans* of debased female numinosity merely attracts admiration and confirms a woman's dependence on the patriarchal approval that watches, names and therefore parodies female reproductivity by bringing women into (a derivatory) existence. Indeed, the phrase 'made up' is virtually synonymous with the construction of femininity. Patriarchal aesthetics have to a great extent been ideological articulations of male judgments on the world. Those judgments have been made possible by a gendered division of the world into looking subjects and looked-at objects. So although aesthetics have actually been politically determined, aesthetic judgments have been *presented* (falsely) as consensual, collective judgments. This artificial consensus has arrogated women's power of self-naming and self-making. For a woman to call *herself* beautiful is either vain or erroneous.

Under these conditions Jane Caputi rightly judges exhortations of women to be made up as demands to cover or deface the power of the

93. Daly, *Pure Lust*, p. 249.

Gorgon with a death mask: 'Naked female faces are taboo. They must be veiled or cosmeticized, for snools [those who sustain the sadostate] cannot look upon the Gorgon and live.'[94] The beauty industry is, then, another daily reenactment of Goddess erasure, most immediately by women who fear their own Gorgon aspect and the potential loss of privileges she implies.

In this context feminism is right to be critical of the energy many women expend in achieving merely 'feminine' beauty. This deflects female energies and persuades them to join a cult of illusion, artifice and air-brushed fakery, maintaining a subculture of manicurists and beauticians whose services are expensive but ultimately futile. Unlike organic female crafts, patriarchal beauty holds artifice and nature in painful tension. Not only is a woman made to fear her own natural physical maturity, the cosmeticization of femaleness captures and romanticizes nature, grooming and taming it for male consumption.[95] And it should not be forgotten that, with honourable exceptions, the profits of the cosmetics industry rely on experiments which have the effect, if not the direct intention, of torturing animals to test the safety of products for humans.

In their justifiable rejection of made-up beauty, many feminists, particularly in the 1970s and early 1980s, have found themselves in odd company. For religious puritanism also condemns make-up and self-decoration as women merely playing to a sexually incontinent male audience. In puritanism a woman's sexual virtue is marked by the absence of coloured paint on her face. She must keep her face as well-scrubbed as her floors. Of course reformist feminism does not have much else in common with puritanism other than its (differently motivated) dislike of blatantly feminine sexual display. But the distrust of self-decoration forgets other, older notions of make-up or body-paint. Self-decoration can celebrate sexual maturity; it can be a form of magical shape-shifting whose camouflage protects the body from harm and is a sign of integration with the landscape. And even though the feminist art of crafting the self is not dependent on such evidence, cosmetics have been found in the earliest of neolithic remains, and nearly all cultures seem to have smeared cosmetics on the body to magically protect, beautify and express its mood.

Through adornment the radical feminist body can become a theatre in

94. *Gossips, Gorgons and Crones*, p. 196.
95. See de Beauvoir, *The Second Sex*, pp. 190-91.

which to raise consciousness of primal powers. Batya Podos has described how feminist ritual theatre awakens these powers in both those enacting the rite and those in the audience: 'They oil their bodies, pound out rhythms on the ground, chant each other's names aloud. They paint their faces and bodies with magical symbols of power, reenact their battles, dip their hands in blood.'[96] Rosemary Sackner describes how a group of spiritual feminists ritually painted themselves with lipstick: 'reclaiming these oppressive, very sexualized feminine things and making them into war paint'.[97] Likewise, Naomi Wolf suggests that women can redefine beauty by enjoying theatrical, creative adornment fed by self-love rather than narcissism.[98] Or again, Kisma Stepanich gives detailed instructions on how women can adorn their bodies according to the stage of their menstrual cycle. She recommends painting a red spiral over the womb area during the period itself—the 'Waning Moon Phase'. Wearing sacred jewellery and 'power tools that are nonthreatening such as medicine bags, woman power shields' and leaving the hair loose are felt to be particularly expressive during the 'Dark Moon Phase'. And during the 'Full Moon Phase' she recommends painting the sign of Venus on the left breast over the heart; 'the inner thigh close to your cunt lips is also another great place, especially if you are planning a love session'.[99] For Stepanich, body art is explicitly hierophanic; as indeed it was in a different way for Hildegard of Bingen, whose nuns resisted criticism and wore jewelled crowns and elaborately embroidered robes in memory of God's clothing the first human beings in light.

Spiritual feminist adornment does not place women outside or above nature but seeks to reintegrate bodies into the rest of the environment of natural forms. When women become the subjects of their experiences of natural energy, their artistic observation of both the human form and those of animals, the wind, waves, hills and celestial bodies in motion are integrated into one free dynamic whole. Hence thealogical representations of naked women such as those of the artist Monica Sjöö and the photographer Cynthia MacAdams are integrated into a pre- or ahistorical reproductive natural environment where, for instance, the representation

96. 'Feeding the Feminist Psyche through Ritual Theatre', in Spretnak (ed.), *The Politics of Women's Spirituality*, p. 305.

97. Quoted in Eller, *Living in the Lap of the Goddess*, p. 103.

98. *The Beauty Myth*, pp. 290-91.

99. *Sister Moon Lodge: The Power and Mystery of Menstruation* (St Paul, MN: Llewellyn, 1992), pp. 100-101.

of the vulva is entirely non-pornographic and may repeat natural or sculpted neolithic forms.[100]

For a woman to draw herself onto her face or body has ancient connections to the religious experience of a holy thing as a concentration or re-presentation of divine power. Make-up and self-adornment need not mask what Estés calls 'the wild woman'; they can be a graphic display of transformatory power that enables a woman to *make up* new and alternative stories about herself, and ritually/theatrically enact (rather than conceal) the changes in her own body. As van der Leeuw puts it, 'pictorial representation is re-presentation, and thus reproduction of power, fixation, and thus concentration of power'. So the more sacred art is stylized and departs from customary aesthetic norms, the more impressive is its evocation of the holy.[101] A self-created, self-mediated woman under patriarchy is 'strange news from another star': she manifests the holy as unfamiliar beauty. And although thealogy celebrates the youthful (but not necessarily physically perfect) Virgin and Mother aspects of the Goddess, it also locates female sacral power and wisdom in aesthetically transgressive physical forms: the Crone's wrathful, wrinkled, lined face; the body stretched and softened by childbirth.

In doing so, thealogy renews a tendency already present in the 'primitive' elements of patriarchal religion in which the sacred or numinous is radically discontinuous with all human value. Rudolf Otto, and those influenced by his work, contested the nineteenth-century identification of moral and aesthetic values with the holy: 'the Holy eludes every human attempt to take it captive and tame it'.[102] Where the Enlightenment had exalted the holiness of beauty, Otto wanted to claim the beauty of holiness, and in doing so, transform the meaning of beauty. For Otto, the numinous evokes a reaction of awed fascination; it is compelling but terrifying. It is barbaric. As such, the numinous is closely identified with what is shocking, fearsome or dreadful. In *The Idea of the Holy* part of Otto wants to say that it is a mark of an undeveloped or 'primitive' religious sensibility to be drawn to the *tremendum*—the awfulness—of the holy as represented in art. Yet he is

100. See, for example, the reproductions of Sjöö's paintings throughout Sjöö and Mor, *The Great Cosmic Mother*; C. MacAdams, *Rising Goddess* (New York: Morgan & Morgan, 1983); and the reproductions and commentary throughout Orenstein, *The Reflowering of the Goddess*.

101. *Sacred and Profane Beauty*, pp. 162, 167.

102. J. Pelikan, *Human Culture and the Holy* (London: SCM Press, 1959), p. 161.

at his most eloquent in his concession that 'the 'fearful' and horrible, and even at times the revolting and the loathsome, arouse the most 'genuine feelings of authentic religious awe'. He elaborates by observing that

[t]he hard, stern and somewhat grim pictures of the Madonna in ancient Byzantine art attract the worship of many Catholics more than the tender charm of the Madonnas of Raphael… Durga, the 'Great Mother' of Bengal, whose worship can appear steeped in an atmosphere of profoundest devotional awe, is represented in the orthodox tradition with the visage of a fiend.[103]

Otto and Jaroslav Pelikan, both in some ways loyal sons of Calvinism, insist that the divine is 'neither lovely nor congenial'.[104] So too, Eliade argues that the 'forbidding countenance' sets people apart: 'this setting-apart sometimes has positive effects; it does not merely isolate, it elevates. Thus ugliness and deformities, while marking out those who possess them, at the same time make them sacred.'[105] Without wanting to say that the 'face' of the Goddess is *only* that of the gargoyle or the Gorgon, thealogy is suspicious of any sanctification of prettiness as a signifier of sexual virtue. Not only is pious religious sentimentalization of the young female body a kind of religious ageism, it is also an attempt to defuse the more politically threatening aspect of female sacrality where this is visually manifest as an angry face or as any other kind of deviance from smallness and fairness.

The 'Black Madonna' of Chartres and other European Marian shrines exemplifies the otherness of female sacral power in ways that plaster statues of Mary painted in pale blue, white and pink cannot. Roger Horrocks, a psychotherapist from a Protestant tradition, describes his first experience of the Black Madonnas on a holiday travelling through France in the early 1980s:

They were totally unlike the rather saccharine, simpering statues of Mary I had seen in England. Here was no symbol of feminine submissiveness and piety. They were stripped down, archaic, fierce. In places like Chartres and Rocamadour, I was also amazed at the popular devotion to the Black Virgin. There was a tremendous aura round the statue—people knelt, prayed, contemplated. A deep silence pervaded everything, and filled my own mind.[106]

103. *The Idea of the Holy*, p. 62.
104. Pelikan, *Human Culture and the Holy*, p. 141.
105. *Patterns in Comparative Religion*, p. 18.
106. 'The Divine Woman in Christianity', in A. Pirani (ed.), *The Absent Mother:*

Without racist intentions Horrocks names the ferocity and rebellion of the Black Virgin's blackness as the sexual/sacral power that has been repressed in the White Virgins. Of course, any comparison of Black and White Madonnas veers into racist stereotyping and Horrocks's discussion cannot help relying to some degree on the implicitly racist archetypes of holiness/purity (whiteness) and profanity/impurity (blackness). But he only assumes these archetypes *in order* to reverse them. Just as radical feminist spirituality has done, Horrocks's remarks demonstrate that the holiest or most powerful images of divinity are also the least anodyne; the least ordinarily human. It should be remembered that the xoanons of the Greek gods and goddesses were rough wooden forms—barely images at all—and it was these rather than their statues in human form that made most impact on the people.[107] Similarly, the fetish is often merely a stone or rock filled with power. In the non-Abrahamic 'primitive' traditions sacral forms have tended to be fetishes in animal or monstrous forms, but rarely literal duplications of the human form.[108] It is this intuition that monstrous otherness is a visual metaphor of the holy that also lies behind the spiritual feminist reclamation of the Gorgon as perhaps the most powerful face of the female sacred.

In recognizing authentic beauty as an otherness which awakens what Otto calls the *sensus numinis*, the feminist reclamation and crafting of the female body recognizes values that are divine rather than literally man-made. This alone rebuts biblical religion's central defamation of paganism as a crude idolatry. The central justification of biblical religion's struggle against paganism has been its apparent worship of natural forms. Feminist self-creation is, however, a prophetic act which shows that the biblical invective against pagan idolatry has been misdirected. Idolatry is more properly patriarchy's worship of its own cultural values. These are so absolute as to anticipate and block the otherness of the holy.

Something of this sense of idolatry already lies behind the Jewish, Protestant and Islamic prohibition of pictorial images of the divine. In Deuteronomy 4.12 the Jews are reminded that God spoke to them from the midst of a fire; they heard a voice and words, but saw no body. Both iconoclasm and iconomachy may originally spring from the same

Restoring the Goddess to Judaism and Christianity (London: Mandala, 1991), p. 100.
   107. See van der Leeuw, *Sacred and Profane Beauty*, p. 163.
   108. *Sacred and Profane Beauty*, p. 169.

sense of reverence for beautiful natural forms as media of the holy. But patriarchal iconoclasm suppresses that reverence in case it mistakes the substance of a thing for its essence or meaning, which is not 'there', but set apart from it in transcendence. Deuteronomy 4.16-20 recognizes the evocative power of nature to evoke the *sensus numinis* in that it is compelled to prohibit any worship of earthly or celestial beauty. In aniconic religions the immanent beauty of natural forms is held to distract attention and love from their transcendent creator. In these religions God's apparent preference for words rather than images devalues whatever does not speak a particular human language—whether they be animals or those humans who are not endowed with the status of intelligent speaking subjects. Iconoclasts preserve God's honour by severing him from natural forms. These are left degraded and available for exploitation. By contrast, in thealogy and other immanentist schemes, the divine is made tangible and, treated with reverence, divine things are not profaned by their 'touchability'.

Although ethnologists have shown how body-paint, masks, tattoos and special clothes are used as signs of self-differentiation marking a rite of passage or separation into a different way of life,[109] I have not intended to recommend that women undergo sacrificial pain to initiate themselves into feminism. The intention is not to turn a woman into a puppet or to make her sweat under grease-paint. It is more that artistic styling of the face and form with make-up, fabric, jewellery, tattoos and so forth are explications and celebrations of the mystery of difference. In this sense, body art may be hierophanic in bringing the meaning of the immanence of the divine within the individual to the surface or skin— the boundary between private self and world.

Here feminist body art precisely resists the domestication and standardization of female beauty. As Dion Fortune's heroine Lilith le Fay says in the novel *Moon Magic*, her lavish decoration of her body gives her the shape-shifting power to be seen as she wishes to be seen.[110] And in Sara Maitland's novel *Virgin Territory* Judy, a lesbian feminist, has a tiny blue leopard with white spots tattooed onto her lower back. Judy argues that the ability to ornament and change one's body is a mark of humanity. She says that if 'the way we see our bodies is socially

109. See Van Gennep, *Rites of Passage*, pp. 72-74.
110. Quoted in B. Koltuv, *The Book of Lilith* (York Beach, ME: Nicolas-Hays, 1986), p. 54. See pp. 54-59 for the entire description of Lilith le Fay's crafting of her self.

constructed with society, then I do want to control my own construction. It makes me feel good.'[111] So too for Judy Grahn, the 'memory' that women 'once took complete charge of the body, shaping it, carving it and decorating it', is a memory of a rite of emergence. The word 'cosmetic' refers, like the word 'cosmos', to the ordering of the world. Grahn interprets cosmetics as another way of ordering or fashioning the world and as therefore bearing traces of cosmogonic meaning.[112]

Like most feminisms, spiritual feminism argues that femaleness has been patriarchally constructed as femininity. But in its thealogical aesthetics it urges women to take control of those powers of construction *as* powers of transformation. Feminist witchcraft, for example, believes that a woman has the capacity to direct the energies of her consciousness to 'bend and shape' reality (as the Old English word *wicca* suggests).[113] As witch, a woman can reclaim and create the beauty of her own self as a representation of the Goddess. Just as a witch might visualize a pot, a piece of embroidery or a tapestry and realize it through her sacral skills into a useful, visible form, so too she can craft her body in ways that celebrate her organic processes of change, for 'in witchcraft the first thing a woman learns to visualize and bring to birth in the world is herself'.[114]

---

111. London: Virago, 1993, p. 145.
112. *Blood, Bread and Roses*, pp. 72-73.
113. Goldenberg, *Changing of the Gods*, pp. 96-97.
114. *Changing of the Gods*, p. 97.

Chapter 4

A FEMINIST MENSTRUAL TABOO

I am covered in snail trails, red snakes.
I am heavy breasted
My milk spills from my nipples.
My tears spill from my eyes.
I am covered in thin milk, thick tears.

Lines from a feminist shamanic drama[1]

In the 1970s pioneering feminist research into the relation of menstruation and religion set the foundations for feminist spirituality's celebration of the menstrual cycle.[2] In 1971 Elizabeth Gould Davis and in 1975 Evelyn Reed, argued that it was women in matrifocal societies who invented the menstrual taboo to withdraw from the male sexual demand. Perhaps most influential of all was Penelope Shuttle and Peter Redgrove's Jungian *The Wise Wound* (1978) which interpreted menstruation as that 'shadow' element of female sexual energy which cannot be confined to reproduction and which is suppressed at the cost of women's mental and physical health. At around the same time Paula Weideger's *Female Cycles*[3] made an important contribution to the argument that menstrual taboos are designed to contain and defuse male fears of menstruating women. She also claimed that our culture has not removed the menstrual taboo but has made it invisible and therefore even more psychologically damaging for women, who suffer increased menstrual pain and depression as a result. Since the late 1970s a large number of spiritual feminist texts, such as Miranda Gray's *Red Moon: Understanding and*

1.   Quoted in Amberston, *Blessings of the Blood*, p. 161.
2.   For a summary of religious feminist studies on this topic see M. Raphael, 'Menstruation and Laws of Purity', in L. Isherwood and D. McEwan (eds.), *Themes in Christian Feminist Theology* (Sheffield: Sheffield Academic Press, forthcoming).
3.   London: The Women's Press, 1978.

Using the Gifts of the Menstrual Cycle,[4] have been written to show women how to use menstrual energy for self-therapeutic purposes. In 1990, Alison Joseph edited a well-balanced collection of comparative essays: *Through the Devil's Gateway: Women, Religion and Taboo*, which reclaimed the meanings of menstruation from within a number of religious feminist perspectives. The most detailed spiritual feminist study of the sacrality of menstrual blood is Judy Grahn's *Blood, Bread and Roses* (1993) which does nothing less than 'menstrualize' human culture. Grahn claims that distinctively human consciousness of the world came into focus through the first ritual separation practices of menstruation: a cyclic division of reality which holds chaos and order in balance. Grahn reads the menstrual taboo as a reminder that female sacral power is a great responsibility—one which is 'phenomenal but also enslaving'—of 'having to hold everything in place, of having the power to destroy everything with a gaze, a touch, or a breath of air whistling through the lips'.[5]

Before taking this discussion further, it should of course be noted that not all radical feminists are religious, and secular radical feminists have not accepted any 'superstitious' or magical account of menstrual blood, especially as these are bound to have continuities with patriarchal superstitions. In *Issues of Blood* Sophie Laws rejects the idea that menstrual blood can still be given a supernatural interpretation in our modern Western society. She argues that female blood is unmentionable not because of religious purity laws but because politically motivated 'etiquette' can mark out social and gender hierarchies devised by patriarchy for secular power. Using Mary Douglas's suggestion in *Purity and Danger* that the profane is matter which is 'out of place', and therefore a threat to the cosmic/social order, Laws regards pollution beliefs as statements posed by those who have the power to define what is and is not out of place.[6] As such, menstruation does not need to be celebrated as any sort of 'cosmic truth'. Mystical power does not, she says, reside in women's reproductive organs, or indeed male fears of them.[7]

However, I am not sure that menstruation and religion can be so simply disengaged. Eliade was, I think, right to insist that the behaviour and values of those who no longer interpret their experience in religious

4.   Shaftesbury: Element, 1994.
5.   *Blood, Bread and Roses*, p. 268.
6.   *Issues of Blood*, p. 36.
7.   *Issues of Blood*, p. 5.

terms, who live a 'desacralized existence in a desacralized world', still reveal the 'fragments of a forgotten or degraded religion'.[8] But whether or not the menstrual taboo has survived or disappeared in modernity is not at issue here. This chapter—and to some extent, the next—will focus instead on the way in which the *concept* of a menstrual taboo can be used to sacralize women's contemporary experience of menstruation and related phenomena.

Patriarchal Menstrual Taboos

To some degree, all spiritual feminist menstrual discourse relies, like Grahn's, on anthropological scholarship. But it does not simply replicate it. Ethnological studies are always subordinated to a spiritual feminist hermeneutic. This filters evidence for customs that could be revived today, and for evidence to present to the secular West that there *are* cultures which acknowledge the numinous power in female reproductivity, even if that acknowledgment can take oppressive forms.[9] All spiritual feminist attempts to resacralize menstruation must negotiate the menstrual taboo—if only to subvert and reinvent it.

Most spiritual feminists are aware that the menstrual taboo is very widespread but not universal, and that the taboo exists in various forms and to various degrees in different cultures. (To that extent, their theories of menstrual taboo are anthropologically literate.) But, apart from their gynocentrism, spiritual feminist studies of menstruation differ from those of secular anthropology in at least three important respects.

8.   *Rites and Symbols*, p. 127.
9.   Spiritual feminist texts are usually aware of the diversity of scholarly opinion on the nature and universality of the menstrual taboo. There is no space here to enter the debate over how ethnographers should read the taboo, but see, for example, Douglas, *Purity and Danger*, pp. 166-69. She observes that menstrual taboos exist where men feel threatened by the danger emanating from women, but in groups where women are completely and violently subjugated (such as the Walbiri of Central Australia) the menstrual taboo is absent. See also A. Gottlieb and T. Buckley, 'A Critical Appraisal of Theories of Menstrual Symbolism', in *idem* (eds.), *Blood Magic: The Anthropology of Menstruation* (Berkeley: University of California Press, 1988). They argue that traditional Western associations of menstruation and evil are commonly projected into ethnographic research. They read 'primitive' cultures as ascribing a potent and prestigious creativity to menstruating women. Separation of menstruating women in these cases conserves potency, rather than protecting society from female evil.

The first is a psychotherapeutic conviction that a woman can achieve a psychically and physically altered experience of her own menstruation within the spiritual feminist paradigm shift. Secondly, there is often a quasi-historical belief that in ancient matrifocal societies menstrual blood was revered rather than degraded. This belief sometimes informs positive readings of menstrual seclusion as a period of rest (a holy/holiday) and perhaps a period to enjoy the collective spiritual power of menstrual sorority with a group of other women. And thirdly, there is a political critique (often subtextual) of the ways in which patriarchy has sacralized male bloodshed in rites of circumcision and subincision, or more commonly, war. To these, spiritual feminists counterpose the life-giving sacrality of female biological bloodshed.

So the spiritual feminist menstrual discourse draws upon anthropology to suit its own purposes. It wants to say that whatever the religio-political intention of the taboo, the taboo is at least an acknowledgment that menstrual blood carries a potent charge. Because the Polynesian word *tapua*, from which 'taboo' is derived, means not only 'sacred' but also 'menstruation', menstruality seems to be integrated into the very meaning of the sacred. As Grahn points out, 'taboo is the emphatic use of imperatives, yes or no, you must or you must not'.[10] It suits the patriarchal purpose to place a negative taboo on menstrual blood since this justifies the close supervision of women that will protect its own social order. Barbaric forms of menstrual seclusion, such as putting women in hammocks and smoking them over the fire, making them lie on beds of nettles for days on end, not letting them lie down, touch their own bodies and so forth,[11] have reinforced that sense that a given community must take precautions against femaleness.

Clearly, menstrual blood has elicited a variety of responses in the world religions. And although indifference has rarely been one of them, menstrual blood has not always evoked disgust. Paula Gunn Allen cites the pre-conquest Native American belief that menstrual blood was the water of life: 'The blood of woman was in and of itself infused with the power of Supreme Mind, and so women were held in awe and

10. *Blood, Bread and Roses*, p. 5.
11. These and other seclusion practices are described by Grahn in *Blood, Bread and Roses* (see esp. pp. 4, 40). She follows Briffault's interpretation of menstrual taboo and suggests that what appears to us to be the torture of women was and is self-imposed by women in the consciousness of their own 'blood power' for the preservation of creation from chaos.

respect.'[12] And traditions such as those of the Celts, early Taoists, Tantrists, Native Americans and ancient Egyptians seem to have honoured menstrual blood and the female numinous in general.[13] But these belief systems are not necessarily femininist in themselves and they are not the traditions most spiritual feminists grew up with or within which they would have experienced menarche. As most late twentieth-century spiritual feminist reconstructions of menstrual power will have been determined to a lesser or greater degree by the attitudes to menstruation these women grew up with, we need to look first at the Western religious context of menstrual experience.

There seems little doubt that the biblical traditions have and continue to find menstrual blood repellent to the holy. It is quite outside or profane to the mechanisms of atonement and salvation which are lubricated by male sacrificial blood. Of course Judaism and Christianity are not Gnostic and the general connection between the fertile wife and God—the source of new life—has been acknowledged and often honoured, particularly in the Jewish traditions of the biblical matriarchs who, even in the 'barrenness' of great age, could become miraculously fertile if that served God's purpose. Even so, God and Moses struck their covenental agreement high on a rocky mountaintop: as far away from women and the fertile valleys and flood plains as God could arrange. Women were not allowed near the mountain which was sealed off by a sacred charge, and the men who were allowed to congregate nearby had not been near a woman for three days (Exod. 19.15). Here, as Judith Plaskow notes, 'the Otherness of women finds its way into the very centre of Jewish experience'.[14] That covenant is still sealed by the blood of each Jewish male baby's circumcision: a blood without the taint of periodicity.

Although they are the actual precondition of any sacred history, the cyclic processes of ovulation and menstruation are not and never have been a dynamic of the biblical scheme of creation, covenant, incarnation, death, judgment, resurrection and new creation. Traditional Christian doctrines of atonement have structural and metaphorical continuities

12. 'Grandmother of the Sun: The Power of Woman in Native America', in Plaskow and Christ (eds.), *Weaving the Visions*, p. 27.

13. L. Owen, 'The Sabbath of Women', *Resurgence* 150 (1992), p. 39.

14. *Standing Again at Sinai: Judaism from a Feminist Perspective* (New York: HarperCollins, 1990), p. 25. Cf. later, but conceptually continuous, warnings such as that of the Jewish legal commentary *Va Yikra* 18.19: 'Do not come close to a woman who is ritually impure because of menstruation'.

with cultic Judaism. At its most transcendental, the Christian scheme requires the sacrifice and sprinkling of male blood: that from Christ's whipped and crucified body, and afterwards in the Eucharistic chalice. Christ's body is rewarded for its blood-loss by being taken into a sphere of deathlessness (or heaven) to sit at God's right hand. Women's blood lacks salvific interest and is left on the earth. And although Protestants and feminist theologians may no longer have the stomach for sacrificial violence, Christian doctrine traditionally concentrates all the redemptive power of male blood in the voluntary death of the circumcised man, Jesus—the man-lamb without the blemish of sin. Through his blood the law of Moses was brought to a close and a new covenant set in place.[15] Of course the Jewish and Christian calenders are not without cyclicity: Christmas and Easter, Rosh Hashannah, Pesach and Yom Kippur are also periodic (though annual rather than monthly) beginnings and ends. But here the cycle is regulated by God's male disembodied will and fuelled by male human and animal sacrificial blood whose flow has not been tainted by menstrual blood.

Orthodox Judaism remains the clearest contemporary example of the Western menstrual taboo. In accordance with such texts as Leviticus 15.19-24; 18.19 and 20.18, Jewish law requires men and women to abstain not just from sex but from all direct contact when the woman is *niddah* (unclean or impure)—about 150 days every year.[16] Since the Jerusalem Temple was destroyed in 70 CE the category of ritual pollution does not, strictly speaking, have any practical application, yet during the Talmudic period the period of *niddah* was extended from five to twelve days. The menstruant is the only person who is still subject to the full laws of ritual purity, and the provision of a *mikvah* (ritual bath) for a Jewish community takes priority over building a synagogue or buying a Torah scroll.

Contemporary Orthodox Judaism and some of its semi-feminist apologists argue that these injunctions are concerned less with women's

---

15. L. Archer, '"In Thy Blood Live": Gender and Ritual in the Judaeo-Christian Tradition', in Joseph (ed.), *Through the Devil's Gateway*, p. 41. Archer's article, and Ruether's which precedes it in the same volume ('Women's Body and Blood: The Sacred and the Impure'), are important contributions to any discussion of the Western gendering of blood.

16. See Abramov, *The Secret of Jewish Femininity*, esp. ch. 7, 'Keeping a Distance'. The laws of 'family purity' are still observed in Orthodox communities, but are not observed in Reform or Liberal communities.

'uncleanness' than with preserving what is known as 'family purity': holy, ethical relations between men and women.[17] However, whether menstrual blood defiles the Temple, the synagogue, the family home or a marriage, and whether that defilement is adjudicated by a rabbi or an ancient Israelite priest, seems to me to be a rather minor distinction. In fact, to render menstrual blood a contaminant of not only the sacrificial apparatus of the Temple, but also the home, family and community is to generalize and widen a woman's bad influence. The domestication of female purity and impurity may therefore have just as systemic a political effect as it would have done as a primarily cultic impurity. There is an early example of this in the book of Job: Eliphaz the Temanite's speculations on how a 'clean' or righteous man can come from the uncleanness of a woman (Job 14.1, 4; 15.14) seem to make moral impurity a function of the female physiology.[18] This derogates women's bodies as much or perhaps to a greater degree than when that impurity is notionally confined to its effect on a cultic institution.

Likewise, Protestantism's anti-cultic concept of holiness as moral perfection makes menstrual women into symbols of sexual and moral defilement or evil rather than impediments to ritual purity. However, the distinction between moral and cultic purity is a false one: moral purity is a precondition of cultic purity. A priest cannot approach the holy in a state of moral sin; he must do more than simply wash his hands. In any case, the effects of cultic and moral ideas of pollution are both systemic and ultimately condition the perceived ontological status of women. For women, there is little to choose between these two closely related moral and cultic concepts of holiness.

Although menstrual practices can be read in a number of ways, even by religious feminists themselves, there are, nonetheless, worldwide associations of menstrual blood with dirt, putrefaction and death. Arapesh women, for example, 'give birth in an area "reserved for excretion, menstrual huts, and foraging pigs"'.[19] (It is no coincidence that 'Zoroastrian demonology has made of the fly a *female* demon, the

17. See B. Greenberg, 'Female Sexuality and Bodily Functions in the Jewish Tradition', in J. Becher (ed.), *Women, Religion and Sexuality: Studies on the Impact of Religious Teachings on Women* (Geneva: WCC Publications, 1990), pp. 27, 29.

18. See further N. Noddings, *Women and Evil* (Berkeley: University of California Press, 1989), pp. 35-58.

19. Cited in Rich, *Of Woman Born*, p. 163.

Nasu, embodying impurity, putrefaction and decay'.[20]) In the West, Aristotle's 'observations' in *On Dreams* and Pliny's *Natural History* depicted menstruation as a monstrous flux and bequeathed Christendom a catalogue of menstrual superstitions. The presence of a menstruant could wither crops, contaminate food, sour milk, dry up milk in udders and breasts, kill bees, stain new mirrors with indelible red marks, rust and blunt metal, make men impotent, and extinguish fires (which were difficult to make). Robert Briffault found examples of beliefs persisting into early twentieth-century rural Europe that menstruants turned wine to vinegar, boiling sugar to a black mess, and butter rancid.[21] Some of these superstitions have persisted into the late twentieth century. Recently, when a student of mine took a job in a local engineering factory, the other workers told her that menstruating women should not touch the iron parts because that would make the metal rust.[22] In India rural Brahmins still advise against hearing a menstruant's voice. The menstruant should not go near seeds or young plants and she should keep away from 'auspicious' events such as weddings in case her presence brings disaster.[23] Although strict menstrual seclusion is no longer widespread in India, vestiges still remain such as the widespread prohibition against a menstruating woman cooking food.[24] Again, fear of disaster can justify a variety of menstrual seclusions to protect patriarchal communities whose stability and prosperity is guaranteed by male supernatural power.

Broadly speaking, in the world's religions menstrual blood is a defiling negative energy because it represents death. Where menstrual blood is absent and the vulva is 'clean' and its discharge is clear or white there is still the possibility of new life. But when the vulva has a copious red discharge it seems to symbolize danger to the masculine supernatural order in that female supernatural energies will not, that month, have been

20. Seligmann, *Magic, Supernaturalism and Religion*, p. 19. (Italics mine.)

21. Cited in Grahn, *Blood, Bread and Roses*, pp. 102-103. See also ch. 5, 'The Moon Cycle', in E. Harding, *Women's Mysteries, Ancient and Modern: A Psychological Interpretation of the Feminine Principle as Portrayed in Myth, Story and Dreams* (New York: Harper & Row, 1976).

22. With thanks to Kim Prosser for this information.

23. Cited by V. Narayanan, 'Hindu Perceptions of Auspiciousness and Sexuality', in Becher (ed.), *Women, Religion and Sexuality*, p. 87.

24. Narayanan, 'Hindu Perceptions', p. 87. See also S.G. Gombrich, 'Divine Mother or Cosmic Destroyer: The Paradox at the Heart of the Ritual Life of Hindu Women', in Joseph (ed.), *Through the Devil's Gateway*, pp. 54-56.

exhausted by providing the community with a child. The menstruant might instead use these energies to mutate the living forms around her. The superstition of the 'evil eye' may originally have been identical with the glance of a menstruant harming crops, food and babies. The veil, beaded headbands, and the downcast gaze so characteristic of women in male-dominated cultures may, then, originate in menstrual taboo.[25]

Significantly, lists of witches' and menstruants' *maleficium* were once almost identical.[26] Witchcraft was demonized as a 'menstrual' anti-religion in that the witch's sacrality was a contaminant. It mediated a variety of social and natural disasters for which women could be blamed. Demonized, the witch was, in every sense, an abortionist. Here the Eucharistic blood of the mass was an antidote to female menstrual sacrality. And this was not only true of Christendom. The Talmud observes that 'if a menstruous woman passes between two men at the beginning of her period her menses will slay one of them'. If she is at the end of her menses, when presumably the evil energy is nearly spent (but may still cause death), the blood will 'cause strife between them'.[27] And nor has this superstitious fear of female power disappeared. Robert Bly, the leader of the New Age men's movement, warns men in his packed seminars to beware of 'the force-field of women'.[28]

The dualism of patriarchal salvific systems can, however, compensate femininity for the negativity of menstrual blood in ascribing purity to the other main female sacral fluid, breast-milk; so much so that in Job 10.10 breast-milk is another metaphor for God's 'female' creative craft. Not only has God fashioned, potted and knitted Job together, he has also poured him out like milk, and curdled him like cheese. Milk-blood is generative and belongs most obviously to what patriarchy would allow as feminine sacrality. Here the female body transforms 'raw' ingested food into 'cooked' food that has been distilled by 'alchemical' processes and turned into breast-milk for a baby. Milk may have been made from female blood, but that blood has made a new life that can now grow *outside* the female body and therefore become subject to patriarchal control. Breast-milk is also morally virtuous because a mother has sacrificially weakened herself by giving her blood to make milk that will,

25. Grahn, *Blood, Bread and Roses*, pp. 87-88.
26. P. Shuttle and P. Redgrove, *The Wise Wound: Menstruation and Everywoman* (London: HarperCollins, 1994), pp. 209-10.
27. Greenberg, 'Female Sexuality in the Jewish Tradition', p. 27.
28. Cited in Faludi, *Backlash*, p. 345.

in turn, make the weak baby strong. It is a 'safe' issue from the female body because the mother drains her supernatural energies in the process. Moreover, her breasts belong to her upper body at some distance from her vulva and can therefore purify her blood. (Hence the asexuality of the lactating Madonna in Christian iconography.)

In the late twentieth century, even when a woman's breast-feeding in public often causes embarrassment to the mother and those around her, breast-milk still symbolizes the moral purity of female nurture. And it is because patriarchy associates breast-milk with female virtue that quite secularized Western women can suffer feelings of quasi-moral guilt or failure if they choose not to breast-feed, if breast-feeding becomes too painful to continue, if the baby is not growing sufficiently on breast-milk alone, or if they fail to find it a fulfilling experience.[29] And even breast-milk can, symbolically, cause the stunted growth associated with the menstrual effect. Excessive female love of male children—a failure to 'wean' them from the mother's breast/love is dangerous in that—like menstrual blood—it can soften men or make them (notionally) impotent or 'queer'. Just as contact with menstrual blood can stunt plants, too much 'milk' can also stop men growing up into patriarchal modes of non-relation.

Both menstrual blood and breast-milk share the instability and unpredictability of all fluid organic substances. Symbolically, this blood can turn into fresh milk or sour into poison. The unpredictability of the female reproductive system, which can either 'waste' its food by clotting it into menstrual blood or use it by clotting it into milk, casts its 'shadow' even onto milk. As the opposite of poison, white breast-milk (life) is held in a dualistic tension with black or purple poison (death). Poison is another fluid associated with women. Menstrual blood is just one of the female fluids that feature in the mythology of poisonous compounds and the poison packets that witches hide in houses to bring death on their inhabitants.[30] Witches or herbalists know how to procure and brew poison from plants, cooks can slip it into their dishes, 'female' serpents inject venom into their victims, and the 'obstructed' or retained 'wise blood' in the veins of menopausal women can turn to magical poison—one of the principal reasons why, until the end of the seventeenth century, old women were suspected of witchcraft on those

29. See, for example, A. Phillips and J. Rakusen (eds.), *Our Bodies Ourselves: A Health Book by and for Women* (Harmondsworth: Penguin, 1979), pp. 458-59.

30. See Grahn, *Blood, Bread and Roses*, p. 130.

grounds alone.[31] In Hindu popular mythology an evil woman either has no milk, or like Putana has poison in her breasts.[32] In the reverse of the mother–child relation, demon goddesses like Kali drink blood—that is, become strong on the blood of the innocent.[33]

Yet spiritual feminism refuses to dualize the body and its fluids into zones of purity/impurity, poisonous/nourishing, life/death. When the words which open this chapter are chanted during a feminist shamanic drama (defying Sartre's notorious disgust of female sliminess) they describe a woman who, covered in sweat, blood and mucus, has just given birth. Here, blood and milk are no longer dichotomized but have become one *unified* religious experience.

Of course, as Sophie Laws points out, in a predominantly secular society menstrual blood is no longer, in any direct sense, feared as dangerous.[34] People usually find it distasteful to some degree but it is not treated as if it had, say, the properties of plutonium.[35] Nonetheless, there is evidence that young girls are acutely self-conscious about menstruation and hide all evidence of it.[36] Menstrual blood is treated as a basically excretory substance that needs hygienic disposal. Menstrual odour and staining on clothes remain shameful and our peculiarly phallogocentric culture advertises the absorbency of sanitary towels with blue ink instead of red.

Yet even if secularism no longer fears that a menstruating woman is harbouring dangerous powers, Jews, Catholics, Protestants (to a lesser extent), Hindus and Moslems would still regard a woman's menstrual blood as polluting their sacred space in a way that a man's blood would not. It is a function of female sexuality and therefore connected to the source of sin and disorder. Many such communities are becoming more conservative or fundamentalist. And where one of the first purposes of fundamentalist religion is to restore 'family values' to counter liberal

31. Walker, *The Crone*, p. 49.

32. W. O'Flaherty, *Women, Androgynes and Other Mythical Beasts* (Chicago: University of Chicago Press, 1980), p. 54.

33. *Women, Androgynes and Other Mythical Beasts*, pp. 41, 42.

34. *Issues of Blood*, p. 37.

35. Plutonium is a substance so dangerous to reproductivity that it should be properly taboo. See R. Bertell, *No Immediate Danger: Prognosis for a Radioactive Earth* (London: The Women's Press, 1985).

36. See S. Prendergast, 'Girls' Experience of Menstruation in Schools', in L. Holly (ed.), *Girls and Sexuality: Teaching and Learning* (Milton Keynes: Open University Press, 1989).

modernity's emancipation of women, menstrual taboos will be more widely and strictly applied, not less.

Spiritual Feminism and the Ambiguity of Menstrual Effects

Menstrual blood is an ambiguous substance in marking the end of one possibility of life and signalling the beginning of a fresh possibility of life. It is a boundary substance: at once a closure and an opening of possibility. As Judy Grahn puts it, 'for some peoples, the menstruant had what might be considered divine powers; she could cause flood or famine; she could make the sun vanish or the sky fall'.[37] So it is hardly surprising that a given religious system would have an ambivalent attitude towards any bearer of that kind and degree of supernatural power. This capacity to effect dramatic change—to accelerate decomposition—informs superstitious beliefs that menstrual blood can avert or cause harm, depending on who controls it and in what context it is being used. For example, in one tribe, that destructive power could be exploited to the collective advantage. A menstruating girl would be made to run naked around a field infested with caterpillars. She was required to turn the force of her destructive power against the insects, so protecting the crops from harm.[38]

Any sort of menstrual taboo puts the blood into the category of sacred/profane things and both of the poles in this category have power. For spiritual feminism it is when the sacred is in the wrong (patriarchal) hands that it will harm its violators, and when it is in the right (feminist) hands that it will make things flourish. Spiritual feminism identifies the sacred with nature's processes of organic change and these sustain life by the constant transmutation of forms. In this vitalist scheme sacred things can harm whatever is harming nature; whatever threatens its own balance. It is the wrong sort of contact with the transforming energy of the sacred that is fatal to the desecrator.[39] It is when a sacred thing is *desecrated* that it will decompose substances. Spiritual feminism partially affirms the negative taboo by saying that in patriarchal hands menstrual blood is indeed destructive because patriarchy has 'misread' or misused its power—and that of the whole of nature. So when patriarchy violates

37. *Blood, Bread and Roses*, p. 129.
38. Harding, *Women's Mysteries*, p. 62.
39. See R. Caillois, *Man and the Sacred* (Illinois: Free Press of Glencoe, 1959), p. 23.

nature by economic exploitation it will, and is now beginning to, suffer the consequences. It is this ambiguity of the effects of menstrual sacrality that spiritual feminism has adapted to its own ethical struggle against patriarchal desecrations of women and nature.

Menstrual taboos point to a potency whose meaning is best contextually derived, for something is tabooed or 'forbidden' when it is *sacer*: either sacred or accursed. The judgment of a thing as sacred or accursed is dependent on the political dynamics of a given religious context. Consequently, where, for whatever reasons, menstruation is deemed a positive charge that makes things flourish, menstruants will be honoured. Conversely, as we have seen, where female sexual blood has a negative charge both the substance and the menstruant have been demonized in superstitions as profaning or causing the objects they touch to deteriorate and decompose.

Yet spiritual feminism honours precisely the reactive quality of menstrual blood that patriarchy fears. In spiritual feminism it is also a catalyst of organic change in other substances. But that change can be a metaphor for divine activity as the dynamic of life; of organic and social change. Where these are outside patriarchal control they are patriarchally named as deterioration and disorder. Yet Kisma Stepanich can speak of menstrual blood as 'the elixir of life; the fluid of the spirit'.[40] Indeed, in the magical worldview of feminist witchcraft that reactive quality of female sacrality is celebrated and turned to women's religio-political advantage. The old account of menstruation's supernatural power is accepted, but only in so far as it can protect women and the environment by decaying and incapacitating patriarchal power. For example, there is a widespread superstition that sexual contact with menstrual blood makes a man impotent and unsuccessful in war. In the spiritual feminist reconstruction of this taboo, menstrual blood will make living things flourish, but will make the death-dealing 'phallic' power of the patriarchal state wither away. In this, menstruation has become the biological ally of radical ecofeminism, witchcraft and all those who seek a secure environment. Luisa Francia, for example, describes menstrual blood as 'protective magic and strong energy. Use it to protect your daughter or your doorway against unwelcome visitors'.[41]

A positive, pro-woman, pro-ecological menstrual taboo does, then, have a place in spiritual feminism. Taboos are protective of the sacred;

40. *Sister Moon Lodge*, p. 5.
41. *Dragontime*, p. 57.

they are not, in themselves, a licence for barbarism. In its resacralization of nature a feminist concept of the sacred would, in a sense, make all things sacramental; but only up to a point. In terms of the immanence of the divine in creation, it is true that all things, *as created*, are sacred. But creation has, as a matter of historical fact, been *de*sacralized and, as deforestation and 'development' continue, the world is more disfigured by profane human projects with every day that passes. Merlin Stone refers to the Goddess as the 'cosmic female energy force [that] fuels and refuels us in our struggle against all human oppression and planetary destruction'.[42] So a total sacramentalism in which all things are an expression of the sacred is the ideal, but not yet the historical reality. If the sacred is to empower the present eco-political struggle, that struggle must presuppose that the sacred—as the divine immanent in nature— has been and is being polluted in a number of ways.

Consequently, ritual purification remains an important element within neo-pagan feminism, though not in any sense as a puritanical purging of personal (sexual) sin. Before a witch casts a circle she will use salt, water, or some other purifying agent which symbolically removes obstructions to power. Here purification is a ritual that 'releases our passage into the place beyond time'.[43] This liminal state is typically a time of danger and the moment of transformation or crossing over from one state to another can be positive or negative depending on the degree to which impure elements have been cast away.

Spiritual feminism's resacralization of the body would not make sense without a concomitant sense of the impurity of the social, environmental and spiritual effects of patriarchal politics. For Mary Daly, it is 'phallocracy' which is a 'polluting' or 'poisoning' cosmic evil. She reverses the history of women as pollutants. Purification for women from phallocracy takes the form of a psychic journey into a different space: a womanspace which will 'release the Spring of be-ing'. To name oneself as a 'hag' (Old English for a witch) is to begin to assume the power of 'mind-washing', which is

> the right rite, the suitable ceremony of the one who has been named
> 'unclean'. She dispossesses her Self of the 'purifiers' who muddy her

42. 'The Three Faces of Goddess Spirituality', in Spretnak (ed.), *The Politics of Women's Spirituality*, p. 66.

43. S. Jayran, 'Circlework: Darklight Philosophy in Practice'. Paper presented at the conference 'Paganism in Contemporary Britain', University of Newcastle upon Tyne, 1994.

mind, who try to master her mind... This cleansing/depolluting of the
Self by the Self is essential to Gyn/Ecology.[44]

Part of the process of spiritual feminist cleansing (I refuse to hand over
that 'female' word to genocidal fascists) is, for Daly, to become
elemental; to realign one's being with the forces of nature: 'For we are
rooted, as are animals and trees, winds and seas, in the Earth's
substance. Our origins are in her elements.'[45] Again, the reversal is clear.
Once the source of women's uncleanness was their closeness to the
'blind' forces of nature. But now spiritual feminists are proposing that,
at this time of ecological crisis, 'femaleness' is a category of generative
being that is resistant to pollution and the modern counter-forces that
are alienating humanity from nature. In that sense, and at this time,
femaleness is the primary medium of divine regenerative energy. In this
new politics of the sacred, menstrual blood is invested with qualities that
make it an *agent of purification* from patriarchal pollution. And like all
sacred things, menstrual blood is dangerous or 'off limits' to all that
would misname or abuse it, in this case contemporary capitalism, whose
hubris sets it in direct, deicidal, opposition to divine immanence. So
spiritual feminists *do still* use elements of the pure/impure distinction for
what they consider to be its original purpose, namely as a means of
conserving the creative power of the earth. If patriarchal science and
economics violate that taboo, they will be exposed to the destructive
effects of those violations in the ecological retribution of the Goddess.[46]

Thealogians are unanimous that the Goddess is inherently re-creative
and healing, but when she is poisoned and therefore obstructed in her
recreative self-expression she is driven to extraordinary destructions. If
nature produces plague, disease and disastrous weather this is not
because the Goddess is as vengeful as the God of the Hebrew Bible can
be when he is jealous of his honour. Natural disasters are occuring
because Gaia's sacred balance has been overturned by greed and must
be righted again. The spiritual feminist reconstruction of menstrual
sacrality must, then, be understood in the broader context of the taboo-
breaking patriarchal 'matricide'.

In its turn, menstrual power—as a sign of cosmic/lunar rhythm and

44. *Gyn/Ecology*, p. 339.
45. *Pure Lust*, p. 4.
46. See M. Raphael, '"Cover Not Our Blood with Thy Silence": Sadism,
Eschatological Justice and Female Images of the Divine', *Feminist Theology* 8
(1995), pp. 87-93 for a critique of thealogy's ecological resolution of evil.

balance—can serve a conserving purpose in restraining patriarchy from its worst violatory excesses: poisoning, burning, deforesting and mining the body of the Goddess. B.E.S. (*sic*), a witch and political activist, rejects the ego-ridden confrontations that occur between some male green activists and the police. She has a vision of menstruation as an alternative form of political agency:

> Imagine a logging road in the bush, bulldozers at the ready when, along with the regular protesters, thirty or fifty women arrive in bloodied skirts, their faces painted with Moon Blood, wailing and chanting and tying their Blood cloths on the old trees as an act of love and protection... This would be a very powerful act.[47]

Here menstruation has been turned into an *ethical effect* in the form of environmental conservation.

In sum, it is not that spiritual feminists deny that menstruation can represent death as the absence of conception. (They are not reviving an ancient view of female parthenogenetic reproduction which claims that foetuses are simply made from clotted menstrual blood.) Clearly, menstrual blood is not straightforwardly generative. Indeed, spiritual feminism does not disavow the patriarchal fear of menstrual blood as a kind of transmutatory fall-out, nor has its 'radioactive' quality disappeared. But the reconstructed taboo only intends danger, of a non-violent sort, to the unjust patriarchal status quo, not to any living forms. Menstrual blood is still 'other' but it is now *respected* as an agent of archaic, cosmic change that, like all sacred things, requires extreme care in handling. In this, menstruality is neither good nor bad; like death and life these two aspects are ecologically interrelated.

47. In Amberston, *Blessings of the Blood*, p. 63.

Chapter 5

The Menstrual Other

[Woman] is unclean in her sex...she is
Created to be a defilement and a temptation

A snake with breasts like a female
A succubus, a flying vagina

So that the singing of God
The secret of God
The name winged in the hues of the rainbow
Is withheld from her

Alicia Ostriker[1]

Menstrual Chaos

We have seen that in the patriarchal mythography of women, men are told to keep away from menstruants because they make things decay, cloud, decompose or otherwise go bad. The widespread superstition that if 'bad' menstrual blood is allowed to fuse with 'good' semen women will give birth to monsters is on the same pseudo-logical trajectory. When, for example, Vishnu had intercourse with the menstruous Goddess Earth the issue was a litter of monsters that nearly destroyed the world. The Zoroastrians believed that intercourse with a menstruant would result in the woman giving birth to demons and the man being forced to swallow filth eternally in hell.[2] Or again, in the seventeenth century we find a tract entitled *Miracle which happened in the city of Geneva in this year of 1609. About a woman who gave birth to a calf, because of disdain for the power of God and of milady Saint Marguerite. Women soiled by blood will bear monsters: Ezra, chap. 5.*[3] It is not hard to

---

1. 'Green Age', in Ostriker, *Feminist Revision and the Bible*, p. 18.
2. Walker, *Woman's Encyclopedia of Myths and Secrets*, pp. 641-42.
3. O. Niccoli, '"Menstruum Quasi Monstruum": Monstrous Births and

imagine how women must have felt giving birth to severely handicapped children in cultures which believed that the shape of the body that came out of a woman's body at birth was an index of her moral virtue. Again, this cruel superstition reflects a view of menstrual blood as an agent of disorder. It skews and jumbles nature by mixing the impurity (the death of a potential life) with purity (provision for a potential life). These superstitions persisted into the nineteenth century, when it was believed that a baby born of a woman who was menstruating at conception would possess occult powers. This was particularly ominous for women because female occult power was treated by the medical establishment at the time as synonymous with insanity and a disordered libido. There are vestiges of this superstitious fear of mixing menstrual fluids with semen in contemporary Jewish law, in which a woman whose period comes on during sexual intercourse

> must tell her husband immediately since he may not separate from her in the normal manner. He must wait until his erection is relaxed and then separate from her. The Shulchan Aruch advises that if the male supports his weight upon his hands and feet, this will help relax an erection.[4]

This chapter will explore how spiritual feminists mix up life and death, purity and impurity after the manner of nature itself and so become monstrous themselves as embodied warnings to patriarchy of the great and dangerous wrong it is inflicting on nature. They also become monstrous on patriarchy's terms as well. For to mix up the processes of life and death is to introduce moral and physical deformity or confusion into patriarchy's/God's social order. Where paganism celebrates mixed, composite forms as harmony, unity or wholeness, biblical religion abominates the confusion of forms and types.[5] It is not that spiritual feminism advocates the incestuous and bestial mixing forbidden in Leviticus, but rather insists that there are ontological continuities between all living things within the shared web of life.

But in the patriarchal imagination a monster—usually a hybrid beast

Menstrual Taboo in the Sixteenth Century', in E. Muir and G. Ruggiero (eds.), *Sex and Gender in Historical Perspective* (Baltimore: Johns Hopkins University Press, 1990), p. 18. On p. 20 of this essay Niccoli rightly concludes that such medical-theological hypotheses were symptomatic of a view of women's genital functions as 'the source of impurity and corruption'.

4.   Rabbi M. Morgan, *A Guide to the Laws of Niddah* (New York: Moshe Morgan, 1983), p. 47.

5.   See, for example, Lev. 18.

of human and animal parts—hypostasizes its own fear of disorder and its punishment. The word 'monster' comes from the Latin *monere* 'to warn' and *monstrare* 'to show'. God punishes promiscuity (the word means 'mixed') with the symbolic warning of a monstrous birth. In seventeenth-century Britain, for example, monstrous births were classified by preachers with floods and comets as signs sent by God to warn the people of the need to repent before they were judged.[6] The monster is, here, a lesson about the chaotic results of an improper reproductive act that disfigures or blurs God's cosmological separations of light and dark, sky and water, and the classification of creatures according to habitat and type.

As a symbol of the chaos of otherness introduced into an ordered system, the female monster motif resurfaces throughout the patriarchal mythography of women. In the Bible, Eve is the first woman to disorder creation and her punishment is to be cursed with difficult reproductivity and subordination to her husband (Gen. 3.16). The Western association of female sexuality and rational/moral unreliability is not, however, exclusively biblical. Aristotle's *Politics* has been almost as instrumental in casting women as ontologically anomalous, misbegotten or defective males, who, like slaves, were excluded from the full operation of a rational soul which alone could subdue irrationality. At conception a woman provided human matter or flesh through her menstrual blood, but men provided the rational soul through his clean seminal fluid.[7] The birth of a female child indicated that her mother's uterus was defective.

Like most others in the history of philosophy, Aristotle did not believe that women were entirely without virtue. But in both ancient and modern Western thought the female state has been depicted as at best morally deficient, and at worst innately deviant. Because women are 'natural' and therefore non-rational their bodies change and decay in ways that (ideologically) men's do not. Men are conserved by the stabilizing influence of reason which orders and pacifies nature. In fact, at least until late middle age, the physical degeneration of bourgeois men is still a mark of their intellectual distinction and ability.

6.   K. Thomas, *Religion and the Decline of Magic* (Harmondsworth: Penguin, 1991), p. 104.

7.   The AIDS virus has meant that 'safe sex' requires the woman to be protected from the semen with a rubber sheath. The 'clean' signification of male sexual fluid and the sense that it is only maleness that needs to be protected from femaleness may therefore diminish in the future.

In the logocentric Western tradition, especially as mediated by modernity, holiness and rationality have been mutually informing. With few exceptions (the semi-Western Russian Orthodox 'holy fool' is one of them) ecstasy or lunacy have not been hierophanic in orthodox religion. The post-Reformation ideology of femininity demanded not exceptional or ecstatic holiness but sensibility, compassion, kindness and obedience to male headship as the *natural* duty of women. These feminine virtues were often the occasion of sentimental praise. But at the same time women's 'natural' impulsive affections and delicate sensibility excluded them *a priori* from moral agency which was properly dispassionate. The patriarchal construction of menstruation as an instability—a nervous and moral debility—has therefore ensured that women have a low religious status. Conversely, as we shall see, the post-patriarchal construction of menstruation as numinous discomposure can be precisely what qualifies women for high religious status.

An amalgamation of religious and Romantic doctrines of the complementarity of the sexes and Enlightenment liberal philosophy underpin this view of female instability. In the modern liberal theory of moral agency the capacities to adhere to abstract moral principle and to own private property are closely allied. Reason is principally attributed to the property-owning head of the household who is also biblically ordained to be male. If, in the same tradition, women are ontologically defined as obedient, maternal beings, dependent on the husbands who have taken their property on marriage, their autonomy as moral subjects is weakened, if not obviated altogether. This is all the more true since the whole rationalist tradition regards a disinclination to emotion and a detached obedience to principle (rather than to other men) as the first qualifications of virtue.

One of the most pronounced features of Western patriarchy—at least since Rousseau—has been its refusal to let women display moral judgment or evidence of intellectual development in public. The development of moral and intellectual judgment would lead women into spiritual corruption and physical degeneration. An immodest display of female intelligence would disorder society because, in this worldview, social order is built on the dual pillars of biological complementarity. Among others, Kant, Schopenhauer and Nietzsche taught that a woman attempting to emulate masculine moral agency, or use her reason to study Greek, mathematics or theology, would not only bring about social chaos, she would first be profaning or perverting her nature: she would become monstrous. (Or as Kant put it, she might as well have grown a beard.[8])

Again, we find the belief that women are prone to *degenerative* metamorphosis. If a woman had the capacity to be as intelligent as men (the sources are ambiguous on this), her intelligence could only be sanctified by its application to non-intellectual domestic issues in the right place: the home. Were her virtues displayed in the wrong place, her femininity would have ceased to complement masculinity and would therefore be profane. And as a woman's being was dependent on and supplementary to masculine being, the independent exercise of her intellect would precipitate a collapse. It would be a greater disordering of nature than her physiology could sustain.

Yet to refuse to attribute the full operation of reason and moral will to a woman is to attribute to her an ontological openness to evil influences that precludes not only the possibility of equal rights but also of true or normative sanctity. The mythography of women's lack of rational resistance to evil permeates the whole Western discourse of 'the problem of evil'. Of course these superstitious prejudices (especially in modern philosophers who considered themselves precisely enlightened from superstition) have not gone unchallenged. There is a broad feminist consensus that men have projected their cruelties and moral weaknesses onto women who are then cast as (covertly) wanton and vicious. The idea that women's bodies endanger men's spirits has been criticized in all feminist writing on the role of female sexuality in religion. The association of female sexuality and evil deflects attention from patriarchy's own responsibility for broken relationships. Ascribing evil and disorder to primal femaleness in the person of Eve allows patriarchy to avoid confronting the true origins of evil. Thus Daly:

> The myth [of Eve and the Fall] takes on cosmic proportions since the male's viewpoint is metamorphosed into God's viewpoint. It amounts to a cosmic false naming. It misnames the mystery of evil, casting it into the distorted mould of the myth of feminine evil.[9]

Some anthropologists have interpreted menstrual taboos as means of harnessing the dangerous power of menstruation and, by keeping it

---

8. See J. Grimshaw, *Feminist Philosophers: Women's Perspectives on Philosophical Traditions* (London: Harvester Wheatsheaf, 1986), pp. 43, 65.

9. *Beyond God the Father*, p. 47.

under control, putting that power to socially beneficent uses.[10] The construction of motherhood from the Reformation, and on into the nineteenth century when motherhood was presented to women as their best opportunity to cultivate feminine virtue, may have perpetuated that process of putting suppressed female *mana* to positive use. In the nineteenth-century ideology of femininity medical and evangelical discourses intersected in the construction of an ideal female type. The sexual energies of a virtuous Christian woman would be contained by marriage or chastity and manifest only in her good influence on her family and the immediate objects of her philanthropic concern. Her subordinated virtues would produce the domestic and national effect of social stability and resistance to vice. Christian motherhood and domesticity set an example of social stability and good order primarily through the instruction and socialization of children into Christian morality and faith.

By the mid-Victorian period any women who had been imperfectly domesticated could rapidly degenerate or 'Fall', especially if subject to the evil influence or contagion of other imperfectly domesticated women. Women who had not been sanctified by their domesticity were sluttish women who had not expended sufficient transformatory energy on ordering and cleansing household mess and dirt, or they were women who had fallen prey to the moral contagion of prostitution (in contemporary slang, another kind of 'slut'). The unclean 'other'—the sexually soiled prostitute of the streets—was the obverse side or antitype of the sanctified, chastely married 'angel in the house'. Her sexual energy was redeemed or rendered positive by her marital obedience and was the polar opposite of that of the promiscuous 'fallen' woman's negative sexual energy. This latter energy was unsanctified by marriage and definitively profane in being available for common use. The aptly named Henry Judge describes prostitution with the archetypal language of temptation, depicting independent female sexuality as a monstrous undulating snake (an image which recalls female sexual arousal). Prostitution is, he says, a 'great gilded snake, a cherub's face, the rest a reptile—that winds its sinuous length through the gay and crowded thoroughfares of London and other populous places, and stifles the youth and health of England in its embraces'.[11]

By the second half of the nineteenth century prostitution was

10. Sanday, *Female Power and Male Dominance*, p. 93.
11. *Our Fallen Sisters* (London: E. Marshall, 1874), p. 33.

perceived by the British government and the church as a threat to the nation's moral and physical health and holiness. The state formulated punitive legislation against prostitutes, most notably the Contagious Diseases Act, while religious bodies punished hardly more subtly and virtually incarcerated women in penitentiaries. (Other evangelicals, such as Josephine Butler and Ellice Hopkins, had kinder and better motives in 'rescuing' or 'befriending' prostitutes.) The associations within the 'National Purity Crusade', as it was sometimes known, included organizations with such names as the Snowdrop Band and the White Cross Army, reflecting the Victorian preoccupation with sacred hygiene. According to Ellice Hopkins, one of its best known rescue workers, prostitutes had been 'cursed'—cast out beyond the boundaries of order and health.[12] She urged the church to 'cease to look supinely on [women's] desecration' because 'this deadliest evil' obstructs 'the divine ideal of womanhood...the fountain of life, and love, and purity to the world'.[13] Hopkins (who was not without recognizably feminist convictions) urged respectable women to sacrifice themselves in 'holy warfare' for the nation's purity: 'There is but one thing that will quench it [prostitution]—life blood, and wherever that is given, God blesses. If you would save England...make sacrifices.'[14]

Feminine—as opposed to female—sexuality is exemplified in Coventry Patmore's famous poem 'The Angel in the House'. Here Patmore exalts in the childlike, prelapsarian innocence of a woman whose menstruation can hardly be imagined.[15] A sweetly childish wife guarantees domestic stability: she will not challenge male judgment. (However, feminine childishness disqualified women from moral or rational knowing and therefore left them vulnerable to medical suspicions that women were particularly subject to nervous disorder.) This nineteenth-century ideology of the biddable wife persists in twentieth-century Christian fundamentalism, especially in the United States. This was evident in the huge sales of Mirabel Morgan's book *The Total*

12. See E. Hopkins, *A Plea for the Wider Action of the Church of England in the Prevention of the Degradation of Women* (London: Hatchards, 1879), p. 8. For a similar sense of the desecration of women, see also anon., *The Perils of Girls and Young Women Away from Home* (London: Dyer Bros, 1884), p. 16.

13. *A Plea for the Wider Action of the Church of England*, p. iv.

14. *The Present Moral Crisis: An Appeal to Women* (London: Dyer Bros, 1886), p. 16. See also pp. 3, 6.

15. See F. Page (ed.), *The Poems of Coventry Patmore* (London: Oxford University Press, 1949), esp. pp. 195-205.

Woman,[16] which urged women to save their marriages by subordinating themselves entirely to their husbands' comfort and pleasure. Here again, female sexuality is childlike, feminine and submissive.

Of course nineteenth-century sexual rhetoric is notoriously difficult to read, and most feminist historians 'read' the crusade against vice as little more than an extension of the criminal justice system. Rescue work seemed to inculcate guilt and the middle-class feminine virtues of chastity, cleanliness and domesticity into working-class women who presumed to own and sell their own sexuality.[17] Given that the Victorian construction of female vice and virtue can be read in a number of different ways, it seems to me that spiritual feminism stands in a tradition of religious feminism that is still negotiating the nineteenth-century ideology of female sexuality as the source of a variety of social effects. For this ideology of femininity is not past history: late twentieth-century conservatism holds fast to this ideology in the face of profound socio-economic change.[18] Religious feminism is therefore forced to engage with a rhetoric that is continuous with that of the nineteenth century, and in the case of spiritual feminism, it subverts it by an idiosyncratic process of co-option. This is not to say that the same historical conditions of belief obtain for spiritual feminists as they did for Victorian evangelicals, but that spiritual feminism has inherited a discourse on female sexuality—still explicit in right-wing evangelicalism—to which it is now adding its own ironical postscript.

Female Sensibility as Madness

The myth of feminine evil comes in large part from the association of menstruality and material, moral and mental instability. And it is in redefining the meaning of menstruality that spiritual feminism, has, I think, made one of the most significant contributions to the redistribution of moral responsibility for evil. But that redefinition involves accepting a very old association of female sexual physiology and mental

16. Old Tappan, NJ: Fleming Revell, 1973.

17. See J. Walkowitz, *Prostitution and Victorian Society* (Cambridge: Cambridge University Press, 1980), pp. 20-29; L. Mahood, *The Magdalenes: Prostitution in the Nineteenth Century* (London: Routledge, 1990), pp. 10, 158, 163.

18. R. Balmer, 'American Fundamentalism: The Ideal of Femininity', in J.S. Hawley (ed.), *Fundamentalism and Gender* (New York: Oxford University Press, 1994), p. 53.

health. To understand these negotiations with the tradition (negotiations secular feminists would not consider entering into) we must first turn back to the nineteenth-century distortion of the lunarity of menstruation into lunacy—the inability to make rational/moral judgments.

The recent history of Western constructions of femininity has largely consisted in ascribing a variety of spiritual sensitivities to women. They succumb more easily to temptation, they are more readily moved to pity, tears and ecstasy, they are physically weak, and in all senses, easily swayed. In 1821, for example, Richard Mant published a characteristically evangelical sermon, arguing that a woman's more 'exquisite' sensibilities and 'ardent' affections made her 'less solid in her judgement and therefore more liable to err'.[19] Like all evangelicals he felt that it was necessary to educate (or more precisely, 'instruct') women because although they were capable of virtue they were also 'constitutionally prone' to the 'misery and disgrace' of a surpassing 'depth and enormity of vice'.[20] The traditional evangelical Christian notion of female weakness-as-power is exemplified by John Angell James's 1853 work, *Female Piety*, in which he writes of 'womankind': 'were she utterly powerless, she could do nothing. Her influence, however, is a kind of passive power; it is the power that draws, rather than drives, and commands by obeying. Her gentleness makes her strong.'[21] Feminine sensibility is what makes a woman at once more caring *and* more *permeable* to evil influence than men. In the same work John Angell James remarks that a woman's 'heart is so made of tenderness, that she is ever in danger of being imposed upon by craft and falsehood'.[22]

Like evangelical Christians, nineteenth-century doctors were also deeply interested in feminine sensibility. Medical opinion often considered that higher education caused infertility and hysteria. Active sexual desire was also hysterical and could, according to Isaac Baker Brown and like-minded doctors, be curbed by clitoral excision.[23] Although there was

19. *The Female Character, A Sermon Preached in the Parish Church of St James, Westminster, 1821* (publisher unknown), p. 13.

20. *The Female Character*, p. 16.

21. Repr. in D. Johnson (ed.), *Women in English Religion 1700–1925* (Toronto: Edwin Mellen, 1983), p. 131.

22. *Female Peity*, p. 132.

23. See J.H. Murray, *Strong Minded Women and Other Lost Voices from Nineteenth-Century England* (Harmondsworth: Penguin, 1984), pp. 129-32; P. Jalland and J. Hooper, *Woman from Birth to Death: The Female Life Cycle in Britain 1830–1914* (Brighton: Harvester Press, 1986), pp. 250-65.

never very widespread approval for this mutilation, the assumption that a woman's sexual physiology could upset her mental balance was not generally challenged. It is notable that as late as 1874 Henry Maudsley, in his article 'Sex in Mind and Education', was using contemporary theories of the conservation of energy to argue that intellectual training would injure girls' brains and eventually lead to sterility and life-long invalidism. Because menstruation was an 'extraordinary expenditure of vital energy' it left 'little vitality to spare' for any other activity which might deprive the menstrual cycle of its necessary energy. So if the exercise of intellectual judgment led to the degeneration of reproductive power, intellectual women would not only become sterile, but unfeminine freaks. Though dressed as women, these creatures would actually be neither male nor female and—unable to reproduce—would be responsible for killing off the human race.[24]

Casting women as almost innately criminal was not only a clinical judgment. Nineteenth-century medicine also intersected with criminological theory. Committed by women, suicide and murder were also hysterical symptoms or 'menstrual psychoses'. As Patricia O'Brien has shown,

> the argument at its most extreme was that all menstruating, lactating, ovulating, pregnant, newly delivered, newly sexually initiated and menopausal women were prone to crime. Most women, therefore, could become criminally deviant during any portion of their adult lives.[25]

And even today, patriarchal apologists for female subordination use female reproductivity as proof that women are not to be socially and politically depended on. Menstruation and the 'failure' to become a mother are both still assumed to cause psychological disturbance.[26]

While spiritual feminism celebrates those female intellectual and sexual liberations that conservative ideologues deplore, it is important to recognize that in both conservative and spiritual feminist views the female reproductive system is a source and index of female mental health.

---

24. E. Showalter, *The Female Malady: Women, Madness and English Culture 1830–1980* (London: Virago, 1987), p. 125. See also P. Atkinson, 'Fitness, Feminism and Schooling', in S. Delamont and L. Duffin (eds.), *The Nineteenth-Century Woman: Her Cultural and Physical World* (London: Croom Helm, 1978), pp. 101-107.

25. *The Promise of Punishment: Prisons in Nineteenth-Century France* (Princeton: Princeton University Press, 1982), p. 68.

26. Neuer, *Man and Woman*, p. 39.

However, spiritual feminism is saying that women will be healthy/holy when their reproductivity is liberated from patriarchal control, but will suffer mental disturbances (such as premenstrual tension and depression) if it is not. By contrast, Victorian sexual ideologues were saying that women's rights would make women ill. The political effect of women's rights would be to take women's reproductivity out of the sanctifying influence of the church and patriarchal state. And to remove female reproductivity from these stabilizing influences would leave it prey to profanity or disorder. Nonetheless, the two worldviews are clearly connected even if one reverses the meanings of the other.

The ambiguous 'female' quality of permeability is crucially important to the spiritual feminist construction of female sacrality. For being permeable to other energies is a prerequisite for mediumship, in a general sense: the capacity to concentrate and diffuse sacred energy into one's own environment. The capacity to become hierophanic is a capacity to open the boundaries of personal identity temporarily in order to unite (as shamans do) divine and human energies in one body.

One of the precursors of spiritual feminist shamanic mediumship was the late nineteenth-century female medium. Mediumship was a largely female profession and one in which a woman could both earn her own living and, in her sensitivity to the spiritual realm, remain obedient to Victorian ideals of femininity as delicate and self-renouncing.[27] A.S. Byatt's novella 'The Conjugial Angel' depicts a medium, Sophy, who is almost destroyed by her profession. In a climactic trance she turns 'a terrible colour, ash and plum and lapis blue together, her lips moving numbly. She snorted, she sucked desperately for breath, as though her life was being sucked out of her.'[28] In this story the medium carried feminine permeability too far: her personal 'transparency' left her unable to withstand spiritual assaults on her identity and she was in danger of losing her Christian self-identity altogether in the multiple possessions of the trance state. 'Mediomania', as it was named by the Victorian medical profession (among them Henry Maudsley), became a psychiatric or hysterical illness. For a woman to regard herself as a medium of special occult power was tantamount to sexual and moral derangement.[29] It was as if some of the more extreme behaviours took feminine sensibility into the realm of self-parody or burlesque, and

27. See Owen, *The Darkened Room*, p. 9.
28. In *Angels and Insects* (London: Vantage, 1993), p. 284.
29. See Owen, *The Darkened Room*, ch. 6, 'Medicine, Mediumship and Mania'.

therefore into the realm of psychological malfunction. Mediumistic (bad) behaviour at seances often involved violent movement, blasphemous outbursts and sexual posturing; in short, it was little less than a 'ritualised violation of cultural norms'.[30]

Now at the end of the twentieth century feminine mental and physical frailty is no longer a qualification for mediating the sacred, even if spiritual feminist sacred madness has by no means disappeared.[31] Although spiritual feminists have not severed the old lunar connection between the cycles of the womb and psychic balance, the feminist medium or shaman is more likely to enjoy a healthy sexuality and mediate the outdoors spirits of the living earth than the indoors spirits of the dead.[32] The female shaman of the woods and the sweat lodge has replaced the domesticated mediumship of the parlour. Even so, the feminist shaman is no more normal in twentieth-century Western society than were her nineteenth-century predecessors. The ritual sublimation of her personality—while still in some senses 'feminine'—remains deviant, if only because modernity construes ecstasy as sub- or countercultural.[33] Ecstacy is unassimilable into the stately religious emotions that have been codified in the art and music of the established Western churches.

As Phyllis Chesler has shown, there is still a gendered asymmetry in the numbers of patients treated for mental illness in psychiatric hospitals and by psychotherapists. This is a statistic whose origins lie at least in part in the cultural representation of madness. Since the seventeenth century women have 'stood for' irrationality and derangement in inverse relation to the ordered rationality of men.[34] (Fashion design

30. Owen, *The Darkened Room*, p. 203.

31. See, for example, G.F. Orenstein, 'Reclaiming the Great Mother: A Feminist Journey to Madness and Back in Search of a Goddess Heritage', *Symposium* 36 (1982), pp. 45-70.

32. For a participant discussion of the reclamation of psychic power in pagan women's spirituality, see D. Stein, *Stroking the Python: Women's Psychic Lives* (St Paul, MN: Llewellyn, 1993), esp. chs. 7–12.

33. See I.M. Lewis, *Ecstatic Religion: An Anthropological Study of Spirit Possession and Shamanism* (London: Routledge, 1989). This comparative study examines why women are particularly attracted to religious ecstasy and spiritual possession in marginal cults—especially those which protest against male dominance and the official religions.

34. *Women and Madness* (Harmondsworth: Penguin, 1979), pp. 3-4. For a more recent study see J. Busfield, *Understanding Gender and Mental Disorder* (London: Macmillan, 1995).

seemed to reflect this. Most eighteenth- and nineteenth-century fashions sapped female energy by constraining or straight-jacketing them in hooked and boned under- and over- garments and, by the second half of the nineteenth century, confining bourgeois women—who were the class most likely to be 'strong-minded' women's rightists—to the padded cells of over-upholstered drawing rooms and parlours.)

At least since Thomas Szaz's article 'The Myth of Mental Illness' (1967) and his book *Ideology and Insanity* (1970), social scientists have suggested that the definition of mental illness is less a clinical judgment than an ideological judgment on a person's inability to function within a set of given social relationships.[35] Second-wave feminist theory has also tended to regard female madness not only as a form of heroic deviancy subverting male norms of sense and reason, but also as an inevitable and rational response to an insane social order that rationalizes itself by projecting its irrationalities onto femininity. In common with contemporary secular feminists (and, to some extent, R.D. Laing),[36] spiritual feminists also refuse to see 'mad' women simply as victims: patriarchy is an ultimately irrational, self-destructive system and perhaps it is more surprising if it does *not* drive a woman crazy.

But through its sacralization of menstrual power spiritual feminism diverges from other feminisms. It inhabits the same magical worldview that produced the suppression of menstrual power. It therefore has to liberate menstruality by accepting—at least in part—the old account of female being as tidal, lunar and periodic in character; an unpredictable flow that mixes, seeps and takes on the character and colours of the underground substances it flows through. Spiritual feminism sacralizes the 'madness' of clairvoyance, divination and premenstrual tension as periodic (lunar) hierophanic oracularity. This position would be familiar to those historians of religion who, like Rudolf Otto, note that in many cultures lunacy is a mark of holiness. In cultures where holiness has not been refined into moral superexcellence, the insane are not loathsome or disgusting, but are divined as seers possessed by an awesome numen.[37]

---

35. See H. Cowen, *The Human Nature Debate: Social Theory, Social Policy and the Caring Professions* (London: Pluto Press, 1994). p. 147.

36. Laing diagnosed irrational symptoms as a rational response to irrational social institutions—especially the family. Laing's later work claimed that schizophrenia was an authentic response to institutional degradation and familial control. For the context of this position, see Cowen, *The Human Nature Debate*, p. 149.

37. Otto, *The Idea of the Holy*, pp. 123-24; 133-34. Of course, historians of

In the light of the ancient association of madness and holiness, spiritual feminism is not willing simply to put aside the history of women's defamation and concede that female sacrality is, after all, identical with the (diminished) feminine sacrality idealized in the self-sacrificial evangelical mother. Nor is it willing to abstract women from the 'wild' realm of nature and transpose them into the 'rational', disenchanted realm of modern science. Instead, it subverts menstrual superstition by suggesting that menstrual otherness does indeed have ambiguous effects but these are precisely *because* it is sacred and should be respected as such. Ever since Rudolf Otto and other early twentieth-century historians of religion angered the Protestant theological establishment by characterizing the numinous as a religious excitement originating outside or beyond human ideas of moral value and therefore neither good nor bad in itself, a scholarly precedent has been set (were one needed) for the spiritual feminist claim that menstruation is also a manifestation of the numinous in female form.

Spiritual feminist reconstructions of menstrual/numinous otherness playfully subvert their patriarchal representation, while sharing the patriarchal understanding of menstruation as a metamorphic energy. Elisabeth Brooke exemplifies this practice:

> A young woman menstruating for the first time enters the world of women's magic, steps over the threshold of another world. When we menstruate, we dream, we are more creative, and if we are denied psychic space we go crazy. Doctors call this pre-menstrual tension, but witches know it is lunacy. Crawling about on all fours and howling like a wolf is a good menstrual antidote to masculine linear consciousness. Eating raw meat and stalking the streets with your Gorgon mask is better still. No mugger I know would take you on. It freezes the blood in their veins and turns them to dust.[38]

Menstrual Oracularity or Seeing Red

In Western culture premenstrual tension can take the form of depression, emotional volatility or mood-swings, insomnia, and bouts of hyperactivity alternating with lethargy and exhaustion. Premenstrual tension is

religion of Otto's generation regarded the uncanny, weird or daemonic as crude hierophanies from which the history of religion was evolving, and to which the civilized Christian West was now largely—though not entirely—immune.

38. *A Woman's Book of Shadows. Witchcraft: A Celebration* (London: The Women's Press, 1993), p. 65.

not normally associated with religious excitement. In fact our society has diffused its fear of the premenstrual temper by making the condition into something of a joke. Premenstrual tension is now a 'blanket' term that can dismiss unhappiness and anger as a hormonal debility. 'PMT', as it is known, may cause temporary familial or marital disturbance, but is hardly regarded as being of political consequence. Yet this negative disturbance of the patriarchal social equilibrium could be both a metaphor and an impetus to political agitation under different conditions. Premenstrual tension may indeed transform women into '*monsters* of behaviour compared to their normal selves'.[39] But this monstrous behaviour could be taken into a different field of meaning where 'monstrousness' would be a sign of the political and spiritual otherness of feminist being. As we shall see, irritability could mean something more than mere bad temper: a spiritual-political irritation inflaming the social body into change.

Again, the possibility of this reconstruction of premenstrual tension derives some of its meaning from reversing the logic of Victorian medicine. Doctors advised bourgeois women to withdraw from normal activities during menstruation in order to conserve their reproductive energies (and perhaps, as a subtext, to protect society from their *de*structive energies). Now in the late twentieth-century neither spiritual feminism nor patriarchal capitalism accepts that menstruation debilitates. Both want, for very different reasons, to represent women as especially energetic around the time of menstruation. Contemporary advertising depicts menstruating women as almost *hyper*active in their diving, water-skiing, dancing and socializing. The actress playing the menstruant is probably not menstruating and is often filmed wearing dazzlingly clean white shorts or a white swimming costume. Her menstruation is taken away from her; patriarchy protects her from it by making the pad and the blood invisible. This new ideology of menstruation keeps a woman sexually and economically available to men and to the workplace. There is no menstrual sabbath—imposed or chosen.

Spiritual feminism *also* wants to represent women as especially energetic at this time. Only here female menstrual energies are not put to secular purposes but to heightening spiritual awareness and to the rigours of creativity, introspection and perhaps self-imposed seclusion, alone or with other menstruating women. In this way, spiritual feminists can use menstruation as a sabbath to replenish their own divine/creative

39. Shuttle and Redgrove, *The Wise Wound*, p. 240. (Italics mine.)

energies. It is commonly believed that before artificial light interfered with the natural rhythms of light and darkness, women enjoyed sister-hood by menstruating synchronically and with the waxing and waning of the moon.[40] As a 'memory', this funds a vision of feminist commu-nity where energy is rhythmically regenerated and pooled through a menstrual sabbath as a source of cooperative social power.

So it is in and through the menstrual cycle that the sacral body gene-rates its energy for psychological and political change. It both reverses and fulfils the patriarchal fear that menstrual blood changes what it touches. Lara Owen, for example, notes how in recent years she has 'noticed extreme sexual energy around ovulation and menstruation. I feel myself particularly a priestess when I'm bleeding.'[41] She reverts to an indigenous belief or experience that menstruation is a time of power: 'if we could just get that, a lot of things would change—the work schedule, our attitudes towards women, sicknesses, more conscious birthing. Everything would change.'[42] Monica Sjöö and Barbara Mor have referred to menstruation as a 'gift (i.e., an advantage and a talent)'.[43] And Judy Grahn claims menstruation as the beginning of knowledge: a proto-scientific measurement of lunar time and astrological space, and in the ancient menstrual symbolism of the snake, a revelation of the divine knowledge of good and evil.[44] These epistemological claims for menstruation must be seen in the context of a religio-political shift in which women and nature have become speaking subjects. In patriarchal religions only the male God and human males speak. The sound of animals, weather and women's voices is precisely that: sound or background noise. It is not speech. Protestantism has not (other than in exceptional periods of sectarian revival) given women outlets for ecstatic utterance. Catholicism has at least allowed women a measure of partici-pation in the numinous through enclosed sisterhoods, but their devotions are usually quiet, well-ordered and contemplative. And in contemporary Western Judaism there is no place for female ecstatic speech.

But with the postmodern 'reenchantment' of nature and the green celebration of the native traditions, there has been a feminist revival of animism where, as Gloria Anzaldua writes, 'stones "speak" to

40. See, for example, Stein, *Stroking the Python*, p. 100.
41. *Her Blood is Gold*, p. 129.
42. *Her Blood is Gold*, p. 130.
43. *The Great Cosmic Mother*, p. 191.
44. *Blood, Bread and Roses*, p. 63.

Luisah Teish, a Santera, trees whisper their secrets to Chrystos, a Native American'. With language that seems to evoke the disturbances of awakening sexual energy, Anzaldua herself remembers

> listening to the voices of the wind as a child and understanding its messages. *Los espiritus* [the spirits] that ride the back of the south wind. I remember their exhalation blowing in through the slits in the door during those hot Texas afternoons. A gust of wind raising the linoleum under my feet, buffeting the house. Everything trembling.[45]

It is as if spiritual feminist animism is the source of countercultural, underground knowledges which no longer come from the urban intelligentsia but spring from nature herself and sometimes the speaking, oracular, womb.

As we have seen, the womb—both a biological organ in the centre of the female body and the unifying symbol of female sacrality—has traditionally constituted a psychiatric problem and a means of excluding women from public rational discourse. The (selective) spiritual feminist historiography of the ancient oracles evokes and promises a different but still 'hysterical' womb knowledge. The original oracle was a female medium through whom prophetic declarations were delivered to a reverent audience who had journeyed to consult her. As a contemporary reconstruction of female insight heightened by the phases of the menstrual cycle, the contemporary oracle represents a female capacity to give solicited, authoritative judgments—or simply a direct self-awareness—unavailable to normal rational thought. Where a contemporary woman's insights are critical of the established order, her prophecy bears some relation to the largely unwelcome, unsolicited tirades against injustice of the Jewish prophets of the eighth century BCE. The more political wing of the Goddess movement tends more towards political prophecy, and the more psychotherapeutic wing to the pagan oracle, but in practice the two forms of prophecy would be hard to distinguish.

Plato's theory of hysteria was that if blood stored in the womb (*hustera*) was not released, the womb would rise or wander and so affect the normal functioning of the mind. The spiritual feminist celebration of women's menstrual connection to the lunar phases recalls this ancient association of femaleness and motion or flux. Elisabeth Brooke quotes Plutarch in her evocation of lunar oracularity as an energy that 'has no

---

45. 'Entering into the Serpent', in Plaskow and Christ (eds.), *Weaving the Visions*, p. 84.

outlet anywhere on the earth nor any single seat, but roves everywhere'. Using Plutarch's words, Brooke invokes the oracular power of Sibyl who 'sang of the future as she was carried about on the face of the moon'.[46] According to Sjöö and Mor the Goddess-worshipping menstruant aligns herself with the moon and so becomes possessed by the lunar snake, 'a pythonic (oracular, menstrual) spirit', for which women were once burned as witches. For 'women's menstrual "mysteries of inspiration" become in war-god worshipping patriarchy, the "mysteries of resisted knowledge"—repression, madness'.[47] Spiritual feminists commonly experience heightened psychic sensitivity and vivid symbolic dreams during the premenstrual phase and may ask their spirit guides for specific dreams to relieve them of the psychic pressure.[48] 'Ana' reports to Diane Stein:

> During waxing moons prior to my flow (at the waxing moon between last quarter and dark) my experiences are heightened, I communicate in various ways to other places at these times. There is no dread, I seek these experiences. I was able to tell people where 'lost' things were, what illnesses they have and what would 'cure' it.[49]

Spiritual feminists can be quite well aware that traditions of the Delphic Pythia's or Python's hysterical frenzy are historically questionable. According to Naomi Ozaniec, the Pythia's possession (*mania* in Greek) has, in its Latin translation, been confused with *insania*.[50] So although there were propitious days to consult the oracle, her possession was probably not manifest as uncontrollable frenzy but as an inspired response to an enquiry. So too, the Pythia herself, as opposed to her priestesses, was not menstruous but post-menopausal.[51] And the sibyls (who were always female and upper class) may only have been mouthpieces for the male Apollo. Moroever, as an important ideological apparatus of the state (even to the point of appearing on Roman coins), the oracle could become a channel for propaganda. However, sibyls did occasionally protest against political hegemonies in the eastern Mediterranean, and above all, the idea of a great female oracle

46. *A Woman's Book of Shadows*, p. 67.

47. Sjöö and Mor, *The Great Cosmic Mother*, pp. 192, 193.

48. Stein, *Stroking the Python*, p. 101.

49. *Stroking the Python*, pp. 101-102.

50. *Daughter of the Goddess: The Sacred Priestess* (London: Aquarian, 1993), p. 277.

51. Stein, *Stroking the Python*, p. 291.

establishes a precedent for female pilgrimage and for female sacred space, knowledge and speech.

Yet contemporary spiritual feminism is also more democratic than ancient paganism and incarnates the Goddess in each woman so that the shrine at which the divinity is consulted is her own body. It is not, then, history alone which links the ancient oracles to Western feminists. It is the spiritual feminist's periodic mediumship or sacrality; her waxing and waning energies which correspond with the ancient Greek oracles' periods of preparation, mediation and recovery from the experience of divine possession.[52] The oracle retreated into a trance state with altered consciousness of reality, so becoming a figure of female authority and transcendent knowledge. Likewise, Judy Grahn describes her period in terms of a rite of initiation into knowledge. She endures each stage of the difficult monthly journey into the menstrual state: first dreams, then pain, self-seclusion, apathy and depression, hunger, and then pain again.

> When the completely gripping pains pass, I begin to feel joyfully renewed and childlike. I am tired and sleep, and awake with fresh insights and perspectives, often with exact solutions to problems of both work and social life puzzling me before my period started. Sometimes toward the end I am ecstatic, experiencing mundane reality as 'freshly washed'.[53]

Grahn says that because this female way of renewing energy and vision is not socially recognized she keeps it inside her as a secret power. The whole process she describes is an internalized journey to consult an oracle who is herself. Again, she describes how she 'menstrualized' her whole existence in order to maximize her creative inspiration for *Blood, Bread and Roses*: 'During the intensive last two and a half years of writing, I stayed in virtual seclusion, wore my hair long for 'flow', ate mostly red foods [and] drank red beer.'[54]

52. Ozaniec, *Daughter of the Goddess*, p. 274.
53. *Blood, Bread and Roses*, p. 42.
54. *Blood, Bread and Roses*, xxiii. It may be that this kind of conception of the female body as a psycho-cosmic theatre, a creative boundary between earthly and cosmic space, owes as much to Eastern Tantric philosophy as it does to Western religions. According to Ajit Mookerjee in *Kali: the Feminine Force* (Rochester, VT: Destiny, 1988), p. 193, the Tantric science of *Amritakala* locates the centres of female bodily energy according to the phases of the moon. In uniting the light and dark sides of the moon the female body becomes an image of wholeness. Sexual intercourse with a menstruant is one of Tantrism's most powerful rites. In *The Wise Wound* Shuttle and Redgrove note that in Tantric philosophy the menstruant is believed to be at the peak of her energies and in incarnating the Red Goddess or

In predominantly Protestant Britain and North America oracular, lunar, metamorphic women are by their own, and patriarchal definition, extra-ordinary. Because patriarchy makes claim to all rational truth Goddess feminists must separate or seclude themselves as 'mad' if they are to succeed in reconstituting primordial knowledge in their own bodies. The ontological transformation of new self-naming within at least notionally post-patriarchal spaces entails that a spiritual feminist loses her 'foreground' self and 'foreground' knowledge. In this liberative but unstable state of psycho-spiritual metamorphosis individuality has fluid boundaries. Any medium (whether electronic, textual or bodily) is, after all, an agency of transmission producing effects that originate in another source. This may lead to a kind of ecstasy (from the Greek *ekstasis*— standing outside or displacing the self) in which the medium at once concentrates and diffuses the sacred. Like the spiralling Goddess, she becomes a vortex drawing all reality into herself and dispersing it again without respect for form and privilege. Ecstasy is therefore both a theaphany and a loss of reason as defined by modernity. But spiritual feminism may not be quite as 'way out' in this respect as it might appear. For all spiritual relationism, including that of reformist Christian feminism, draws on the postmodern spiritual drive to reintegrate the private, rational, competitive, autonomous human (male) subject within the organic unitary pulse of life. All organicist theories have, therefore, a different epistemology: a non-rational holistic mystical knowing that is easily, but wrongly, confused with irrationality.

In sum, it is only when menstrual energies are repressed that they dissipate as depression, intolerance and irritation with immediate friends and family, rather than being creatively directed into transformatory energy and knowledge. This is of course the marginal, 'fringe' or alternative knowledge that is mythically analogous to that of the Fates (*fatum* is the Latin word for a prophetic oracle). The ancient and globally attested Fates or Weird Sisters were crones who inhabited the 'edge of the depths of woods, water, and the unconscious—places where things can turn into their opposites'.[55] It is from these magical margins that feminist Fates derive their oracular knowledge. Similarly, the spiritual feminist Gossip is not a woman who wastes her time bearing petty,

Dackini her blood is an intoxicant performing the muse-like function of wine or drugs in inspiring poetry and philosophical illumination (p. 193).

55. N. Hall, *The Moon and the Virgin: Reflections on the Archetypal Feminine* (New York: Harper & Row, 1980), p. 206.

malicious tales about others (men have also gossiped, nagged and scolded but these habits were never attributed to them as titles). In Caputi's feminist etymology, the Gossip is a god/*sib*: a person held in a matrix of relationships through whom divinity speaks. A Gossip's storytelling is prophetic, 'menstrual' 'word-magic' through which she can 'avert (or cause) disasters, and conjure Powers through the utterance of words'.[56]

Patriarchal Demonography and Feminist Monsters

With Caputi's remythologization of women, we come back to female monsters. Throughout her *Woman's Encyclopedia of Myths and Secrets* and *Dictionary of Symbols and Sacred Objects* Barbara Walker provides comparative particulars of female monsters and divinities (Lilith, the Gorgon, the Moirai, Sirens, the Banshee and so forth). I shall not, therefore, give an inventory of female monsters here, but shall instead reflect on the way that the monster—always a powerful metaphor in any ideological armoury—has been reclaimed by spiritual feminism, turning the patriarchal association of female menstruality with monstrous disorder on its head.

Under patriarchy the monstrous person is a warning, a portent and a punitive lesson. The otherness of those who are unassimilable into the social order is dramatically paraded before the rest, allowing the dominant 'normal' group to be distinguished from the other. The old European anti-Semitic superstition that Jews had cloven hooves inside their shoes and goats' horns under their hats is just one example of ideologically motivated therianthropism—the conjoining of animal and human bodies. As an imaginal and political device, feminist therianthropism breaks down and synthesizes patriarchy's oppositional principles. It challenges the patriarchal ontology of ideally pure essences by proposing an intermediate, evolving, changing woman; a woman who is mutating: turning her sacral power of metamorphosis on her own body. Half civilized and half wild, she is in the process of returning to naturalness. As such, monstrousness can be reclaimed by spiritual feminists as a sign of the feminist numinous.

Spiritual feminist monsters and mythical creatures are derived from the history of the Western demonography of women who, failing to conform to stereotypical feminine virtuousness, are demonized because they

56. *Gossips, Gorgons and Crones*, pp. 74, 78.

are unassimilable into masculine salvific institutions. Various psychological explanations have been given by spiritual feminists to account for this kind of demonization of women.[57] But unmarried women who manifest apparently autonomous unfeminine sexual desire and give birth outside the sanctity of the masculine institutions, and women who choose to abort an unwanted foetus, are particularly unassimilable.

The unmarried mother belongs to a specific historical demonography of women that has not disappeared in contemporary conservatism. Adrienne Rich traces punitive attitudes to unmarried mothers and illegitimate children to the male need to prove that he too has the elemental power of procreation.[58] But more than that, lacking the complement of a masculine partner, the unmarried mother lacks the ontological completion and therefore stability of being in a union blessed by the church or state. The man who impregnated her has 'disappeared'—or been 'devoured' by her unsanctioned desire.[59] She no longer has any visible cause of her impregnation. (During the witchcraze the church taught that witches had intercourse with demonic supernatural powers, reversing Mary's impregnation by the Holy Spirit.) Without the complementary rationality of a sanctified permanent union with a man, a woman and her children are perceived as vulnerable to a variety of social and genetic disorders.

There are over a million women in Britain bringing up children on their own and 90 per cent of all lone parents are women.[60] It may be

---

57. Generally speaking (and as I discussed in Chapter 1), spiritual feminism argues that men are jealous of female powers of conception. Birth would, by its miraculous nature, constitute a primary locus of numinous awe in human religious history. The male body cannot conceive and give birth to new life and may therefore denigrate or demonize women's capacity to do so out of a jealous desire to appropriate its power. Organizing religion around transcendental masculine sacrality, women's immanent reproductivity becomes largely unassimilable into masculine salvific mechanisms—especially if that reproductivity has not been defused by subordination to a husband.

58. *Of Woman Born*, p. 119.

59. The danger that 'man-eating' female desire castrates men is globally attested in primal and world religions in the patriarchal superstitions of the *vagina dentata* or 'toothed vagina'. There are voluminous records of this, especially where the history of religions intersects with psychology and anthropology. Barbara Walker summarizes these in the *Woman's Encyclopedia of Myths and Secrets*, pp. 1034-37.

60. Faludi, *Backlash*, p. 11. The million British female heads of household are not all unmarried; some are divorced or widowed.

that an unmarried mother is socially marginalized or made profane to society as a punishment for having used her womb outside the sanctification of marriage and for making herself the female head of household with children who will take her female name and property. Patriarchy warns her that she will have to face the practical consequences of her profanity: financial ruin, loneliness and isolation. All these are summarized in the symbol (and often the reality) of her being placed away from society on the top floor of a tower block with the lifts permanently out of order, so becoming the anti-type of the sacred princess kept locked in a tower by a wicked witch. Whether symbolically or actually, the single mother's offspring will also bear the quasi-genetic taint of her promiscuity or profanity (both words refer to the indiscriminate mixing or confusion of unsorted elements): criminal deviancy, lower educational achievement and emotional instability. Sometimes these threats come true, but this is largely because the state puts single mothers into a larger sub-class of people (often ethnically mixed) who cannot earn enough to be financially independent and consume in sufficient quantity to earn the protection of the state. And so, in substantial part, the state produces these effects itself.

The legal right to abortion is a significant element of spiritual feminist politics, as it is in the wider feminist movement, and one which is also demonized in fundamentalist circles. Traditionally, witchcraft and abortion have always been two closely associated evils and the witch and the abortionist incarnate the child-killing female monsters of global folklore. In the past, local midwives probably had knowledge of abortifacients, and equally, miscarriages were often imputed to witchcraft. During the witch-hunts the local midwife was always one of the first to be suspected of witchcraft. The legacy of this mixed association of women with the passage of life and death has been that even in countries where abortion is legal, women who have chosen (usually in great spiritual pain) to have an abortion can feel that they are committing a monstrous crime. Without in any way celebrating abortion, spiritual feminism integrates abortion into thealogy as a painful element of the divine ecology. Life and death meet in the Goddess. Nature can appear to be wasteful of its bounty, but apparent waste is endlessly recycled and so never dies. In this, spiritual feminism refuses the demonography of the independent operation of female reproductivity, while refusing to give patriarchy any reassurances about feminine nurture.

This understanding, which releases women who have chosen to have abortions from excessive moral guilt, is exemplified in Ginette Paris's book, *The Sacrament of Abortion*. Despite this book's disturbing title (which has suffered in translation), Paris presents a pagan feminist argument that women should have the *religious* choice of abortion as a sacrificial act that expresses the religious responsibility of a mother to her own self, to her womb, to the sacred connection between a mother and a child, and to the ecology around her. Abortion demands wise moral agency: it is a balancing act of loving responsibility, not a failure of maternal love. To force a woman to give birth is, for Paris, the real violation of the sacred; of the sanctity of life.[61] Our culture 'needs new rituals as well as laws to restore to abortion its sacred dimension, which is both terrible and necessary'.[62] These rituals would help to heal the grief of a lost opportunity for love. Yet it is unlikely that any patriarchal institution would provide for this spiritual need, since women's choice to abort has been presented as wickedly selfish. Paris argues that abortion is monstrous to patriarchy because femininity should be 'naturally' *self-sacrificing*; it does not sacrifice others. Even though human beings have always been sacrificed by men in wars, patriarchy cannot allow that 'a woman has the power to make a moral judgement that involves a choice of life or death. That power has been reserved for men.'[63]

The patriarchal demonography of women tells us more about male fears and fantasies than about women themselves. However, it may be that some female mythological monsters are not irredeemably misogynistic patriarchal constructions of femininity gone to the bad. If the ownership of myths is a dialectical political process then the meaning of female monsters can change. Patriarchy has itself altered and added to mythology to suit its own political purposes. Across two Testaments Mary's passive obedience to God rectifies Eve's wilful disobedience when in Luke 1.38 she surrenders her will to God's. That late twentieth-century religious women are making up myths *about themselves* and *for themselves* seems to be largely unprecedented in the history of religion and is a profoundly important phenomenon in itself. It is true that the mythological beings spiritual feminists invoke to express the relation between women and the divine are largely reclamations of male myths about women, but mythology's lack of clear authorial intention means

---

61. Dallas: Spring Publications, 1992, p. 62.
62. *The Sacrament of Abortion*, pp. 92-93.
63. *The Sacrament of Abortion*, p. 25.

that myths can be endlessly recycled to suggest multiple and diverse meanings.

In patriarchal, and now spiritual feminist, schemes two animals in particular have hypostasized menstrual/monstrous female power: the snake and the mare. To take the snake first, there is a feminist consensus that 'Christianity, Judaism, Islam and other Father God religions trace the evil of women to menstruation. Menstruation is the visible bloody sign of the serpent, of the Devil, in the female body.'[64] The Christian archetype of the good woman, Mary, is sometimes depicted crushing the serpent under her foot, an image which 'seems to call on Christian women to repudiate their earlier powers and demean their own physical functions'.[65]

All spiritual feminists reclaim the serpent as a female symbol of cosmogony, healing and prophetic wisdom which only became a symbol of evil during patriarchy's religio-political manoeuvres to discredit ancient goddess worship. And in contemporary spiritual feminism, the snake, 'the one creature that most looks like a disembodied vagina', flowing across the ground like blood snaking down a woman's leg, emerging from the waterhole of the womb, shedding its skin like the lunar shedding of the womb's menstruous lining, has become 'a kind of subconscious lingual/menstrual configuration'.[66] It is no surprise, then, that the spiritual feminist collective noun for a group of menstruating women is a 'dragon'—a giant snake. This reclamation of the mythical snake is informed by a Jungian conviction that where patriarchy drives female divinity underground (in all senses) that divinity is turned into a fearsome monster, lurking in the hellish recesses of pits and caves. But the monster is only dangerous or 'unbalanced' because it represents the schizoid splitting of female being/divinity into false polarities of black earthiness and bad temper, and milk-white nurture and good temper.[67] When these polarities are held in balance its power is not profane/ destructive but sacred/creative.

The widespread mythology of the mare is also a good example of how patriarchal demonography can be turned to the advantage of (Dalyesque) hagiography. Wendy O'Flaherty has shown that the English

---

64. Sjöö and Mor, *The Great Cosmic Mother*, p. 192.
65. Noddings, *Women and Evil*, p. 55. For her discussion of the snake symbol see pp. 53-55.
66. Grahn, *Blood, Bread and Roses*, pp. 58-59.
67. See Anzaldua, 'Entering into the Serpent', p. 77.

word for a female horse, 'mare', interconnects throughout Indo-European language and culture with *mer* and *mare* (French and Latin for sea), *mère* (French for mother), and *mor* (French and Latin for death).[68] The word 'nightmare' is associated with the witch's mare who flies through the night, but this word refers to the woman rather than the horse. The word 'nightmare' comes from the Old English 'hag' or *mare* (a night spirit) and refers to the visitation of a female monster who suffocates people in their beds at night. People look haggard or 'hag-rid' when they awake without energy from their night's rest, just as witches or hags ride mares and men to exhaustion through the night.[69]

The hybrid, snaky, 'nightmare' body of the Lilith unites these two monsters—the snake and the mare—in her own person. She is usually depicted with long flowing hair, a beautiful woman's face, a serpent's body and animal's feet. (Feminist neo-pagans use hybrid or composite symbols to show that the Goddess 'is a force, not solely human'.[70]) Lilith is, in fact, a paradigm case of the political dialectics of mythography at work. She therefore deserves closer attention. In the first-century Jewish legend recounted in the *Alphabet of Ben Sira*, Lilith was the first woman. She was created at the same time as Adam and was his first wife. She was banished into exile by God and Adam for daring to want to have intercourse sitting astride Adam; that is, for demanding sexual equality with Adam. As she flew away she cried out the secret name of God. Her punishment for persistently refusing to give in and come home to Eden was that she would lose her original status of being the mother of all living things,[71] and she would give birth to one hundred demon babies a day. These babies—the result of her promiscuous sex with men and other demons—would all die and in her rage and grief she would come up at night from the depths of the Red Sea and circle the earth, taking her revenge forever. Lilith, then, epitomizes the idea of a menstrual demon who, like the cosmogonic snake, lives at the bottom of the Red Sea: within, as it were, her own menstruous womb. Like the night mare she swoops in the night, riding sleeping men as if they were horses; exhausting their potency by her voracious, limitless sexual energy.

68. O'Flaherty, *Women, Androgynes, and Other Mythical Beasts*, p. 203.
69. *Women, Androgynes, and Other Mythical Beasts*, pp. 202-203; Walker, *The Crone*, pp. 87-88; Daly, *Gyn/Ecology*, pp. 14-15.
70. Budapest, *The Holy Book of Women's Mysteries*, p. 228.
71. Carmody, *Mythological Women*, p. 92.

When spiritual feminists come to tell this story *for themselves* they are making several strategic moves at once. First, they are playing with a long-standing Indo-European mythological tradition in which female sexual energies drain men of their sexual energy and therefore, according to the logic of myth, kill off the male name and line. (Traditionally, Jewish women have worn amulets depicting Lilith both to promote fertility and to ward off harm from their babies.[72]) But the Lilith myth is also an available imaginal repertoire for witches and others who want to say that female erotic energies will *not* obstruct the passage of new life, but *will* obstruct the patriarchal obstructions to new life. In other words, Lilith will drain the patriarchal energies of pornography, war, battering and environmental degradation. In symbolically draining men of their semen or potency, Lilith (in the name of radical feminism) deprives patriarchy of its purported power to transcend nature and time through technology and the immortality of the male name and line. In its place, she will replenish one hundredfold the non-patriarchal energies born of erotic connectedness. Jewish feminists sometimes wear images of Lilith as necklaces, not to ward her off, but to warn the Jewish establishment that she has returned from exile. Spiritual feminism tells the Lilith story in a spirit of irony, conscious that it is patriarchal systems, not Lilith, which vampirically consume the fruits of female embodiment.

Secondly, the myth can be used to reclaim female erotic lust. Jungian spiritual feminists use Lilith as an archetypal representation of women's potential for initiating self-defining sexual pleasure. Lilith *is* shocking, but therapeutically so. As mistress of the 'one-night-stand', entering and leaving a man's bed in the space of a few hours, she transgresses a widespread romanticization (and often actuality) of female sexuality as more in search of affection than genital pleasure.[73] Lilith's bestial desire shocks a woman into recognition of her 'Lilith nature'; it shows her that

72. B.B. Koltuv, *The Book of Lilith* (York Beach, ME: Nicolas-Hays, 1986), p. 81. Koltuv does not, however, note that amulets worn to protect women and babies during childbirth often depicted Lilith in chains and sometimes accompanied by the three angels who captured her from the Red Sea. See D. Goldstein, *Jewish Folklore and Legend* (London: Hamlyn, 1980), p. 26.

73. It is often the case that women's sexual pleasure is more focused on touching and emotional imtimacy than on orgasm. Shere Hite's survey showed a universal female desire for more tenderness and emotional intimacy during sex. This came top of women's lists of sexual pleasures, not penetrative sex and orgasm. See *The Hite Report* (London: Pandora, 1989), pp. 553, 559-63, 630.

she is 'connected to the Great Goddess in her original collective orgiastic aspect'.[74]

Thirdly, Lilith—who is childless—can represent the angry menstruous woman who is frustrated by her inability to conceive. She can be 'the raging premenstrual witch' who carries women off to 'the desolate wilderness and bitterness of the menstrual hut'.[75] Spiritual feminism recognizes that menstruation can be a manifestation of the 'dark side' of the Goddess; a traumatic theaphony. The onset of a period can mean the loss of hope for a baby that month. And menstrual blood is a horrific sight when a wanted baby miscarries. Here Lilith has 'killed' a potential child and is a symbol of dashed hopes. Lilith's power is, like all sacred power, ambivalent in its effects. She stands as a reminder that thealogies of embodiment are not sentimental.

Fourthly, Lilith is paradigmatic of the spiritual feminist refusal to submit to the moral dualism of traditional Western theism—which often forgets that in the Hebrew Bible the divine *summum bonum* can be capricious, jealous and liable to desert those who have served him well. Lilith's behaviour is similarly ambiguous. In the traditional Jewish myth she tickles children and makes them smile in their sleep; she might also strangle the new-born. As in male monotheism where God can be terrible in his punishments, female polytheism includes a numinous-demonic element that would be cast out at the expense of power. Barbara Koltuv interprets the mythology of Lilith as a seductress and child-killer as patriarchy's recognition that women's 'Lilith power' is 'greatest at the instinctual crossroads of a woman's life: at puberty, at each menstruation, at the beginning and end of pregnancy, motherhood and menopause'.[76] These are all points when a woman's reproductive life is *itself* in a state of transformation. As such, these moments of transformation are (differently) for spiritual feminism and for patriarchal religions, the moments of a woman's greatest sacral power. Lilith is the other side of Shekhinah, the receptive, nurturing face of female divinity; she is: 'that part of the Great Goddess that has been rejected and cast out in post Biblical times'.[77]

---

74. Koltuv, *The Book of Lilith*, p. 30.
75. *The Book of Lilith*, p. 81.
76. *The Book of Lilith*, p. 81.
77. *The Book of Lilith*, p. 121. In *Mythological Women*, p. 149, Denise Carmody charitably suggests that in the figure of Shekhinah 'traditional Judaism made its apologies to the femaleness it had denigrated in creating Lilith and put a

Judith Plaskow also shows how Lilith completes a feminist conception of womanhood. In her feminist midrash on Lilith she and a group of other feminist theologians imagine Eve, Adam's second wife, escaping from the garden she shared with God and Adam and meeting the exiled Lilith she had long wanted to meet. They befriend and teach one another; they cry and laugh together until 'the bond of sisterhood grew between them... And God and Adam were expectant and afraid the day Eve and Lilith returned to the garden, bursting with possibilities, ready to rebuild it together.'[78] Here Lilith is the 'other' side of Eve and their reunion develops women's holistic power and knowledge.

But Lilith is a challenge to patriarchy in ways that Eve is not. Unlike Adam or Eve, she knows God's secret name (and therefore has magical power over him). She is amphibious: she can fly, swim and walk and therefore disperses her elusive power in all dimensions and spaces. Here God is sadistic and she is tragically brave. She has paid an unjustly high price for her independence and political beliefs. As Aviva Cantor points out, before Lilith is a child-killing witch she is a rebel, refusing to be complicit with an unjust social order: 'Lilith, it must be emphasized, is a fighter and a fighter in a good cause'.[79] So it is not that religious feminism relishes Lilith's murderousness (as presented by patriarchy), but rather her commitment to justice that no patriarchal mythology of female evil can obscure.

I have little doubt that liberal, secular feminists would resist *any* remythologization of women. Probably the majority of feminists have no wish to be fantastic, but want to get on with the more ordinary liberations of equal pay for equal work, free pre-school childcare and so forth. Mary Daly's radical feminist cast(e) of hags, Nag-Gnostic Archelogians and such like has been criticized as the cultivation of a new elite sorority who are separated off from the everyday realities of ordinary women's lives.[80] There is more than an element of truth in this. Daly may indeed have created an aristocracy of *Überdamen* and a far larger corresponding set of 'ordinary' women who are (differently) monstrous: the 'fembots' who are too 'lobotomized', 'tokenized' and 'misbegotten' to

gracious womanliness within the reality of the Holy itself'.

78. 'The Coming of Lilith: Toward a Feminist Theology', in Christ and Plaskow (eds.), *Womanspirit Rising*, p. 207.

79. 'The Lilith Question', in S. Heschel (ed.), *On Being a Jewish Feminist* (New York: Schocken Books, 1983), p. 42.

80. Grimshaw, *Feminist Philosophers*, p. 158.

join the Race of Lusty Women. Lynne Segal suspects that Daly (who reputedly declines to speak to 'stupid women') is actually 'A-mazingly anti-woman' in her categorical divisions. Segal remarks that Daly 'does not say women must be affluent, highly educated, white, Western, free of needy dependents and all exhausting commitments. She does not say that the weary night-cleaner cannot enter into her Gnostic Nag-nation of Dreamers, as she dreams only of sleep.'[81]

But this is true not only of Daly's spirituality, but of all those spiritual/ psychotherapeutic practices which presuppose a fairly high level of education, time, space, energy (and sometimes income) to devote to them. There is no doubt that, whether feminist or otherwise, the advocates of contemporary (often esoteric) spiritualities are usually middle class. And the spiritual feminist remythologization of women would hardly make any sense without some degree of mythographic literacy. The remythologization of women is not, however, indifferent to political oppression—indeed it resists it by taking control of a narrative means of liberation from false consciousness. And even if this remythologization does require a relatively educated leap of the religio-political imagination, that does not make the *spirituality* wrong, but the present economic and educational context it is practised in.

Spiritual Feminism and the Defamation of Women

Spiritual feminists are not alone among postmodern feminists who want to relinquish the moral righteousness of female victimhood. For feminists to cast women *only* as victims is to assume a helplessness and a passivity that may obscure the complexities of their history of resistance as well as their suffering. Religious feminism is a non-violent means of personal and collective empowerment. All religious feminists try to steer their way through the Scylla of idealized femininity in which women represent convenient accumulations of moral capital, and the Charybdis of defamatory ideologies in which female power confirms patriarchy's worst fears of female deceit and sexual degeneracy. Some Christians in the feminist spirituality movement have made motherhood a paradigm of divine–human relations.[82] Postbiblical feminists have been more likely

---

81. *Is the Future Female? Troubled Thoughts on Contemporary Feminism* (London: Virago, 1987), pp. 20, 21.

82. See, for example, M. Hebblethwaite, *Motherhood and God* (London: Cassell, 1984); C. Ochs, *Women and Spirituality* (Totawa, NJ: Rowman & Allenheld, 1983).

to remythologize themselves as feral or wild. In thealogy the divine–human relation includes maternity, but is first an ecological connection that is not necessarily nurturing. Here the patriarchal mythography of female evil is not simply replicated in feminist mythography but nor is it reversed into feminine virtue.

Of course, spiritual feminism might well be criticized for reviving superstitious worldviews that are too defamatory of women to be anything but dead and buried with the inquisitors who invoked them. On the one hand, most feminists would not like to find themselves back in the sort of kabbalistic world evoked by the stories of Isaac Bashevis Singer where, for instance, Taibele takes a demon-lover and fears giving birth to an imp or a mooncalf, but is reassured by the demon that the Jewish laws of menstrual purity do not apply to those who have sex with monsters. Singer's imaginary world of she-devils who variously deprive men of their potency, spit fire and venom, or, helpfully, knead dough for housewives when they are ill,[83] is a world in which women are persuaded to be afraid of themselves; of what they might do next. And of course one must hesitate before representing anyone as a monster when in popular culture that word is usually reserved for sex criminals and sadists. On the other hand, for women of a Romantic religious temperament, religio-political liberation may demand the invocation of powers that patriarchy *itself* recognizes as frightening in order to compel its recognition of the awesome power of the Goddess in women. To invoke female numina is to say that this power not only should be respected now, but in a back-handed way, *always has been.*

Religious feminism wants to integrate the imagination into the dynamics of political change. And yet the available mythical personifications of female transmutational power and commotion are precisely those hypostases of female sacrality that *patriarchy* has named as evil. Patriarchy has *mis*used these female numina to scare the credulous with stories of the miserable fates awaiting any woman powerful (evil) enough to transgress the contemporary codes of feminine behaviour. Under patriarchy, female psychic energy and resistance are personified by women who are promiscuous, vain, cruel and jealous. These are women who have not used up, or have misused, their reproductive power as mothers. They are either spinsters without children, women who are cruel to children, or stepmothers: the 'fake' mothers of the

83. 'Taibele and her Demon', in *The Collected Stories of Isaac Bashevis Singer* (London: Jonathan Cape, 1982), pp. 134, 135.

children they care for. (Hansel and Gretel are hounded by two of these murderous women at once.) The powerful knowledge of cursing, putting the evil eye on someone and casting spells are feminized and attributed to women immediately to hand: local women who are usually unmarried or widowed; women who have (suspiciously) outlived or have never been subject to a husband's ownership of their reproductive energies.

The problem for spiritual feminism is that stories about the independent exercise of female supernatural power belong to an essentially local, domestic tradition of negative, destructive purposes like cursing, hexing and poisoning. Understandably, most feminists would be unwilling to have their sexual-political energies associated once again with what is stationary, private and fearful rather than just. Furthermore, the revival of the self-styled witch is a gift to evangelical propagandists on the Christian far right. The Reverend Pat Robertson, for example, believes that the Equal Rights Amendment would encourage women to 'leave their husbands, kill their children, practise witchcraft, destroy capitalism, and become lesbians'.[84] Of course, like the authors of the *Malleus Maleficarum* who believed that most of the world's great kingdoms had been overthrown by women, Robertson credits feminists with a political force few would recognize as their own. Yet the language of feminist witchcraft is easily misrepresented and persecuted as a kind of female Satanism. This can have serious social consequences for practising Wiccans—feminist or otherwise—such as the removal of children into 'care' or the loss of jobs. As ever, it is in the interests of conservative politics to preserve the social order from the chaos of women stirring and brewing social transformation.[85] For to mix up those categories that permit one class of being to exploit another is precisely the spiritual feminist project.

So it is only proper that the feminist sacred should evoke some degree of political anxiety in patriarchal commentators. If it did not, it would hardly be worthy of the name 'feminist'. Not only is the spiritual feminist sacred politically subversive, it is also mediated in self-consciously archaic modes and forms. This is a symbolic function of sacred things which embody or reveal something other than what superficially 'appears' and so evoke both veneration and fear. The otherness of new,

---

84. Roundtable discussion on 'Backlash', *Journal of Feminist Studies in Religion* 10 (1994), pp. 91, 107.

85. See N. Jay, 'Gender and Dichotomy', in Gunew (ed.), *A Reader in Feminist Knowledge*, pp. 103-104.

unusual, monstrous, unique and perfect things can all be kratophanic (manifestations of power). Eliade reminds us that in all forms of culture 'the strange and the monstrous are expressions frequently used to emphasize the transcendence of the spiritual'.[86] The terror and veneration sacred things evoke are continuous emotions.[87] If this is true of the archaic patriarchal sacred, it is all the more true of spiritual feminism's contemporary self-sacralization which is wholly at odds with the religious temper and manners of twentieth-century Western Christianity.

So the evangelical far right's equation of (all) feminism with witchcraft has some element of justifiable fear for its own interests. Marxist and radical feminisms do indeed challenge capitalism and uncritical preservation of the traditional heterosexual institutions of marriage, family and church. Feminist witches would certainly want to say that to bring about the end of patriarchy would involve, among other things, a magical exercise of directed will and consciousness. However, feminist witchcraft and spiritual feminism as a whole also belong to the tradition of *non-violent* political action. Christina Feldman's *The Quest of the Warrior Woman: Women as Mystics, Healers and Guides*, for example, disowns the masculine tradition of the invincible warrior who was 'compelled by fear and pride into the battleground'. The authentic warrior is, for her, the woman or man who renounces machismo and 'is willing to be visible or invisible but is committed to freedom, healing and understanding and is rooted in a profound sense of interconnectedness'.[88]

Feminist witchcraft is a biophilic spiritual practice. Nonetheless, feminist witches continue to call themselves witches, not in spite of the numinous horror the word invokes, but because of it. The word 'witch' is, as Otto would say, *unheimlich*—an untranslatable word roughly meaning odd, eerie, strange—and it therefore awakens the *sensus numinis*.[89] Yet the title is far from being used as an incitement to mischief. On the contrary, the spiritual feminist historiography of witchcraft is that of a rural religion practised mainly by independent

---

86. *Rites and Symbols*, p. 28. See also *Patterns in Comparative Religion*, p. 13.
87. Caillois, *Man and the Sacred*, p. 21.
88. London: Aquarian, 1994, p. 14.
89. In *Truth Or Dare*, p. 8, Starhawk describes herself and others like her as 'witches' because 'witch' forces people to confront the reasons *why* they fear the word and its connotations and it shows her commitment to the Goddess and to recalling the outlaw status of the immanent. She also likes the way it 'reeks of holy stubborness'.

women whose first purpose was and still is a healing one. The two most influential interpretations of the witchcraze have been Margaret Murray's *The Witch-Cult in Western Europe*[90] (1921), which argued that the witchcraze was Christianity's attempt to stamp out the Old Religion (identified by feminists as a female wisdom religion of the Goddess); and Barbara Ehrenreich and Deirdre English's book, *Witches, Midwives and Nurses*[91] (1972), which has also informed a widespread spiritual feminist view of witches as unlicensed village midwives-healers or wise women whose competition the new male medical profession wanted to eliminate.

But it is notable that these and Starhawk's discussion of what she calls the 'Burning Times' are quite lacking in numinous elements. Starhawk vindicates the moral and spiritual worth of female spiritual power by her claim that witchcraft legitimately belongs to the history of European religion. She rationally adduces various causes of the persecution of (mainly) peasant women as witches, attributing the persecution less to perceived *powers* in women, than to the social and ideological upheaval of the sixteenth and seventeenth centuries. The witch-hunts were, she writes, 'linked to three interwoven processes: the expropriation of land and natural resources, the expropriation of knowledge; and the war against the consciousness of immanence which was embodied in women, sexuality and magic'.[92]

The patriarchal concept of magic as a solitary and basically mercenary practice must always be distinguished from a feminist concept of magic. It is true that in common with many other forms of witchcraft around the world, feminist witches use the coven system and, even if only symbolically, cultivate shape-shifting powers. But witchcraft is traditionally accused by Christians of reversing and perverting the order of nature and allying itself with evil powers.[93] We have seen that feminist witchcraft does precisely the opposite: it restores nature's own order and allies itself with all struggles for justice and life. This implies that it is patriarchy and not women who are guilty of the wrongs patriarchy calls witchcraft. The feminist magical will is a will collectively attuned to the

90. Repr.; New York: Oxford University Press, 1953.

91. New York: Glass Mountain, 1972.

92. *Dreaming the Dark*, p. 189.

93. See, for example, M. Douglas, *Natural Symbols: Explorations in Cosmology* (London: Barrie & Jenkins, 1973), p. 138; Durkheim, *Elementary Forms of the Religious Life*, p. 44.

creative energies of the cosmos for life-affirming, relational ends. The sacred is a creative, protective power when it is respected. It is, however, capable of incapacitating its abusers. And it is this magical ambivalence of the sacred that lies behind the controversy in spiritual feminist circles over the use of hexing. All spiritual feminists recognize the dangers of hexing. And the majority of feminist witches believe that hexing must never be used for personal vendettas because magic is dangerous and can rebound threefold on the one who sent it out. Moreover, a hex binds the hexer to the hexed, and also violates its object's freedom of will. But a very small minority of feminist witches feel that hexing can be used *in extremis*. Zsuzsanna Budapest and Luisah Teish, for example, feel justified in retaliating or sending back harm to rapists and other attackers if they are proved to be guilty. They argue that the attacker needs to be taken out of circulation for the sake of other women and for his own sake as well.[94] For Budapest, who instructs her readers in the making of hexes and the preparation of a black altar, the power to hex is as much a function of her sacrality as her power to heal, and so 'a witch who cannot hex cannot heal'.[95]

It is clear that while spiritual feminism never celebrates or romanticizes evil, contemporary radical feminism does not present a wholly unified front on the moral agency of women. On the one hand, the maternalist camp is exemplified by Nel Noddings's and Sara Ruddick's emphasis on caring and nurture as a model of feminine moral agency.[96] On the other hand, Daly, Caputi and others (who are also profoundly anti-militarist) are metaethically guided by reconnection with female elemental power. This latter is often driven less by agapeistic, self-sacrificial love than by the exercise of liberated gynergy. Indeed, in Daly's vitalist, almost Nietzschean,[97] philosophy of female self-affirmation, neo-pagan feminist resistance is not the domesticated moral influence of the nineteenth-century ideal mother, but the turbulence of wind and waves, the mutterings of crones and hissings of snakes. This liberation movement is

94. This account of the controversy over hexing is from Eller, *Living in the Lap of the Goddess*, pp. 123-29.

95. *The Holy Book of Women's Mysteries*, p. 43.

96. See N. Noddings, *Caring: A Feminine Approach to Ethics and Moral Education* (Berkeley: University of California Press, 1984); S. Ruddick, *Maternal Thinking: Towards a Politics of Peace* (London: The Women's Press, 1990).

97. For a brief discussion of the Nietzschean elements in Daly's philosophy see Grimshaw, *Feminist Philosophers*, p. 157.

made in the image of the ancient mythological dragons who, like menstruants, had the power to cause floods, storms, hurricanes and tornadoes.[98]

These are women who want to recall the Maenads: fierce, drunken, oracular priestesses of Dionysus whom patriarchy records as having orgiastically consumed their male sacrificial victims; the African and Mediterranean Amazon warrior women who fought for matriarchy and Macha the raven goddess of psychic warfare are just some of the spiritual feminist personifications of female resistance. But it must be stressed that their revival has little or nothing to do with violence as such and much more to do with the tradition of ecstatic, instinctual, anti-industrial counterculture that can be traced from early nineteenth-century Romantics like Shelley and Godwin to Jim Morrison and the twentieth-century hippies.[99] Goddess feminism is also a Romantic movement in that it embraces Dionysian chaos, a mixing and confusion of given elements for the purposes of wholeness, over and against the rational Apollonian rules of the establishment. Numinous power is generated by 'dionysiac madness: the churning of the essence of life surrounded by the storms of death'.[100]

Spiritual feminism, then, both refuses and selects from the history of women's moral defamation. It is not, in any straightforward sense, a complete disowning of negative female sacral transformations, where these could be used to decay patriarchal structures of destruction. After all, the sacred itself can have destructive powers, and periodic destructions are an integral part of the ecology of the cosmos.

So feminist monsters are, in an ecological sense, salvific. They hypostasize nature's warning of imminent destruction. And more than this, through direct political action, ritual reenactment, and psychological identification (or 'aspecting', a form of spiritual feminist spirit possession), women *become* present embodiments of archaic female power. Margot Adler describes hearing the eerie ululating yells of radical women at political protests and says, 'Amazons are coming into existence today. I have heard them and joined with them. We have howled with the bears,

98. On the association of dragons and menstruants see Grahn, *Blood, Bread and Roses*, p. 69.

99. Cf., F. Musgrove, *Ecstasy and Holiness: Counter-Culture and the Open Society* (London: Methuen, 1974), pp. 65-80.

100. This phrase is borrowed from J. Sanders, 'Dionysus, Cybele and the "Madness" of Women', in Gross (ed.), *Beyond Androcentrism*, p. 126.

the wolves, and the coyotes.' Their elemental cries express their animal strength and will to 'ally themselves with all that is female in the universe and wage a war for Mother Nature. These women are creating their own mythologies and their own realities.'[101]

In sum, in spiritual feminism menstruality no longer signifies madness, failed motherhood and abortion. But it *does* signify liberation from patriarchal prohibitions which are associated with these, namely, prophetic inspiration and a woman's freedom of procreative choice. Here maternal reproductive power includes but also transcends female biology and is ecologically integrated with the periodic rhythms of cosmic creation, destruction and re-creation. The 'menstrual' woman is, then, more than a woman who happens to be menstruating. She represents a spiritual-political type: a woman embodying the sacral energy to resist nature's violation and to preserve it (and therefore other humans as well) from harm. Resurrecting slain menstrual monsters in order to teach patriarchy one of its own lessons and to sabotage its ontological categories may not be as perversely obscurantist as it might appear.

101. *Drawing Down the Moon*, p. 191.

Chapter 6

THEALOGY FROM THE EDGE OF CHAOS

There was an old woman tossed up in a basket,
Seventeen times as high as the moon
Where she was going I could not but ask her
For in her hand she carried a broom
Old woman, old woman, old woman, said I
Where are you going to up so high?
To brush the cobwebs off the sky!
May I go with you?
Yes, by-and-by.

Traditional Rhyme

Boundaries and Ideology

In recent years old boundaries have been disappearing. The demolition
of the Berlin Wall began in 1989 and the Iron Curtain was lifted during
the first year or so of the 1990s. Uncensored information and monetary
transactions flow across global cyberspace with no regard for territorial
boundaries. Mass air travel facilitates the rapid spread of diseases that
might otherwise have burned out locally. And mass ownership of televi-
sions in the West has meant that human compassion and political effort
is being extended across national boundaries to suffering peoples and
animals that the donor will probably never physically encounter. Recent
technology may be removing any clear distinction between the artificial
life of computers and the biological life of living organisms. And the
spiritual and scientific work of the green movement has shown that
areas of environmental damage cannot be isolated forever; that damage
to one part of the ecosystem effects the whole web of life. Among other
related hypotheses, James Lovelock and Lynn Margulis's 'Gaia' model
of planetary and cellular dynamics has shown that the earth is a unified,
self-organizing system.[1]

1. See, for example, J. Lovelock, *Gaia: The Practical Science of Planetary
Medicine* (London: Gaia Books, 1991).

Most significantly, postmodernism (as intellectual analysis rather than a new sort of cultural consumerism[2]) has subjected the whole basis of modernity to intense and profound criticism. The modern understanding of reality as no more than the sum of material things whose behaviour can be empirically tested, measured, engineered and controlled has been shown to be an ideological construction. This construction has allowed a Western male elite, whose reason and rule look suspiciously like that of their monarchical God, to colonize and regulate the world as if it were their intellectual and material property. Although the numbers of people actually participating in the postmodern spiritual, scientific and political paradigm shift towards an organicist worldview are relatively small and it is still marginal to the *realpolitik* of free-market capitalism, its way of thinking about the world is becoming increasingly pervasive and influential—even in a patriarchal milieu. Above all, organicism questions the absolute separation of God from nature and the cognate separation of mind or spirit and the matter it controls. (Though not everyone will be able to dismiss this pair of separations as nonchalantly as Gregory Bateson: 'we won't be bothered by that any more except to look at it with curiosity as a monstrous idea that nearly killed us'.[3])

Modernity is in flux, and although the effects of postmodern intellectual and spiritual turbulence and resistance are not wholly predictable, its importance can hardly be underestimated. One source of that turbulence is the feminist spirituality movement, which is itself a product of and a contributor to the new eclectic, globalist networks of contemporary spirituality that are so troubling to exclusivist traditions. As we will see in the course of this chapter, spiritual feminism shares in the globalist attempt to erase or transcend all forms of barbed wire frontiers and boundaries in the interests of dialogue and common environmental and humanitarian concern. It is in the nature of a paradigm shift that the old view is gradually left behind, and a new one begins to unfold on the edges of the old. It is this latter phenomenon of the boundary as the leading edge of a repressed but emergent vision—spiritual feminism—that will be the theme of this chapter.

2.   This latter meaning of postmodernism as a form of theme-park culture of shallow eclecticism, pastiche and simulacra has been described by D. Lyon, *Postmodernity* (Buckingham: Open University Press, 1994), esp. p. 68.

3.   'Men are Grass: Metaphor and the World of Mental Process', in W.I. Thompson (ed.), *Gaia, A New Way of Knowing: Political Implications of the New Biology* (Great Barrington, MA: Lindisfarne Press, 1987), p. 41.

There are of course menacing countertrends to spiritual globalism and the (at least intellectual) dissolution of hierarchical relations. Far-right nationalists also benefit from global communication networks, but nonetheless work to erect violently exclusive racial and national boundaries around themselves. Their boundaries are militarized frontiers, places of crossfire; fissures in which all respect for life is suspended. National boundaries normally define adjacent territories as either allied, neutral or hostile. But when democratic 'low level' nationalism turns to fascism, frontiers are used to defend a 'pure' national space whose racial pollution might be 'ethnically cleansed' by the deportation and the mass murder that 'washes' the nation by blood sacrifice. And contemporary global divisions are not only ethnic and national. The gulf between the rich and poor continues to widen. The richest people in the world usually live on the prosperous green edge of cities and erect 'security' boundaries of alarms, flood-lights and guarded fences around their manicured persons and property. They form a fortified circle around the poor and dispossessed who are held inside decayed, unkempt inner cities. (It is an ironical twist in the topology of privilege when the rich speak from the centre but inhabit the periphery).

Or again, the Internet may be an alternative connectedness, a kind of global cybercommunity, but it may also encourage a new Western transcendentalism in which those who are computer literate and can afford a computer that is connected to the Internet[4] can depart the earth and its needs for a clean, disembodied cyberspace, leaving the poor, the cities and the environment to their dereliction. The exponential growth of information can become a proliferating glut of data rather than knowledge. And through technology Western and Westernized lives are becoming ever more permeable to information and accessible to an insistent electronic contact that erodes the necessary sense of the boundaries that define personhood—even personhood in biophilic connection.

Some of the most fervently upheld exclusive boundaries are those that divide one fundamentalist religion from another and which segregate the sexes according to divinely ordained gender roles. There are a number of ways of doing this. To take just two examples: in fundamentalist Islam women are separated by making them invisible under the veil and by varying degrees of seclusion in the home, and in Judaism, orthodoxy

---

4.   For a radical feminist appraisal of the Internet see C. Woodbine, 'Women's Webs: Will We Use Computer Networks?', *From the Flames* 14 (1994), pp. 10-12.

retains the *mehitzah*—a screen which separates men from women in orthodox synagogues. Women are kept to the rear by a variety of partitions: iron grilles, a wooden lattices, curtains or upstairs galleries. Contemporary orthodoxy upholds the use of the *mehitzah* as the main distinguishing feature of an orthodox synagogue.[5] The claimed purpose of separating men and women is to isolate men from female sexual distraction and to protect women's modesty from the sexually objectifying attentions of men. Nonetheless, as Peggy Reeves Sanday has observed, 'whether men and women mingle or are largely separated in everyday affairs plays a crucial role in the rise of male dominance. Men and women must be physically as well as conceptually separated in order for men to dominate women.' So too, sexual separation will predominate 'when the natural environment is seen as hostile. When it is a partner, there is mingling.'[6] In other words, sexual equality, unbounded movement and biophilia belong together in ways that this chapter will explore.

But fundamentalism opposes the mixing that blurred edges allow. Clearly-drawn, non-negotiable boundaries secure the purity of the religious system which, like any totalizing social or conceptual system, is vulnerable to invasion, dilution and other adulterations of its truth claims. To fundamentalist systems, open boundaries do not invite entry as much as threaten the departure or assimilation of the faithful through apostasy or secession. The constraints placed upon members to remain within these boundaries are principally worked out through dietary and sexual control of the body—in particular the orifices which open or close the body to the other (whether that other is something genital, edible, or intellectually foreign). Mary Douglas (following Marcel Mauss) has described the ancient religio-cultural tendency to see the body as a microcosmic symbol of society. Society's image of itself has, like the body, a bounded form: 'Its outlines contain power to reward conformity and repulse attack. There is energy in its margins and unstructured areas.'[7] If the female body models the tensions within the structure of a fundamentalist community, then invasion or pressure on that structure

---

5.   M. Ydit, 'Mehiza', *Encyclopaedia Judaica*, XI, pp. 1234-35. The Reform movement has abolished the *mehitzah* and men and women sit together on the grounds that the Bible does not command the separation of men and women during worship.

6.   *Female Power and Male Dominance*, p. 7.

7.   *Purity and Danger*, p. 137.

is held at bay through the control of the female bodies within the community.[8]

Fundamentalism opposes secular modernity as a threat to its truth claims, practices and values. Modernity and all that is confusingly other to the strictly defined identity of the group is commonly projected onto the morally and intellectually 'weak' female body. This body, and its debilities, can be kept under control by inhibiting its movement within clearly delineated spaces like the home or a segregated area in a place of worship. As John Hawley and Wayne Proudfoot have pointed out, if women do not keep within their divinely appointed margins this is 'a symptom and a cause of cosmic dislocation'. Women are uniquely fitted to their function as screens on which to project male anxiety because they are 'close enough to serve as targets, yet pervasive enough to symbolize the cosmic dimensions of the challenge'.[9]

Toril Moi has made the point that because women's bodies mark out the symbolic order they also share in the problematic properties of all boundaries, namely, that they belong neither in nor outside a communal space. As she says,

> It is this position that has enabled male culture sometimes to vilify women as representing darkness and chaos, to view them as Lilith or the Whore of Babylon, and sometimes to elevate them as the representatives of a higher and purer nature, to venerate them as Virgins and Mothers of God. In this first instance the border line is seen as part of the chaotic wilderness outside, and in the second it is seen as an inherent part of the inside: the part that protects and shields the symbolic order from the imaginary chaos.[10]

Male ownership of female sexual choice is an investment in the purity and stability of the community. When women's bodies are 'closed' or pure as virgins or wives their bodies represent an inviolate, secure community.[11] So again we see that in patriarchal religions women are

8.   See Douglas, *Natural Symbols*, pp. 16, 98-99. Douglas's discussion here is conducted largely without reference to gender.

9.   In their 'Introduction' to Hawley (ed.), *Fundamentalism and Gender*, p. 27.

10.   *Sexual/Textual Politics: Feminist Literary Theory* (London: Methuen, 1985), p. 167.

11.   See G. Sahgal and N. Yuval-Davis, 'Fundamentalism, Multiculturalism and Women in Britain', in *idem* (eds.), *Refusing Holy Orders: Women and Fundamentalism in Britain* (London: Virago, 1992), pp. 8-9. Here they note that within fundamentalism, controlling women is 'the panacea for all social ills and failure to do so, a recipe for social disaster'.

not simply and straightforwardly profane. If the female body consitutes a boundary between order and chaos it can be sacred or profane depending on where a given patriarchal system is locating the sacred and which 'side' of that body is visible. In a slightly different context René Girard has observed how, 'by reason of [a woman's] weakness and relatively marginal social status...she can be viewed as a quasi-sacred figure, both desired and distanced, alternately elevated and abused'.[12]

Although present forms of fundamentalism have been growing numerically and in influence since the late 1970s, Ewart Cousins believes that what he calls the 'forces' producing global consciousness are 'immeasurably stronger than those causing the conservative reaction'.[13] The history of human consciousness can be divided, as Cousins does, into three key periods. The first has been known as the Pre-Axial Period of archaic consciousness, in which there was little or no individuation of self from the tribe. During the first millennium BCE humankind passed into the second stage, the Axial Period, during which consciousness of individual identity emerged independently in China, India, Persia, and the Eastern Mediterranean. The sense of a (male) self as a private individual allowed the spiritual separation of humans from their natural and tribal environment that could and did produce the detached, transcendental judgments that constitute the teachings and revelations of the major world religions. But now, as we approach the new millennium, there is a widespread sense that human history stands on the threshold of a Second Axial Period, 'a transformation of consciousness that is as momentous as that of the First Axial Period and that will have comparable far-reaching effects'.[14]

Spiritual feminism is very much a part of this dynamic transformation of consciousness—politically as well as spiritually. And its ontology is part of that dynamic: female sacrality is itself an agency of transformatory change. This entails a new understanding of spirituality, and one which will bear little relation to the punitively ascetic disciplines that

12. *Violence and the Sacred* (Baltimore: Johns Hopkins University Press, 1979), pp. 141-42.
13. 'Spirituality in Today's World', in F. Whaling (ed.), *Religion in Today's World* (Edinburgh: T. & T. Clark, 1987), p. 332. This was Cousins's opinion eight years ago, and although both fundamentalism and globalism have continued to grow, it is my impression that at least the sense of ecological urgency has become more widespread since then.
14. This classification of the periods of human consciousness is from Cousins, 'Spirituality in Today's World', pp. 324-31.

have characterized some forms of spirituality. Charlene Spretnak's definition of spirituality corresponds closely with female sacral practice. She defines spirituality as 'the aspect of human existence that explores the subtle forces of energy in and around us and reveals to us profound interconnectedness'.[15] This chapter takes that recreative energy into an/other space whose conditions of possibility are both the source and the end or purpose of spiritual feminist activity. In other words, female sacral energy can drive and sustain transcendence of patriarchal ontological and political constraints and distortions in a movement towards what Daly calls 'ontological Metamorphosis'. For when feminists recover ownership of the meaning of their own bodies, that entails redrawing the body's boundaries so as to become impermeable to the profanity of pornographic naming and intrusion. And it entails resituating the body in one of the forms of feminist sacred space that I shall discuss in this chapter.

Spiritual Feminist End-Times

Postmodern spirituality (to which spiritual feminism has made one of the most comprehensive contributions) is hopeful that this period of spiritual-cognitive shift will be a sacred period of time: a threshold onto new global patterns of communication and reverence for life. (This, despite knowing that the earth could also become inhospitable or uninhabitable through a series of nuclear wars and accidents, and the interactive effects of global warming, ozone depletion, resource wars and migrations through loss of human habitat.[16])

And spiritual feminism has its own reasons for believing that the modern period of world history is coming to an end. The spiritual feminist configuration of the sacred is one in which the eternal is manifest through the pulse and flow of organic processes of change in time. And this is as true of political change as it is of organic change. There are numerous reasons why Goddess feminists believe that at least the modern phase of patriarchy may be beginning to 'break up'. But one of the most central reasons is the reemergence of Goddess worship in the West after an absence of about 1500 years, and the revived vocation of

15. Appendix C, 'The Spiritual Dimension of Green Politics', in C. Spretnak and F. Capra, *Green Politics: The Global Promise* (London: Paladin, 1990), p. 240.

16. Starhawk sets her novel, *The Fifth Sacred Thing*, half a century into the future, depicting both of these possibilities coexisting at once in adjoining territories.

priestess (reckoned to have been suppressed since the middle of the second millennium BCE with the advent of Jewish monotheism).

A combination of the general postmodern feeling for end-times,[17] and green apocalypticism in particular, suggests to many spiritual feminists that this period is not the end of one patriarchal millennium and the beginning of a new one, but is rather a boundary onto a new religio-political reality ushered in by the reemergence of the Goddess. Her return is understood in quasi-eschatological terms as the resurrection of a divine presence that is not salvific in the classical sense of redeeming humanity from divine punishment, but is certainly a sign that life is open to regeneration. At this end-time it is a female divinity that is returning and she is ushering in an era of new eco-spiritual consciousness that will end the alienation of what Asia Shepsut calls 'The Dark Age of Monotheism'.[18] Similarly, Paula Gunn Allen believes that 'this is the time of the end—the end of patriarchy, the end of the profane. It is the time of the Grandmother's return, and it is a great time indeed.'[19]

Agreeing with Caitlin Matthews that we are on the threshold of a new Goddess religion and a new historical epoch, Naomi Ozaniec believes that 'we are in a time of transition, the classic initiatory sequence, death and birth on a grand scale'. Consequently, she believes that we need a female priestesshood to mediate between the spiritual and material in a 'potent and potentially dangerous time'.[20] This is a priestesshood which is, according to Asia Shepsut, about to be born: 'The long atrophied gifts of the priestess are on the brink of painful re-emergence.'[21] In the language of Goddess feminism, the spiralling chaotic vortex of the Goddess's womb is churning creation into a new order; the yawning mouth of chaos is opening to swallow the religious, scientific and philosophical patriarchal order. Thus Caputi:

> Chaos is (re)emerging. The Goddess—that is, turbulent and transmutational powers in which both males and females participate—is returning. And this unpreventable event is occurring despite the degree to which patriarchal sciences and religions have tried to prevent it.[22]

17. See F. Jameson, *Postmodernism, or, The Cultural Logic of Late Capitalism* (Durham, NC: Duke University Press, 1991), p. 1.

18. *Journey of the Priestess*, p. 6.

19. In her 'Foreword' to Caputi, *Gossips, Gorgons and Crones*, p. xviii. See also Goldenberg, *Changing of the Gods*, p. 109.

20. *Daughter of the Goddess*, p. 300.

21. *Journey of the Priestess*, p. 5.

22. *Gossips, Gorgons and Crones*, p. 281.

Political and intellectual developments are also cited as signs of an end-time and include the emergence of the women's movement and Christian and Jewish feminist theological revision, the emergence of the green movement and green science, and the psychotherapy movement and its reunion of rationality and intuition. Scientific discoveries, both negative and positive, are both signs of and contributions to a new age. These include the discovery that human beings can end their own history by nuclear annihilation; the opening of the ozone hole; the discovery of black holes and the emergence of 'chaos consciousness' itself.[23] For spiritual feminism these holes symbolize the 'thinning' or wearing away of the decaying fabric of patriarchal systems. These holes are small openings onto big new spaces.

Classical theism's doctrine of an immutable, omnipotent, omniscient, discarnate God has funded patriarchal concepts of both the holiness of spirit and the profanity of organic matter, and a modern science in which matter is predictable and manageable because it is without spirit.[24] But the emergent patterning is not one that is assimilable into patriarchal categories organized around the distinction between sanctity and profanity. The old boundaries of the sacred and the profane will be, and already are, subject to dislocation.

Contrary to modern empirical philosophy and science, postmodern science has shown that at the quantum level matter does not behave according to laws of prediction and spirit/energy and matter cannot be separated. Indeed the 'reenchantment' of nature and of science itself is the central project of postmodern science, which realizes that the modern mechanical view of the earth is not only a false description of the world, it is also a destructive one. Postmodern science and postmodern spirituality are therefore inseparably connected, implying that the sacred is unpredictable in that it cannot be staked out and down by human reason. The postmodern theological/thealogical shift from a God

23. See, for example, Caitlin Matthews's list of twentieth-century developments that are cited as evidence of our living in a period 'when the Goddess walked among us', in *The Goddess* (Shaftesbury: Element, 1989), pp. 6-7.

24. This is, of course, a generalization. Jewish law covers almost all actual or possible circumstances and therefore in some senses sanctifies the whole of a Jew's mundane or profane existence—but still under patriarchal criteria. So too, the Christian doctrine of the incarnation of God in the man Jesus shows God willing to enter the conditions of finitude. However, if Jesus' sinlessness consists primarily in his asexuality, then his masculine embodiment constitutes at best divine indifference to female sacrality and at worst, dishonour.

of law presiding over a cosmic machine to a divinity holding creation in a nexus of complex relations has—like one of its forerunners, process theology—brought the divine into the very heart of change: the Goddess does not sit and watch the cosmos but is dancing at its very centre. The sacred becomes less an instrument of God's will or law staking out the parameters of his operations, than the unfolding dynamic energy of creation stirring and disturbing the world; disordering what human patriarchal arrogance has posited as eternal order. The Goddess is an iconoclast: human conceptions of the sacred end up in the pot with everything else. This is a cosmology of permanent underlying apocalypse in the sense that dissolution is a continual ecological process and the 'doomsday Crone' is an integral aspect of the thealogical trinity.

But spiritual feminist apocalypse is not the sudden shock of time having run out as it has been in millenarian schemes. The spiritual feminist end-time marks both the beginning and the end of the sacred/profane distinction. By this I mean that beyond or 'after' patriarchy, distinctions are reversed and dispersed and what was silent—women and nature—speaks. Although some spiritual feminists are suspicious of any conceptual dualities (mistaking them for dualisms), a spiritual feminist end-time should, I think, also mark the beginning of a new sacred/profane distinction. Throughout this book I have argued that, under patriarchy, feminist reclamation of the sacred/profane distinction is ecologically necessary if sacred living things are to be religiously and politically protected from patriarchal evil-as-profanization. In this case 'post-patriarchy' is less a present state than a boundary point of departure. It is a point of departure from the patriarchal pollutions that constitute the real profane, and a point of entry into a liberative sacred space which, by its imaginal nature, is out of bounds to the violatory patriarchal 'touch' (namely, whatever exploits creation as a means to accumulate profit and power).

This period, which for spiritual feminists is one of quasi-eschatological reversal, does not simply swap around the elements of the sacred/profane distinction. It is not that what was once on the left of the boundary is now on the right and what was on the right is now on the left. Spiritual feminist boundaries are not just mirrors. A boundary between the sacred and the profane still exists (or should exist). It has changed its shape and its permeability, but it is still a boundary that demarcates absolute moral difference. In an actually post-patriarchal world that boundary would no longer be needed and would disappear: everything would be sacred. But until patriarchy has disappeared (a circumstance of eschatological proportions) non-violent feminist boundaries must remain both to defend nature and, more dynamically, as leading edges of change.

The Resacralization of Profaned Space

One of the ways in which religio-political boundaries have been contested have been the various green defensive occupations of threatened natural space. The green movement has developed the methods of student protest occupations of the late 1960s and 1970s. Radical ecofeminist networks have also decentralized and spiritualized the androcentric revolutionary politics of occupation. Without official leaders, ecofeminist organization is a network within which actions spring up, disappear and emerge elsewhere like the branching elements of a fungal mycelium. This is, as we will see, the organicist politics of chaos.

In its religious dimension, occupation of contested space has sacralized direct action to the point of ritual. Mary Daly's presence in the Harvard Memorial Church in 1971, to which she had been invited to be its first woman preacher, was significant in its brevity. Her transgression was not to enter the space, but to *leave* it in exodus with a number of other women. An action which will become a part of British post-Christian feminist legend was that of Monica Sjöö and other women from a weekend gathering who walked into Bristol Cathedral on the morning of 9th May 1993 and disrupted the service. Sjöö was carrying a placard of her 'blasphemous' painting, 'God Giving Birth', and they all lined up in front of the altar, facing the congregation—reclaiming the ground for the Goddess, drumming, singing and declaring the end of patriarchy.[25]

By their sheer bodily occupation of space, women embodying the energy of the Goddess reclaim and change the energetics and use of a place perceived to have been profaned. Spiritual feminist presence is non-violent, prophetic and sacralizing and as such protects a space— usually a piece of land—from the desecration of 'development' or military use. The choreography of feminist consecration could be witnessed, for example, when the US Cruise missile base at Greenham Common was (magically) encircled and closed by linked hands on 12th and 13th December 1982.

But the wholly female presence at Greenham was demonized in

---

25. M. Sjöö, 'Breaking the Tabu—Doing the Unthinkable', *From the Flames* 10 (1993), pp. 22-23.

conservative religion and culture. In the logic of Mary Douglas's conception of the relation of the sacred and the profane, radical ecofeminists were certainly manifesting female virtues of nurture, but in the wrong place: that is, out of the safe containment of the patriarchal private home and in an open public place that symbolized and actualized patriarchal power over the future of all that lives. In the patriarchal ideology of *feminine* sacrality, the Greenham women's pacific virtues would have sanctified their proper place—the nurturing female home—but their ritualized pacifism profaned this public open space. According to the religious ideology of femininity, a woman's bodily presence is the still centre of a peaceful home, but in this place it would (and did) cause the chaos of conflict with police and bailiffs, and the muddy mess of improvised shelter.

The sense that women were interfering with, obstructing and messing up the patriarchal order—that they were, in other words, monstrous—was differently noted at the time by the right-wing press and by cultural historians. Of the latter, Allon White and Peter Stallybrass wrote that 'the women of Greenham Common are drawing (in some cases self-consciously) upon historical and political resources of mythopoeic transgression and conjuring from their antagonists not dissimilar reservoirs of material symbolism'.[26] In the popular right-wing press Greenham women were collectively labelled lesbians (as a term of abuse rather than a description). And the mythological language of female monstrosity resurfaced once again. Such words as 'hefty', 'gruesome', 'harridans', and 'Amazons' were used of the women, connoting patriarchy's sexual rejection of them as women who were confusing the 'natural' sexual order.[27]

Of course Mary Daly would herself use some of this family of words to describe all-female activism. Large numbers of the women at Greenham were indeed lesbians who, in Daly's understanding of lesbianism, had violated the ultimate patriarchal taboo: the 'Taboo against expression/expansion of Ontological Female Connectedness'.[28] Yet it seems to me

26. P. Stallybrass and A. White, *The Politics and Poetics of Transgression* (Ithaca, NY: Cornell University Press, 1986), pp. 24-25. Cited in J. Emberley and D. Landry, 'Coverage of Greenham and Greenham as "Coverage"', *Feminist Studies* 15 (1989), p. 487.

27. Newspapers using these words are cited in Emberley and Landry, 'Coverage of Greenham', p. 493.

28. *Pure Lust*, p. 244.

that any feminist transgressor violates the boundaries of the 'fore-ground'. Whether or not they are lesbians, women participating in 'women-only' political actions are transgressing the heterosexual arrangement of female bodies and male bodies as sets of complementary opposites. These transgressors cross the patriarchal boundary into *female* profanity:

> We pass beyond our own former limits. We become and are Other. Finding our Original Otherness, we break the Terrible Taboo. We *become* Terrible, Taboo. By this crossing we are outrageous, contagious. Taboo, we are Tidal, transgressing coasts, coasting freely.[29]

Here female sacrality can be understood as the propulsive power by which a feminist transposes her being into the (open) sphere of the feminist sacred. It is an ontological mutation. But like most phases of transition it is also a struggle.

On a visit to Greenham in 1984 I found, as everyone did, that the women camped there had to expend a great deal of spiritual and physical energy fending off continual assaults from the state, from local vigilante groups and, differently, from the tabloid press. In *Greenham Common: Women at the Wire* one woman wrote about how 'actions involving physical confrontation exhausted and, in some ways, damaged us'.[30] Another woman recorded:

> During July and August we had containers of maggots, blood and faeces thrown over the benders. Tents were trampled over and slashed with knives. Quick-drying cement was poured into the water supply and the standpipe was stolen. Women were attacked—two women were sprayed with blue dye.[31]

(It seems significant that patriarchy pelted women with the byproducts of organic decay in order to desecrate or profane this feminist sacred space.)

In its pacific intentions and its sheer power of endurance, the camp, and indeed the very word 'Greenham' has come to symbolize female prophetic presence—whether at Greenham itself, or at Aldermaston, Menwith Hill, Sellafield or any other women's peace camp.[32] As Julia Emberley and Donna Landry have written, 'the camp has a rich history

29. *Pure Lust*, pp. 244-45.

30. B. Harford and S. Hopkins (eds.), *Greenham Common: Women at the Wire* (London: The Women's Press, 1984), p. 139.

31. *Greenham Common*, p. 157.

32. All these sites are in England. Sellafield is a nuclear power and processing plant, Aldermaston manufactures nuclear weapons, and Menwith Hill is a US spy base.

of representation resonating beyond the issue of nuclear disarmament'. The term 'Greenham' has become a linguistic space in which many different radical women's symbolic protests can be represented.[33]

I would go further and suggest that Greenham was not only a new form of political action, but that the dynamics of this action were also a new manifestation of female sacrality. A female sacral space (literally a no-man's-land) was established at the very heart of patriarchal power. Here the feminist sacral will exorcised patriarchal colonization of the mind and the land. In this verse of her poem 'Bad Weather', Bryony Dahl expresses the transition between the ordinary or 'profane' privation of the Greenham women surviving the winter sleet under blankets in benders, and the sacred realm of ontological possibility whose new spiritual and political conditions they were gestating:

> What I hear tonight
> Is that violated by nuclear missile warheads
> Stealthily we are
> As witches in the ditches
> Pregnant with new babies, great sea-faring girls.[34]

The Separatist Womanspace

The establishment of a separate womanspace—as a communal organization rather than for the temporary purpose of a direct action—is sometimes advocated as a political act through which women can freely define and develop their own identity. In this short section I shall primarily discuss *spiritual* separatism and its implications for a renewed concept of female sacrality, rather than the choice to live in a permanently separate community that has as little to do with men as possible. (Nonetheless, spiritual feminism, a strong identification of men as a sex with patriarchy, and living in women-only lesbian separatist households often go together.)

In its *religious* form, one of the main purposes of lesbian separatism is to gather and concentrate female energy to 'psych out' (for want of a better phrase) patriarchy.[35] The separatist bonding of women—whether

33. 'Coverage of Greenham', p. 485.

34. In L. Hurcombe (ed.), *Sex and God: Some Varieties of Women's Religious Experience* (London: Routledge & Kegan Paul, 1987), p. 45.

35. See S. Gearhart, *The Wanderground: Stories of the Hill Women* (Watertown, MA: Persephone, 1978).

in community or at a women-only retreat—involves a massing of female sacral power through ritual, friendship, and a kind of erotic touch that has never been sanctified by patriarchal religion. In attempting to heal the wounds patriarchy has inflicted on women's psyches and often bodies as well, spiritual feminist separatism draws a magical ring around the female community/consciousness—a kind of 'white light' that repels male influence. (In the early years, separatist communities barred male children from decision-making since their 'male energies' violated or disturbed the energies of female space.[36]) Daly also urges that gynergy can only be fully liberated in a (paradoxical) separation from separation. That is, radical feminist separatism separates women from 'phallic separatism, which blocks and bars Life-Lust—the desire for ontological communication' and allows women to 'live our radical connectedness in biophilic be-ing'.[37]

In an interview in 1984, Daly said that she refuses to submit to feminine socialization and 'feel sorry for men and try and include them'. In her experience, energy is generated by being with women rather than men, and women must absent themselves from what has drained them of energy by objectification and abuse:

> The other side of our power of presence to ourselves is our power of absence. That means we are absent very often physically or we can be there physically but absent in the sense that we will not be used, we will not be objectified.[38]

While Daly regards radical feminist lesbianism as an end to objectification and almost a prerequisite mediatory state for the transmission-by-touch of the tabooed power of female wholeness/holiness, I would want to extend the possibilities of this power of connection beyond lesbianism. It is not only lesbians whose sacrality is sourced in an erotic connection with nature. A variety of paganisms and heterodox forms of Christianity have been conducted at least in this spirit and despite their patriarchal contexts. Any separatist language of female holiness as strictly or

36. V. Taylor and L. Rupp, 'Women's Culture and Lesbian Feminist Activism: A Reconsideration of Cultural Feminism', *Signs* 19 (1993), p. 43.

37. *Pure Lust*, p. 364. Daly expresses justifiable reservations about the term 'separatism' and calls it a 'second order' term. For her, separatism for the sake of 'ontological Metamorphosis' is made necessary by the conditions of patriarchy, but should not be mistaken for metamorphosis itself.

38. K. Peader, 'Rejecting Theology for a Religionless Spirituality', *One World* 98 (1984), p. 21.

formally dichotomous to male profanity can be destructive. Certainly, the line between the feminist sacred and the patriarchal profane is non-negotiable. But it may be that separatist notions of female purity draw too absolute a distinction between maleness and femaleness, in insisting on women's belonging and therefore having 'rights' to a moral, imaginal or physical space that men, by virtue of their biology rather than their values, do not.

Of course separatists separate from the rest of society for positive reasons; not just for the sake of separation itself. And it can be argued that communitarian lesbian separatism has preserved and nourished radical feminist culture within and outside the separatist community in times of backlash or decline in the wider women's movement.[39] Even so, I hope that some of the images that I discuss in this chapter may suggest more spiritually and politically fertile conceptions of female sacral space than separatist ones. For to sever absolutely femaleness and maleness to produce a wholly unified female subject is also to foreclose existential possibility by controlling all outcomes.

Although sexual and racial separatism are definitely *not* the same thing, they both engage in the prevention of plural identity. Fascism categorizes lesbians, 'queers', transvestites, 'half-castes', Anglo-Jews and other compound identities as impure and that over and against which its own purity is defined. Fascism seeks to destroy or confine this otherness within a ghetto—a small separate space that is vulnerable to attack. Lesbian separatists feel compelled to *choose* a separate, small space for *themselves*. Whether in the mind or in a house, feminist separatism, which is non-violent, holds threatening masculine otherness at bay. (Refuges for battered women and children do so with very good reason.) While staving off 'other' values and practices (perhaps more than overcoming them), feminist separatism also multiplies hostile alterities and severs possibilities of connectedness. Yet spiritual feminism, with other organicisms, insists that whatever cuts the threads of inter-dependence in the natural web of life will eventually wither away. It is for this reason that I do not believe that separatism (other than when it is appropriate for the purposes of direct action) is congruent with spiritual feminism.

The Jewish term *herem* usefully describes the ambiguous meaning and effect of the separatist community. *Herem* connotes things which are

39. This is the contention of Taylor and Rupp in their article, 'Women's Culture and Lesbian Feminist Activism'.

separate or set apart from common use either because they are excommunicate and, as abominations, set apart for destruction; or because they are sacred and consecrated to God. Spiritual feminist separatism is under a *herem* that is partly self-imposed and partly a response to the banned or excommunicate status of women who have come out as lesbians. (Lesbians and gays cannot even walk hand in hand in a public place without fear of derision, hostility or attack.) Yet what is *herem* is also taken out of circulation; it is going nowhere. And to be out of circulation is to defeat the means and purpose of female sacrality whose transformations are by their nature relational, symbiotic, interactive and transmutational, and whose outcomes are therefore not wholly figurable in advance.

Of course, the female consciousness/body cannot be permeable to invasion and possession, and separations—as from damaging relationships—can be necessary and healthy. So too, excluding boundaries are important in feminist witchcraft, one purpose of which is to secure bodily integrity or wholeness/holiness from male sexual attack. Contrary to the secular feminist notion that spiritual feminism reduces femaleness to pure receptivity, the magical will can be used as a protective power of exclusion. A witch may, in Elisabeth Brooke's examples, repel attackers by tapping into the 'hag within', by visualizing herself as a cobra and fixing her attacker with an unblinking stare, or by surrounding herself with 'white light'. She may also protect spaces sacred to herself such as her home by 'sealing' the doors and windows with white light. With or without ritual, all that is needed is 'unbending intent'.[40] Here the witch does not so much stand on a linear boundary, or remove her body and property from patriarchal ground (which is in some senses impossible to do), but *wraps* a protective boundary around her.

What Brooke describes is a way of protecting the sacred without removing one's consciousness or body altogether from the mixed community of persons and ideas. The capacity of female sacrality to ferment material, political and spiritual change from within is evoked by Maria Lugones when, speaking of culturally mixed *mestizaje* women such as Mexican-Americans, she urges that transgressive feminist 'impurity' resists and threatens modern control of subjects as *either* masculine *or* feminine. To be *mestizaje* is to be complex, plurivocal and in process. 'Curdled' women are practised in the art of metamorphosis and transformation by mixing. They inhabit a crosscultural space that is

40. *A Woman's Book of Shadows*, pp. 144-45.

'in the middle, anomalous, deviant, ambiguous, impure. It lacks the mark of separation as purity. If it's hybrid, it's in the middle of either/or twice.'[41] This ontological curdling (which Lugones likens to making mayonnaise) seems to me to be sacrality in action. Although, it is true, I have throughout this book used the word 'female' as demarcating a political and spiritual orientation, that word is not closed. Spiritual feminist shape-shifting allows women to elude the ontological stasis of patriarchal classifications. It mixes up the old divisions of women by race, class, religion, and sexual virtue, and yet remains sensitive to the richness of multiple but distinct identities within the whole.

The Spiral Labyrinth

Spiritual feminist boundaries are not battle-lines of massed female troops facing male troops in hatred. To situate oneself on a boundary (rather than being pushed onto it) is to be oppositional and resistant, but neither of these qualities is necessarily adversarial. Some activism, such as lying down in front of diggers and squatting trees to stop the clearance of land for more roads, shops and offices, interjects female bodies as a human frontier between nature and oncoming patriarchal destruction. For spiritual feminists the boundary may also be a point of spiritual, political and intellectual crossing. Asia Shepsut, for example, says that she 'took the decision to walk back, psychologically, over the Bridge of Monotheism, which spans what turns out to be only a narrow divide between our modern world and the old'. Her boundary crossing was psychological and also physical. She travelled to ancient Goddess sites and monuments whose atmosphere 'sang in the ears at high frequency, electrifying the soul as it reconnected with far memory'.[42]

The spiritual feminist boundary is curved or spiralling because its reality has a different shape to that of linear modernity. There are no straight lines in nature. It is modernist patriarchal efficiency that has resisted organic spread. Modernism has erected brutalist estates of tower blocks in contrast to the pre-modern clusters of cottages and the warren-like alleyways of old cities; electric fences instead of hedgerows; lines of chickens in battery cages instead of mingling and scratching for food in the yard. By these and other means, whatever is chaotically alive can be confined in easily managed linear, square or flat spaces. By contrast, the

---

41. Lugones, 'Purity, Impurity and Separation', p. 462.
42. *Journey of the Priestess*, p. 9.

natural terrain bears the shape of generative turbulence: the drift and
shift of land masses and the passage of water have kinked and coiled the
landscape, pushing up mountains and cutting gorges through the rocks.

In its antipathy to the straightening, flattening and regulation of nature
in industrial modernity, contemporary feminist iconography proposes
the spiral as a new/old symbol of a characteristically 'female' way of
knowing and travelling through time and space. The spiral is also a
'female' formation in nature. As a variety of matrifocal cultures attuned
to the rhythms of nature have observed, the snaking, winding passages
of the vagina, womb and ovaries, the curved phases of the moon, the
designs engraved on the stone passageways and chambers of some
neolithic burial sites, and the sea shells in whose shape one can listen to
infinity are all spiral formations. So too, the feminist passage into
spiritual/bodily integrity-in-connection is a spiralling, rhythmic, dance-like
process that periodically loops back on itself, enclosing, absorbing and
dissolving the 'foreground' or 'underworld' (the alienation to be faced
and overcome) within one's own body.

The ethnologist Arnold Van Gennep's *Rites of Passage* usefully
summarizes how a person's shifting sense of the relation of the sacred
and the profane will entail a complete social and psychological shift in
her or his life. He writes: 'such changes of condition do not occur without disturbing the life of society and the individual, and it is the function
of rites of passage to reduce their harmful effects'.[43] The spiralling spiritual feminist journey can be a ritualized rite of passage that effects and
contains the trauma of a woman's separation from a previous political
and spiritual identity (death), and incorporates her into a feminist one
(rebirth). This is a psychotherapeutic journey into the submarine or
underworld labyrinth where the minotaur of patriarchy is finally faced in
a quasi-shamanic trance. When the subject emerges from her underworld she is reborn as one who has transformed (but not destroyed) the
power of patriarchal monsters, or forces of non-being, into feminist
existential and political energy.[44]

43. *Rites of Passage*, p. 13.
44. See for example, Starhawk's account in *Dreaming the Dark*, pp. 66-70, of
'Joy's' shamanic wrestling with her 'monster'—especially her early religious
upbringing. She eventually transforms that monster by becoming its animating spirit,
using its power to realize her own maturity: 'The dark has been transformed; it is no
longer fearful. Now it holds brightness, And in what was the monster, a beautiful
woman who radiates light and power. . .'

The shamanic capacity to be in an ordinary and a mythical space at the same time is built into feminist witchcraft. An ecstatic trance can be induced by drumming and dance and is particularly valued as a way of ritually defining the edges of patriarchy beyond whose boundaries women will be able to construct a new identity. In the ecstasy of the trance they become literally self-possessed. Drawing on the healing traditions of Native American religion, feminist shamans may guide and protect women who are travelling across biological and psychological boundaries to access sacred energy for healing, self-knowledge and the courage to confront patriarchal force without paralysing fear.[45] The feminist shaman is practised in the art of travelling between worlds and dissolving the boundaries of the sacred and the profane through dreams, dance and trance. In doing so, she connects a 'tamed', over-civilized woman or community with the untamed, liberative numinous realm. And since dreams, dance, trance and menstrual insight are available media for all spiritual feminists,[46] not just professional shamans, the very form of feminist spirituality is shamanic in character. The purpose of shamanism and the purpose of spiritual feminism can be one and the same. For as Starhawk points out, sacred or shamanic possession 'reminds us that the sacred is immanent'. It develops the knowledge that is the beginning of liberation from patriarchal consciousness: 'the knowledge of how to become possessed is also the knowledge of how to become unpossessed'.[47]

The numinous space of the healing trance is not, then, a resting place but a labyrinthine space of religious and political struggle with a self whose energies have been diffused and therefore profaned by patriarchal false consciousness. Any labyrinth represents a problem. As Eliade puts it, the path to the 'centre' of one's being is 'arduous and fraught with peril because it is, in fact, a rite of passing from the profane to the sacred'.[48] In the mythology of the Malekulan islanders of the New Hebrides archipelago the entrance to the underworld is guarded by the female monster Le-hev-hev who has before her a drawing of the labyrinth, half of which she has rubbed out. If the soul has been properly

45. See, for example, V. Noble, *Shakti Woman: The New Female Shamanism* (New York: HarperSanFrancisco, 1991); Jamal, *Shapeshifters*.

46. For the relation of menstruation and shamanism, see Stepanich, *Sister Moon Lodge*, pp. 74-75.

47. *Truth or Dare*, p. 96.

48. *Patterns in Comparative Religion*, p. 382.

initiated in life she or he will know the design of the labyrinth and can restore the map. If not, the soul will be devoured by the monster.[49] This mythological image perfectly illustrates the spiritual feminist's drama: either she will be devoured by the patriarchal monster which will lead her again and again into states of non-being, or she must summon her primal integrity, wit, courage, and knowledge to devour the monster herself.

Recently, some spiritual feminists have tried to move away from the dehistoricizing, subjectivizing quality of the interior shamanic journey. Inspired by the pilgrimages of primal peoples to actual natural sites, they are trying to journey to the mountains, caves and sites associated with the Goddess.[50] But not all spiritual feminists can afford the costs of such a journey or are able or willing to leave young children. Usually the feminist's shamanic journey is a journey into her own embodied consciousness and onwards out into the cosmos of which it is a part. That journey is not complete with one ritual. It is also a long process of introspection, (often) depression and recovery. The journey is commonly imaged in and through one of the variations of the myth of Demeter and her daughter Persephone, in which Demeter descends into the underworld to find her abducted daughter. In her grief Demeter has suspended all growth above ground until she finds Persephone. After their reunion Persephone is able to return to the upper world with Demeter for nine months of the year during which all living things grow and bloom. The underworld is, then, the winter of the soul: a place where the patriarchal woman has to die, gestate in the lightless earth, and re-flower or be reborn into the summer of liberation.[51]

In the spiritual feminist context the term 'reborn' does not imply that there was anything wrong with being born from a mother (as it does in patriarchal religions). On the contrary, it is the departure from necrophilic patriarchy that promises new life. Of course not all such journeys into the underworld are explicitly political. Christine Downing found that her menopause was a 'transformatory mystery' that demanded her passage through the underworld:

49. Falk, 'Feminine Sacrality', p. 305; Eliade, *Rites and Symbols*, p. 62.

50. Orenstein, *The Reflowering of the Goddess*, p. 31.

51. For a wholly feminized version of the myth in which Persephone is not abducted by Hades but is instead taken to be educated by Hecate, see D. Stein, *The Women's Spirituality Book* (St Paul, MN: Llewellyn, 1987), pp. 40-41.

my journey through menopause has brought me to Hestia. She comes bearing none of the usual attributes of the goddess but carrying a book with blank pages, the unwritten volume of the new. I am only beginning to sense what will be written there.[52]

Psychical regeneration is through reconnection with the cosmic whole. It is magical in that it liberates previously unconscious sacral energies. And these energies can empower a woman to make significant changes in a life that has been fragmented and therefore weakened by patriarchy.

Living On and Beyond the Edge of Patriarchy

Postmodern feminism is aware that female marginality may entail powerlessness but is not synonymous with it. To be on the margins is not necessarily to be on the sidelines of power if power is not perceived as a space one is either absolutely in or out of. But even within the traditional spatial model of power, the margin or edge can also be a place from which the transformative, liberative vision and language of otherness can be generated.[53] To choose marginality as a political state-ment might almost be called a *posture*; a deliberate transgression of the alienating politics which distinguishes centre and edge, top and bottom. Far from being a posture of flight, religious feminist criticism engages prophetically with the patriarchal centre from a position of vocational marginality. In liberal democracies at least, intellectual marginality can be uncomfortable and tiring but is not usually dangerous. Liberal patri-archal culture tolerates relatively minor irritations to the body politic, especially when countercultural criticism is perceived as a merely spiritual, intellectual or textual production whose author has refrained (unlike the industrial picket line) from disrupting the flow of capital, production and the passage of goods. Although, for example, Starhawk and Daly justifiably claim to be activists and their books are quite other to the content and temper of most of the work done in religious studies, they are widely known, published, and are employed as teachers. They

52. Quoted between two sections of D. Taylor and A. Sumrall (eds.), *Women of the 14th Moon: Writings on Menopause* (Freedom, CA: The Crossing Press, 1991), p. 320.

53. Daly and Caputi define 'Boundary Living' in the *Wickedary* as 'Realizing Power of Presence on the Boundaries of patriarchal institutions; Presentiating [*sic*] the Background in the midst of foreground conditions by communicating contagious Courage, Pride, and Other Volcanic Virtues'.

have not been silenced by their marginality in the way that, say, most elderly or disabled people are silenced by their marginality.

Spiritual feminists are usually white, educated, and of Jewish or Christian middle-class origins.[54] They have made a moral and existential choice to position themselves on the alternative fringes of social and religious practice, regarding that fringe as a threshold onto a different way of being. In a somewhat reductionist sociological discussion of spiritual feminist marginality, Cynthia Eller claims that spiritual feminists often prefer to feel that they are persecuted outsiders who will eventually be punished by fundamentalists and fascists because that gives them a sense that they are a genuine threat to patriarchal power. In fact, at present, Goddess feminists are rarely ostracized in urban America. And seeing themselves as seers, prophetesses and wise women, they can 'rest secure in a spiritual specialness that will not be confused with insanity'.[55]

But this seems to me to miss the *religious* point of marginality as a religio-political protest, as a sacral sign, and as a magical state from which to draw transformatory power. In short, marginality can be a womanspace that derives its power by the freedom of being both here and not here; separate and connected. For Daly, who is a separatist, 'womanspace' is a

> Space created by women who choose to separate our Selves from the State of Servitude: FREE SPACE; Space in which women actualize Archimagical Powers, releasing the flow of Gynergy; Space in which women Spin and Weave, creating cosmic tapestries; Space in which women find Rooms, Looms, Brooms of our Own.[56]

Some spiritual feminists are fortunate in being able to dwell physically as well as spiritually in an/other space. The priestess Hallie Iglehart Austen

> lives in the hills above Point Reyes in northern California, in a round house that sits in a hollow in the land, surrounded by tall fir trees... She writes in a small, cozy room at the top of a spiral staircase, with windows on three sides that look out at the swaying treetops and the blue blur of the ocean in the distance. It seems fitting that she should live and work here, in this beautiful, still wild part of the planet, surrounded by earth and water, trees and sky.[57]

54. Eller, *Living in the Lap of the Goddess*, p. 18. See also pp. 19-23.
55. *Living in the Lap of the Goddess*, p. 223. For her whole discussion see pp. 217-23.
56. This is the *Wickedary* definition of 'Women's Space', cited in *Outercourse*, p. 95.
57. Owen, *Her Blood is Gold*, pp. 125-26.

Mary Daly moved to the moon in November 1991: 'My workshop is on the side of a beautiful mountain with a gorgeous view of the sky. Both Wild Cat and the cow helped me to build it, which wasn't hard, since it's largely a natural formation... We have lived together happily ever after.'[58] Austen at the top of her spiral staircase, and Daly on the other side of the moon can write about the world from the transcendent vantage point of the sacred. They situate themselves like the wise old women in fairy tales who live in the forest and appear to good travellers to help them find their way through its dark tangle.

For those who do not live in sacred places[59]—real or imaginal— Brooke Medicine Eagle has popularized the Native American Moon Lodge as a place for women to absent themselves from the mundane or profane realm of everyday constraints and oppression. It is also a place where menstruous women can give back female blood to the earth in a kind of ritualized blood/energy transfusion from the healthy/holy daughter to her endangered, profaned mother.[60] Unlike the Underworld, the Moon Lodge is a place of rest and withdrawal (though not enforced seclusion):

> In this quiet questing place, we have the ability to see deep into mystery, and to draw forth from the deep starry womb of the feminine, the visions, ideas, discoveries, and creative sparks which need to be made real in the lives of our people.[61]

The Moon Lodge can be an improvised space in the wild, in a house, or failing that, in the mind alone.

It is also common for spiritual feminists (North American in particular) to spend weekends going out into the wilderness together. As in most religions, the wilderness is a sacred space in whose vastness one at once encounters and loses the self. A feminist wilderness is not required to be a parched, mountainous desert in which men are tested by themselves and by God to prove that they have transcended their embodiment. Here 'wilderness' signifies an untouched area of 'female' earth which has not yet been violated by the male hand of environmental degradation.

58. *Outercourse*, p. 346.

59. See Javors, 'Goddess in the Metropolis', pp. 211-14. This short paper avoids any sense that the sacred is a privileged state. Javors sees the sacred in profane places and in those who are socially outcast without that having been a political choice.

60. See Eller, *Living in the Lap of the Goddess*, p. 87.

61. Brooke Medicine Eagle, 'Introduction', in Francia, *Dragontime*, p. xiv.

Margot Adler's description of one such event is crowded with the motifs of weaving, spirals, oracularity, marine questing and female spiritual collectivism that have filled this book. The women, she says, 'slept in a circle with their heads together, facing inward, their bodies like the spokes of a wheel. They wove "dream nets" from wool and fibres and sewed "dream pillows" filled with mugwort and psyllium seeds.' One of the women dreamed that she was with a 'mass of chanting women', rowing across the sea and walking on a spiral path in a wood by the water's edge, guided by an old woman.[62]

Another ritualized concentration of female sacral power for mutual healing is circle-casting in feminist witchcraft. The circle is a symbol of the womb, of the trust between the women, and a traditional (pan-religious) protective encircling of the sacred. American feminist covens usually declare the circle a 'safe space' for women.[63] The circle holds sacred space and time within itself; so much so that if a woman has to leave the circle she may trace a doorway in the air and step out of it, closing it behind her in mime.[64] In the rotating incarnation of the Goddess each woman takes it in turn to be the priestess casting the circle. As is customary in all forms of witchcraft, women purify themselves on entering the circle and the circle is cast by calling the four points of the compass. A cone of power is raised by chanting and dancing to invoke and share in the cosmic creative energy which is magically sent round and out of the circle for healing purposes.

Feminist witchcraft also develops visualization or 'pathworking' skills. These enable a witch to evoke magically and be transported into a highly detailed mental image or narrative whose content will have empowered the subject on her or his return. Pathworking generates, gathers and releases power as the narrative reaches its climax. In one pathworking, women find themselves in

> a sea weed room... Sands of different colours make a spiral pattern on the floor. The spiral leads to a large cauldron in the centre. Standing around the cauldron are three women... the women of the waters... they speak to-gether... This is the threshold between the worlds. We are your guides.[65]

62. *Drawing Down the Moon*, pp. 199-200.

63. Eller, *Living in the Lap of the Goddess*, p. 94. In non-separatist covens the circle can include men as representatives of the male principle.

64. *Living in the Lap of the Goddess*, p. 95.

65. This account of pathworking, and the cited example, are from Luhrmann, *Persuasions of the Witch's Craft*, pp. 209-10.

All these practices that I have described are techniques of encircling, protecting and releasing the sacred under political conditions which require the redemption of space from patriarchal profanization. As patriarchy attempts to own and mediate all experience of time and space, that colonization of reality has to be resisted by some form of ritual and imaginal dislocation.

The Regenerative Boundary

Since the late 1960s holistic science has come to understand the universe as a 'seamless web':

> Patterns and codes that manifest themselves on earth are part of a universal, unfolding whole. The forces and agents of change operate within existing codes and patterns, but also create new ones. These forces constantly defy entropy and are of a self-organizing nature.[66]

Holistic or postmodern science differs significantly from modern science in accepting that nature behaves in non-linear ways that cannot be precisely, mathematically predicted.

Perhaps the most important development of this insight has been chaos theory or chaology. This science of 'complexity' studies the dynamic interaction of systems and recognizes that human life is just one element in an infinitely complex web of interacting elements. The whole universe is in flux and its organic systems—as well as some of those devised by humans—can be characterized as 'chaotic' when they lose form, and 'anti-chaotic' when they spontaneously reorder. The 'moment' when a system is balanced between emergent order and disorder is the 'edge of chaos', and it is this mysterious edging onto transformatory turbulence that will be particularly significant in these two final sections of this chapter.

For it may be that this model of human and non-human systems is one that is particularly applicable to a thealogy of political activism in which spiritual and political systems and processes of change are encompassed by a divine reality that holds all these dynamic processes in balance. Jane Caputi has suggested a chaos model for feminist political strategy in her Conclusion to *Gossips, Gorgons and Crones*.[67] I have

66. A. Stikker, *The Transformation Factor: Towards an Ecological Consciousness* (Rockport, MA: Element, 1992), p. 126.
67. *Gossips, Gorgons and Crones*, pp. 275-90.

found her discussion (and invocation) inspirational and would like to develop it here. The interaction of thealogy, activism and the possibility of actual change in the human world order are, I think, better represented as an edge of chaos than by traditional political models which remove human activity from the complexity of the whole ecosystem and seek to impose one cause and one explanation on the historical process. For in both nature and political history,

> [t]he edge of chaos is where new ideas and innovative genotypes are forever nibbling away at the edge of the status quo, and where even the most entrenched old guard will eventually be overthrown... where eons of evolutionary stability suddenly give way to wholesale species transformation. The edge of chaos is the constantly shifting battle zone between stagnation and anarchy, the one place where a complex system can be spontaneous, adaptive and alive.[68]

During the same period in which spiritual feminism has developed, and participant in the same web of ideas, postmodern science has been developing complexity theory: one of the most significant discourses to have undermined modern Newtonian determinism. At the same time, spiritual feminism has been developing a thealogy which similarly, but in its own way, undermines modernity. Thealogy refuses to submit its ideas to modernity's rationalistic systems and with a playful elusiveness proposes, for example, paradoxical or even contradictory descriptions of the Goddess. Whether the phrase 'the Goddess' stands for the Great Mother (a biological fertility symbol) or the Great Goddess (a metaphysical symbol of cosmic oneness),[69] the ontological priority of a divine female cosmogonic principle, a private sense of the divinity of the female self, a purely psychotherapeutic symbol of self-affirmation, a conflation of the qualities of numerous ancient goddesses, or some degree of all these, is not clear. Some spiritual feminists are thealogical realists and others are not. (Indeed, I am not sure that thealogy need postulate one or more Goddesses at all. For myself, thealogy refers to a conceptual and imaginal shift through which one can construct a plurality of ideas and experiences of the divine in female terms.) All that is unanimously agreed is that she is not God's wife or 'God in a skirt'.

But it is not that Goddess feminists lack the intellectual will and ability

---

68. M.M. Waldrop, *Complexity: The Emerging Science at the Edge of Order and Chaos* (Harmondsworth: Penguin, 1994), p. 12.

69. See Ursula King's discussion of this distinction in *Women and Spirituality: Voices of Protest and Promise* (London: Macmillan, 1989), p. 148-49.

to propose a careful systematic thealogy. Their refusal to do so shows that no human system transcends biography and the history of ideas. All human conceptual systems are in process. Just as under scientific observation the behaviour of matter at the quantum level is altered by the very fact and manner of its being observed, so too analysis of human conceptual systems alters them by the addition and subtraction of meaning. (I have been conscious of this process in thinking and writing about spiritual feminism.) Conceptual systems are conditioned and mediated knowing and as such their structures are never immune to constant pressure or pushing from their own margins. If creative change comes from the outer edges of systems, that is why thealogy is, in all senses, always on the edge of chaos.

Although knowledge and property has belonged to men for at least 5000 years, human history *has*, as I mentioned at the beginning of this chapter, witnessed momentous shifts in consciousness. These have occurred at around 1000 BCE and now at around 2000 CE. In post-modern, post-Holocaust Europe and America students of religion are now unwilling to rank religions according to the Christian triumphalist evolutionary schemes that were proposed in the nineteenth and early twentieth centuries.[70] With Jacques Derrida, some postmodern philosophers are deconstructing the epistemological foundations of modernity. Less nihilistically relativist, 'constructive' or 'revisionary' postmodernism has criticized modernity as a threat to the survival of life on this planet, and is urgently revising the modern conceptions of personhood, nature and divine reality to secure the conditions of survival.[71]

So, using the language of chaos theory, it is possible to deconstruct patriarchal social organization as another sort of complex dynamic system that is subject to a variety of unpredictable fluctuations, one of which is the turbulence of feminist reaction. Turbulence is introduced into a given system when dissonant rhythms or frequencies mount up to the point at which a given system becomes stormy, 'cacophonous', incomprehensible and finally enters a state of collapse. Industrial capitalism has probably not passed the onset of turbulence, though its logistical

70. See P. Byrne, *Natural Religion and the Nature of Religion* (London: Routledge, 1989), p. 192-94.
71. For this distinction between the two related but different types of postmodern theory, I am indebted to David Ray Griffin's introduction to the SUNY series in constructive postmodern thought in *The Reenchantment of Science: Postmodern Proposals* (Albany, NY: State University of New York Press, 1988), pp. x-xi.

complexity and social discord seem to be pushing it towards that state. Feminist activism or turbulence (including hermeneutical turbulence) attempts to break up the ordered but unjust patterns of the patriarchal system, 'freeing up' consciousness and space for new biophilic patterns of social organization to form. So too, in chaos theory, at the onset of turbulence 'all the rules seem to break down. When flow is smooth, or laminar, small disturbances die out. But past the onset of turbulence, disturbances grow catastrophically.'[72] Feminist spirituality's 'menstrual' behaviours, rituals, directs actions, magical visualizations and so forth can then be likened to that one grain of sand that added to the sand-pile will cause an avalanche and irreversibly change the shape of the whole pile. The chaologist's sand-pile seems a particularly apt metaphor when the complexity of the capitalist economic system and the ecological system it depends on are perceived by many commentators (not just spiritual feminists) to be poised by their very nature on the edge of collapse.

Numerically, organicism is in the minority and spiritual feminists are a minority within a minority. This paradigm shift is, at present, a quantum shift. But just as the minute turbulence caused by a butterfly flapping its wing on one side of the world can affect the weather on the other (the 'butterfly effect'), so too slight and relatively powerless feminist turbulence could bring about new social conditions not strictly predictable in present political forecasting or logic.[73] For if the system is sufficiently unstable—or, to use Ilya Prigogine's phrase, 'far from equilibrium'— then one grain of sand can stimulate an avalanche. Like other sorts of systems, the patriarchal system has a breaking point when critical mass is reached and it will change into another form. If the time is right an idea or network of activists comparable to a grain of sand can cause change to the system beyond the sum and scope of its own personal efficacy as a discrete agent or group. But if the patriarchal system is stable it will be less susceptible to such effects.

However, the late twentieth-century patriarchal system *does* show signs of instability—as have all rising and falling civilizations in the past. Its own money markets periodically crash. Since the Second World War these crashes (such as that of 19th October 1987) have been damaging but relatively minor. But economists do not rule out the possibility that a

72. J. Gleick, *Chaos: Making a New Science* (London: Sphere, 1990), p. 122.

73. Mary Daly makes the related point in *Gyn/Ecology*, p. 379, that the power generated by female bonding cannot be calculated by normal quantitative methods.

series of small fluctuations in the money market could theoretically cause such turbulent dealing that the whole system could be seriously damaged or collapse. The capitalist free market is a non-linear system: an economic climate is created by millions of separate consumer choices, themselves already conditioned by the buying decisions that have shaped the boom or recession in the first place.[74] Or again, when the flow of traffic comes to a halt on congested roads; when the simmering grievances of the poor in the inner cities boil over; when the proliferation of organized crime cannot be checked by the police and infiltrates the government and judiciary by bribes and intimidation; and when plutonium is illegally sold to governments indifferent to world opinion, the population fears that the moral order is collapsing and that a good future for their children is in doubt. As in the economy, politics is dangerously subject to loss of confidence.

But the very complexity and instability of the patriarchal system also opens it to possibilities of spiritual and social transformation. A chaos theory of altered political consciousness could equally show that non-violent, quantitatively slight, 'butterfly' changes of consciousness could transfigure the whole without first fighting for a privileged position at the top or centre of a hierarchical stack. Without resorting to coercion, the superficial, apparent equilibrium of the patriarchal status quo could be stirred simply by introducing small pockets of turbulence into the machinery of domination. Politically insignificant rituals and revisions on the alternative fringe may be minutely turbulent but could act upon the global consciousness in an unpredictable and far-reaching manner. Changing the chaos image from that of weather to plants, if the spiritual feminist consciousness is likened to a seed pod or puff-ball, it could swell, burst and waft clouds of minute pollen grains, spores and seeds to bear the fruit of change in the waste places of patriarchy, freely transgressing all its frontiers in ways that cannot be plotted (and therefore pre-determined) before they happen.

Capitalist social Darwinianism has justified ruthless competition as 'natural': species or humans must compete for limited space and resources if they are to survive. The popularized theory of the survival of the fittest pits life against life: a successful player or team drives the losers to the edge of the field and then out of the game. However, new biological research suggests that symbiotic cooperation is at least as

74. Waldrop, *Complexity*, p. 65.

important to evolution as competition.[75] Added to this, one of the most important social implications of chaos theory is that the old hierarchical privileges dispensed from the top down are displaced by the chaotic equality of all conscious subjects. Each conscious agent has a impact on the environment which cannot be empirically measured and which may or may not accrue transformatory socio-spiritual power exponentially in collectivized action or ritual.

This is, I think, what Jane Caputi is moving towards when she urges women to 'develop chaotic political strategies. We must stir the Crone's turbulent cauldron.'[76] To be poised on the edge of feminist chaos is to be dancing on the edge of new existential possibility. Chaos is not only a threat to the status quo, it is also a threat to one's own identity (most of us have grown up and spent *some* years of adulthood with a map of patriarchal values that has helped us make some sense of its world and what we are supposed to do in it). Therefore, as Caputi puts it, 'to speak both of and with chaotic Powers, we must journey into the chasm. We must begin to speak with the tongues of dragons and monsters.'[77]

In the patriarchal politics of confrontation, unyielding boundaries protect the social order from the assault of difference. They demarcate races and classes and establish the limits of tolerable behaviour. By contrast, within the cooperative, organicist politics of spiritual feminism, boundaries are pliant and permeable to change. In other words, the envisioned culture is one that, like nature, is constantly evolving, renewing itself by adaptation from within; change is 'cooked' with the leaven of sacral energy. Barbara Walker defines 'Chaos' as the 'Greek word for the undifferentiated nature of raw elements supposed to occupy the World-Goddess's womb before creation and after destruction of each recurrent universe'.[78] The eighteen-billion-year[79] history of the unfolding universe can be imaged as the Goddess Chaos stirring the cauldron: a spiralling motion through which the fluid of life churns into and out of stability, just as complex interactions produce constantly changing social patterning.

75. See, for example, L. Margulis, *Symbiosis and Cell Evolution* (San Francisco: Freeman, 1981).

76. *Gossips, Gorgons and Crones*, p. 283.

77. *Gossips, Gorgons and Crones*, p. 286.

78. *The Woman's Encyclopedia of Myths and Secrets*, p. 160.

79. The age of the universe is of course contested. This widely agreed approximation is from Stikker, *The Transformation Factor*, p. 122.

Thealogy's transgressive conception of the world as constantly subject to the primordial dynamics of chaos disorders patriarchal theology by undermining the cosmological foundations of its divinely ordained social order. As we will see in the next chapter, by its very nature, thealogy's chaotic model of the cosmos as a spiral of convulsive, self-regenerative openness to change undermines (as Darwinian theories of evolution did in their time) patriarchy's cosmological claim to be the eternal, God-given social system that was set out in the first three chapters of Genesis. The leaven of all organicist conceptions of the world is introducing a radical change in our perception of reality as the product of infinitely variable interactivity whose stability cannot be autocratically engineered or predetermined from without. It is, as Mitchell Waldrop remarks,

> essentially meaningless to talk about a complex adaptive system being in equilibrium: the system can never get there. It is always unfolding, always in transition. In fact, if the system ever does reach equilibrium, it isn't just stable. It's dead.[80]

However, to give chaos a female gender is not to confirm the old stereotype of women as ontologically amorphous, diffuse, and whose reason is threatened by their reproductive ability to become two in one. While it is true that many mothers feel that the boundaries of their personhood have indeed become amorphous in the experience of pregnancy and birth, the 'femaleness' of chaos is less to do with female biology than with the feminist subversion of modernity's rectilinear political and religious project. 'Masculine' modernity has imposed an unnatural order on 'female' nature. Chaotic activism is spiritual politics in (com)motion. Here change is conducted through a flow of energy, whereas even with the most honourable egalitarian intentions, most patriarchal revolutions have maintained (an often notional) equality by traditional methods of suppression. Thought, behaviour and organization have been changed by force—often at gunpoint or with the threat of incarceration. To resist this form of revolution is not to propose a merely 'feminine' politics without teeth, but a vision of a world that is sustained by ecological energies other than violence.

It cannot be emphasized too strongly that a transitional boundary between patriarchal order (as control) and the chaos of unmapped, unfolding being is a creative or sacred destabilization. Its passage is not,

---

80. *Complexity*, p. 147.

and could not be, the terrifying trail of havoc left by war. The purpose of feminist chaos would be to restore the ecological balance of generation, decay and regeneration from the disorder of technological acceleration and interference; to crack open the materialist carapace and allow the free passage of biophilic relations. As Asia Shepsut tells her readers (albeit in the patriarchal idiom), 'You are to be a spiritual revolutionary conducting subtle guerilla warfare against lapses from cosmic law which lead to human degradation!'[81] Ilya Prigogine has argued that living systems self-organize and their chaotic entropy creates new order.[82] So too, by its ecological nature, spiritual feminist activism perturbs those smooth-running, but destructive and ultimately entropic political structures which mechanistically and continuously channel production into the global market of goods and information.

In *Violence and the Sacred*, René Girard claims that religious violence is a form of sacral generativity. In the world's religions, 'the operations of violence and the sacred are ultimately the same process'. He goes on to say that the sacred 'involves order as well as disorder, peace as well as war, creation as well as destruction'.[83] But spiritual feminist turbulence is not blindly destructive: it demands no sacrificial victims; no cycle of war, cease-fire and war. Spiritual feminism is not an organized religion and its 'violence', if it has any, is that of the Crone-power of nature which does not require sacrifice because everything dies in its own time. Ecological dissolution is not to be confused with violence. The task of spiritual feminism is to obstruct the tendency of capitalist entropy not to exhaust its own markets but to dissipate the energy of living systems by exploitation, clear-cutting and combustion (even though it will, finally, destroy itself).

One of the main achievements of the organicist vision has been to dissolve the artificial boundaries between theory and experience, and nature and culture. These boundaries gendered theory and culture as male and experience and nature as female. Secular feminists tend to think that thealogy redraws those boundaries in virtually the same place. But this is not true: as we saw in Chapter 3, thealogy does thoroughly displace those boundaries by including culture in the ecology of living

81. *Journey of the Priestess*, p. 241.

82. See Renée Weber's interview with Prigogine—one of the originators of chaos theory—in her collection, *Dialogues with Scientists and Sages: The Search for Unity* (London: Arkana, 1990), p. 182.

83. *Violence and the Sacred*, p. 258.

things (and often by tracing the beginnings of culture to matrifocal social organization). Although its mood is, broadly speaking, Dionysian rather than Apollonian, that does not preclude the peacefulness of its utopian vision. Spiritual feminism postulates that love and justice flourish in a harmonious social environment kept in balance by the circular relation of biophilic practices of production that are informed by the teachings, rituals and periodic festivals that align social and cosmic law.[84] As Asia Shepsut expresses it, thealogical 'measure is more understanding of organic subtleties—not inclined to accept man-made, often machine-like or robotic rhythms which jar against cosmic intervals'.[85] And thealogians often claim that the words 'motherhood', 'measure', 'mental' and 'menstrual' have an etymological family relation to one another which reunites intellection and female biology.

Spiritual feminism has, then, an inalienable but idiosyncratic rationality or good sense that unites pre- and postmodern ways of thinking. Spiritual feminist consciousness is not that of pure sensibility. Judy Grahn's *Blood, Bread and Roses* is a celebration of the first women's menstrual rites as the origins of human culture: the emergence of human consciousness from the undifferentiated consciousness of primate groups. Or again, reconstructed Wisdom goddesses such as Ma'at are honoured in the contemporary feminist pantheon. Ma'at was the Egyptian goddess of truth, right and justice. Her name means a measure of land and she demanded that the dead souls who appeared before her confess that they had 'not made any to weep'. Both Ma'at's name and her practice reflect the ways in which the harmony of the whole cosmos depends on the divine maintenance of an exact cosmic balance of nature and, interdependently, the ordered, just, compassionate conduct of human society.[86] As Rosemary Ruether points out, ancient Near Eastern

84. For an outstanding description of this social possibility see Starhawk's novel, *The Fifth Sacred Thing*.

85. *Journey of the Priestess*, p. 24. She describes this measure as 'matriarchal', but I do not find that misleading word helpful, especially as her point is relevant to thealogy as a whole. Also see her account of the duties of a priestess, pp. 234-35.

86. See, for example, Stone, *Ancient Mirrors of Womanhood*, pp. 263, 242, 276, 367; Long, *In a Chariot Drawn by Lions*, pp. 69, 85, 110-11, 117. See also Raphael, '"Cover Not My Blood with Thy Silence"', pp. 85-105 for a discussion of thealogical possibilities for the reclamation of the form and processes of justice from patriarchy. I am grateful to Asphodel Long for drawing my attention to the fact that recent African goddess worship indicates that the African goddesses have played an important role in the preservation of social justice. In a personal letter to me, Long

goddesses represented 'the wisdom and order that restore the harmony not only of the natural environment but also the humanly managed urban and agricultural worlds, rescuing them as well from threatened disruption by the forces of death and chaos'.[87] (I would read the latter phrase as referring to the 'death and chaos' of patriarchy, not nature.) It is not surprising, then, that the 5000-year-old story of Inanna who gained from her drunken father Enki the power of the *Me*—the measures governing human life (including the *Me* of decision and judgment)—now has almost the status of a feminist sacred text.

Feminist chaos is not, then, to be confused with punk anarchy or heavy-metal 'chaos magic(k)'. 'Chaos magic' is inspired by the work of the late magician Aleister Crowley. By shattering all social conventions and conditioning by violent and often degrading means, chaos magic is believed to release personal power. Even if only in the imagination (as it usually is), to confront and enter the maelstrom of chaos is itself believed to be empowering. Tanya Luhrmann notes that 'the fantasy often has a bizarre, bleak form. The indubitable logic of [chaos magic] philosophy presses the role of violence, murder, sexual degradation: the most stringent regulations should yield greatest power when violated.'[88]

Spiritual feminist chaos, however, belongs to the natural generative rhythms of the universe. To take just three examples, the creativity and beauty of chaos is manifest in psychology, music and biology. For Jane Caputi, acceptance of inner psychic chaos is vital in the process of developing what she calls 'female Powers' and what I would call 'female sacrality':

> If we can know and accept within ourselves that which is chaotic, dark, creative, turbulent, female, and wild, our fear will leave us. We will see that female Powers are not at all forbidding, repulsive, or frightening, but are, in a word, *attractive*.[89]

So too, musical harmony can be richly textured by the use of counter-point and the minute irregularities of human beat rather than the sterile

---

writes that 'all over Ikwerre land there is a common saying "Nye Kratwatru, Eli chekwetaa" (the goddess earth protects the just)'. See W.O. Wotogbe-Weneka, 'Eli. Earth Goddess, as a Guardian of Social Morality among the Traditional Ikwerre of Rivers State Nigeria', in *King's Theological Review* 11 (1988), pp. 50-54.

87. 'Goddesses and Witches: Liberation and Countercultural Feminism', *The Christian Century* September 10–17, 1980, p. 845.

88. *Persuasions of the Witch's Craft*, p.104.

89. *Gossips, Gorgons and Crones*, p. 288.

and uninteresting beat of mathematically regular computer-generated music. Again, chaos as an agency of renewal can be detected in the findings of recent biological research which shows that slight irregularities in heartbeat and the patterns of white cell production are necessary to the body's health. Heart disease and leukaemia both appear to produce (respectively) *over-* regular beats and cell production.[90]

In sum, organicist politics mirror nature as understood by the science of complexity. Sacral turbulence such as that of radical ecofeminist activism attempts to stir or disorganize patriarchal order into a chaotic state of change. Chaos theory reminds us of the mysterious ability of systems to degenerate and then, out of the chaos, to self-organize into new patterns of order and complexity. So Caputi's exhortation to stir the cauldron is not to incite ruin. It is rather to begin a process analogous to that which makes a snowflake. A snowflake is the product of both chaotic weather conditions and the sublimely beautiful ordering of the sixfold symmetry of crystal formation. (By analogy, Emily Culpepper found that her experience of organization in the women's movement unified and patterned the chaotic quality of her radically eclectic spirituality.[91])

Chaotic political thealogy is not yet a fully emergent discourse, but in my own understanding it defuses the coercive force which holds nature and society in the artificial grip of uniformity and conformity. It refuses the monocultural standardization that stunts healthy human and natural biodiversity. Instead, the natural capacity to self-organize can be imaged by the sudden flocking of birds into patterned formations, and thealogically imaged as the Goddess who, like the chaologists' 'strange attractor', exerts a mysterious spiral 'pull' on dynamic systems, introducing a beautiful stability and regularity into irregularity.[92] The Goddess is the

90. J. Briggs, *Fractals: The Patterns of Chaos* (London: Thames & Hudson, 1992), p. 129.

91. 'The Spiritual, Political Journey of a Feminist Freethinker', in P.M. Cooey *et al.* (eds.), *After Patriarchy: Feminist Transformations of the World Religions* (Maryknoll, NY: Orbis Books, 1991), p. 151.

92. Cf. Gleick, *Chaos*, p. 152. When strange attractors became manifest in random points plotted on a computer, they 'seemed like a face they [the scientists] had been seeing everywhere, in the music of turbulent flows or in clouds scattered like veils across the sky. Nature was *constrained*. Disorder was channelled, it seemed, into patterns with some common underlying theme.' In *Gossips, Gorgons and Crones*, p. 290, Jane Caputi discerns in the owl-like 'face' of this strange attractor 'the classic spiralling eyes of countless ancient goddess images'.

principle of anti-chaos who brings in a new order from the edge of the old.

Spiritual Feminist Politics/Poetics as 'Weather'

In this final section of the chapter I would like to look at one particular element of chaos: weather, and its effects on the topology, so to speak, of feminist transformation. As the meteorologist Edward Lorenz discovered in 1961, weather patterns are not predictable. The constantly changing variables of wind speed, humidity, air pressure, changes in vegetation, snow cover, the extent of pack ice, and the interactions of all these and others, make precise long-range forecasting impossible.[93] Even with satellite photography meteorologists can only forecast accurately three to seven days in advance.[94]

To image feminist activism as 'weather' is to evoke a parallel dynamic patterning in sacral transformation and emergence. Just as contemporary environmental pollution by 'greenhouse' gases seems to be negatively altering the earth's climate, so too, when spiritual feminist activism is imaged as weather it evokes feminist sacral power to provoke a positive change in the political climate. With its magical capacity to turn the smooth flow of patriarchal systems to turbulence, spiritual feminism dissipates their destructive energies; erases their check-points and frontiers and defines new spaces whose language and patterns of organization have yet to unfold. (As in some Christian eschatologies, the regenerated world is both now and not yet.)

The text which best exemplifies the sacral dynamics of ontological transformation as 'gyn/ecology' in motion is Mary Daly's *Outercourse*, and I will quote fairly extensively from it because to paraphrase Daly is not only a literary sacrilege, but a diminution of meaning. For Daly, Crones who hear the 'Call of the Wild' spin counterclockwise 'beyond the compass and off the map' and 'between the left and right hemispheres of the brain' where the word-magic of metaphor carries crones off and out of the foreground on wings, winds, threads and pathways.[95]

---

93. See E. Lorenz, 'Large-Scale Motions of the Atmosphere: Circulation', in P.M. Hurley (ed.), *Advances in Earth Science* (Cambridge, MA: MIT Press, 1966), pp. 95-109; W.J. Burroughs, *Watching the World's Weather* (Cambridge: Cambridge University Press, 1991), p. 3.

94. Burroughs, *Watching the World's Weather*, p. 5.

95. See, for example, *Outercourse*, pp. 311-12.

Sacred shape-shifting and the spiritual amphibiousness of biophilic women empowers them to 'Hop, Leap and Fly' out of the 'foreground': 'I can feel the pull of my Sister the moon and I feel mySelf rising, rising. I thought it was a dream until I heard mySelf scream: "Power to the Witch and to the woman in me."'[96]

Daly is carried away by a 'Great Wind which calls and carries Wild, Deviant Women on our True Course'.[97]

> It's been very Windy lately, in every sense of the word. So I've been thinking about Blasting. When I thought about Blasting out of the foreground I saw mySelf riding a Blast of Wind, in my Craft, of course, which can also be a broom. But what I also wanted to do was to Blast a hole in the wall between the foreground and the Background—a hole so big that everyone who is really Alive can get through. I decided that the way to do that was just to be my Natural Self, who is Extreme.[98]

As 'Outlandish Outsider' the radical feminist Self possesses the energies of disruption and departure. Blasted by patriarchy as a witch, her own blasting is both a curse on patriarchy and a summoning of the volcanic propulsive energy that hurls her up into the transcendence of air and across the immanence of the earth and seas. It sustains her at the high altitudes of metapatriarchal consciousness, and keeps her buoyant on its uncharted seas. In short, it propels her towards the magical extremities of extremism. On a flight to Seattle in 1980 the aircraft Daly was travelling in passed the volcano Mount Saint Helens. The volcano was belching white smoke prior to a subsequent eruption a few days later. Daly writes of this auspicious moment:

> I felt a deep kinship between her need to explode and my own...Mount Saint Helens spoke to me of the Elemental Biophilic Powers of the Earth and of women, as distinguished from destructive man-made necrophilic nuclear, chemical, and political pseudo-powers. That volcano said to me: 'Come on! Explode with me! Our Time is coming.'[99]

One of the most numinous agencies of disorder is a storm. At its greatest pitch of spiritual/political energy female sacrality can be imaged as (bad) weather: a tornado buffeting, eroding, scattering patriarchal structure. Like wind and rain, gynergy is a dissident, dissonant counterblast

96. *Outercourse*, p. 343.
97. *Outercourse*, p. 52.
98. *Outercourse*, p. 341.
99. *Outercourse*, p. 242.

to the destructive, consumptive energies of patriarchal systems. Gynergy blows, shakes and courses through the architecture of patriarchy like the volcanoes, rivers and climate changes that have changed and will change the world's terrain over time. Although, under industrial capitalism, air and water have been burdened as the principal carriers of environmental pollution, as the elemental carriers of gynergy they also purify. When a window is opened a breeze wafts through a fusty room; water washes away accretions that have obscured and defaced the beauty of the material beneath.

Of course it needs to be said that *actual* tornadoes, tidal waves, earthquakes and volcanic eruptions only have a numinous grandeur when viewed from a safe distance. Abnormal weather conditions are usually catastrophic for all the human beings and many of the animals in a given environment. Freak weather conditions like long-term drought wreak immense suffering through starvation, homelessness and death, as well through their longer-term impact on the poor within a damaged national economy. Thealogians are well aware of this and do not romanticize nature. On the contrary, despite its ultimate vitalism, 'deep green' thealogy is not a triumphalist conceptual system: it can be very bleak, almost nihilistic in its recognition that the natural phenomena that cause human pain are part of a larger cycle of cosmic death and regeneration in which human experience may not count for very much. There are natural extinctions and most animals are preyed upon or suffer the effects of seasonal climate change and die in some degree of pain. Thealogy does not see this ecological suffering as a sign of divine moral evil. But at the same time thealogy would never claim that natural destruction could justify deliberate, self-gratifying human destruction. Natural death is necessary for regeneration, but human cruelty is not. Any possible spiritual regeneration after a period of historical cataclysm (like the claim of some Zionist Jews that the state of Israel arose from the ashes of Auschwitz) happens by default; it has no inherent relation to evil. Thealogy does not impute moral evil to the Goddess and nor does it justify human evil, but its ecological model reminds us that the Goddess has not created as easy or as joyous a paradise as we might have liked.

Postmodern cosmology, like thealogy, presents a bubbling universe in which

> dynamical chaotic forces… operate among the planets in the deep space
> beyond. Here collapsing neutron stars spin at frantic rates, supernovas

slowly explode in shock waves that trigger the birth of new stars, suns—spinning balls of turbulence—spew out magnetic storms across millions of miles, and black holes chew up passing energy.[100]

The Goddess has not, then, created a world whose history can be forecast as the conditions for 'man's' progressive apotheosis at the expense of all that lives. Instead, the Goddess situates female sacral power as a cosmic power to generate and change life without either diminishing or aggrandizing itself: an ultimate image of liberation from its centuries of seclusion, separation, confinement, invisibility and hiddeness. Here the creative energies of women and the Goddess are dynamically related as are streams to the seas. On the turbulent regenerative boundary, the Goddess is, like those who consciously seek to embody her energy, a great river in full flow; a very stormy sea. And this means that feminist spirituality must also brave its uncertainties. The destinations of feminist voyages over the turbulent seas of spiritual/political struggle are not mapped or promised by covenantal agreement. A radical feminist diaspora will not enjoy the security of God's covenantal blessing on their wanderings. They have not already been promised a territory filled with the (female) blessings of milk and honey.

A sub-metaphor of the spiritual feminist voyaging metaphor is that of the sea mist. Like other sacred things, the mist is ambiguous in being both protective and dangerous. The 'mist' evokes the hazard of a boat running aground or sailing round and round in circles. But mist also offers protection to the sailor from attack. Daly's piratical, wind-tossed voyages smuggling liberative knowledges into the havens of radical feminist coves are dangerous. The mists that swirl around her Craft reveal subliminal meanings, but their vapours also confuse; mists that arise from the sea contain Background knowledge but are also are filled with illusionary contaminants or 'man-made mind-pollutants' and the feminist sailor has to navigate through them.[101] Yet in Marion Bradley's *The Mists of Avalon* the mists are a magical boundary that descend to veil the holiness of the Isle of Avalon from the profane world, thereby hiding and protecting this female space from patriarchal sight.[102] For spiritual feminists, the mists warn voyaging women of the danger of drifting into a state of limbo as they attempt to re-map the sacrality of the material world and the profanity of what pollutes and exploits it. When the mists

100. Briggs, *Fractals*, pp. 50-51.
101. *Outercourse*, pp. 130, 150.
102. London: Sphere, 1984.

come down there is a sense that the earth itself conspires with women, in their liberation and its own. Above all, the mist is a watery veil, and like other veils it marks a woman's passage from one state to another. The veil of water becomes a symbolic element of the rite of passage into spiritual feminist consciousness and is in some senses comparable to a nun's 'taking the veil', which marks her passing from the novitiate to permanent incorporation into a community of sacred women.

Daly has set sail on a turbulent sea of subliminal, archaic knowledge that has been forbidden to women under patriarchy. As *sub*liminal it is underneath or in front of a boundary that must be crossed in order to contact and actualize its knowledges.[103] When spiritual feminists lift the heavy patriarchal anchor and cast themselves off into the sea and winds of ontological transformation they are neither in patriarchy nor out of it and so are compelled to be migratory, rootless and transplanted. They have different ways of speaking and reading the world. They do not have the right papers: the patriarchal guarantee of identity, prosperity and freedom of movement.[104] Boundary feminists are a threat to patriarchy because—unlike refugees who cast themselves in gratitude and humility on the mercies of their host—their oppositional political vision makes them unassimilable. The physical body of the 'terrible Tabooed woman' may still inhabit the patriarchal 'foreground', but the recognizably other meaning and intentionality of her body is tabooed or shunned. Divorced from the patriarchal Adam, a spiritual feminist can find herself in Lilith's desolate blood-drenched wilderness of thistles by the Red Sea, with only owls, ravens and jackals for company.[105]

Translated into 'foreground' language, this means that she may be subject to discrimination. The outlawed (profane) woman has renounced her claim to the physical protection and rights that patriarchy can offer to some wives and to women of property. The edge of patriarchy is no place for the faint hearted.[106] Nor is it a place for secular feminists who

---

103. *Outercourse*, pp. 13, 129.

104. There are some affinities between my conception of the sacred/profane borderland and that of Gloria Anzaldúa in *Borderlands / La Frontera: The New Mestiza* (San Francisco: Spinsters / Aunt Lute, 1987), pp. 3-4.

105. Isa. 34.14: 'And wild beasts shall meet with hyenas, and satyr shall cry to his fellow; yea, there shall the night hag [Lilith] alight, and find for herself a resting place.'

106. See, for example, Maggie Lowry's account of the blockade at Greenham when 150 women chained themselves for 24 hours to the eight main gates of the

have no wish to be divorced and exiled from language and history once more, even if by the agency of other feminists. The very *point* of reformist feminism is to change patriarchy on its own best terms. The purpose of bourgeois secular feminism is precisely to be accepted into patriarchal hierarchies on equal terms. Exile or banishment from history would defeat that object. For many, perhaps most feminists, the images of religio-political activism as wandering, abnormal weather or seismic disturbance would be too random and transcendental to be politically engaging. In an immediate sense, perhaps they would be right, but when it finally dawns on patriarchy that there is no material division between humans and nature, between 'doers and done-to',[107] then the terms of political engagement will have to change.

base; in D. Thompson (ed.), *Over Our Dead Bodies* (London: Virago, 1983), esp. pp. 73-74.

107. This is a phrase Mitchell Waldrop uses in *Complexity*, p. 333.

Chapter 7

THE COSMOGONIC WOMB

The first vibrations of the egg of the world which unfold to the edges of
the universe are both expanding and contracting, emerging from the
source and pulsing outward to disappear into a spherical vortex. The still
center (the heart) is the axis of creation—the universal continuum
perpetually unfolds, pulses outward, contracts—perpetually spinning
through its own center...

Monica Sjöö and Barbara Mor[1]

Male sacrality is almost universally associated with the sky. And because
the celestial configurations of stars, moon and sun appear to be relatively
fixed, this cosmic stability is commonly regarded by historians of religion as the source of the masculinization of rules, laws, institutions; in
short, all those things which establish permanence. Male deities tend to
set down the immovable elements in the landscape such as sacred mountains and boulders; they set out the permanent moral and legal institutions and all the accompanying cultural and religious rites that legitimate
and perpetuate them. And as M.H. Klaiman notes, 'virtually without
exception, human societies exclude women from the most sacred
religious rites, as well as from manipulation of the most sacred objects of
cult'. So while masculine sacrality is associated with what Klaiman calls
'stability and essentiality', female sacrality is associated with the 'change
and materiality' of outer substances: 'The masculine may be associated
with the potential, inactive form of being; the feminine, with kinetic,
active being. The masculine is one and/or integrated; the feminine is
plural and/or diffuse.'[2]

Female cosmic energy is variously expressed in the world's religions.

---

1.   *The Great Cosmic Mother*, p. 55.
2.   M.H. Klaiman, 'Masculine Sacrality', in Eliade (ed.), *Encyclopedia of
Religion*, IX, p. 257. This whole discussion of masculine sacrality is indebted to
Klaiman's article.

For example, in Indian Yoga philosophies *sakti* is 'the energy that activates the ever-changing material universe'. It is dangerous and 'rampant'
if it is not balanced by the masculine principle of *purusa* (meaning
'man'). Or again, female cosmic energy is manifest in the Navajo female
earth divinity, born of First Girl and Boy, and called—significantly—
Changing Woman.[3] Female change and male permanence are also
reflected in the world's religious rituals. Rituals that mark decisive
beginnings or ends, origins and culminations, are male dominated. The
material, domestic roles are consigned to women because productivity,
process and change are feminine. These are, according to Klaiman,
'more or less universal tendencies'.[4]

It is also generally agreed that the world's 'feminine' cosmogonies are
associated with water and earth and female divinities usually create from
the body—the archetypal 'Great Container', as Neumann would put it.
Male creators, however, tend to create from up in the sky and if they
fashion or transform material into existent things this is done outside
their own bodies.[5] Charlene Spretnak's beautiful image of the Goddess
birthing the world by a bursting forth of female reproductive vitality
conforms to this gendered cosmological typology:

> From the eternal Void, Gaia danced forth and rolled Herself into a
> spinning ball... from Her warm moisture She bore a flow of gentle rain
> that fed Her surface and brought life. Wriggling creatures spawned in tidal
> pools, while tiny green shoots pushed upwards through her pores. She
> filled oceans and ponds and set rivers flowing through deep furrows.[6]

Now it could be said that spiritual feminism merely confirms and
perpetuates both traditional religious practice and the androcentric
assumptions of the scholars who have documented and analysed it. But
my point has been that 'female' sacrality is not the same as 'feminine'
sacrality. The word 'female' has a feminist intention of ridding sacrality
of its delimitation by men to the secondary, non-political, private sphere
of the profane or semi-profane. To celebrate the female instead of the
feminine is to rid the sacred/profane distinction of the false polarities that
have dogged the history of its application to women—namely, casting

3. Klaiman, 'Masculine Sacrality', p. 257.
4. 'Masculine Sacrality', p. 257.
5. Sanday, *Female Power and Male Dominance*, p. 58.
6. In Spretnak and Capra, *Green Politics*, p. 250. She is citing her own work
from *The Lost Goddesses of Early Greece: A Collection of Pre-Hellenic Myths*
(Boston: Beacon Press, 1981).

domestic feminine sacrality as safe and public female sacrality as dangerous.

Instead, the feminist sacred can be evoked and described with language and practices historically attributed to women *in so far as* these seem to be biophilic and relational in character. In this way contemporary feminists have an ethical, practical and spiritual say in the naming of the sacred, and yet retain some dialogical link with women of the past and non-feminist women of the present, as well as the possibility of dialogue with religious scholarship. In other words, the sacred will have been reconstructed within a feminist context and yet the term will not have degenerated into private language. This dialogical character of the spiritual feminist sacred is particularly apparent in its cosmology.

In Europe humanity's 50,000-year-old religious history of cosmological myths came to an end with the rise of mechanistic, reductionist, abstract science.[7] Cosmology and theology survived the Enlightenment, but in a desacralized form. The Enlightenment God was, broadly speaking, a deist God who wound up the universe as if it were a clock and then retired into absolute transcendence, leaving its maintenance to a male technocracy. However, postmodern science, and chaology in particular, substantiates a thealogical cosmology in which the universe is generated by the pulse of 'female' energy. This might be expected. Each successive cultural and scientific paradigm furnishes a new cosmology. Historically, political and cosmological models have been mutually informing and affirming. In the present Western world, postmodern cosmologists tend to be people who are apprehensive of centralized military and technological power; for whom race and gender difference are not social disqualifications; and for whom the consciousness and ensoulment of matter are not (as they were for Descartes) in question. In the postmodern milieu power and information are being democratized (up to a point) through a variety of web- or net-like relationships that are making hierarchies look dated: all these factors are contributing to the reimaging of the cosmological process.[8]

The developments in postmodern science I discussed in the previous

7.   B. Swimme, 'The Cosmic Creation Story', in Griffin (ed.), *The Reenchantment of Science*, p. 49. Brian Swimme is a physicist who is committed to collaborative work with other advocates of creation spirituality such as Matthew Fox.

8.   Although I discuss cosmology as a set of metaphors—as something that is, in a Ricoeurian sense, both like x and not x, there are of course those who would claim that their myths are not metaphors but descriptive histories.

chapter undermine the still dominant patriarchal picture of the cosmos as a fixed, mapped entity. Its matter both eludes objective, fixing description and is in constant flux (at the quantum level light can be observed as a wave or a particle depending on one's experimental procedure). And chaos theory has shown that change and transformation are the chief characteristics of living systems.[9] In the light of this, it is arguable that the masculine way of setting and fixing the religious, legal and material landscape in concrete is less of a metaphorical 'fit' with the contemporary model of the cosmos than are the 'female' cosmologies of chaos and complexity. So when creation and subsequent social organization are imaged as, say, a dance,[10] rather than a divine taxonomic exercise, female sacrality becomes cosmologically appropriate. It can no longer be contained as a secondary, private, domestic energy because the old stable boundaries between nature, domesticity and culture have disappeared into an ecologically connected model of reality.

The current 'feminization' of cosmology could be supportive of late twentieth-century feminist sexual politics. After all, patriarchal readings of Genesis have played a central role in the Western history of sexual polemics; patriarchal cosmology has underwritten its own sexism. If that is so, then sexism could be overcome *ab origine* by a spiritual feminist reclamation of cosmology that has already been set in process in postmodern science and in its own reconstruction of female embodiment as replicating the cosmogonic activity of the Goddess. As cosmogonic stories unify time and are models of all subsequent creation, the embodied immanence of the Goddess in women or 'female' modes of being makes all biophilic creativity cosmogonic to some degree. Female sacrality casts a whole circle. This last chapter takes female sacrality through a full circle that unites craft, menstruality and spiritual/political activism as one embodied cosmogonic process. In the course of this chapter I shall explore several cosmological metaphors that propose 'female' modes of creation. It will be noticed that I do not always attribute particular cosmological metaphors to particular writers. That is

9. For a readable survey and commentary on the 'magical' character of postmodern science see Roney-Dougal, *Where Science and Magic Meet*, pp. 65-89.

10. The 'dance' of creation is a common postmodern cosmological image. Spiritual feminism's use of the image recalls the great cosmogonic dance of the Hindu goddess and god Shakti-Kali and Shiva who danced creation in and out of being. In this, spiritual feminist cosmology has more in common with the Eastern than the Western tradition.

because, as with other parts of spiritual feminist discourse, no one writer adopts one metaphor as her own and dismisses the rest. There is a common pool of imagery into which all writers dip at will.

Feminist Cosmology

When nature, culture and cosmos are organically related in the generative processes of the Goddess who, in her immanence, is not ontologically other to women, female sacrality becomes gestatory in all dimensions: biological, cultural and ultimately cosmogonic:

> The Goddess is not separate but is in everything. We are her and she is us. Her agency is our energy: it is in all of us at a deep personal level as a source of power and we have many choices as to how we may wish to express this power... We are all individual sources of energy but we are also all joined as one great pool of power, strength and creativity as are all things in the universe and beyond.[11]

Or again, Starhawk's poem 'A Story of Beginnings' urges women to feel the Goddess in their belly, pulse and nerves. Repeating the refrain 'you are alive in her as she in you', Starhawk writes,

> You are alive in her as she in you
> You are her
> Your misty breath great clouds of gases set in motion
>   by your spinning dance
>   swirl and cool and rain
>   for thousands and thousands of years.[12]

The continual biological and cultural generation that is human history participates in continual cosmic generation—that which takes all other generativities into itself. A cosmogonic story is therefore an inaugural but open-ended, indeterminate story of possibilities. In Goddess feminism, where beginnings and ends are cyclic, cosmogony is a continually renewed promise of transformation and new beginnings. And as such, cosmology should exercise the feminist imagination since the primeval signifies a truly pre-patriarchal, non-colonized time and space. It signifies the beginning of all possibility.

---

11. From a cyclostyled paper by a group of women in the Matriarchy network. Quoted in King, *Women and Spirituality*, p. 146.

12. In J. Plant (ed.), *Healing the Wounds: The Promise of Ecofeminism* (Philadelphia: New Society, 1989), p. 116. See whole poem, pp. 115-17.

However, thealogical creation myths are not as common in the literature as might be expected. This may be because of the monotheistic overtones, the apparent centralization of power, and the imposition of a linear scheme of beginnings and ends that creation narratives usually suggest. Also thealogy would want to avoid establishing one single, definitive, canonical creation text. Patriarchal canons have notably encouraged authoritarian orthodoxies, literalism and the foreclosure of other imaginative possibilities.

It may also be that those spiritual feminists who are concerned to avoid essentialism, biologism and the assumption that all Goddess feminists are 'earth-mothers' with very full laps would be uneasy with an ontology of femaleness as that which *primarily* gives birth—and on a cosmic scale. This unease would not be groundless. For example, while being a profoundly spiritual labour, Judy Chicago's collaborative work 'The Birth Project' illustrates the maternalist nature of most spiritual feminist cosmogony. It is a piece of needlework to which many women contributed from across the United States. It depicts a woman in labour whose wave-like contractions echo the regenerative ebb and surge of cosmogonic energy.[13] Female cosmogony inevitably places a good deal of emphasis on the womb as the central symbol and source of generativity. But for women who do not want children or who cannot have children, the womb is either an irrelevant or a traumatic symbol that has not played a role in their erotic-creative agency. And for women who have not been able to bear children, or for the large numbers of women who have had hysterectomies,[14] or who have had a difficult menopause, the womb can be a symbol of loss; an empty space.

So feminist unease with female cosmogonic myths is partially justified. To primordialize, biologize and situate female power in a cosmic womb can be emotionally problematic and can appear to ignore women's cognitive creativity. If giving birth (even to the universe) is proposed as the highest, most powerful female state, that might appear to devalue other forms of female being, and indeed, other manifestations of female

13. See Orenstein, *The Reflowering of the Goddess*, pp. 93-94.
14. According to Dorin Schumacher's statistics in 'Hidden Death: The Sexual Effects of Hysterectomy', in Rosenthal (ed.), *Women, Ageing and Ageism*, pp. 54-55, only 63% of American women reach the age of 65 with their uterus intact. Between 1970 and 1984 only 10.5% of hysterectomies were medically indicated; it is usually a preventative operation. However, its effects can include depression and the loss of a woman's sexual desire and her ability to reach orgasm.

sacrality in culture. The attribution of cosmic generativity to women also seems to propose that female existence will be an exhausting effort of continual giving and activity which does not ring true to women's actual need to be given *to*, to rest, and to do nothing for a while. Yet a maternalist creation myth would, by its nature, imply the normative ontological status of motherhood for women. To remember the first state of womanhood in its maximal creativity might be to remember it in its pristine and therefore true state. But few feminists would want to impose biological motherhood as the first, final and maximal state of femaleness.

However, to reduce 'female' cosmology to a purely biological process may also be to submit to the history of its derogation. As Christine Downing has pointed out, the biblical reduction of the Canaanite goddesses to fertility goddesses ignored the fact that the Canaanite goddess's title was usually Queen of Heaven, not 'earth mother'. The Goddess was, according to Downing, 'not associated only with fertility, whether agricultural or human, but was also viewed as creatress of all; she was spoken of as prophetess, as inventor, healer and warrior'.[15] Here cultural as well as biological sacrality is continuous with cosmogonic sacrality. Moreover, the Goddess's qualities and practices can be less than ordinarily maternal. In her parthenogenetic forms she is androgynous; she is also a destroyer, a goddess of the underworld and of lunacy: 'She is the poppy as well as the grain, the giver of intoxicants (and poisons) as well as food.'[16]

Female cosmogony is not, then, simply an amplification of human women's experiences of motherhood and its generativity is not the same thing as the fertility patriarchy attributes to women. The common patriarchal conception of female fertility is that of passive undifferentiated clods of ploughed earth whose vulval furrows are tilled by the active, linear passage of the phallic plough.[17] Spiritual feminism, however, argues that divine and human female generativity is not antithetical to culture: it is a continuous energy that in itself knows no human theoretical, temporal or spatial differentiations. And accordingly, female sacrality is immanent, active and culturally diverse. Any person with the spiritual intention of transformation—even if that is just recycling household waste—is exercising a form of cosmic regeneration. (After all, the whole cosmos is made of recycled matter.)

15. *The Goddess*, pp. 14-15.
16. Downing, *The Goddess*, pp. 12-13.
17. See for example Qur'an 2:223.

And in those traditions which pre-date full knowledge of the role of male sperm in conception, the Goddess's cosmogonic processes are not, in any case, those of normal human reproductive biology. The Goddess fashions, transforms herself, or churns things into existence. She might fashion the primordial materials that are to hand, or she might change her body into that of the earth, with her breasts becoming mountains, her womb becoming the sea and so on. In this way, the Goddess is in nature but is more than the sum of its parts. So too, women's crafted products are organically expressive of their being, but do not exhaust the meaning of their being (as can the drudgery of patriarchal domesticity and motherhood). To project those crafts onto the reproductivity of the universe does not render women mere cosmic drones. On the contrary, it sacralizes women's lives by a radical imaginal expansion of their scope and meaning.

As the Celtic goddess Cerridwen, the northern goddess Wyrd, the Hindu goddess Kali, the Mycenaean Demeter, or the Babylonian Siris, the Goddess stirs her menstrual (or sometimes milky) womb/cauldron to generate, destroy and regenerate all living things.[18] In this great steaming menstrual soup all that will be curdles, coagulates and churns. The cosmogonic cauldron's undifferentiated, unclotted elements of possibility without form are probably alluded to in Genesis 1.2, where *tohu* and *bohu* are often translated pejoratively as the mere 'waste and void' of the primordial state. Her creation has no beginning and will have no absolute end. It is a continuous cycle: she bears all the temporal aspects of Virgin, Mother and Crone at once. Change is an inseparable part of the meaning of the Goddess's existence, hence the recurrent crescent moon, chrysalis and butterfly symbols found in the archaeological remains of 'Old Europe'.[19] The chaotic cauldron metaphor is perhaps most significant of all thealogy's cosmological metaphors as it is fruitfully connected to those of new science and ecology, widely distributed in the world's mythologies, antithetical to the most harmful elements of the biblical cosmologies, and unsentimental in its image of both women and divinity.

In Genesis God does not create *ex nihilo*: that is a later Christian doctrine.[20] Nonetheless, classical theism is premised on the assumption

18. For details of the cauldron motif see Walker, *The Crone*, pp. 92-122.
19. See M. Gimbutas, *The Goddesses and Gods of Old Europe 6500–3500 BCE: Myths and Cult Images* (Berkeley: University of California Press, 1982), p. 237.
20. See R.R. Ruether, 'Patriarchy and Creation: Feminist Critique of Religious

that God created *ex nihilo* and therefore the world began as the best of all possible worlds. Whatever has gone wrong subsequently is the moral failing and the responsibility of human beings. By contrast thealogy's cosmology of the Goddess as a vortex from which all things emerge and to which they return entails a theadicy in which the Goddess is 'responsible' for suffering and loss only in so far as these are 'natural' evils and have ecological and cosmological origins. As such, spiritual feminist menstrual cosmology has returned to an ancient cosmology in which chaos and harmony belong together in a creation where perfection is both impossible and meaningless.

Here again, thealogy has not simply projected human maternity onto the cosmos. Its cosmogonic symbols are female-referring and immanent in the material realm, but they are also divinely other. And yet even in its divine otherness female cosmogony is interwoven with human generativity in ways that masculine cosmological metaphors are not. Masculine cosmological sacrality is typically remote, inactive and withdrawn. And male divine epiphanies are typically manifest in thunder, or the flight of eagles, or the appointment of a son or other second-in-command to continue the male god's activities on earth.[21] Although spiritual feminist cosmogonies, or 'cosmogynies' as some would prefer, are distinctive in intention and form, they are, I think, best understood in relief against the biblical cosmology that, in one form or another, almost all spiritual feminists grew up with and have spent many years dissociating themselves from. One of the central claims of spiritual feminism is that in patriarchal cosmologies a male divinity overpowers a female divinity or female creative principle, usurps and derogates her creativity, and takes the credit for creation himself. So over half of this chapter will use spiritual feminist cosmological motifs to draw out those elements of patriarchal cosmology—that of the biblical Priestly writer in particular—that have had a significant influence on the status of female sacral creativity.

Thealogical cosmology is, like its object, a discourse in process. It is also a very new discourse, as discourses go. Although female cosmologies are an ancient phenomenon, their feminist reconstructions are only about 20 years old and have not had the millennia to develop that patriarchal cosmology has had. Some spiritual feminists are either making up their own creation story, rewriting the biblical one, or borrowing one

and Scientific Cosmologies', *Feminist Theology* 2 (1993), p. 63.

21. See Klaiman, 'Masculine Sacrality', pp. 252-55.

from a primal religion which honours the female principle.[22] Or they might be doing something between all three. The details of any one or other feminist cosmogony are less important to the present discussion than that spiritual feminism has rejected biblical cosmology as a political device that establishes patriarchy as an order that originated with time, space and the creation of matter. It has adopted instead a thealogy of periodic destruction and renewal that makes non-sense of patriarchal politics' cosmological pretensions.

Spiritual feminism's continuous reproductive cycle of creation renders the clock-time of human historiography problematic, since beginnings and ends cannot be distinguished (other than the humanly observable point at which, say, a human being's heart ceases to beat). Beginnings and ends occupy the same points on the revolving circle. So although some feminists see this present period of ecological crisis as the possible end of a 'micro' world-cycle, the 'macro' cycle of nature as independent of human life is a continuous process of transformation with no absolute boundary between life and death.

So too, the establishment of a moral code whose foundations are set down at creation is largely redundant. Spiritual feminism is not, I hasten to say, without moral implications and responsibilities. But good human behaviour need not be ordained at creation and remain so under threat of punishment. It is ideally a 'timeless' obligation of love and gratitude to the earth and its creatures for sustaining one's life. When Anne Cameron was a child an old woman taught her about ethical obligations:

> She taught me without me knowing I was being taught... She taught me you do not put garbage or waste in your drinking water, she taught me you do not heedlessly cut every tree and leave the earth to erode, unprotected and insulted... She taught me you do not move on this earth disrespectfully and cruelly.[23]

22. See for example Anne Cameron's 'First Mother and the Rainbow Children', in Plant (ed.), *Healing the Wounds*, pp. 54ff. This is a re-telling of the Native American myth of origins which begins with the cracking of the Great Egg from which flows the River of Life after which the Creator makes First Woman from the earth, with bones and teeth made of seashells, hair of grass, and shining eyes from the sun, moon and stars.

23. 'First Mother and the Rainbow Children', p. 56.

Eggs, Snakes and Water

As well as the cauldron, there are at least three other recurrent motifs in spiritual feminist cosmological discourse: eggs, snakes and water—and these latter two are interconnected with the cauldron. Taking the egg motif first, it is at once apparent that the feminist emphasis on the primacy of the egg contests that theology in which the biblical promise is carried through the male seed in the passive vessel of the female womb. In the Hebrew Bible God's will is carried in the seed or sperm; the matriarchs' wombs are simply vehicles and the egg is more or less invisible in the texts.

Paganism is usually more balanced and has many myths in which before time begins the earth mother pairs with a male fecundator and their separation (not always an amicable one) forms the sky and land with light in between. The union and separation of the Greek Gaia and Ouranos, the New Zealand Rangi and Papa, and the North American Earth Mother and Sky Father are examples of these.[24] Neo-pagan thealogy recognizes the oddity of the dominant biblical creation myths in which a father creates the world without a mother. The Goddess commonly enjoys relationship with a male lover or consort—sometimes the Horned God—who fecundates the Goddess but does not generate life. But Dianic witchcraft can be guilty of tipping the balance the other way. Here the male fecundating principle plays no role at all. The contemporary parthenogenetic Goddess recalls those early cultures which were unaware of the role sperm played in pregnancy; children were sometimes believed to have been placed in the mother's womb—having previously lived in caves, wells, trees and so forth. The strong lesbian element in spiritual feminism would be inspired by these parthenogenetic images of birth as the product of women's erotic connection with the conscious female body/earth. Similarly, the emergent cosmos is sometimes pictured in contemporary thealogy in the ancient image of the world egg which simply cracks when the time is right. As Sjöö and Mor put it (in terms that mix science and mythology), 'at the pole of contraction, our universe existed as an invisible point of dark light, of compacted *potentia* or energy. This was the world egg.'[25]

24. Falk, 'Feminine Sacrality', p. 304.
25. *The Great Cosmic Mother*, p. 55. See the section entitled 'Female Cosmology and the Creation of the Universe', pp. 55-56. This book is a valuable participant

In all forms of Goddess religion, the cyclic energies of menstruation and ovulation are realigned with the Crone-Goddess's cyclic energies of cosmic death and regeneration. The unbroken but dismediated biological /ontological continuity of ovulation and menstruation from Goddess to woman and from primordial creation to the present makes female reproductivity a carrier or stream of cosmogonic power. In these lines from her poem 'Blood Stop', Katherine Wells expresses her sense of bodily female connection with the beginning of all possibility (a connection that is all the more poignant in that the poem is about menopause—the end of biological reproductive possibility):

> Even in my mother's womb
> I had my own womb
> and a million little possibles
> jostling for the signal to travel.
> Such overkill. Enough to start a planet.[26]

In thealogy the snake has as important a role to play as it does in Genesis, but it is honoured instead of vilified and its wisdom hypostasizes female knowledge of the transformatory mysteries. Female dragon-snakes are global mythological symbols of the energies of the elements and of rebirth. And according to Barbara Walker, the biblical snake is derived from a far earlier widespread mythology in which the primal couple were originally just the Goddess and a snake living in the paradisal garden of the Goddess's own womb.[27] This powerfully knowledgeable cosmogonic/menstrual snake is a primordial symbol of female regenerativity in that both the snake's skin and the menstrual lining of the womb are periodically shed and renewed with wave-like, 'tidal' or lunar contractions.[28]

The primal pagan mythologies have also informed the spiritual feminist reclamation of the snake. The serpent's open oracular mouth is, like the dilated cervix and vagina of a woman giving birth, a point of entry onto the earth. (Trobriand and West African myths claim that their ancestors emerged from female holes in the ground and 120 versions of such earth emergence stories have been recorded from Native North

source of spiritual feminist cosmology. See esp. pp. 55-65.

26. From Taylor and Sumrall (eds.), *Women of the 14th Moon*, p. 321.

27. *The Woman's Encyclopedia of Myths and Secrets*, p. 642.

28. Shuttle and Redgrove, *The Wise Wound*, p. 249. The Tantric philosophy of the female Kundalini sexual snake-energy coiled at the base of the spine has also been influential in the spiritual feminist reclamation of the snake.

Americans alone.[29]) The snake is, above all, a female symbol of regeneration. As Eliade notes, 'the snake is an animal that "changes"'. Mediterranean goddesses like Artemis, Persephone and Hecate hold snakes in their hands, and Gorgons and Erinyes have snakes for hair. There is a European superstition that if some hair is pulled from the head of a menstruating woman (a woman under lunar influence) and buried in the earth, it will turn into snakes.[30] In other words, the moon, the female head, and snaking menstrual blood flow can come together as a cosmogonic node through which energy passes and branches out into the earth, water and sky.

It is a testament to the snake's hold over the patriarchal imagination that the dragon/snake must be repeatedly slain before patriarchal order can be secured. Tiamat was slain by Marduk, the Python by Apollo, the Medusa by Perseus, Leviathan by Yahweh, and the Hydra by Hercules. Perhaps the best-known example of the female cosmogonic dragons usurped by patriarchy is the first of these, where in the Babylonian myth the world-mother Tiamat ('the Deep') was the sea dragon who created the world out of the chaotic sea of her menstrual blood. She was slain by the warrior-god Marduk. He stole her power and out of the two halves of her dismembered carcass made a heaven and earth for himself to rule.

In something approaching an eschatological gesture, spiritual feminism sews the severed limbs of the cosmogonic dragon back together, presaging the feminist wholeness of a re-created world. Spiritual feminists commonly call menstrual blood 'dragon blood': its flow 'turns women into dragons'.[31] The metaphor of spiritual feminists as dragons is a way of regenerating female sacral power as symbolized by the numerous cosmogonic female dragons who have been slain by men. But just as a salamander can regenerate its lost limb or tail, so too the cosmogonic dragon incarnates female sacral powers of self-replication and she is now envisioned as re-membering her own power. Spiritual feminists can only recreate the world, or, differently expressed, establish new possibilities for life to flourish, in so far as they embody that cosmogonic dragon power of the Goddess. Patriarchy often refers to strong, assertive women as 'dragons'.[32] But in spiritual feminism dragonish qualities are

29. Falk, 'Feminine Sacrality', p. 303.

30. *Patterns in Comparative Religion*, p. 168.

31. Francia, *Dragontime*, p. 44.

32. J. Hoult, *Dragons: Their History and Symbolism* (Glastonbury: Gothic Image, 1987), p. 7.

not those of elderly domestic tyrants whose energies and abilities have been frustrated by the remnants of a Victorian ideology of femininity; the dragon is a sexually autonomous, defiantly creative woman.

This parallelism, which reciprocally models the state of the cosmos on that of the body, and the body on that of the cosmos, is not new. In most religious systems, the health/holiness of the human body symbolically (and often in fact) represents the health, unity or wholeness of the social body and the cosmos. Spiritual feminist holiness is modelled on the holistic holiness of the Goddess, that is, her oneness with the living whole. As for deep ecologists, the spiritual feminist cosmos is a unified whole and its value ultimately resides in its wholeness, not in the contributions of individual human creatures or species. While this should not mean that the real needs of individuals are ignored, these must be contextualized within those of the whole. As John Cobb says, writing of deep ecology and other anti-mechanistic worldviews, 'to this whole, a strong sense of sacredness attaches itself; to its violation, a strong sense of evil'.[33] The image of the cosmos/dragon cut up by patriarchy and made whole or resurrected by spiritual feminism is, I think, the most powerful meaning of the snake symbol and a precondition of all its other feminist meanings.

The difference, then, between thealogical and other organicist concepts of holiness as cosmic wholeness and the Priestly concept of holiness as separation is an instructive one. In Priestly Judaism, the body is to be kept holy or separate from profane life forms according to the classifications God laid down at creation when he made humanity in his own image. Throughout Leviticus, God issues instructions that will make Israel a socially and spiritually separate or distinct people. These instructions are summarized in the words, 'You shall be holy to me; for I the Lord am holy, and have separated you from the peoples, that you should be mine' (Leviticus 20.26). Spiritual feminist holiness bears *some* likeness to Priestly holiness in that its own community's holistic holiness makes it spiritually distinguishable from what is morally and spiritually wrong with the practices of the majority of people that surround its community. But that is one of the only points of contact. Priestly and feminist cosmologies diverge from the outset because the Priestly God's divine power is only resident in his mind and will. This entails that the most valuable attributes of human agency will be intellectual and

33. 'Ecology, Science, and Religion: Toward a Postmodern Worldview', in Griffin (ed.), *The Reenchantment of Science*, p. 106.

moralistic detachment—the qualities that patriarchal philosophy identifies as male and in which Eve showed herself to be deficient in Eden.

The holy or righteous man conducts himself as God conducted himself at creation: thinking, willing and resting in a state of apartness. Religious feminism has not forgiven those biblical figures like Hezekiah who in 2 Kings 18.3-5 destroyed the pagan 'high places', cut down the Asherah or sacred tree, and broke up Moses' bronze serpent. Such leaders together instituted the process in which human and animal intelligence were severed. The snake's knowledge belongs to an animist worldview which may attribute intelligence and the power of speech to any living form. In the anti-animist worldview the snake and its blatant sexual energy (whether female or phallic) would have nothing to do with the proper constitution of the world. The banishing of animism from religious experience can, by its own logic, lead to the desacralization of organic process and, finally, the ecocide which 2 Kings 3.19 chillingly prefigures: 'you shall fell every good tree, and stop up all springs of water, and ruin every good piece of land with stones'.

Protestant aniconism also left nature (and therefore embodiment) non-sacramental or profane. The *mysterium tremendum* of holiness as a material manifestation within natural forms was lost and holiness began to be interpreted solely as a requirement of moral perfection.[34] By the nineteenth century, Protestant virtue and holiness bore a quantitative relation to one another as grades of moral perfection, but were not qualitatively different. Only the biblical text could reveal God's will and everything else in creation must listen.

The third recurrent feminist cosmological motif is water. Although men sweat, spit, urinate and ejaculate semen, femaleness is usually symbolically associated with fluids and maleness with solids.[35] There are a great many related creation traditions in which the world is born from and sometimes destroyed by female water.[36] Symbolically, the distinction between swirling waters and solid land marks a primary distinction between historical order and primordial chaos. Of course, the actual

---

34. Paul Tillich's discussion of the moralization of holiness is useful here. See his *Systematic Theology*, I (London: SCM Press, 1978), pp. 216-17; *The Protestant Era* (London: Nesbit, 1955), pp. 120-22.

35. O'Flaherty, *Women, Androgynes and Other Mythical Beasts*, p. 33. Her discussion of women and fluids relates to the Eastern tradition.

36. Eliade, *Patterns in Comparative Religion*, p. 191. See the whole of ch. 5, 'The Waters and Water Symbolism'.

distinction between land and water is not absolute: cliffs and rocks fall into the sea; water flows into the land through streams and rivers; and the pull of the tides, the rising of sap and the flow of menstrual blood follow the phases of the moon. Those ancient pagan mythologies, of the ancient Near East in particular, in which water forms a primeval, female cosmogonic matrix from which all life emerges reflect how water circulates through the planet. Because all watercourses—streams, rivers and pools—are connected as if by veins and blood vessels to the sea and moon, these waters are often feminized in pagan traditions, as for example in the Goddess/rivers of India and Mexico, and the water nymphs who inhabited the ponds and springs of the Mediterranean.[37]

As 'water', femaleness is an agency of both chaos and purification. It is ambiguous. The derogation of female cosmogony in patriarchal religion plays on its own ambivalent feelings about those female fluids in which matter gestates, clots and spawns new life. Nor are female fluids easily and safely contained. They are active: the amniotic waters 'break' before a woman gives birth and milk seeps and spurts from the engorged breasts a few days after giving birth. Female water can also signify the periodic flood which engulfs and dissolves the world, taking back what it has given and then, when the waters recede, revealing a renewed, 'washed' reality. On the one hand, the flood is a human catastrophe—more or less the end of history. 'Male' civilization is overwhelmed and washed away by a tidal wave of 'female' water. On the other hand, whatever human possibility survives the flood has been purified of its iniquities and the cosmos sparkles—drenched through and dripping with the numinous energy of life. It is as if the Goddess has laundered the fabric of the world.[38] This regenerative quality of female water is recognized by Eliade when he writes that without the flood, life forms would 'crumble, exhaust their powers of creativity and finally die away'.[39]

Something of the 'female' regenerative power of water remains in patriarchal rites of purification that use water. Rites such as Christian baptism—at once a purification and an initiation rite—allow the subject to drown (die) and be reborn from the realm of the material/female/ profane into the realm of the spiritual/masculine/sacred without the

37. Falk, 'Feminine Sacrality', p. 305.
38. Estés, *Women Who Run with the Wolves*, p. 95.
39. *Patterns in Comparative Religion*, p. 211.

intervention of a female body or a female priestly officiant.[40] The baptismal font and the Jewish *mikvah* (ritual bath) are containers filled with water. This water shares some of the sustaining attributes of female 'amniotic' fluid, but has been masculinized. Although the *mikvah* is filled to a depth of about four feet with pure rainfall, lake or sea water, or a mixture of piped and natural water, these 'female' waters are subject to male divine law and can therefore cleanse a woman of the danger of her menstrual association with death.

Like small glass phials of holy water from Catholic (once pagan) shrines and wells, these carefully *measured* quantities of male-controlled water can purify as an ablution or regenerate through temporary immersion. But unfathomable, unquantifiable expanses of water like seas and lakes elicit patriarchal anxiety. Among others, the mermaids, the Ladies of the Lake, water nixies and sirens are all female bodily forms symbolizing female fluid less as an amniotic cosmic matrix in which all possibility is held in suspension, than as a lure or bait; a fatal attraction. Certainly, anxiety about deep water is not unreasonable. Water may be reminiscent of the primordial sea of creation—a source of life—but it is also fearful in its impenetrable, claustrophobic, lightless depths. Nonetheless, for spiritual feminists, the sea goddesses and female marine monsters are not *sexually* dangerous. If their appearance is portentous it is as a warning to those patriarchal sailor-theologians whose metaphysical expeditions have plundered the female numinous. In short, both for patriarchal religion and for spiritual feminism water evokes the *sensus numinis* and (differently) symbolizes the ontological fluidity of women who will not stay in their place. Water is re-creating, refreshing and nourishing but it is also hard to contain: it seeps, bursts, overflows and washes things away—the very qualities that inspire patriarchal fears for its own order, and inspire spiritual feminists as the regenerativity of sexual revolution in motion.

Cosmology and Patriarchal Order

In the Hebrew Bible there are several intertwined traditions which differently position God in relation to the world. Some traditions are

---

40. Eliade interprets male initiatory subincision practices as ways in which men let out the mother's blood that they have carried since being a foetus in the womb. The male is strengthened by his purification from a female fluid. See *Rites and Symbols*, p. 27.

more open to positive feminist readings than others. John Armstrong has argued that the pre-Mosaic Hebrew God has not yet lost all immanence; his proximity is expressed

> in the simple phrase 'I will be with thee'. At the same time he is specially to be met in a variety of sacred places, if ominously few. His principal function is to give and renew the blessing, a role fulfilled by constant life-giving activity.[41]

And in the more esoteric Wisdom tradition *Hochmah* is a playful female divinity who co-creates the world with God; only later in Jewish tradition is she subsumed into the monotheistic God as an attribute of his personality. However, the most historically influential cosmological positioning of God and matter has been the Priestly creation myth in the first chapter of Genesis. Here God creates light *ex nihilo* but brings order from the chaotic sea (and perhaps land) by a series of verbal commands and instructions. God calls matter to order in two ways: first, by the classification that assigns each creature with its feet, wings or fins to its respective and fitting element of earth, air or water. These classifications are the basis of the Jewish dietary laws defining which animals and parts of animals are and are not fit (kosher) for human consumption. Secondly, God commands Adam to subdue and dominate every living thing that moves over the earth.

In the book of Job this cosmology resurfaces and we read that God has had to 'shut in the sea with doors when it burst out from the womb', commanding it with the words 'Thus far you shall come and no further...here shall your proud waves be stopped' (Job 38.8-11). (Later the medieval Christian doctrine of continuous creation warned that if God relaxed the vigilance of his creative will for one instant the universe would revert to chaos.) In its sense that organic change was a vestige of chaos, and therefore profane, Priestly Judaism required that whatever was to be offered back to God as a sacrifice should retain its original ordered form as far as possible; it should not be returned in any sort of mess. If an animal was offered it would have to be free of any discharge or disease since discharge, like disease, presages the decomposition of form in a corpse—the most unclean object of all. Meat would need to be salted to preserve its freshness and if bread was offered it would have to be without leaven because a raising agent would work changes in the flour. More generally, good and evil were codified as whatever affirmed

41. *The Idea of the Holy and the Humane Response*, p. 16.

or disrupted the order God established at creation. Moral goodness was achieved by controlling unruly emotions and by punctilious attention to divine rules.[42]

God ruled both human and natural chaos. Passion or rebellion against God was punished by his unleashing natural chaos onto humanity, thereby making nature an instrument of punishment. Patriarchal cosmology emptied female cosmogenesis of its creativity and only the terrifying destructive element remained. In Genesis 6–10 God repented of having made humankind and, although he graciously spared one family and the animals they had collected, he filled the earth with flood water for 150 days, drowning everything else. Chaos was also prophesied as an eschatological punishment. Isaiah 24.18-19 threatens that the windows of heaven will open; the earth will shake from its foundations, break open and disintegrate.[43]

In Priestly theology, the holy is whatever belongs to God's being or sphere of activity and whatever is appointed to that becomes holy—the result of which is that the holy must separate from the earthly sphere.[44] The stages in between holiness and profanity form a complex system of graded holiness which could be crudely simplified as running from the High Priest and other consecrated human males who were fit to minister in the holy sanctuary, to ordinary men, to women, to Gentiles, down to reptiles, scavengers, crawling insects and dead things (the unclean or profane). Perhaps the most significant aspect of the Priestly system in the present context is that 'anomaly is as much an offense against an ordered world as is the destructive power of death'.[45]

But as we have seen in the course of this book, spiritual feminism

42. This discussion of Priestly cosmology summarizes G.G. James's paper, 'The Priestly Conceptions of Evil and Practice in the Torah', given at the Inter-Religious Foundation for World Peace conference on 'The Reality of Evil and the Response of the World's Religions', Seoul, Korea, April 1994.

43. See Ruether, *Sexism and God-Talk*, p. 77.

44. P. Jenson, *Graded Holiness: A Key to the Priestly Conception of the World* (JSOTSup, 106; Sheffield: JSOT Press, 1992), p. 48. Here Jenson notes that modern scholarship generally agrees that holiness does not, etymologically, mean separation, but that separation is its necessary consequence. However, from a feminist point of view, the association of holiness and separateness excludes or certainly marginalizes women and all of nature from the cult and therefore from full relationship with God.

45. Jenson, *Graded Holiness*, p. 88. Jenson's remark is descriptive, not critical, of this ordering.

celebrates anomaly and otherness as signs of change and of new life. Its monsters are spiritually amphibious and move through the elements of earth, sky and water regardless of women's bipedal created form. Hybrid creatures of the sort represented by Lilith, who is both woman and snake, disorder these classifications and presage the female chaos that patriarchy wanted God to have conquered at creation and, knowing that he has not, has feared thereafter. In this, spiritual feminism is the religious anti-type of Priestly Judaism.[46] Spiritual feminists deliberately place themselves in the realm of the biblical unclean. Priestly holiness maintains the stable order of creation by keeping its categories from joining, mixing, inter-breeding, and transsexual behaviour. But it is social and imaginal cross-breeding or hybridization—as eclecticism and pluralism within a common biophilic matrix—that spiritual feminists believe will reinvigorate the gene pool of religious language and ideas.

The church did not maintain the Priestly cosmic ordering through dietary regulations. In Acts 10.9-16 the apostle Peter has a vision on a rooftop in Joppa of a sheet descending from heaven in which all manner of unclean animals, birds and reptiles are being carried. God tells the hungry Peter to kill and eat these animals. Peter replies, 'No, Lord, for I have never eaten anything that is common or unclean.' And the voice comes to him again a second time, 'What God has cleansed, you must not call common [profane].' Instead, in substantial part the church ordered creation through its social hierarchies whose primary division was the subordination of women to men. The Protestant systematic theologian Werner Neuer, who himself proposes a pyramidal social order as salvific, argues that from the time of the early church the biblical ordering of male and female was evident in the church's theology, daily life, and in the giving of pastoral and teaching offices to men alone. Neuer goes on to trace the sacred history of male headship—where women approach God in and through their husbands—from the early church through to the modern period and down to twentieth-century Protestant systematic theologians such as Karl Barth, Emil Brunner and Dietrich Bonhoeffer.[47]

The patriarchal fear that women are too 'naturally' chaotic to be

---

46. Zoroastrian texts also classify creatures in this way. Snakes, bugs, flies, lice and the like are considered imperfect and are held to be the products of processes of corruption, not semen. This implies that these animals are products of the demonic realm (Seligmann, *Magic, Supernaturalism and Religion*, p. 18).

47. *Man and Woman*, pp. 142-43.

contained even by their subordination to men, and that their organic materiality will 'go off' regardless of religious law, was graphically illustrated in medieval Christendom when nature was represented by the duplicitous *Frau Welt*: a beautifully dressed woman from the front, but from the back a swarming, crawling mass of reptilian, maggoty uncleanness. Women were also likened to a painted tomb-stone covering a rotting corpse.[48] Here it is feared that the thin skin of civilization, already infected by the female chaos beneath, will break open and its liquifying decay will ooze to the surface. And these images did not originate in the medieval period. In the patristic period, for example, women were similarly imaged as temples built over sewers. In ascetic patriarchal religions the beauty of female flesh is a hallucination; a vaginal trap which opens onto the pit of death. To die is, again, to be punished by chaos. Patriarchal death is not the transformation of human into non-human living forms. In traditional Catholic mythology, hell, the pit of the unredeemed dead, is contained by the bowels of the female earth. Even God's most ungovernable human creations are not allowed to die. Hellish eternal life is that of unceasing punishment; of bodily torments—often of a sado-sexual kind. This house of everlasting correction is starkly opposed to heaven: the celestial realm of perfect, eternal life that awaits the elite of the righteous. Christianity and Judaism *do* have eschatologies of bodily resurrection, but Platonic philosophy has influenced them both. In Pauline Christianity the resurrected body is no longer subject to organic change. It has the immortal fiery character of the matter from which planets and stars are formed.[49]

The biblical concern to keep all things to their appointed place has not only permitted exploitative hierarchical social conservatism, it may in the near future permit technocrats to hold a new artificial line against imperfection and change. While it has not yet degenerated into fascist eugenics, genetic engineering is working to control human physical defects and prolong, perfect and standardize vegetal life. (The intention to perfect and the intention to standardize are not always clearly distinguishable.) This modification or reordering of life-forms so as to arrest natural flux reduces the mystery and value of life to a set of engineered chemical conditions for perfection. If human perfection were to become possible,

48. These two examples are from Ruether, *Sexism and God-Talk*, p. 81, but the gloss is my own.
49. Ruether, 'Patriarchy and Creation', p. 63.

or even philosophically meaningful, that perfection would bear no relation to holistic holiness.

Spiritual feminism and one of its close relatives, creation spirituality, do not confuse holiness and physical perfection. The *telos* of creation (if it has one at all) is not to achieve a static perfection. As Matthew Fox has observed, there are 'serious problems' with a creation story that says that humanity was created in a perfect state from which it quickly fell. It is, he says, the idea that human life can be perfect that has informed the consumerist dream of a perfect home and perfect bodies. In fact,

> in nature, in creation, imperfection is not a sign of the absence of God. It is a sign that ongoing creation is not an easy thing. We all bear scars from this rugged process. We can—and must—celebrate the scars. The alternative is to opt out of the ongoing work of Dabhar [the Hebrew word for divine creative energy].[50]

If God has created not a static cosmos, but an unfolding one, then holiness is not a static perfection, but in humans, a movement towards fullness or wholeness.[51] This is a wholeness/holiness that is utterly absent in the attempt to recreate creation genetically 'without spot or blemish' by a scientific elite.

An important patriarchal device for (re)calling society to order has been its sabbath. The patriarchal sabbath remembers God's understandable need for rest on the seventh day of creation, and allows humans and animals a day of rest from their labours as well. In this the patriarchal sabbath is not without merit.[52] Yet God rests not only because he has brought aspects of the cosmos into being, but also because he is recovering from the exhausting imposition of his will upon chaos. In its contemporary Western form, the sabbath erects a temporal

50. *Original Blessing: A Primer in Creation Spirituality* (Santa Fe: Bear & Co., 1983), pp. 110-11.

51. *Original Blessing*, pp. 111-12.

52. The Hebrew Bible is of course a complex set of texts—some of which are implicitly self-critical and remain spiritually instructive. Lev. 25.10ff. sets out instructions for a Jubilee: one holy year in every 50 which provides a foretaste of an ecological and eschatological Shalom where relationships are restored to justice and the land rests. The biblical religions also have death and regeneration cycles built into their calendars. The Jewish new year, for example, bears traces of a cyclicity which was marked in its ancient form. But Jewish and Christian regenerations are historicized and moralized and while they celebrate new life they do not honour the decay and death that spiritual feminism celebrates in the 'dark' or crone side of the Goddess.

boundary to fend off a chaos *of its own making*. For one day a week the turbulence of its economic system returns to apparent calm (though in the late 1990s, the interests of escalating trade and consumption threaten even this gesture towards Shalom).

But the sabbath was also once a part of female menstrual cosmology. Some ancient goddesses were believed to menstruate, especially those lunar goddesses with the power of death and regeneration. At the full moon the Babylonian goddess Ishtar was thought to be menstruating. The 'sabbatu' on which she menstruated and work ceased was not a day of rest as such, but an inauspicious day of unpredictable effects during which it was unwise to undertake any work.[53] Again we see how the meaning of the sacred pivots on a political axis. Judaism and then Christianity sanctified the sabbath by attributing its origins to the cosmological activity of God whose rational word could subdue female chaos at the beginning of time and now for one day of restrictive quietness in every week. This preserves the patriarchal sacred equilibrium from the threat of all sorts of 'female' chaos. Spiritual feminism has its own sabbath rest—that of the menstrual period. But this menstrual sabbath celebrates both the expected and the unexpected. Although menstruation is a lunar phenomenon and therefore comes roughly every 28 days, its onset has an 'predictable unpredictability. You never know exactly when it is going to come, and sometimes it completely surprises you. And not only is it inconsiderate of timetables and schedules, it is also messy. Hooray!'[54]

Owen's remark hints at what the advocates of the patriarchal sabbath would oppose in the feminist sabbath. For as a way of ridding the social order of unpredictability, the sabbath became another means by which patriarchal religion could justify its dominance, this time as protecting the social order from the chaos of female religions. The witches' sabbat, for example, was described in Christian polemics as the four times in the year when witches and other demons came together at night and were most actively maleficent: participating in the orgies, cross-dressing and counterclockwise circular dances that reversed and muddled Christian order and encouraged promiscuous, random fertility.

For those who are employed, the pace of contemporary Western labour and consumption makes a sabbath spiritually and ecologically necessary. It may be the only time in the week that can be spent with

53. Noddings, *Women and Evil*, pp. 38-39.
54. Owen, 'The Sabbath of Women', p. 41.

friends and family. However, the masculine cosmology of the sabbath as not only rest but imposed stillness has eradicated the cosmogonic meaning of female chaos as positive, primordial possibility. A contemporary feminist religion would not want to end the institution of sabbaths and holy/holidays. A feminist sabbath would not only bring temporary rest, it would bring the authentic Shalom of a slower, less frenetic society that would keep pace with the seasonal, menstrual rhythms of the moon. An ecologically harmonious culture that listened to the rhythms of infinity would show patriarchal production to be the dissonant negative chaos that it is. (The dealing floors of international stock exchanges are some of the most powerful manifestations of patriarchal cacophony.) Patriarchal religion has replaced female generative chaos with the destructive chaos of free-market economics and war, drawing a flotsam of refugees, homelessness and environmental desolation in their wake.[55] And from this the world needs a very long sabbath indeed.

'Feminine' Cosmologies

Cosmologies that use female imagery are not necessarily feminist. Feminine and feminist cosmologies have points of intersection but they also need to be politically distinguished from one another. In *The Sacred and the Feminine* (1982) Kathryn Rabuzzi advocates a 'feminine cosmization' in which women's ritualized housework enacts the (re)creation of the world out of the chaos of familial mess. She claims that the rituals of a woman's housework are hierophanic because through these a housewife-priestess enters the primordial, sacred time 'in which the gods and goddesses originally created order out of chaos'.[56] Rabuzzi is aware that an over-ordered house is a lifeless museum, and purification can tip over into a neurotic obsession. But in her concept of domestic female sacrality a traditional housewife's cleaning is an act of purification ensuring that this female space—'home'—becomes symbolically and morally distinguished from negative female spaces such as brothels. Housework stakes out the physical and spiritual safety of the home.[57]

---

55. In *The Goddess*, p. 15, Christine Downing reminds us that 'the arrival of Yahweh in Canaan was that of an invader who brought havoc and destruction'. And it was only in times of national crisis that this god was turned to. Goddess worship was maintained for the peaceable daily round of agriculture and worship.

56. *The Sacred and the Feminine*, p. 97.

57. *The Sacred and the Feminine*, pp. 114, 115.

Gratingly, Rabuzzi even sacralizes the bourgeois housewife's possessions. A 'silk print cocktail dress', a 'gold filigree lighter' are, she says, 'icons', and for a woman

> to lose one [of these] is to lose touch with the past that helps sacralize her existence by telling her who she is. But the world she creates is not only rooted in the sacred past. It simultaneously looks forward, too, being a continuous creation rather than an entity fixed once and for all.[58]

Rabuzzi stands partly in the Victorian tradition that contained femaleness as a domesticity that soothed male philosophical angst and sheltered bourgeois men from the social anomie of their own creating. Rabuzzi's work recalls John Ruskin's sentimental eulogy of the home as a refuge from the threat of both modernity and nature. He says of the housewife, 'The stars only may be over her head; the glow-worms in the night-cold grass may be the only fire at her foot: but home is yet wherever she is.'[59] Susan Thistlethwaite is at least superficially correct in criticizing Rabuzzi's *The Sacred and the Feminine* as being 'a treatment of housework...made exclusively from the perspective of one who could choose to hire someone for this work'.[60] It is true that Rabuzzi's study seems only barely feminist and often falls into a bourgeois romanticization of (usually) alienated female labour. But perhaps Rabuzzi's belief that women can experience the sacred obliquely and in the most mundane conditions is more useful than its illustrations.

Nonetheless, *feminine* spirituality largely ignores the way in which, since the beginnings of industrial modernity, domesticity has been used as an ideological tool. The Protestant capitalist cult of domesticity has stabilized society by its imposition of middle-class values and culture. The cosy home has compensated society for its social and racial divisiveness and the dis-ease of its economic competitiveness. The patriarchal home represents a bastion of tidy female virtues: sexual and material purity, subordination to male authority, and self-denial. These virtues have set feminine piety apart from the moral turmoil of industrial capitalism.[61] Harriet Beecher Stowe, for example, wrote of the home as

---

58. *The Sacred and the Feminine*, pp. 106-107.

59. 'Of Queen's Gardens', in *Sesame and Lilies* (London: Cassell, 1907), p. 74.

60. *Sex, Race and God: Christian Feminism in Black and White* (London: Geoffrey Chapman, 1990), pp. 49-51.

61. There have been numerous accounts of the origins and function of nineteenth-century domestic ideology. See, for example, K.K. Sklar, *Catharine Beecher: A Study in American Domesticity* (New York: Norton, 1973), pp. 158-67; C. Hall,

'more holy than cloister, more saintly and pure than Church or altar'.[62]

In this, the ideology of femininity does grant *some* sacral power to women, but its operations are bricked into a confined space where they are easily monitored by the male head of household. If the patriarchal home has any symbolic cosmological power it is not that of a radical feminist 'menstrual' cosmological power. Feminine sacrality as pious hygiene merely holds the line against daily bacterial and sexual stain and disorder. Here feminine sacrality assists the ordering work of the patriarchal God and reassures patriarchy that it has turned over the 'right' side of women: the obverse side of the witch, namely, the virtuous, chaste, biblically-instructed woman. In nineteenth-century evangelicalism this feminine 'side' of femaleness was credited with the power not only to purify a woman's home and body with moral and physical hygiene, but to regenerate the morals of the nation (without the need for any radical redistribution of wealth and privilege).[63]

Right up to the 1960s, domestication kept women's power away from that of nature under a form of the policy of divide and rule. With the arrival of affordable household appliances and the postwar demolition of many urban slums, domesticity not only transcended nature morally, but technologically and spatially as well in new blocks of flats. The domestic ideal became a germ-free suburban home with linear, modernist furniture that was easy to keep clean. The family's clothes were machine-washed to a 'blue' whiteness. (Even in 1982 Rabuzzi was still divinizing housework and this view of housework as a rite of purification has not yet disappeared.) Female failure was now less a sexual fall than that of losing the struggle against chaos—especially germs and a fertility uneducated by contraception.

Female sacrality remained domesticated as a kind of spiritual embourgeoisement until the green movement and feminist neo-paganism took root. Now at the end of the twentieth century the green movement has reversed the equation of purity with white, rational, technological sterility. For spiritual feminism 'order' signifies the *artificial* peace of the suppression of nature's primordial unruliness. Order can now be distinguished from the authentic Shalom of cooperative harmony. Feminist

'The Early Formation of Domestic Ideology', in S. Burman (ed.), *Fit Work for Women* (London: Croom Helm, 1979).

62. *The Minister's Wooing* (New York: Derby & Jackson, 1859), p. 566.

63. See, for example, S. Lewis, *Women's Mission* (London: John Parker, 1839), pp. 20, 128, 135, 152.

sacrality is no longer synonymous with rules of hygiene laid down at the patriarchal creation in Genesis. It is muddy, seething Nature that is a clean realm to be saved from the pollution of technology. Even the advertising industry is aware that for the consumer the words 'organic' and 'natural' now signify any product that is morally wholesome: a virtuous purchase. For the green movement, dazzlingly white sheets and clothes become profane when the washing powder and energy to keep them artificially bleached pollutes rivers and streams. Ecofeminists are now aware that domestic purity (as distinct from ordinary cleanliness) is established at the expense of nature. So feminist neo-pagans are doing something quite different with female sacrality than quasi-feminists who call that sacrality 'feminine'. Both use female sacrality as a cosmological agency, but by taking it outdoors, neo-pagan feminists release and disperse its power as an agent of sexual-political transformation and change.

Of course, the split between indoors and outdoors is in many ways an artificial one, and spiritual feminist sacrality may *also* be a domestic agency. Luisah Teish describes dishwashing as 'an exquisite ritual'. She washes dishes with music playing and adds to the dishwater, 'an ounce of river water, an ounce of ocean water, an ounce of rain water, and some lemon oil'. She writes that 'women's work has been degraded and it never should have been. It's what preserves life.'[64] But this life-preserving sacrality is no longer *automatically* walled into the patriarchal domestic space where its energy is restricted to the transformation of food into meals, fabric into clothes, and children into young adults. Spiritual feminists have returned female sacrality to its elemental origins and, like the wolf in the story of the three pigs, it will huff and puff and blow the patriarchal house down. The broom takes to the skies; spiritual feminists prophesy against the destruction of nature from the whirlwind—from within nature itself, not just from the hearth.

Female Sacrality as an Alchemical Process

So far I have discussed the relation of biblical and postbiblical models of creativity where, broadly speaking, the former creates by ordering and the latter by mixing. But the spiritual feminist model of the creative process is also related to another, heretical, tradition of the generation of

---

64. Interview with Luisah Teish, quoted in Eller, *Living in the Lap of the Goddess*, pp. 108-109.

matter: alchemy. Through the processes of fermentation, putrefaction, heat, sublimation, facilitating prayers and meditations, and sometimes the cooperation of an actual female *soror mystica* representing the female energy principle, the alchemists attempted to transform ordinary matter or base metals into 'gold': an elixir that would give eternal life. The transformation was to take place inside the egg-shaped *vas Hermeticum*, a vessel regarded as a matrix or womb from which the 'philosopher's stone' or gold was to be born. Even in its patriarchal forms alchemy is closer to the female sacral process than the biblical, and since the metaphor is now resurfacing in spiritual feminist discourse it merits investigation.

Alchemy is an ancient occult art which has recently awakened interest in New Age and other circles as a proto-scientific discourse whose practices recommend themselves as being apparently free from modern scientific desacralization. The Christian ecofeminist Catharina Halkes, for example, contrasts alchemy favourably with modern science. She notes that the alchemists were mystical, organicist and anti-rationalistic in their approach to knowledge. They also sexualized knowledge and power as a sacramental quasi-coital union of the male and female principles which were symbolically equal and related to one another as are the sun and the moon and a king and queen. The alchemists did not enslave and subordinate the female principle as did Baconian science.[65]

And alchemy has other apparently metapatriarchal features. It is a common claim that Western alchemy was originally a female art which developed in the first four centuries CE and was notable for its female practitioners, particularly Maria the Jewess and Theosebia.[66] And alchemy has immanentist elements: in the first half of the sixteenth century the physician-magus Paracelsus urged alchemists to approach their science with the wonder of children, and to see the *prima materia*—the primary ingredient for alchemical transformations—at work in the lives of the poor, in children at play and in the contemplation of nature. In her alchemical manual Maria the Jewess instructed alchemists first to summon a black and white snake in their retort to symbolize the material unity of perfection and imperfection.[67] And medieval alchemists invoked the presence and the wisdom of the

---

65. *New Creation*, pp. 58-61.
66. Seligmann, *Magic, Supernaturalism and Religion*, p. 80.
67. See Seligmann, *Magic, Supernaturalism and Religion*, pp. 87, 90.

goddess Sapientia (or Sophia) as the female primordial principle without whom the magic would not work.[68] For those seeking to reunite science and spirituality, there is little doubt that alchemical mysticism is preferable to modern science which proceeds without any concept of, let alone consideration for, the sacrality of matter. The etymology of the word 'laboratory' gives some clue to the sacral intentions of early science as conducted in alchemical laboratories: the Latin *labor* means 'labour', and *oratorium* means a 'place devoted to prayer'.[69] (The alchemist's modern successors in chemistry and metallurgy sought no divine assistance and the spaces in which they worked, their apparatuses and their transformations were wholly desacralized.)

Yet however spiritualized its contemporary readings might be, spiritual feminism should be suspicious of patriarchal alchemical discourse. There are numerous reasons for this, some of which I shall set out below—not in order to pursue an esoteric debate but to illustrate how misleading the conflation of female and feminine sacrality can be. Within the patriarchal scheme, the alchemical metaphor may only represent the *mystification* of femaleness, which is something very different from a mystical feminist conception and experience of femaleness. Here the alchemical metaphor can powerfully evoke female sacral processes and must be reclaimed on spiritual feminism's own terms.

In spiritual feminist mythopoeics the womb replicates the divine cosmogonic cauldron of menstrual *prima materia*. Yet, figuratively speaking, patriarchal alchemy subjects women to a hysterectomy in which this vessel of creation is removed from its natural place inside the female body and relocated in the laboratories of alchemists. In its quest for the philosopher's stone, alchemy refuses female change and death and seeks for itself a materiality which, like gold, will not corrode or perish but will share in the immortality of the gods. Indeed, in attempting to liberate the divine essence of matter, alchemy became an almost priestly task of mediation—of bringing the immutability of the divine realm to birth in the present finite order. As in the biblical account of creation, the alchemist perfects, completes and redeems the work of chaotic nature by his reason. Alchemical theory proposes that elements in the earth would, if left to themselves, eventually purify into gold. But that process could be accelerated by alchemists whose work

68. Walker, *The Crone*, p. 117.
69. Seligmann, *Magic, Supernaturalism and Religion*, pp. 88-89.

dispensed with the gestatory geological aeons of natural time.[70] The philosopher's stone was often calculated to form over a period of nine months and was then intended to be used as a kind of powdered yeast that, like the pregnant female body, could multiply and transmute substances without diminishing its own potency. That the Western alchemists recognized that women's bodies were both an explanation of and an obstruction to the alchemical process is clear from Paracelsus's injunction that the male practitioner must return to his mother's breast and be reborn from her womb. In this sense, patriarchal alchemy can be interpreted as yet another instance in the history of religions in which men must be born twice in order to take the mother's generative power but rid themselves of the pollution and delimitation of her biological finitude.[71]

The rhetoric of alchemy claimed that the science perfected female nature whose non-golden products were the freaks or abortions of an imperfect or obstructed process. The laboratory and the crucible replace the womb and the earth as sacral spaces: 'The seeker not only shrinks time but reproduces the dimensions of the universe within the confines of his laboratory.'[72] The alchemist, then, attempts to surpass God's creation by conquering all natural and temporal process. Although alchemy was not primarily about financial gain, it *was* about seizing a kind of power that is more fundamental than economic or military power. Esoteric systems have revered four elements or essences as the sacred ground of reality: fire, water, earth and air. The fifth sacred element is a quintessence—the animating world soul. For the alchemists, 'he who can free the fifth element from the matter that it inhabits shall hold in his hand the creative power with which God has endowed the world of matter'.[73]

Alchemy's attempt to usurp and improve on divine creativity was, then, paradigmatically patriarchal. Alchemy is one logical outcome of characterizing divine generation as a male process, and one which men, who were made in the male divine image, would be entrusted to preside

70. M. Eliade, 'Alchemy: An Overview', in *idem* (ed.), *Encyclopedia of Religion*, I, p. 184.

71. For a discussion of masculine rebirthing rites, see Eliade, *Rites and Symbols*, pp. 57-60.

72. N. Sivan, 'Chinese Alchemy', in Eliade (ed.), *Encyclopedia of Religion*, I, p. 187.

73. Seligmann, *Magic, Supernaturalism and Religion*, p. 96.

over here on earth. But alchemy tried to do more than merely assist God's work on earth: it can be read as a parable of patriarchal *hubris*: the (failed) attempt of men to depose their own gods, to shrink the universe to human territorial dimensions, and to exalt patriarchy in God's place.

Since alchemy promises quasi-divine powers to its practitioners it is hardly surprising that the secrets of its transmutations were encoded in an obscure symbology. But the church could not own such a heresy: alchemical *gnosis* was regarded as a revelation from the demonic realm. This discourse was suppressed by Christianity and as a self-styled key to all knowledge of creation it was deliberately shrouded in secrecy by the alchemists themselves. It was learned by revelation and initiation to an elite few. To have made it available for common practice would have profaned the mystery.

The history of religions now usually interprets alchemy as having had a spiritual intention of realizing and releasing the energies of divine presence, 'the divine secret', in any base matter, including that of the body.[74] But neither that, nor Jung's influential claim that alchemy was a discourse on the psychic processes of a quest for the Self couched in the language of science,[75] makes the spiritual intentions of classical alchemy in any sense feminist. After all, Maria the Jewess is reputed to have said 'invert nature and you will find that which you seek', which is precisely

74. J. Campbell, *The Masks of God*. IV. *Creative Mythology* (New York: Arkana, 1991), pp. 271-72.

75. See C.G. Jung, *Psychology and Alchemy* (New York: Pantheon, 1952). But it is his wife Emma Jung's work with Marie-Louise von Franz in *The Grail Legend* (London: Hodder & Stoughton, 1971) which, for Jungian spiritual feminists, established the Grail legend as an allegory of the womb and vagina as a goblet filled with blood: an alchemical medium through which the quest for the connection between the individual and the divine could be realized. Shuttle and Redgrove follow Emma Jung in regarding the menstrual womb as 'the buried feminine secret', completing and bringing into balance the masculine and feminine principles. See also their new book, *Alchemy for Women: Personal Transformation through Dreams and the Female Cycle* (London: Rider, 1995). However, Jungian doctrines of essential sexual complementarity may be unhelpful for many spiritual feminists who would resist the Jungian account of femaleness as incomplete in itself. The Grail legend can contain many meanings and some might prefer to follow those mythographers of the womb who interpret the eucharistic goblet holding Christ's magical blood as a misappropriation of the power of the womb-chalice (see for example Francia, *Dragontime*, p. 26).

the process of reversal which feminists criticize as denigrating women and threatening the life of the planet.

The alchemical dragon that appeared in the retort had to be (once more) sacrificed and dismembered by the alchemist. It was to vanish into black smoke to show his transcendence of material imperfection and natural passions. The earth goddesses summoned for their assistance were no more significant than emblems of the generative power of the philosopher's stone.[76] And the symbol of the pregnant moon simply reflected the rays of the male sun but had no creative energy of its own. The dualism on which alchemy is founded, in which maleness is generative, active and redemptory, and femaleness is base, vegetative, and fertile *prima materia* waiting to be perfected by male interference, should have nothing to recommend it to spiritual feminism. In short, the contemporary reconstructions of alchemy as an alternative model of science and as a Jungian self-transformation mystery lack the critical, political edge that would read this discourse as another patriarchal theft of female sacred cultural/biological arts and the metaphors those engender.

As we have seen, feminine—though not feminist—metaphors permeate this discourse on (re)creativity. However, the honour given to female sacrality is nominal. Alchemy's use of female metaphors and principles illustrates patriarchy's lethal and futile attempt to play not only God, but in doing so, woman. The laboratory, with its furnace and vessels, displaces the female womb in which female energy turns food and blood into flesh, and the oven whose fire women have traditionally used to cook, ferment and and craft raw materials into cultural products of value. Spiritual feminism has a magical view of the female body (especially the womb) and its products and arts. But these are magical in that they are a replication rather than an interventionary redemption of the ecological processes of transmutation.

The patriarchal acceleration of natural gestatory processes established its power as a developing system—particularly through metallurgy and the proto-industrial production of metal arms. In the spiritual feminist account of prehistory the sacred tabooed art of metallurgy was taken from the protection of the Goddess, leaving the earth's iron ores available for the Bronze and Iron Age production of durable and effective weapons. These destroyed the Goddess cultures and subdued and tapped

76. Seligmann, *Magic, Religion and Supernaturalism*, pp. 90-92, 96. His account of alchemy is entirely androcentric. The feminist reading is my own.

human and natural energies, making them servants of male private property. It was metallurgy that gave men the sense of power over life and death that had once been revered as female. As Monica Sjöö and Barbara Mor put it, 'now *he* had the power, and he found he could also easily invent his own sacredness, by fiat. God became male—a warrior male—in his own image.'[77] They speculate that this may be why 'even today, witches must not touch iron. Metal mining and smelting remain the most male-dominated of all professions, and access to ores remains a major criterion of male power states.'[78] (Though now the use of information technology in contemporary warfare means that the war machine requires less metal and more electronics.)

A spiritual feminist reading of alchemy is not only a reminder of the abuse of female sacral power, it is also a warning of the consequences of its misuse. For tragically, the alchemical arts do not so much imitate as recruit and then parody female sacrality. In doing so, they exemplify the Promethean dangers of *hubris*. One of the alchemical retort's most contemporary forms is in its mirror image: the nuclear reactor. Nuclear technology's transmutation of matter to generate energy is so total that nuclear accidents and bombs can smash, combust, mutate and poison life. This chaotic fission is the polar opposite of the female natural alchemy which creates life by the infinitely complex filtering and organization of elements in the womb. Nuclear technology develops and stockpiles weapons, using transformatory power as a threat of punishment to all those other powers planning territorial or political transgression. In the occult art of alchemy spiritual capital is generated as power and glory for the alchemist alone. By contrast, in spiritual feminist ethics, spiritual power is generated in the womb/furnace/mind with the sole purpose of mediating the transformatory, biophilic energy of the divine.

In its affinity with all natural energies, this generative power or leaven is also chaotically unpredictable or indeterminate. Unlike the patriarchal 'Fordist' production-line which produces vast quantities of identical objects, feminist creation is analogous to a series of catalytic reactions. It fuses and recycles elements whose product (like a baby's physical characteristics) cannot be entirely predicted. But, in this, feminist alchemical processes name a natural process of change and diversification

77. Sjöö and Mor, *The Great Cosmic Mother*, p. 240.
78. *The Great Cosmic Mother*, p. 238. See also Sjöö, *New Age and Armageddon*, pp. 157-58.

that is essential to the planet's ecology. Consequently, in the feminist spirituality movement a daughter's menarche is a sacred rite of passage; a moment of political and spiritual metamorphosis that must be marked by ritual:

> Like the butterfly that emerges from the cocoon in beauty and flight, so is she who bleeds and blooms now a caretaker of the magical and transformative blood of life, and her womb a fertile seed chamber. She is a guardian of Mother Nature, and her uterus a chalice carrying the life force that women have embodied throughout the ages.[79]

Although the discourse of alchemy has been largely taken over by Jungians of various types, the alchemical metaphor is also prevalent in spiritual feminist texts and art. Here alchemy has been variously recast as a scholarly/imaginal method of transmuting knowledge across political and semantic boundaries,[80] as the miracle of female reproductive embodiment,[81] and as a rite of transformation. This latter rite symbolizes

> psychic death, change, and re-birth through the alternating fusion and dissolution of opposite elements. [Alchemy] is a psychic rite, an earth-spirit ritual, retaining much of the ancient Goddess mysteries in distilled form, within each individual psyche.[82]

Or again, the artist Edith Altmann has used alchemical symbols and processes to reverse the history of patriarchal destruction. In her piece 'Rebuilding the Temple: We Are Given a Gold Tent and All of Life is the Folding and Unfolding of the Tent' (1987), Altman helped to heal her father of his experience of being turned into nothingness in Buchenwald. She placed the alchemical symbol of the golden tent in front of pictures of the concentration camp. The sacred energy within the tent/womb/

79. S. Valadez, 'The Eye of the Cobra', *Snake Power* (Hallowmas 1989), p. 25, quoted in Eller, *Living in the Lap of the Goddess*, p. 86.

80. In *Outercourse*, p. 157, Daly refers to herself as an alchemist/scholar who re-creatively studied patriarchal philosophy and theology and distilled and reset their meanings in the context of radical feminist philosophy: 'Each time I returned from my adventures in the Mists of the Subliminal Sea I quickly settled down to work in my Cove and Conjured my Alchemical craft. With this Craft I transformed the damaged but partially genuine gems of insight that I had acquired in my High Sea adventures.'

81. Owen, *Her Blood is Gold*, p. 130. According to Owen women 'naturally' understand transformative processes because of their experience of their own alchemical embodiment.

82. Sjöö and Mor, *The Great Cosmic Mother*, p. 132.

furnace replaced the profaned energy generated by the crematoria.[83] Alchemical symbols require careful handling: the Nazis' crematoria were an alchemical symbol gone horribly wrong. The Nazis brought the Jews together from the dispersal of their exile and processed them through apparatuses of asphyxiation and combustion in order to purify the German blood and land of its imperfections. The Nazis were to be immortalized by turning the 'impurities' of their social body into smoke. As André Schwartz-Bart expresses it at the end of his novel *The Last of the Just*, in the crematory ovens, '*Luftmensch* became *Luft*. I shall not translate... For the smoke that rises from crematoria obeys physical laws like any other: the particles come together and disperse according to the wind, which propels them.'[84] The alchemical metaphor is dangerous under patriarchy because it uses natural processes to destroy and re-create according to its own specifications. Post-patriarchal feminism, by absolute contrast, creates in and with the natural processes of creation and destruction. There is no hiatus between nature and female embodiment in which spiritual feminism could interject its own purpose.

These lines from a poem called 'Autumn Alchemy' by the lesbian feminist poet Heather (no surname) summarize female reproductivity as a form of cookery in which the womb becomes an alchemical kitchen:[85]

> My body simmers like a kettle,
> round and steamy;
> the elemental brew is changing
> in my blood
> I'm percolating in a tropic time,
> slow and humid;
> the damp leaf compost of my fall
> is heating up.[86]

It is this *idea* of a woman's body as a *krater* or vessel of trans-formation—a 'cauldron of regeneration'—that is significant here and which summarizes much of the content of this book. It must again be

83. For an account of this piece and other feminist alchemical art see Orenstein, *The Reflowering of the Goddess*, pp. 100-101.

84. Harmondsworth: Penguin, 1977, p. 383.

85. Art is also described as alchemical cookery by Gloria Orenstein in *The Reflowering of the Goddess*, p. 63. She writes that 'art is a magical food which we ingest through the eyes, but which brings a subtle chemistry to our beings in a way that is similar to what we experience when we eat. Art transforms us and makes us into what we see in the same way that food transforms us into what we eat.'

86. In Taylor and Sumrall (eds.), *Women of the 14th Moon*, p. 205.

emphasized that women are not being imaged as mere passive recept-
acles. Admittedly, in associating female sacrality with any hermetic
philosophy, spiritual feminism is still pursuing an ontology of femaleness
as that which *contains* things (a hermetic seal is an air-tight closure). But
the spiritual feminist containment of power is the generative precondition
of its active, magical and erotic release.

From their own experience and from the history of religions spiritual
feminists have constructed an image of women as inventive persons who
can combine and transform seeds, yeasts, raw foods and fire into edible
and palatable states that have been purified of harmful bacteria and will
maintain human energy; who can use dust, water and fire to make
vessels that store and stabilize the energies of food and fluids; who can
spin and weave thread to conserve the energy of the body as heat; and
spin words that turn ideas and images into the fabric of a text. It is this
idea of female activism which informs spiritual feminism's belief in
women's magical energies to bring existing substances together to make
new ones; to transform one thing into another; to change consciousness:

> A German fairy tale tells of an old witch who agrees to teach a man
> magical cooking skills. First she gives little Jacob a bowl of soup to eat.
> The soup tastes both strange and wonderful... When he's eaten it all,
> he's changed into a dwarf. Then his lessons begin.[87]

In the course of this book it should have become clear that, with
Daly,[88] I believe that the women's movement is or should be an ontological movement: a radical, dynamic regeneration of being. And as
human and natural being is continuous, the women's liberation movement is also an ecological liberation movement. I have argued that justice
and reverence for female sacrality is a precondition of the ontological/
ecological regeneration made necessary by the depletions and exhaus-
tions of modern patriarchy. Spiritual feminism's conception of the
'femaleness' of the sacred has at the very least brought that regeneration
within the realm of the imaginable.

87. Francia, *Dragontime*, p. 24.
88. See, for example, *Beyond God the Father*, p. 24.

SELECT BIBLIOGRAPHY

Abramov, T., *The Secret of Jewish Femininity: Insights into the Practice of Taharat HaMishpachah* (Southfield, MI: Targum, 1988).

Adler, M., *Drawing Down the Moon* (Boston: Beacon Press, 1986).

Alba, D., *The Cauldron of Change: Myths, Mysteries and Magick of the Goddess* (Oak Park, IL: Delphi, 1993).

Allen, P.G., 'Grandmother of the Sun: The Power of Woman in Native America', in Plaskow and Christ (eds.), *Weaving the Visions*.

Amberston, C. [Cornwoman], *Blessings of the Blood: A Book of Menstrual Lore and Rituals for Women* (Victoria, BC: Beach Holme, 1991).

Anzaldùa, G., 'Entering into the Serpent', in Plaskow and Christ (eds.), *Weaving the Visions*.

—*Borderlands/La Frontera: The New Mestiza* (San Francisco: Spinsters/Aunt Lute, 1987).

Archer, L., '"In Thy Blood Live": Gender and Ritual in the Judaeo-Christian Tradition', in Joseph (ed.), *Through the Devil's Gateway*.

Armstrong, J., *The Idea of the Holy and the Humane Response* (London: George Allen & Unwin, 1981).

Atkinson, P., 'Fitness, Feminism and Schooling', in S. Delamont and L. Duffin (eds.), *The Nineteenth-Century Woman: Her Cultural and Physical World*.

Awekotuku, N.T., 'He Wahine, He Whenua: Maori Women and the Environment', in Caldicott and Leland (eds.), *Reclaim the Earth*.

Balmer, R., 'American Fundamentalism: The Ideal of Femininity', in Hawley (ed.), *Fundamentalism and Gender*.

Bartky, S.L., 'Foucault, Femininity and the Modernisation of Patriarchal Power', in I. Diamond and L. Quinby (eds.), *Feminism and Foucault: Reflections on Resistance* (Boston: Northeastern University Press, 1988).

Bateson, G., 'Men are Grass: Metaphor and the World of Mental Process', in W.I. Thompson (ed.), *Gaia, A New Way of Knowing*.

Beardsworth, T., *A Sense of Presence* (Oxford: The Manchester College Religious Experience Unit, 1977).

Beauvoir, S. de, *The Second Sex* (Harmondsworth: Penguin, 1982).

Becher, J. (ed.), *Women, Religion and Sexuality: Studies on the Impact of Religious Teachings on Women* (Geneva: WCC Publications, 1990).

Bell, R., *Holy Anorexia* (Chicago: University of Chicago Press, 1985).

Berger, A., 'Mircea Eliade: Romanian Fascism and the History of Religions in the United States', in N. Harrowitz (ed.), *Tainted Greatness: Anti-Semitism and Cultural Heroes* (Philadelphia: Temple University Press, 1994).

Bertell, R., *No Immediate Danger: Prognosis for a Radioactive Earth* (London: The Women's Press, 1985).

Bordo, S., 'Feminism, Postmodernism and Gender-Scepticism', in Nicholson (ed.), *Feminism/Postmodernism*.
—*Unbearable Weight: Feminism, Western Culture, and the Body* (Berkeley: University of California Press, 1993).
Bovery, S., *Being Fat is Not a Sin* (London: Pandora, 1989).
Bradley, M., *The Mists of Avalon* (London: Sphere, 1984).
Briffault, R., *The Mothers: A Study of the Origins of Sentiments and Institutions*, I (repr.; New York: Johnson, 1969); II (London: George Allen & Unwin, 1952).
Briggs, J., *Fractals: The Patterns of Chaos* (London: Thames & Hudson, 1992).
Brooke, E., *A Woman's Book of Shadows. Witchcraft: A Celebration* (London: The Women's Press, 1993).
Brown, P., *The Body and Society: Men, Women and Sexual Renunciation in Early Christianity* (London: Faber & Faber, 1990).
Brownmiller, S., *Femininity* (London: Hamish Hamilton, 1984).
Budapest, Z., *The Holy Book of Women's Mysteries* (Oakland, CA: Wingbow Press, 1986).
Burroughs, W.J., *Watching the World's Weather* (Cambridge: Cambridge University Press, 1991).
Busfield, J., *Understanding Gender and Mental Disorder* (London: Macmillan, 1995).
Byatt, A.S., *Angels and Insects* (London: Vantage, 1993).
Bynum, C.W., *Holy Feast, Holy Fast: The Religious Significance of Food to Medieval Women* (Berkeley: University of California Press, 1987).
—'The Female Body and Religious Practice in the Later Middle Ages', in *Fragmentation and Redemption: Essays on Gender and the Human Body in Mediaeval Religion* (New York: Zone, 1991).
—*Fragmentation and Redemption: Essays on Gender and the Human Body in Medieval Religion* (New York: Zone, 1991).
Byrne, P., *Natural Religion and the Nature of Religion* (London: Routledge, 1989).
Caillois, R., *Man and the Sacred* (Illinois: Free Press of Glencoe, 1959).
Caldicott, L., and S. Leland (eds.), *Reclaim the Earth: Women Speak Out for Life on Earth* (London: The Women's Press, 1983).
Campbell, J., *The Masks of God. I. Primitive Mythology* (New York: Arkana, 1991).
—*The Masks of God. IV. Creative Mythology* (New York: Arkana, 1991).
Cantor, A., 'The Lilith Question', in S. Heschel (ed.), *On Being a Jewish Feminist* (New York: Schocken Books, 1983).
Caputi, J., *Gossips, Gorgons and Crones: The Fates of the Earth* (Santa Fe: Bear & Co., 1993).
Carmody, D.L., *Mythological Women: Contemporary Reflections on Ancient Religious Stories* (New York: Crossroad, 1992).
Carse, J., 'Shape Shifting', in M. Eliade (ed.), *The Encyclopedia of Religion*, XIII, pp. 225-29.
Chamberlain, M., *Old Wives' Tales: Their History, Remedies and Spells* (London: Virago, 1981).
Chernin, K., *The Hungry Self: Women, Eating and Identity* (London: Virago, 1985).
—*Womansize: The Tyranny of Slenderness* (London: The Women's Press, 1993).
Chesler, P., *Women and Madness* (Harmondsworth: Penguin, 1979).
Christ, C., 'Mircea Eliade and the Feminist Paradigm Shift', *Journal of Feminist Studies in Religion* 7 (1991), pp. 75-91.

—'Why Women Need the Goddess: Phenomenological, Psychological and Political Reflections', in Christ and Plaskow (eds.), *Womanspirit Rising*.

Christ, C., and J. Plaskow (eds.), *Womanspirit Rising: A Feminist Reader in Religion* (New York: HarperSanFrancisco, 1992).

Christ, C., and C. Spretnak, 'Images of Spiritual Power in Women's Fiction', in Spretnak (ed.), *The Politics of Women's Spirituality*.

Clark, E., and H. Richardson (eds.), *Women and Religion: A Feminist Sourcebook of Christian Thought* (San Francisco: Harper & Row, 1977).

Cobb, J., 'Ecology, Science and Religion: Toward a Postmodern Worldview', in Griffin (ed.), *The Reenchantment of Science*.

Cousins, E., 'Spirituality in Today's World', in F. Whaling (ed.), *Religion in Today's World* (Edinburgh: T. & T. Clark, 1987).

Coward, R., 'Naughty but Nice: Food Pornography', in E. Frazer, J. Hornsby and S. Lovibond (eds.), *Ethics: A Feminist Reader* (Oxford: Blackwell, 1992).

Cowen, H., *The Human Nature Debate: Social Theory, Social Policy and the Caring Professions* (London: Pluto Press, 1994).

Craighead, M., 'Immanent Mother', in Giles (ed.), *The Feminist Mystic*.

Culpepper, E., 'The Spiritual, Political Journey of a Feminist Freethinker', in P.M. Cooey *et al.* (eds.), *After Patriarchy: Feminist Transformations of the World Religions* (Maryknoll, NY: Orbis Books, 1991).

Daly, M., *Pure Lust: Elemental Feminist Philosophy* (London: The Women's Press, 1984).

—*Beyond God the Father: Towards a Philosophy of Women's Liberation* (London: The Women's Press, 1985).

—*Gyn/Ecology: The Metaethics of Radical Feminism* (London: The Women's Press, 1991).

—*Outercourse: The Be-Dazzling Voyage* (London: The Women's Press, 1993).

Daly, M., and J. Caputi, *Webster's First New Intergalactic Wickedary of the English Language* (Boston: Beacon Press, 1987).

Delamont, S., and L. Duffin (eds.), *The Nineteenth-Century Woman: Her Cultural and Physical World* (London: Croom Helm, 1978).

Diamond, I., and G. Orenstein (eds.), *Reweaving the World: The Emergence of Ecofeminism* (San Francisco: Sierra Club Books, 1990).

Diamond, J., *The Rise and Fall of the Third Chimpanzee* (London: Vintage, 1991).

Douglas, M., *Natural Symbols: Explorations in Cosmology* (London: Barrie & Jenkins, 1973).

—*Purity and Danger* (Harmondsworth: Penguin, 1970).

Downing, C., *The Goddess: Mythological Images of the Feminine* (New York: Crossroad, 1990).

DuBois, P., *Torture and Truth* (London: Routledge, 1991).

Durkheim, E., *The Elementary Forms of the Religious Life* (repr.; London: George Allen & Unwin, 1971 [1915]).

Dworkin, A., *Pornography: Men Possessing Women* (London: The Women's Press, 1981).

Ehrenreich, B., and D. English, *Witches, Midwives and Nurses: A History of Women Healers* (New York: Glass Mountain, 1972).

Eilberg-Schwartz, H., 'Witches of the West: Neopaganism and Goddess Worship as Enlightenment Religions', *Journal of Feminist Studies in Religion* 5 (1989), pp. 77-95.

Eliade, M., 'Alchemy: An Overview', in *idem* (ed.), *The Encyclopedia of Religion*, I, pp. 183-86.

—*Patterns in Comparative Religion* (London: Sheed & Ward, 1958).

—*The Sacred and the Profane* (New York: Harcourt, Brace & World, 1959).

—*Rites and Symbols of Initiation: The Mysteries of Birth and Rebirth* (New York: Harper & Row, 1965).

Eliade, M. (ed.), *The Encyclopedia of Religion* (New York: Macmillan, 1987).

Eller, C., *Living in the Lap of the Goddess*: *The Feminist Spirituality Movement in America* (New York: Crossroad, 1993).

Emberley, J., and D. Landry, 'Coverage of Greenham and Greenham as "Coverage"', *Feminist Studies* 15 (1989), pp. 485-98.

Estés, C.P., *Women who Run with the Wolves: Contacting the Power of the Wild Woman* (London: Rider, 1992).

Falk, N.A., 'Feminine Sacrality', in M. Eliade (ed.), *The Encyclopedia of Religion*, V, pp. 302-12.

Faludi, S., *Backlash: The Undeclared War against Women* (London: Vintage, 1992).

Feldman, C., *The Quest of the Warrior Woman: Women as Mystics, Healers and Guides* (London: Aquarian, 1994).

Figes, K., *Because of Her Sex: The Myth of Equality for Women in Britain* (London: Macmillan, 1994).

Firestone, S., *The Dialectic of Sex* (New York: Bantam, 1970).

Foucault, M., *Discipline and Punish: The Birth of the Prison* (Harmondsworth: Penguin, 1977).

—*Power/Knowledge: Selected Interviews and Other Writings 1972–1988* (ed. C. Gordon; London: The Harvester Press, 1980).

Fox, M., *Original Blessing: A Primer in Creation Spirituality* (Santa Fe: Bear & Co., 1983).

Fox-Keller, E., *Reflections on Gender and Science* (New Haven: Yale University Press, 1986).

Francia, L., *Dragontime: The Magic and Mystery of Menstruation* (Woodstock, NY: Ash Tree, 1991).

Frymer-Kensky, T., *In the Wake of the Goddesses: Women, Culture, and the Biblical Transformation of Pagan Myth* (New York: The Free Press, 1992).

Fuss, D., *Essentially Speaking: Feminism, Nature and Difference* (London: Routledge, 1989).

Gearheart, S., 'Womanpower: Energy Re-Sourcement', in Spretnak (ed.), *The Politics of Women's Spirituality*.

—*The Wanderground: Stories of the Hill Women* (Waterton, MA: Persephone, 1978).

Gennep, A. Van, *The Rites of Passage* (repr.; London: Routledge & Kegan Paul, 1965 [1908]).

Gerike, A., 'On Gray Hair and Oppressed Brains', in Rosenthal (ed.), *Women, Ageing and Ageism*.

Giles, M. (ed.), *The Feminist Mystic and Other Essays on Women and Spirituality* (New York: Crossroad, 1982).

Gillespie, F., 'The Masterless Way: Weaving an Active Resistance', in G. Elinor *et al.* (eds.), *Women and Craft* (London: Virago, 1987).

Gimbutas, M., 'Women and Culture in Goddess-Orientated Old Europe', in Spretnak (ed.), *The Politics of Women's Spirituality.*

—*The Goddesses and Gods of Old Europe 6500–3500 BC: Myths and Cult Images* (Berkeley: University of California Press, 1982).

Girard, R., *Violence and the Sacred* (Baltimore: Johns Hopkins University Press, 1979).

Gleick, J., *Chaos: Making a New Science* (London: Sphere, 1990).

Goldenberg, N., 'Dreams and Fantasies as Sources of Revelation: Feminist Appropriation of Jung', in Christ and Plaskow (eds.), *Womanspirit Rising.*

—*Changing of the Gods: Feminism and the End of Traditional Religions* (Boston: Beacon Press, 1979).

Goldstein, D., *Jewish Folklore and Legend* (London: Hamlyn, 1980).

Gombrich, S.G., 'Divine Mother or Cosmic Destroyer: The Paradox at the Heart of the Ritual Life of Hindu Women', in Joseph (ed.), *Through the Devil's Gateway.*

Grahn, J., *Blood, Bread and Roses: How Menstruation Created the World* (Boston: Beacon Press, 1993).

Gray, E.D., 'Women's Experience and Naming the Sacred', *Woman of Power* 12 (1989).

Gray, M., *Red Moon: Understanding and Using the Gifts of the Menstrual Cycle* (Shaftesbury: Element, 1994).

Greenberg, B., 'Female Sexuality and Bodily Functions in the Jewish Tradition', in Becher (ed.), *Women, Religion and Sexuality.*

Grey, M., *Redeeming the Dream: Feminism, Redemption and the Christian Tradition* (London: SPCK, 1989).

Griffin, D.R. (ed.), *The Reenchantment of Science: Postmodern Proposals* (Albany, NY: State University of New York Press, 1988).

Grimshaw, J., *Feminist Philosophers: Women's Perspectives on Philosophical Traditions* (London: Harvester Wheatsheaf, 1986).

Gross, R., 'Androcentrism and Androgyny in the Methodology of History of Religions', in *idem* (ed.), *Beyond Androcentrism.*

Gross, R. (ed.), *Beyond Androcentrism: New Essays on Women and Religion* (Missoula, MT: Scholars Press, 1977).

Gulczynski, J.T., *The Desecration and Violation of Churches: An Historical Synopsis and Commentary* (Washington, DC: Catholic University of America Press, 1942).

Gunew, S., (ed.), *A Reader in Feminist Knowledge* (London: Routledge, 1991).

Halkes, C., *New Creation: Christian Feminism and the Renewal of the Earth* (London: SPCK, 1991).

Hall, C., 'The Early Formation of Domestic Ideology', in S. Burman (ed.), *Fit Work for Women* (London: Croom Helm, 1979).

Hall, N., *The Moon and the Virgin: Reflections on the Archetypal Feminine* (New York: Harper & Row, 1980).

Harding, E., *Women's Mysteries, Ancient and Modern: A Psychological Interpretation of the Feminine Principle as Portrayed in Myth, Story and Dreams* (New York: Harper & Row, 1976).

Harford, B., and S. Hopkins, *Greenham Common: Women at the Wire* (London: The Women's Press, 1984).

Harraway, D., 'A Manifesto for Cyborgs: Science, Technology, and Socialist Feminism in the 1980s', in Nicholson (ed.), *Feminism/Postmodernism*.

Harvey, D., *The Condition of Postmodernity: An Enquiry into the Origins of Cultural Change* (Oxford: Blackwell, 1989).

Hawley, J.S., (ed.), *Fundamentalism and Gender* (New York: Oxford University Press, 1994).

York: Collins, 1989).

Hebblethwaite, M., *Motherhood and God* (London: Cassell, 1984).

Herik, J. van, 'Simone Weil's Religious Imagery: How Looking Becomes Eating', in C. Atkinson *et al.* (eds.), *Immaculate and Powerful: The Female in Sacred Image and Social Reality* (Boston: Beacon Press/Crucible, 1985).

Heyward, C., *Touching Our Strength: The Erotic as Power and the Love of God* (New Hite, S., *The Hite Report* (London: Pandora, 1989).

Hopkins, E., *A Plea for the Wider Action of the Church of England in the Prevention of the Degradation of Women* (London: Hatchards, 1879).

—*The Present Moral Crisis: An Appeal to Women* (London: Dyer Bros, 1886).

Horrocks, R., 'The Divine Woman in Christianity', in A. Pirani (ed.), *The Absent Mother: Restoring the Goddess to Judaism and Christianity* (London: Mandala, 1991).

Hoult, J., *Dragons: Their History and Symbolism* (Glastonbury: Gothic Image, 1987).

Hurcombe, L. (ed.), *Sex and God: Some Varieties of Women's Religious Experience* (London: Routledge & Kegan Paul, 1987).

Husain, S. (ed.), *The Virago Book of Witches* (London: Virago, 1994).

Ind, J., *Fat is a Spiritual Issue: My Journey* (London: Mowbrays, 1993).

Isherwood, L., and D. McEwan, *Introducing Feminist Theology* (Sheffield: Sheffield Academic Press, 1993).

Jamal, M., *Shapeshifters: Shaman Women in Contemporary Society* (New York: Arkana, 1987).

Jameson, F., *Postmodernism, or, The Cultural Logic of Late Capitalism* (Durham, NC: Duke University Press, 1991).

Javors, I., 'Goddess in the Metropolis: Reflections on the Sacred in an Urban Setting', in Diamond and Orenstein (eds.), *Reweaving the World*.

Jay, N., 'Gender and Dichotomy', in Gunew (ed.), *A Reader in Feminist Knowledge*.

Jenson, P., *Graded Holiness: A Key to the Priestly Conception of the World* (JSOTSup, 106; Sheffield: JSOT Press, 1992).

Johnson, D. (ed.), *Women in English Religion 1700–1925* (Toronto: Edwin Mellen, 1983).

Joseph, A. (ed.), *Through the Devil's Gateway: Women, Religion and Taboo* (London: SPCK, 1990).

Judge, H., *Our Fallen Sisters* (London: E. Marshall, 1874).

Jung, C.G., *Psychology and Alchemy* (New York: Pantheon, 1952).

Jung, E., and M.L. von Franz, *The Grail Legend* (London: Hodder & Stoughton, 1971).

Keller, E.F., *Reflections on Gender and Science* (New Haven: Yale University Press, 1986).

Kenton, L., and S. Kenton, *Raw Energy* (London: Century, 1985).

Kieckhefer, R., *Unquiet Souls: Fourteenth-Century Saints and their Religious Milieu* (Chicago: University of Chicago Press, 1984).

King, U., 'A Question of Identity: Women Scholars and the Study of Religion', in *idem* (ed.), *Religion and Gender*.

—*Women and Spirituality: Voices of Protest and Promise* (London: Macmillan, 1989).

King, U. (ed.), *Religion and Gender* (Oxford: Blackwell, 1995).

Klaiman, M.H., 'Masculine Sacrality', in M. Eliade (ed.), *The Encyclopedia of Religion*, IX, pp. 352-58.

Klein, R., and D. Steinberg (eds.), *Radical Voices: A Decade of Feminist Resistance from Women's Studies International Forum* (Oxford: Pergamon, 1989).

Koltuv, B.B., *The Book of Lilith* (York Beach, ME: Nicolas-Hays, 1986).

Kuryluk, E., *Veronica and her Cloth: History, Symbolism, and Structure of a 'True' Image* (Cambridge, MA: Blackwell, 1991).

Laws, S., *Issues of Blood: The Politics of Menstruation* (London: Macmillan, 1990).

Leeuw, G. van der, *Religion in Essence and Manifestation* (London: George Allen & Unwin, 1938).

—*Sacred and Profane Beauty: The Holy in Art* (London: Weidenfeld & Nicolson, 1963).

Lewis, I.M., *Ecstatic Religion: An Anthropological Study of Spirit Possession and Shamanism* (London: Routledge, 1989).

Lewis, S., *Women's Mission* (London: John Parker, 1839).

Long, A., *In A Chariot Drawn by Lions: The Search for the Female in Deity* (London: The Women's Press, 1992).

Lorber, J., 'Dismantling Noah's Ark', in *idem* and S. Farrell (eds.), *The Social Construction of Gender* (Newbury, CA: Sage Publications, 1991).

Lorenz, E., 'Large-Scale Motions of the Atmosphere: Circulation', in P.M. Hurley (ed.), *Advances in Earth Science* (Cambridge, MA: MIT Press, 1966).

Lovelock,J., *Gaia: The Practical Science of Planetary Medicine* (London: Gaia Books, 1991).

Lugones, M., 'Purity, Impurity and Separation', *Signs* 19 (1994), pp. 458-79.

Luhrmann, T., *Persuasions of the Witch's Craft: Ritual Magic in Contemporary England* (London: Picador, 1994).

Lyon, D., *Postmodernity* (Buckingham: Open University Press, 1994).

MacAdams, C., *Rising Goddess* (New York: Morgan & Morgan, 1983).

MacIntyre, V., 'writing at risk', *From the Flames* 11 (1993), pp. 18-22.

MacKinnon, C., 'Pornography:.Not a Moral Issue', in Klein and Steinberg (eds.), *Radical Voices*.

Magee, P., 'Disputing the Sacred: Some Theoretical Approaches to Gender and Religion', in King (ed.), *Religion and Gender*.

Mahood, L., *The Magdalenes: Prostitution in the Nineteenth Century* (London: Routledge, 1990).

Maitland, S., *Virgin Territory* (London: Virago, 1993).

Mant, R., *The Female Character, A Sermon Preached in the Parish Church of St James, Westminster, 1821* (publisher unknown).

Margulis, L., *Symbiosis and Cell Evolution* (San Francisco: Freeman, 1981).

Mariechild, D., *Mother Wit: A Guide to Healing and Psychic Development* (Freedom, CA: Crossing Press, 1988).

Matthews, C., *The Goddess* (Shaftesbury: Element, 1989).

McCrickard, J., 'Born-Again Moon: Fundamentalism in Christianity and the Feminist Spirituality Movement', *Feminist Review* 37 (1991), pp. 59-67.

McGlynn, C.M., 'Nudity', *The Deosil Dance* 36 (1993, pp. 3-5.

McNay, L., *Foucault and Feminism: Power, Gender and the Self* (Cambridge: Polity Press; Oxford: Blackwell, 1994).

Mernissi, F., *Beyond the Veil: Male–Female Dynamics in a Modern Muslim Society* (Cambridge: Schenkman, 1975).

Miller-McLemore, B., 'Epistemology or Bust: A Maternal Feminist Knowledge of Knowing', *Journal of Religion* 72 (1985), pp. 229-47.

Millet, K., *Sexual Politics* (London: Sphere, 1972).

Minces, J., *The House of Obedience: Women in Arab Society* (London: Zed, 1982).

Moi, T., *Sexual/Textual Politics: Feminist Literary Theory* (London: Methuen, 1985).

Mookerjee, A.K., *Kali: The Feminine Force* (Rochester, VT: Destiny, 1988).

Morgan, M., *The Total Woman* (Old Tappan, NJ: Fleming Revell, 1973).

Morgan, Rabbi M., *A Guide to the Laws of Niddah* (New York: Moshe Morgan, 1983).

Muir, E., and G. Ruggiero (eds.), *Sex and Gender in Historical Perspective* (Baltimore: The Johns Hopkins University Press, 1990).

Murray, J.H., *Strong Minded Women and Other Lost Voices from Nineteenth-Century England* (Harmondsworth: Penguin, 1984).

Murray, M., *The Witch-Cult in Western Europe* (repr.; New York: Oxford University Press, 1953 [1921]).

Musgrove, F., *Ecstasy and Holiness: Counter-Culture and the Open Society* (London: Methuen, 1974).

Narayanan, V., 'Hindu Perceptions of Auspiciousness and Sexuality', in Becher (ed.), *Women, Religion and Sexuality.*

Neuer, W., *Man and Woman in Christian Perspective* (London: Hodder & Stoughton, 1990).

Neumann, E., *The Great Mother: An Analysis of the Archetype* (Princeton: Princeton University Press, 1955).

Niccoli, O., '"*Menstruum Quasi Monstruum*": Monstrous Births and Menstrual Taboo in the Sixteenth Century', in E. Muir and G. Ruggiero (eds.), *Sex and Gender in Historical Perspective.*

Nicholson, L. (ed.), *Feminism/Postmodernism* (London: Routledge, 1990).

Noble, V., *Shakti Woman: The New Female Shamanism* (New York: Harper-SanFrancisco, 1991).

Noddings, N., *Caring: A Feminine Approach to Ethics and Moral Education* (Berkeley: University of California Press, 1984).

—*Women and Evil* (Berkeley: University of California Press, 1989).

O'Brien, M., *The Politics of Reproduction* (Boston: Routledge & Kegan Paul, 1981).

O'Brien, P., *The Promise of Punishment: Prisons in Nineteenth-Century France* (Princeton, NJ: Princeton University Press, 1982).

O'Flaherty, W., *Women, Androgynes and Other Mythical Beasts* (Chicago: University of Chicago Press, 1980).

Ochs, C., *Women and Spirituality* (Totawa, NJ: Rowman & Allenheld, 1983).

Odeh, L.A., 'Post-Colonial Feminism and the Veil: Thinking the Difference', *Feminist Review* 43 (1993), pp. 26-36.

Orbach, S., *Fat is a Feminist Issue: The Antidiet Guide to Permanent Weightloss* (London: Paddington Press, 1978).

Orenstein, G.F., 'Reclaiming the Great Mother: A Feminist Journey to Madness and Back in Search of a Goddess Heritage', *Symposium* 36 (1982), pp. 45-70.

—*The Reflowering of the Goddess* (New York: Pergamon, 1990).

Ortner, S., 'Is Female to Male as Nature is to Culture?', in M.Z. Rosaldo and L. Lamphere (eds.), *Women, Culture and Society* (Stanford, CA: Stanford University Press, 1974).

Ostriker, A., 'Entering the Tents', *Feminist Studies* 15 (1989), pp. 541-48.

—*Feminist Revision and the Bible* (Oxford: Blackwell, 1993).

Otto, R., *The Kingdom of God and the Son of Man* (London: Lutterworth, 1938).

—*The Idea of the Holy* (New York: Oxford University Press, 1958).

Owen, A., *The Darkened Room: Women, Power and Spiritualism in Late Nineteenth-Century England* (London: Virago, 1989).

Owen, L., 'The Sabbath of Women', *Resurgence* 150 (1992), pp. 38-41.

—*Her Blood is Gold: Reclaiming the Power of Menstruation* (London: Aquarian, 1993).

Ozaniec, N., *Daughter of the Goddess: The Sacred Priestess* (London: Aquarian, 1993).

Page, F. (ed.), *The Poems of Coventry Patmore* (London: Oxford University Press, 1949).

Paris, G., *The Sacrament of Abortion* (Dallas: Spring Publications, 1992).

Parker, R., *The Subversive Stitch: Embroidery and the Making of the Feminine* (London: The Women's Press, 1984).

Peader, K., 'Rejecting Theology for a Religionless Spirituality', *One World* 98 (1984), pp. 20-21.

Pelikan, J., *Human Culture and the Holy* (London: SCM Press, 1959).

Philips, A., and J. Rakusen (eds.), *Our Bodies Ourselves: A Health Book by and for Women* (Harmondsworth: Penguin, 1979).

Plant, J. (ed.), *Healing the Wounds: The Promise of Ecofeminism* (Philadelphia: New Society, 1989).

Plaskow, J., 'The Coming of Lilith: Toward a Feminist Theology', in Christ and Plaskow (eds.), *Womanspirit Rising*.

—*Standing Again at Sinai: Judaism from a Feminist Perspective* (New York: HarperCollins, 1990).

Plaskow, J., and C. Christ (eds.), *Weaving the Visions: New Patterns in Feminist Spirituality* (New York: HarperSanFrancisco, 1989).

Podos, B., 'Feeding the Feminist Psyche through Ritual Theatre', in Spretnak (ed.), *The Politics of Women's Spirituality*.

Prendergast, S., 'Girls' Experience of Menstruation in Schools', in L. Holly (ed.), *Girls and Sexuality: Teaching and Learning* (Milton Keynes: Open University Press, 1989).

Rabuzzi, K., *The Sacred and the Feminine: Toward a Theology of Housework* (New York: Seabury Press, 1982).

Raphael, M., 'At the East End of Eden: A Feminist Spirituality of Gardening Our Way Past the Flaming Sword', *Feminist Theology* 4 (1993), pp. 101-10.

—'Doing Green Justice to God: Immanentism in the Contemporary Feminist Spirituality Movement', *Theology in Green* 5 (1993), pp. 34-41.

—'Feminism, Constructivism and Numinous Experience', *Religious Studies* 30 (1994), pp. 511-26.

—'"Cover not our Blood with thy Silence": Sadism, Eschatological Justice and Female Images of the Divine', *Feminist Theology* 8 (1995), pp. 85-105.

Reed, E., *Woman's Evolution: From Matriarchal Clan to Patriarchal Family* (New York: Pathfinder, 1975).

Rich, A., *Of Woman Born: Motherhood as Experience and Institution* (London: Virago, 1992).

Roney-Dougal, S., *Where Science and Magic Meet* (Shaftesbury: Element, 1993).

Rosenthal, E. (ed.), *Women, Ageing and Ageism* (New York: Harrington Park Press, 1990).

Rowland, R., 'Reproductive Techniques: The Final Solution to the Woman Question', in R. Arditti *et al.* (eds), *Test-Tube Women: What Future for Motherhood?* (London: Pandora, 1984).

Ruddick, S., *Maternal Thinking: Towards a Politics of Peace* (London: The Women's Press, 1990).

Rudolph, K., *Historical Fundamentals and the Study of Religions* (New York: Macmillan, 1985).

Ruether, R.R., 'Goddesses and Witches: Liberation and Countercultural Feminism', *The Christian Century* (10–17 September 1980), pp. 842-47.

—'Renewal or New Creation? Feminist Spirituality and Historical Religion', in Gunew (ed.), *A Reader in Feminist Knowledge*.

—'Women's Body and Blood: The Sacred and the Impure', in Joseph (ed.), *Through the Devil's Gateway*.

—*Sexism and God-Talk: Towards a Feminist Theology* (London: SCM Press, 1983).

—*Womanguides: Readings Toward a Feminist Theology* (Boston: Beacon Press, 1985).

—'Patriarchy and Creation: Feminist Critique of Religious and Scientific Cosmologies', *Feminist Theology* 2 (1993), pp. 57-69.

Ruskin, J., *Sesame and Lilies* (London: Cassell, 1907).

Sahgal, G., and N. Yuval-Davis, *Refusing Holy Orders: Women and Fundamentalism in Britain* (London: Virago, 1992).

Saiving, V., 'Androcentrism in Religious Studies', *Journal of Religion* 56 (1976), pp. 177-97.

—'The Human Situation: a Feminine View', in Christ and Plaskow (eds.), *Womanspirit Rising*.

Sanday, P.R., *Female Power and Male Dominance: On the Origins of Sexual Inequality* (Cambridge: Cambridge University Press, 1981).

Sartre, J.P., *Being and Nothingness: An Essay on Phenomenological Ontology* (London: Methuen, 1969).

Schumacher, D., 'Hidden Death: The Sexual Effects of Hysterectomy', in Rosenthal (ed.), *Women, Ageing and Ageism*.

Schwartz-Bart, A., *The Last of the Just* (Harmondsworth: Penguin, 1977).

Segal, L., *Is the Future Female? Troubled Thoughts on Contemporary Feminism* (London: Virago, 1987).

Seligmann, K., *Magic, Supernaturalism and Religion* (London: Allen Lane, 1971).

Sheldrake, R., *The Rebirth of Nature: The Greening of Science and God* (London: Rider, 1993).

Shepsut, A., *Journey of the Priestess: The Priestess Traditions of the Ancient World* (London: Aquarian, 1993).

Showalter, E., *The Female Malady: Women, Madness and English Culture 1830–1980* (London: Virago, 1987).

Shuttle, P., and P. Redgrove, *The Wise Wound: Menstruation and Everywoman* (London: HarperCollins, 1994).

—*Alchemy for Women: Personal Transformation through Dreams and the Female Cycle* (London: Rider, 1995).

Simonon, L., 'Personal, Political and Planetary Play', in Caldicott and Leland (eds.), *Reclaim the Earth*.

Singer, I.B., *The Collected Stories of Isaac Bashevis Singer* (London: Jonathan Cape, 1982).

Sireling, L., 'The Jewish Woman: Different and Equal', in Joseph (ed.), *Through the Devil's Gateway*.

Sjöö, M., *New Age and Armageddon: The Goddess or the Gurus? Towards a Feminist Vision of the Future* (London: The Women's Press, 1992).

—'Breaking the Tabu—Doing the Unthinkable', *From The Flames* 10 (1993), pp. 22-23.

Sjöö, M., and B. Mor, *The Great Cosmic Mother: Rediscovering the Religion of the Earth* (New York: HarperSanFrancisco, 1991).

Sklar, K.K., *Catharine Beecher: A Study in American Domesticity* (New York: Norton, 1973).

Söderblom, N., 'Holiness (General and Primitive)', in J. Hastings (ed.), *The Encyclopaedia of Religion and Ethics* (Edinburgh: T. & T. Clark, 1913), VI, pp. 731-41.

Spignesi, A., *Starving Women: A Psychology of Anorexia* (Dallas: Spring, 1983).

Spretnak, C. (ed.), *The Politics of Women's Spirituality: Essays on the Rise of the Spiritual Power within the Feminist Movement* (New York: Doubleday, 1982).

Spretnak, C., and F. Capra, *Green Politics: The Global Promise* (London: Paladin, 1990).

Starhawk, 'Witchcraft as Goddess Religion', in Spretnak (ed.), *The Politics of Women's Spirituality*.

—*The Spiral Dance: A Rebirth of the Ancient Religion of the Great Goddess* (New York: Harper & Row, 1979).

—*Truth or Dare: Encounters with Power, Authority and Mystery* (New York: HarperSanFrancisco, 1987).

—*Dreaming the Dark: Magic, Sex and Politics* (London: Unwin Hyman, 1990).

—*The Fifth Sacred Thing* (New York: Bantam, 1994).

Starrett, B., 'The Metaphors of Power', in Spretnak (ed.), *The Politics of Women's Spirituality*.

Stein, D., *Stroking the Python: Women's Psychic Lives* (St Paul, MN: Llewellyn, 1993).

—*The Women's Spirituality Book* (St Paul, MN: Llewellyn, 1987).

Stepanich, K., *Sister Moon Lodge: The Power and Mystery of Menstruation* (St Paul, MN: Llewellyn, 1992).

Stikker, A., *The Transformation Factor: Towards an Ecological Consciousness* (Rockport, MA: Element, 1992).

Stone, M., 'The Three Faces of Goddess Spirituality', in Spretnak (ed.), *The Politics of Women's Spirituality*.

—*Ancient Mirrors of Womanhood* (Boston: Beacon Press, 1991).

Stowe, H.B., *The Minister's Wooing* (New York: Derby & Jackson, 1859).

Swimme, B., 'The Cosmic Creation Story', in Griffin (ed.), *The Reenchantment of Science*.

Taylor, D., and A. Sumrall (eds.), *Women of the 14th Moon: Writings on Menopause* (Freedom, CA: Crossing Press, 1991).

Taylor, V., and L. Rupp, 'Women's Culture and Lesbian Feminist Activism: A Reconsideration of Cultural Feminism', *Signs* 19 (1993), pp. 32-61.

Thistlethwaite, S., *Sex, Race and God: Christian Feminism in Black and White* (London: Geoffrey Chapman, 1990).

Thomas, K., *Religion and the Decline of Magic* (Harmondsworth: Penguin, 1991).

Thompson, D. (ed.), *Over Our Dead Bodies* (London: Virago, 1983).

Thompson, W.I. (ed.), *Gaia, A New Way of Knowing: Political Implications of the New Biology* (Great Barrington, MA: Lindisfarne Press, 1987).

Tillich, P., *The Protestant Era* (London: Nesbit, 1955).

—*Systematic Theology*, I (London: SCM Press, 1978).

Waldrop, M.M, *Complexity: The Emerging Science at the Edge of Order and Chaos* (Harmondsworth: Penguin, 1994).

Walker, A., *In Search of Our Mothers' Gardens* (London: The Women's Press, 1984).

—*Possessing the Secret of Joy* (London: Jonathan Cape, 1992).

Walker, B., *The Woman's Encyclopedia of Myths and Secrets* (New York: Harper-SanFrancisco, 1983).

—*The Crone: Woman of Age, Wisdom and Power* (New York: HarperCollins, 1988).

—*The Women's Dictionary of Symbols and Sacred Objects* (New York: HarperCollins, 1988).

Walkowitz, J., *Prostitution and Victorian Society* (Cambridge: Cambridge University Press, 1980).

Weber, R., *Dialogues with Scientists and Sages: The Search for Unity* (London: Arkana, 1990).

Weideger, P., *Female Cycles* (London: The Women's Press, 1978).

Weinstein, D., and R. Bell, *Saints and Society: The Two Worlds of WesternChristendom 1000–1700* (Chicago: University of Chicago Press, 1982).

White, E., 'Religion and the Hermeneutics of Gender: An Examination of the Work of Paul Ricoeur', in King (ed.), *Religion and Gender*.

Wolf, N., *The Beauty Myth: How Images of Beauty are Used against Women* (London: Vintage, 1991).

Woodbine, C., 'Women's Webs: Will We Use Computer Networks?', *From the Flames* 14 (1994), pp. 10-12.

Wooley, O., S. Wooley, and S. Dyrenforth, 'Obesity and Women—II. A Neglected Feminist Topic', in Klein and Steinberg (eds.), *Radical Voices*.

Ydit, M., 'Mehiza', in C. Roth *et al.* (eds.), *Encyclopaedia Judaica* (Jerusalem: Keter, 1972), XI, pp. 1234-35..

INDEX